Research findings about Alzheimer's disease are growing at such a pace that few scientists, let alone care-giving professions can keep abreast of them. The first two volumes of *Care-Giving in Dementia* integrated up-to-date neurobiological information about dementia with specific developments in care-giving. The third volume of *Care-Giving in Dementia* takes the same multi-disciplinary approach and draws on contributions from leading practitioners to explore the latest rapid and palpable findings of this complex field. Key themes in volume three include:

- The Alzheimer Café concept and new support groups for people with dementia.
- Extended use of the concept of attachment in dementia care.
- Ethical issues in the care of elderly people with dementia.
- Support programmes for caregivers of people with dementia.

Illustrated by case histories, the wealth of practical advice in this third volume will prove invaluable to all health and mental health professionals caring for people with dementia.

Gemma M.M. Jones is a freelance educator about dementia care with all types of health care professionals and family carers, and consultant on specialist care facility design for persons with dementia.

Bère M.L. Miesen is a psychogeriatric advisor in Nursing Home A.H.S. 'De Strijp' in The Hague, and in the Department of Health and Clinical Psychology of the University of Leiden, The Netherlands.

Care-Giving in Dementia

Research and applications

Volume 3

Edited by Gemma M.M. Jones and Bère M.L. Miesen

Brunner-Routledge
Taylor & Francis Group

HOVE AND NEW YORK

First published 2004 by Brunner-Routledge
27 Church Road, Hove, East Sussex, BN3 2FA

Simultaneously published in the USA and Canada
by Brunner-Routledge
29 West 35th Street, New York, NY 10001

Brunner-Routledge is an imprint of the Taylor and Francis Group

Typeset in Times by Graphicraft Limited, Hong Kong
Printed and bound in Great Britain by Biddles Ltd, King's Lynn
Paperback cover design by Sandra Heath

British Library Cataloguing in Publication Data
A catalogue record for this book is available from the British Library

Library of Congress Cataloging in Publication Data
Care-giving in dementia : research and applications / edited by
Gemma M.M. Jones and Bère M.L. Miesen.– 3rd vol.
  p. cm.
  Includes bibliographical references and index.
    ISBN 1-58391-188-X (hardback : alk. paper) – ISBN 1-58391-189-8
  (pbk.: alk. paper) 1. Senile dementia. 2. Psychotherapy in old age.
3. Senile dementia–Patients–Care. 4. Community mental health
services. I. Jones, Gemma M.M., 1957– II. Miesen, Bère M.L.,
1946– III. Title.

RC524.C37 2004
618.97′683–dc22   2003024917

ISBN 1-58391-188-X (hbk)
ISBN 1-58391-189-8 (pbk)

To all of our former students and course participants: with gratitude for their hard work and enthusiasm, and with the hope that they will continue to make their presence felt in this new field, as caregivers, understanding persons and educators.

Contents

Figures

Tables

Contributors

Thomas Arendt is Professor of Neuroscience at the University of Leipzig where he runs the Department of Neuroanatomy at the Paul Flechsig Institute for Brain Research and the Alzheimer Centre. He was trained in psychiatry, biochemistry and neuroanatomy. He is working in the field of cell biological and molecular biological mechanisms of neurodegeneration and made contributions to the understanding of cholinergic dysfunction and neuroplasticity in the pathomechanism of Alzheimer's disease.

Co Bleeker works as a training psychiatrist in the regional mental health care organization 'De Grote Rivieren' and as a forensic psychiatrist in the Penitaire Inrichting Overamstel (Bijlmerbajes Prison) in Amsterdam. From 1988 to 1996 he was a member of the board of directors of the International Psychogeriatric Association.

Elles Breebaart is a social gerontologist and works at the department of care of the province of North-Brabant in 's Hertogenbosch. Between 1994 and 1996 she was an assistant researcher at the department of Psychiatry of the Vrije Universiteit (Amsterdam) on the research project 'Development and Effectiveness of the Meeting Centres Support Programme for Persons with Dementia and their Carers'.

Mariëtte Broersen has a wide range of experience as a music therapist with persons with dementia in nursing homes. In 1993 she completed her masters of science of music at the Universiteit van Amsterdam with a thesis on 'Muziektherapy with Alzheimer Patients: A literature study'. She has written articles in this field, given lectures and conducted related workshops. She was involved with the television programme about memory 'Vertrouwd en o zo vreemd' in 1994, broadcast through the VPRO.

Terry Connors is a psychologist and researcher who has carried out three research projects for Sonas aPc since 1999.

Rose-Marie Dröes is a human movement scientist, specializing in psychogeriatrics. Since 1992 she has worked as a senior researcher at the department of Psychiatry and the Alzheimer Centre of the Vrije Universiteit medical centre and at the regional mental health care organization GGZ Buitenamstel in Amsterdam. She led several research projects in the field of psychosocial intervention for persons with dementia and their carers, including studies into the effects of psychomotor therapy and emotion-oriented care for persons with dementia in nursing homes. She has written many articles and several books on these subjects. In 1999 she received the Prof. Schreuder Award of the Dutch Association for Gerontology for her research. In 1997 the 'Meeting Centres Support Programme for Persons with Dementia and their Carers' that she developed was awarded the Ter Haar Award by the Dutch Alzheimer Association. Her research into the effectiveness and nationwide implementation of this programme was given the Van Beresteyn Gerontology Award in 2002.

Mia Duijnstee is a district nurse and a psychologist (University of Utrecht). She received her doctorate in 1991 (University of Nijmegen). In 1994 she was appointed as professor at the University Medical Center Utrecht, Dept of Nursing Science. Research on family care is her special area of interest. In 2001 she became director of the Academy of Health Sciences Utrecht. In 2003 she was appointed reader in nursing and paramedical care at Hogeschool of Utrecht.

Hilda Flint's experience in homes for the elderly and of people with dementia has been with Building Community Through Arts, an outreach programme of the community-based Kew Studio. Her chapter comes from her recent MA in philosophy/religion. She is a Church of England reader and hospital chaplaincy visitor, experimenting with storytelling to 'build community' between residents and care staff. Widowed in 1995, she has an extensive family of daughters and grandchildren.

Joy Goffin is a human movement scientist and works as a psychomotor therapist at the regional mental health care organization GGZ Buitenamstel in Amsterdam. From 1990 until 1996 he worked as an assistant researcher for the project 'Development and Effectiveness of the Meeting Centres Support Programme for Persons with Dementia and their Carers'.

Rosemary Hamill, BSc MRCSCT is a speech and language therapist who works with Sonas aPc on a consultative basis in training and development. She has made great contributions to the development of the quality of the Sonas approach over the last ten years.

Cees Hertogh is an MD geriatrician and has a PhD in philosophy. He is senior researcher at the Institute for Research in Extramural Medicine of the Free University Medical Center, Amsterdam, and a geriatrician at the Naarderheem Centre for geriatric rehabilitation and long-term care. He is (co-)author of several books and articles on nursing home medicine and medical ethics, and is also a member of the editorial board of the Dutch *Journal of Gerontology and Geriatric Medicine*. His current research is about the moral problems and challenges of care-giving in dementia.

Anne-Marth Hogewoning-van der Vossen studied philosophical and empirical pedagogy at the University of Leiden. She was involved with research on impact of attachment on the cognitive development of children. She worked in the business sector and studied organizational psychology at the Open University. In 1996, she started work at De Strijp nursing home in the Hague as a personnel and organization advisor. In 1998 she was closely involved in the process of introducing the lifestyle concept within this home as care manager and interim project manager. As the current director, she is focusing on working with other organizations in the region. This has led to the introduction of a regional Alzheimer Café, waiting list care, and setting up small-scale group living arrangements for older persons with dementia.

Gemma M.M. Jones currently works as a freelance educator about dementia care with all types of health care professionals and family carers. She also consults about care facility design for persons with dementia. Her doctorate, from the University of London, Institute of Psychiatry, is on the neuropsychology of Alzheimer's disease. She also holds degrees in cell biology and nursing. She helped set up and run the first Alzheimer Café in Farnborough, UK, three years ago.

Neil Mapes graduated with a BSc (hons) in human psychology in 1996 and has been working with people with dementia since 1994. After graduating he spent 18 months as an assistant psychologist for people over 65 years old. During this post he first became involved in memory groups for people with dementia in a community day care setting and found them to be successful for all concerned. He is now a support and advocacy worker for Alzheimer's Concern Ealing in London and has held this post for nearly two years. He is committed to improving the lives of people who have dementia by distributing more helpful understanding of the illness and by developing local services that are available to people with dementia in Ealing. He is a keen writer of short stories and is working on his first wood sculpture.

Ann Marshall qualified as a clinical psychologist at the Institute of Psychology in 1981 and specialized in work with older adults in 1988. She works in a community mental health team for older adults and in a memory clinic in the West Hampshire NHS Trust. Since 1997, she has been running support groups for clients following a diagnosis of dementia and in 2001 completed a doctorate with a study in this area.

Bère Miesen is a clinical psycho(geronto)logist NIP who has been working in the Netherlands with people with dementia since 1970, their families and professionals. He is a clinician, therapist, teacher, researcher, author and poet. Today he works as psychogeriatric advisor in the nursing home A.H.S. De Strijp in The Hague and in the Dept of Health and Clinical Psychology of the University of Leiden. He has received several national awards for his efforts in emancipating all 'parties' involved in the field of dementia. In 1997 he started the Alzheimer Cafés as an ongoing, low threshold, psychosocial intervention for persons with dementia and their families.

Clare Morris worked for ten years as a speech and language therapist in a variety of acute and community settings with people with neurological conditions. She studied personal construct psychology and applied it to her work, becoming a UKCP registered psychotherapist in 1994. In 1997 she joined the Dementia Research Group at the National Hospital for Neurology and Neurosurgery and the MRC Prion Unit at St. Mary's Hospital in order to set up a therapeutic service for younger people with dementia and their families. In addition to providing counselling for individuals and couples affected by the diagnosis of dementia, she is involved in training and supervision, and writes on the experience of the symptoms of dementia for family and professional caregivers.

Gilda Newsham qualified as a nurse in 1958 and worked in various areas of nursing, including Ear, Nose and Throat and general medical wards. She became a district nursing sister in 1974 and worked in this capacity for 10 years. In 1984 she became nursing officer for district nursing in Slough, Berkshire and in 1986 became patient care manager for community nursing in East Berkshire. In 1990 she transferred to the Southampton and South West Hampshire Health Authority as the senior nursing home inspector and registration officer. Following her retirement from nursing in 1998 she has worked with the New Forest branch of the Alzheimer's Society acting as facilitator for 'Care Giving in Dementia' training. At present she is the chairman of the New Forest branch.

Niek van Nieuwenhuijzen completed his cello studies at the conservatory in Amsterdam and thereafter completed a study in social pedagogics-andragogics on music therapy and family therapy. He is a registered music therapist (RMTh) and since the 1980s has specialized in working with persons in psychogeriatric settings. He also researched receptive music therapy and its effects on depressed persons in 1995. Since 1970 he has worked as music therapist and head of department at the Psychomedisch Centrum Parnassia in Den Haag. Since 1999 he has been a staff lecturer, and since 2000 head of the music therapy programme at the Conservatorium van de Saxion Hogeschool in Enschede. Between 1973 and 1990 he was member of the Society for Music Therapy and chair of the professional society for creative therapy (NVKT). He has written numerous articles on music therapy. He has lectured on music therapy at European and world conferences in Noordwijkerhout (1989), Cambridge and Sittard (1992), Vitoria Gasteiz (1993), Aalborg (1995) and London (1997).

Anne Margriet Pot is a clinical psychologist, researcher and educator. She is affiliated to the Dept of Nursing Home Medicine (GERION) and the Institute of Extramural Medicine (EMGO) of the VU Medical Center, Amsterdam. Her interests relate to dementia and depression and the care of the elderly. She is (co-)author of several publications and chapters on these topics, and is chair of the Dutch Society of Psychology and the Elderly.

Elsbeth de Rooij is a human movement scientist and in 1996 worked as a graduate student at the Vrije Universiteit (Amsterdam) on the research project 'Development and Effectiveness of the Meeting Centres Support Programme for Persons with Dementia and their Carers'.

Wynand Ros is a health psychologist at the Dept of Nursing Science and Medical and Health Psychology of Utrecht University Medical Centre. He is researching coping, social support and quality of life in persons with cancer and other chronic illnesses and their families, with a special interest in nursing interventions.

Willem van Tilburg is Professor in Clinical Psychiatry, head of the department of Psychiatry of the Vrije Universiteit medical centre, and Medical Director of the regional Mental Health Care Organization GGZ Buitenamstel in Amsterdam. Since 1996 he has been the President of the Dutch Association of Psychiatry. He is (co-)author of many scientific articles, especially in the fields of gerontopsychiatry and dementia.

Han Vissers is a human movement scientist and works as a physiotherapist in the nursing home De Landrijt in Eindhoven. As a graduate student at the Vrije Universiteit (Amsterdam) between 1995 and 1996 he participated in the research project 'Development and Effectiveness of the Meeting Centres Support Programme for Persons with Dementia and their Carers'.

Introduction to Volume 3

Gemma M.M. Jones

This third volume of *Care-Giving in Dementia* follows the thematic pattern of the previous volumes. Looking back at why and how these volumes were compiled is very encouraging because it shows how much has changed, and that the speed of change is palpable. The first efforts to bring out such a book were met with much scepticism and rejection. Publishers were wary of launching out without a defined market for such work, and many persons working innovatively in clinical settings did not have an arena in which communicate their ideas or experience.

Volume three comes out at a time when the first Alzheimer Café in the UK is in its fourth year. There are 60 such cafés in the Netherlands, over a dozen in Belgium, one in Greece; two have been started in Australia. Specialist journals about dementia care and research have also started to fill an important niche. What this represents is a new and significant shift in the type of information and support available to persons with dementia and their family members.

The Alzheimer Café movement is not the only change: new support groups are coming into being for persons with rarer types of dementia; scientists are making their work more understandable to the public; specialist journals for dementia care have been launched and are reaching more and more professional caregivers; documentaries and even television serials are increasingly including dementia as a subject worthy of attention.

Professionals such as clinical psychologists are starting to define their own specialist area with regard to working with persons with dementia. In the Netherlands, where they are about 1000 strong, they are working towards a national curriculum. Groups such as Psychologists Special Interest Group for the Elderly (PSIGE) in the UK are also considering how best to further their work with persons with dementia, and their professional numbers. Such is the growth in this field of care-giving in dementia that the contributions for volume four are largely ready and will follow closely on the heels of this book.

Perhaps the most recurring theme in this volume is 'valuing': valuing feelings, perceptions, beliefs, realities, persons, objects and environments.

There have been many changes in way that dementia is referred to in the past four decades. The research findings about Alzheimer's disease are growing at such a pace that few scientists, let alone care-giving professions, will be able to keep abreast of them. The metasynthesis (Chapter 1) offers a very important overview about how many variables and facets are involved in trying to put together the puzzle pieces, which will finally allow us to answer the question 'What causes Alzheimer's disease?'

We are especially pleased that more difficult subjects like abuse, ethics and spirituality are broached in a clear way in this volume. Case histories make these chapters all the more pointed. The bottom line is that we cannot escape having to discuss these things, and most professional staff in this field have never had formal training about how to think through and discuss these topics. It is hoped that presenting this material here will be of practical help, particularly since so many caregivers report feeling compromised when they are asked 'difficult' questions by family carers.

Readers will also note the strides that have been made in trying to identify and analyse a literature base for assessing various approaches to group work. The ways in which small groups are specializing is extremely encouraging. This is true for support as well as therapy groups, for both persons with dementia and their families.

In editing a volume where contributions have been translated, it is important to note that there are differences in nomenclature which are difficult to reconcile satisfactorily. For example, the terms *psycho-gerontology* and *psycho-geriatrics* are in common usage in the Netherlands, but not in the UK. (The term 'psycho' does not have the pejorative connotation that it does in English, but is much used as in the term 'psycho-social causes'.) Another point of difference comes from how the diagnosis of dementing illnesses is made. In the Netherlands, aside from diagnoses of dementia being made earlier than in the UK, neurologists and neuropsychologists are key figures in memory clinic multidisciplinary teams. In the UK, old-age psychiatrists and clinical psychologists would be the norm. In Germany and the Netherlands, a person with dementia would be referred to as a 'dementia patient' (being under the care of a specialist team). In the UK, with the current efforts to use the best term possible, 'person with dementia' is the norm. We have tried to normalize and equalize such word usage to the best of our ability, but acknowledge that such problems are not easy to overcome. There is not yet an ideal universal vocabulary to overcome such differences.

Throughout all of this, what remains key is that understanding what a person with a dementing illness is experiencing helps us to understand how 'individual' behavioural responses can be. If the 'practical consequences of the illness' and the subsequent 'emotional responses to these consequences' are increasingly seen as important points of intervention, then perhaps there will be less nihilism in society about dementia, and among those health care professionals who still prefer not to be involved with this population of persons. Reality is telling us that dementia is definitely with us for the time being, and that we will all be confronted with its effects, whether in the health care service or in our community and private lives. Although it is a very tragic illness, when our understanding of it reduces our fear of the 'craziness' that is still too often associated with dementia, we can see a meaning and logic to how persons continue to struggle to be themselves and problem solve, despite increasingly severe limitations. This view is one which will help quell another fear that is prevalent – the fear that one might someday have the illness oneself. This fear can only be lessened if we know that, should we ever get a dementing illness ourselves, we will be cared for by knowledgeable, caring others who will continue to see the real us shining out from the mists with which dementia can surround us.

N.B. The term 'carer' denotes a family member, the term 'caregiver' is used to refer primarily to paid professionals caring for a person with dementia.

Part I

Models and theories

Chapter 1

Metasynthesis of the neurobiology of Alzheimer's disease

Thomas Arendt

Dementia is a major public health problem

Dementia affects both genders and all socio-economic and ethnic groups. Dementia is not a disorder in its own right; it is rather a complex syndrome of brain dysfunction with a number of potentially different underlying causes. Dementia can be defined in the following way (WHO 1986):

> Dementia is the global impairment of higher cortical functions, including memory, the capacity to solve the problems of day-to-day living, the performance of learning perceptuo-motor skills, the correct use of social skills and control of emotional reactions, in the absence of gross 'clouding of consciousness'. The condition is often irreversible and progressive.

Alzheimer's disease (AD) is by far the most common cause of dementia. It appears to have several causes, some of which are very rare. These are discussed later in the chapter. AD accounts for about one-third of all dementia cases in the elderly. Another third is of vascular origin (resulting primarily from the accumulation of strokes or infarcts), and the last third are mostly mixed cases of both AD and vascular dementia. Dementia, and in particular AD, occurs primarily in elderly persons (Arendt 2001; Terry *et al.* 1999).

Aging in itself, however, is a physiological process, and AD is not an inevitable consequence of age. (AD can also occur in persons in their fourth and fifth decades, though this is uncommon.) In the absence of dementia, cognitive performance can remain relatively stable with age. This apparently stable performance does not exclude the possibility of some age-related cognitive deterioration, because learning can potentially counteract against small declines.

During a lifetime, an individual can accumulate a number of small (though possibly deleterious) impacts. Each impact, in and of itself, might be insufficient to cause functional impairment, however when they accumulate progressively they could reduce the *reserve capacity of the brain*. In this sense, aging influences the onset and course of a number of disorders, and it is the most important risk factor for dementia.

The incidence (i.e. the number of newly diagnosed cases) of dementia rises drastically with age, and its prevalence doubles every five years. At the age of 65, about 1 per cent of the population has a dementing illness of some sort. Thereafter, the *prevalence* (i.e. the percentage of people that is affected by a disease) has been estimated to increase up to 30 per cent (some say 50 per cent depending on which criteria for diagnosing dementia are used), for persons aged over 85. AD is the most common form of dementia in the Western industrial countries and affects about four million people in Europe and a similar number in the USA. The continuing growth of the elderly population is leading to an ever-increasing number of dementia patients worldwide. Within the next 20 to 30 years, the number of people aged over 60 years will double and the number of persons with dementia will rise accordingly. While so far age-related disorders have been a major health problem only in the Western world, the less developed countries will catch up with these figures within the next 50 to 60 years.

AD is a chronic progressive disorder

In the absence of dementia or other diseases, older adults may expect relatively stable cognitive function and few difficulties with everyday performance of accustomed activities, a process referred to as 'successful aging'. A decline that is considered to be age related may thus reflect the effect of unrecognized very mild dementia. Some persons requesting a diagnosis have cognitive complaints of uncertain significance and may only demonstrate questionable deficits on quantitative testing. It may thus be difficult to classify such persons as either 'normal' or 'having dementia'. Hence, the term mild cognitive impairment (MCI) has been coined. For many persons with MCI, this may indeed represent the initial presentation of AD. It has been estimated that about 25 per cent to 40 per cent of these progress on to having officially diagnosable dementia within two and three years, respectively.

Dementia usually starts with relatively slight impairments and progresses to a point where all skills of communication and self-care are lost. The rate of progression depends on both internal and external factors. With the help of a scale such as the dementia rating scale, one can place a patient into one of five stages along a continuum from healthy to severely demented (Table 1.1).

The development of the NINCDS/ADRDA criteria have made a more standardized clinical diagnosis of AD possible. These criteria establish three levels of diagnostic certainty. *Probable AD* is present when dementia is characterized by gradual onset and progression, when deficits are present in

Table 1.1 Functional levels of AD and corresponding developmental ages during childhood according to Reisberg

Functional level	Behavioural Stage when function is lost	Stage of AD when function is lost	Stage when function is acquired
Smiles; holds head up independently	4	7e & f	1–4 months
Sits up independently	4	7d	6–10 months
Walks independently	3	7c	12 months
Responds with over one clearly heard word when questioned	3	7b	12 months
Responds with over six clearly heard words when questioned	2–3	7a	15 months
Maintains fecal continence; urinary continence	2–3	6d & e	2–5 years
Performs toileting & bathing correctly, independently	2	6b & c	4 years
Dresses self properly, independently	2	6a	5 years
Selects proper clothing for season & occasion	2	5	5–7 years
Performs complex activities of daily life independently (e.g. managing finances, shopping, planning & making a meal)	1	4	8–12 years
Performs competently in demanding employment settings	1	3	Adolescence

Source: Adapted from Reisberg *et al.* (1999) *International Psychogeriatr*, 11: 7–23, incorporating Behavioural Staging mentioned in chapters 3 and 12, G.M.M. Jones, this volume.

two or more cognitive areas, and when other disorders that could cause dementia are absent. *Possible AD* is present when the patient has variations in the presentation of dementia (e.g. disproportionate language dysfunction early in the course). *Definite AD* can only be diagnosed when the clinical diagnosis is histopathologically confirmed by biopsy or autopsy. The clinical diagnosis of 'probable AD' has an accuracy of 90 per cent or greater, if made by a memory clinic or specialist multidisciplinary diagnostic team.

The histopathology of Alzheimer's disease

The diagnosis of Alzheimer's disease is mainly based on the exclusion of other possible causes of dementia and disorientation. This careful exclusion process is particularly important for the identification of those forms of illness which are treatable and, therefore, at least partially reversible. Remember

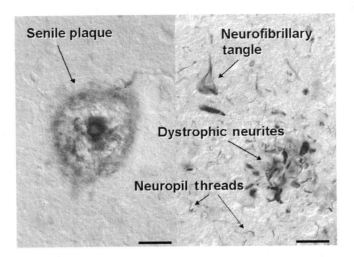

Figure 1.1 Senile plaques, consisting of aggregated amyloid ß-peptide (left) and neurofibrillary tangle, dystrophic neurites and neuropil threads, consisting of paired
helical filaments made up by the cytoskeletal protein tau (right). Scale bars,
left: 50μm, right: 20μm.

that a 100 per cent certain diagnosis can only be established after post-
mortem examination, which confirms the clinical diagnosis in most cases.
The appearance of plaques and neurofibrillary tangles in the cerebral cortex
is the typical pathology of Alzheimer's disease. Both plaques and tangles are
cause by protein deposits, but by two different ones. In the case of a plaque,
the protein (beta-amyloid), accumulates outside of the nerve cell. In the case
of tangles, the protein, called tau, accumulates within nerve cells (also called
neurons or neurites).

On the basis of their presence the post-mortem diagnosis of AD is established (Figure 1.1). The occurrence of both senile plaques and neurofibrillary
tangles, however, is not absolutely specific for Alzheimer's disease. They
are also found in other dementing disorders such as elderly with Down's
syndrome, post-traumatic dementia (boxing dementia) and to some very
small extent are sometimes found even in normal elderly who show no
mental impairment.

Plaques

Plaques, also referred to as 'senile plaques', are extracellular (outside of the
cell) deposits of a small peptide (a chain of organic compounds called amino
acids which are required for the production of proteins) called 'amyloid-ß-
peptide', that have become intermingled with 'glial cells' (a type of brain cell

which is part of the immune system) and 'processes' of neurons (called axons and dendrites, which are the equivalent of arms and legs on a human, which bring the cell into electrochemical contact with other cells) which have been damaged. The amyloid-ß-peptide is formed by the 'proteolytic processing' (made from the breakdown of other proteins) of a larger cell surface protein (called amyloid precursor protein, APP). Beta amyloid progressively accumulates into plaques and into the walls of blood vessels. Plaques are thus rather compact spherical structures with diameters of up to 200µm (200 millionths of a meter) that eventually occupy a considerable portion of the brain tissue. The mechanisms leading to the generation and deposition of the amyloid-ß-peptide (and thus to the formation of plaques), are still not understood very well.

A number of enzymes (a protein which speeds up biochemical reactions) have been identified that control the formation of the amyloid-ß-peptide from its precursor protein. These enzymes have been called 'secretases' since they regulate the 'secretion' of the peptide. Secretases are one target for a number of potential therapeutic approaches currently under way. These strategies aim to reduce the generation of amyloid-ß-peptide and thus the formation of senile plaques. It remains questionable, however, whether reducing the levels of amyloid-ß-peptide will be of any benefit, since its production appears to be a consequence, rather than a cause, of cell death. Accumulation of amyloid-ß-peptide in the brains of AD patients is most likely the result of impaired clearance of amyloid-ß-peptide through the vascular system. Under normal conditions, in the non-diseased human brain, amyloid-ß-peptide is produced at very low amounts and cleared through the vascular system. If it is produced at a much higher rate, as in AD, its clearance through the blood is insufficient and it seems to passively accumulate into plaques.

Neurofibrillary tangles

Neurofibrillary tangles (see Figure 1.1) are localized within the cell bodies of neurons. They consist of twisted filaments (called paired helical filaments), which are formed from a small cytoskeletal protein called 'tau'. The normal function of the tau protein is to stabilize the cell's 'microtubules'. (Microtubules are pipe-like protein structures in the cell's axonal process. In additional to providing structural support for a cell, they also provide a sort of 'rail track' for the transport of many nutrients and substances within the cell.) In AD, the binding of the tau protein to the microtubules is altered, resulting in twisted pairs of tau which destroy the shape of the microtubules, reducing their ability to transport substances normally.

The binding of tau protein to microtubules is regulated by a process known as 'protein phosphorylation' (i.e. the binding of phospho-residues to the tau protein). If protein phosphorylation is high, i.e. a lot of phospho-residues are bound to the tau protein, its interaction with microtubules is made unstable, or 'labilized'. As a consequence, the 'rail track' structure of the microtubules breaks down and the 'axonal transport' fails.

For reasons that are unknown, the phosphorylation of the tau protein is elevated in AD. The microtubule structure is disturbed, and the tau protein, which does not bind efficiently to the microtubules, accumulates in the cell body (the main part of the nerve cell, not its processes) of the affected neuron in the form of 'paired helical filaments', which are the major component of neurofibrillary tangles. These twisted filaments (paired helical filaments) also occur in degenerating neurites (dystrophic neurites) and in the neuropil (neuropil threads) (see Figure 1.1).

Similar 'intraneuronal (inside the cell) inclusions' of the tau protein also occur in other neurodegenerative disorders that share clinical features with AD and are commonly referred to as '*tauopathies*'. These include Down's syndrome, progressive supranuclear palsy, corticobasal degeneration, Pick's disease, and frontotemporal dementia with Parkinson's linked to chromosome 17.

It is important to note that, during the stage of 'neuronal fibre outgrowth' in brain development, this tau protein is highly phosphorylated, and also destabilizes the structure of microtubules. This developmental destabilization of the microtubule structure is exactly the same as what happens in AD. However, during the developmental stage, it is a necessary prerequisite for the axon to be able to grow, and does not lead to harmful, deleterious effects.

Parkinson's disease

The second most frequent neurodegenerative disorder after AD is Parkinson's disease (PD). PD clinically involves extra-pyramidal (nerve cell groupings associated with involuntary control of muscle activity) motor system abnormalities and is characterized (pathologically) by the presence of *Lewy bodies*. Lewy bodies are intracellular spherical inclusions of a synaptic protein called 'alpha-synuclein'. It is not known what their presence does to the cell, or what causes their formation. Lewy bodies are found within neurons of the part of the brain called the 'substantia nigra' (Figure 1.2). Other than PD, Lewy bodies have also been associated with AD, where they are found in cortical neurons. This suggests an important interaction and common mechanism in the pathogenesis of the two diseases. About 25 per cent of patients with PD also develop dementia. Conversely, about 30 per cent of patients with AD develop extrapyramidal motor disturbances. An association between cortical Lewy bodies and dementia has recently started to be increasingly recognized, and 'Dementia with Lewy bodies' is now regarded as an independent dementing disorder that can be distinguished from AD on the basis of particular visual hallucinations and extrapyramidal signs.

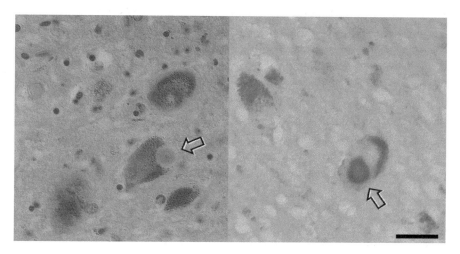

Figure 1.2 Lewy bodies (arrows) in the substantia nigra of incidental Lewy body disease (left: hematoxilin-eosin staining; right: immunostaining for alpha-synuclein). Scale bar: 20µm.

Which neurons degenerate in AD?

While plaques are more uniformly distributed throughout the cortex, neurofibrillary tangles show a typical sequence of formation throughout different parts of the cortex (Figure 1.3). The number of neurofibrillary tangles, moreover, correlates with the degree of mental impairment while such a correlation is not observed for senile plaques. The formation of neurofibrillary tangles within a neuron apparently critically impairs its viability and after years or even decades might eventually result in cell death. This process is called neurofibrillary degeneration. The development of neurofibrillary tangles first starts in the transentorhinal and entorhinal cortex.

At this very early stage of the disease, no mental impairment is apparent. During further progression of the disease, tangle formation begins to involve the limbic cortex and also occurs in the neocortex where it first affects the cortical association areas. This process is associated with the development of first clinical symptoms. With progression of the disease, tangle formation expands more and more over the cortex and progressively involves additional cortical areas. At late stages of the disease, primary sensory cortical areas and cortical motor areas are also affected. As the formation of tangles critically impairs the specific function of the affected area, progression of clinical symptoms parallels progression of neurofibrillary degeneration throughout an increasing number of brain areas.

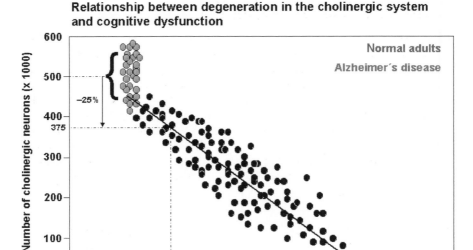

Figure 1.3 Relationship between loss of cholinergic neurons and progressive cognitive dysfunction. Normal adults have about 400.000 to 600.000 cholinergic neurons in the brain (grey). This number is greatly reduced in AD. The reduction in number of neurons is paralleled by cognitive dysfunction. The Mini Mental Scale (MMS) can evaluate cognitive function. A MMS score above 24 points is normal. As can be seen from the graph, a 25 per cent cell loss is functionally tolerated, as the MMS score still is between 30 (normal) and 24 (borderline). Only a cell loss beyond 25 per cent is associated with cognitive dysfunction (MMS score below 24).

Limbic system: memory, learning and behavioural symptoms

From an evolutionary point of view, the limbic system is an old part of the brain, whereas the neocortex (the structure surrounding the limbic system) is the newest part of the mammalian brain. It is in the hippocampal/limbic area that the damage in AD starts, and continues. In effect, neurofibrillary degeneration in the entorhinal cortex and efferent neurons of the subiculum disconnect the hippocampus from the neocortex. Since the hippocampal-neocortical connection is critically involved in information processing in the brain, this disruption contributes to learning and memory disabilities. It is thought that further lesions/damage to the limbic and paralimbic systems contribute to some of the behavioural symptoms of AD.

Temporal-parietal-occipital association cortex: visual impairment, aphasia, apraxia, agnosia

Within the neocortex, the multimodal association cortex is highly prone to neurofibrillary degeneration, resulting in visual impairment, aphasia (inability to speak), apraxia (inability to make purposeful movements) and visual disorientation in AD. Dysfunctions of the posterior association areas correlate with several disturbances in higher cortical function that usually follow the development of amnesia (memory loss). Visuospatial impairment occurs relatively early during the course of the disease. Disturbances of language are regarded as typical for AD and correlate with other indicators of disease severity. Apraxia is frequently present in AD, and in most cases characterized by clumsiness in object manipulation and in executing complex goal-directed activities.

Prefrontal cortex: insight, abstraction, planning, judgement, personality change, behavioural disturbance and relative preservation of social propriety

Apathy, impaired insight and lack of judgement are common clinical observations in AD. Perseveration and inefficient problem solving are frequently noted in psychometric assessment. This contrasts markedly with Pick's disease, which shows a constant involvement of prefrontal cortex. In comparison to Pick's disease, persons with AD show relatively well-preserved social graces and appropriateness.

Subcortical projection: memory, learning, behaviour

Several subcortical projection systems, which innervate the cerebral cortex (such as the 'cholinergic basal forebrain system', the 'serotoninergic raphe nuclei', the 'noradrenergic locus coeruleus', and to a lesser extent, the 'dopaminergic substantia nigra'), are affected by neurodegeneration in AD. The cholinergic basal forebrain projection system shows a most early and most constant cell loss in AD (Figure 1.4).

This system is involved in cortical information processing through regulation of cortical arousal. A failure in this system, which occurs early during the course of AD, results in difficulties in 'the gating' or controlling of specific sensory information. This results in impaired memory storage and retrieval. Through the application of acetylcholinesterase-inhibitors (substances which prevent acetylcholine from being broken down as quickly as normal), it is possible to inhibit the degradation of acetylcholine, which is the neurotransmitter (conducting fluid) used in the cholinergic system. This might be of some benefit to the patients during the early stages of the disease,

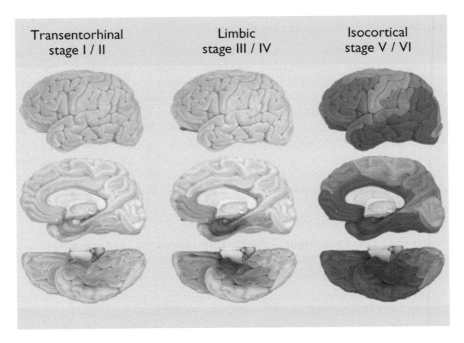

Transentorhinal
stage I / II

Limbic
stage III / IV

Isocortical
stage V / VI

Figure 1.4 Progression of neurofibrillary degeneration throughout different cortical areas. Degeneration starts in the entorhinal and transentorhinal cortex (stage I and II), progresses through limbic cortical areas, such as hippocampus and amygdala (stage III and IV) and eventually reaches isocortical areas, where it first affects association areas, while primary sensory and motor areas are affected only very late (stage V and VI).
Source: Adapted from Braak and Braak (1991: 239).

as it enables the brain to make more intensive use of this neurotransmitter that is only available in reduced amounts.

Why do neurons degenerate in AD?

As can be seen from the sequence of progression of neurofibrillary degeneration throughout the cortex, different cortical areas are vulnerable to tangle formation to different extents. For reasons that are unknown so far, cortical areas that mature very late during brain development are particularly vulnerable to damage. Conversely, those brain regions that mature very early during development are quite resistant to such degeneration. The brain regions that develop and mature late (of late ontogenetic development) are also those that, from an evolutionary point of view (phylogenetically very young, only acquired or at least have recently reorganized), represent those parts of the

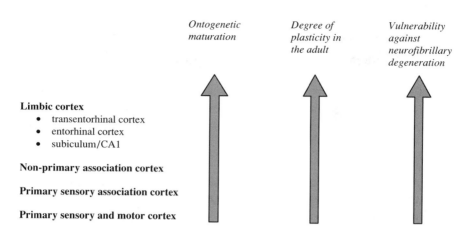

Figure 1.5 Hierarchical pattern of the developmental sequence of maturation, the degree of neuronal plasticity and the vulnerability against neurofibrillary degeneration in the human cerebral cortex.

brain that are unique to the human. These most vulnerable brain regions are the ones which subserve the so-called 'higher brain functions' such as learning, memory, reasoning and self-consciousness. Brain functions that are acquired late during childhood are affected first, according to the principle 'last in – first out' (Figure 1.5).

Accordingly, functions already acquired very early in childhood remain unimpaired until the most advanced stages of the disease. Hence, the developmental sequence of symptoms in AD is the opposite of the functional maturation experienced during childhood ('last in – first out'). This systematic sequence of loss of function provides an important basis for the anticipation of further disease progression and the organization of patient's care that matches defined aspects of care in childhood. That is only at the level of some aspects of physical care, however. In addition, the changes to language, the perceptual deficits and the emotional and sensory memory sparing through to late stages of AD, make an understanding of the progression of the illness essential so that care interventions can be adapted throughout the course of the illness. This sequence of neurobiological changes in the brain has its functional expression (Table 1.2).

Why are brain regions that have been acquired only very recently during evolution so vulnerable?

Neurons are organized into networks. The number of neurons in the human brain amounts to about 10^{12}. Thus, each neuron receives about 10^4 to 10^5

Table 1.2 Clinical dementia rating (CDR)

Behavioral Stage	Healthy CDR 0	Questionable dementia CDR 0.5	Mild dementia CDR 1	Moderate dementia CDR 2	Severe dementia CDR 3
	0	0–1	1–2	2–3	3–4
Memory	No memory loss or normal forgetfulness	Mild consistent forgetfulness, incomplete recall of events	Moderate memory loss, normally for recent events, affects everyday activities	Severe memory loss, highly learned material retained, new information quickly lost	More severe memory loss, some fragments remain
Orientation	Fully oriented to person, relationships, place, time		Some difficulty with some relationships, may have some spatial disorientation	Usually disoriented in time, often in place	Oriented to person only
Judgement and problem solving	Solves everyday problems well, judgement good compared to past	Only doubtful impairment in solving problems, similarities, differences	Moderate difficulty solving complex problems, social judgement usually maintained	Severe impairment solving problems, similarities, differences	Unable to make judgement or solve problems
Community affairs	Independent function at usual level in job, shopping, business and financial affairs, social activities	Doubtful or mild impairment in these activities	Unable to function independently in these activities; may appear engaged and normal at casual inspection	No pretence of independent functioning outside home	No significant independent functioning
Home and hobbies	Home life, hobbies and intellectual interests well maintained	Home life, hobbies and intellectual interests maintained or slightly impaired	Mild but definite impairment of home life; withdrawal from complex chores, hobbies and interests	Only simple chores preserved, very limited interests, poorly sustained	No significant functioning in home outside of his/her own bedroom
Personal care	Independent in self-care		Needs occasional prompting and reminding	Needs help in dressing, hygiene, keeping track of personal effects	Needs full assistance with personal care, often incontinent

Source: Adapted from Hughes et al. (1982) British Journal of Psychiatry, 140: 566–72, incorporating Behavioural Staging in chapters 3 and 12, G.M.M. Jones, in this volume.

synaptic (i.e. the contacts of nerve cell processes with other nerve cells) contacts from other cells. This means the brain contains at least 10^{16} (10,000,000,000,000,000) synaptic contacts. By comparison, the human genome contains less than 100,000 genes. That means only a minor part of the information necessary to build the human brain is derived from one's genes. Where does the other major part of information come from? It comes from the environment. This 'environmental information' (also called epigenetic information) shapes the brain through the interactions of the organism with the environment and provides the basis for what we call 'experience'.

For example, we know from the classical case of Kaspar Hauser, who behaved like an animal as he was reared under very deprived conditions in a dungeon, that environmental influence is particularly important during childhood when the brain develops. Fortunately though, even when brain development has come to an end, the brain remains highly 'plastic', or changeable. It is continuously reshaped through environmental influences. In other words, neuronal networks are continuously reorganizing themselves through a process called 'synaptic plasticity'. This is a lifelong process that also operates in the adult and even in the aging brain.

Variations in plasticity of different brain regions

The degree of synaptic plasticity, however, varies for different brain areas and neuronal types. The so-called 'higher brain functions' that are highly experience-dependent (such as learning, memory, reasoning and self-consciousness) are based on a particular high degree of synaptic plasticity and require a lifelong process of new synapse formation. On the other hand, brain areas that subserve more 'static functions' (such as in the motor system) are based on neuronal networks that are rather stable and well-established. They exhibit a much lesser degree of 'synaptic plasticity'. For example, riding a bike needs to be learned only once; speaking a foreign language however, requires continuous practice in a process of stabilization and relearning.

In other words, it is the high degree of 'structural synaptic plasticity' that enables our brain to subserve those very functions that are the basis for uniquely human behaviour. However, it is exactly this high degree of structural plasticity that makes neurons vulnerable to such diseases as AD, which is also unique to humans.

Why are higher plastic functions more vulnerable to AD?

What is the reason for this? The answer to this question lies in understanding how synaptic plasticity has evolved. At the stage of biological evolution when multicellular systems evolved from single cellular systems, intercellular communication became an important tool to regulate tissue formation. One of the major mechanisms to guarantee regular growth and development of a multicellular system was to stop cell division through 'contact inhibition' by neighbouring cells. That means a cell stops dividing and multiplying itself when it makes contact with another cell. This way, a tissue, for example, 'skin', can be formed without encroaching on other tissue types such as muscle. Correspondingly, cells start dividing again when this 'contact inhibition' is lost. (The latter is observed, for example, during the processes of wound healing. New skin cells are produced until exactly enough have been formed to fill the wound without excess.) Under certain conditions, the control of 'contact inhibition' can be lost, as happens during cancer development, which is characterized by uncontrolled cell division that does not stop on contact with other cells. Similar mechanisms operate in neurons. Once a neuron has been integrated into a network, through synaptic contacts, it does not divide anymore. As said before, however, intercellular contacts of a neuron, i.e. synaptic contacts, are not permanent: in the process of synaptic plasticity they are restructured, lost and newly formed. This plasticity of synaptic contacts puts the neuron at permanent risk of losing control over the proliferation restraint. Neurons with a high degree of synaptic plasticity are, therefore, at a particularly high risk of starting to divide again.

This is exactly what happens in Alzheimer's disease. Prior to cell death, the neuron rejuvenesces and attempts to divide again. As in differentiated neurons, however, cell division is irreversibly blocked, and in the adult brain there is no other outcome from a partly initiated cell division, the cell dies. Thus, we have to face the problem that evolution of the human brain has created a structure that through its flexibility is extremely powerful, but at the same time this flexibility renders the brain very fragile. The potential to develop AD is, thus, an essential consequence of how the human brain is organized. Since AD occurs after the reproductive period, there is no evolutionary pressure on this 'constructive error'. In this sense the human brain is probably an evolutionary cul-de-sac. In summary so far:

1   AD is a synaptic disorder. Degeneration starts at synaptic junctions and preferentially involves molecules critical for modifying synaptic connections, such as synaptic molecules, adhesion molecules, molecules involved in membrane turnover, cytoskeletal proteins, growth-inducing and growth-associated molecules, etc. Mutations leading to functional deficits of these molecules increase the risk of AD.

2   The spatial and temporal distribution of AD pathology follows the pattern of structural neuroplasticity in the adult brain. From this both the sequence of structural involvement into degeneration of defined brain regions and the development of functional impairment can be anticipated.

3   Life events that place an additional burden on the plastic capacity of the brain or that require a particularly high plastic capacity of the brain might trigger the onset of the disease or might stimulate a more rapid progression of the disease. In other words, they might increase the risk for AD.

4   The highly plastic nature of the brain might provide some reserve compensation ability which can prevent the manifestation of the disease or at least delay the onset of the symptoms. All measures that contribute to increase this 'plastic capacity' will offer protection against getting the disease.

From this we can derive three major conclusions:

1   Alzheimer's disease is a long chronic progressive process. It apparently starts (like cancer) long before the first symptoms occur. Once the disease is recognized it progresses inevitably in a more or less predictable way. Only the rate of progression can be modified to some extent but not the progressive process itself.

2   The cause of AD, the mechanisms of the disease and its progression, although still not fully understood, are intimately linked to how the brain is organized and how higher cerebral functions are executed. To interfere with the disease process, thus, means to interfere with basic mechanisms of cortical information processing. It appears that strategies of this kind, in principle, will bear a considerable risk.

3   If we are able to understand the molecular mechanisms that regulate structural plasticity in the human brain, we might also be able to understand how Alzheimer's disease develops and how we can interfere with these mechanisms to develop a neuroprotective strategy. As long as this process is still incompletely understood, the best we can do is to define the risk factors for the disease, and conditions that will to some extent slow down the progression of the disease.

AD: the risk factors and possible protective factors

There are some very rare forms of AD that together amount to less than 1 per cent of all patients which are familiar forms due to a mutation in the genome of the person. These mutations are transmitted from parent to child. Every child who is a carrier of these mutations (located either in the gene that codes for the amyloid precursor protein or for presenilin), will definitely get the disease. Moreover, the onset of this familiar form of the disease occurs at a rather young age, typically before the age of 60 years, often many years before that.

In the majority of cases, however, AD occurs 'spontaneously', which means there is no particular familial transmission. This spontaneous form of

AD is a combination of some inherent genetic disposition and harmful environmental influences. That means if you carry the genetic disposition and you are not exposed to these bad environmental factors you will not get the disease. Conversely, if you are exposed to these bad environmental factors but do not have the genetic predisposition you will not get the disease. The disease will only become manifest if both genetic and environmental factors come together. This form of AD occurs later in life, typically above the age of 65 years or even much later, and can be very variable because of the complex interactions between the environment and genetic factors.

Genetic risk factor: Apolipoprotein E

Apolipoprotein E (ApoE) is a lipid (fat) carrier in the brain. It also serves a function in intercellular and intracellular signal relay (transduction). In particular, it is involved in molecular transport and the cellular take-up and metabolism of cholesterol. Cholesterol is one of the most important constituents of cell membranes. It is highly needed for turnover of synaptic membranes involved in the process of neuronal plasticity. ApoE exists in three different types (isoforms) that are alternatively determined genetically: epsilon 2, epsilon 3 and epsilon 4. Carriers of the ApoE epsilon 4 isotype have a significantly increased risk for AD. A likely explanation for this link is an alteration of cholesterol binding ability of the epsilon 4 isoforms, which results in a dysfunction of cholesterol transport required for synaptic plasticity.

Age

The most important non-genetic risk factor is age. As already mentioned, it is very rare to get AD before the age of 50. About 1–2 per cent of persons aged about 60 have AD. By age 80, more than 10 per cent of persons have AD. The reason for this age-related increase is not the ageing process itself, but rather the accumulation of 'life events', each of which in itself would be insufficient to provoke the onset of AD. Altogether, however, such life events are thought to diminish the plastic reserve capacity of the brain. So, eventually a limit will be reached and the disease will become manifest.

Gender

Life expectancy for women throughout most countries is much higher than for men. As a result, women represent the majority of the aged population being at high risk for Alzheimer's disease. Therefore, females with AD are more frequent than males. Researchers are looking at whether there might also be a definite higher risk for women, on an aged-matched basis, that becomes manifest after menopause. A potential explanation might lie in the reduction of estrogen levels, which are known to regulate 'neuroplastic processes' in the brain. In the male brain estrogen is also involved in these processes, but probably to a lesser extent. It is possible that the male brain has developed additional mechanisms to regulate plasticity.

The usefulness of an estrogen replacement therapy, however, is still unproven and controversial. There might not be much benefit of estrogen application after the disease has become manifest. Some researchers are looking at whether the risk of getting AD might be somewhat lowered if estrogen is supplemented earlier in life. The basis for this is not understood very well. Bearing in mind, however, that the process underlying the disease starts rather early in life, estrogens might slow down this process (which shows no symptoms in very early stages) in persons who are at risk of getting AD for some other reason.

Metabolic dysfunction, thyroid disease

Besides estrogens, there are other factors involved in regulating brain plasticity. One of these is thyroid hormone. It is likewise possible, but not yet proven, that untreated thyroid disease might thus increase the risk of AD.

Brain trauma

Brain injury or trauma, even a closed contusion to the head without loss of consciousness, appears to increase the risk of getting AD. Naturally, severe trauma such as that which occurs during boxing, will drastically increase the risk. The explanation for this is that minor brain damage puts an additional burden on the plastic capacity of the brain to repair the damage. As a result of this, the reserve capacity of the brain is used up and the critical threshold will, thus, be reached more quickly.

Other environmental factors

There is the potential of increasing the risk of AD, or some other form of dementia, by other noxious agents to the brain. Among them is alcohol and it seems tobacco, as well as the occupational exposure to organic solvents, although the role of these factors is less clear. Other researchers are investigating whether environmental factors such as certain kinds of social stress might also increase the likelihood of getting AD, since they might place an additional burden on the plastic capacity of the brain. This has not yet been proven though.

Mental activity and education

Potentially, all factors that can increase the plastic capacity of the brain stand a chance of diminishing the risk of getting AD. Some researchers are looking at whether this plastic capacity can be potentially increased through continuous mental activity and exercise, particularly in early life. This involves looking to see if achieving a high level of education and securing a demanding (but not overdemanding) occupation might lower the risk for the disease. For the same reasons, others are looking to see if certain types of mental activity could be beneficial to those who already have AD (whether disease progression might be slowed down) if remaining abilities are still exercised. With brain plasticity in mind, it seems better if stressful events are avoided, so as to minimize the rate of disease progression. This principle seems a practical one for planning care during progression of the disease.

Conclusions

Much has been learned in recent years about the neurobiological correlates of functional impairment in Alzheimer's disease. We know what type of neuron dies, and in what way the process of cell death eventually progresses throughout different areas of the brain. This knowledge has enabled us to develop symptomatic treatment approaches aiming at counteracting the acetylcholine (a neurotransmitter which is critical for information processing) losses, which occur early during AD. Although this approach might be beneficial in early stages of the disease, it certainly is not a cure.

The cause of the disease and the mechanisms of neuronal death are still not understood. The lack of insight into the part of the disease mechanism still prevents us from developing available strategies that will prevent the disease, cure it, or at least slow down its progression for significant periods of time.

What we have begun to understand, however, are critical aspects of what the initiation and progression of neuronal death is about and how it relates to basic principles of brain organization and function. Although this is a major achievement for cellular and molecular neuroscience, it is not linked yet to a major benefit for persons with AD. Still, this emerging knowledge provides a better basis for caring for persons and coping with the disease.

There is still a long way to go before a cure will become available. The help for the persons who are ill at present and in the near future will thus not come from basic research so much as from highly motivated, educated and skilled caregivers. It is a demanding task for the whole of society to support the efforts being made, both at the lab bench and at the bedside.

References

Arendt, T. (2001) 'Alzheimer's disease as a disorder of mechanisms underlaying structural brain self-organization. Commentary', *Neuroscience* 102: 723–65.

Braak, H. and Braak, E. (1991) 'Neuropathological staging of Alzheimer related changes', *Acta Neuropathol.* 82: 239–59.

Hughes, C.P., Berg, L., Danziger, W.L., Coben, L.A. and Martin, R.L. (1982) 'A new clinical scale for the staging of dementia', *British Journal of Psychiatry* 140: 566–72.

Reisberg, B., Kenowsky, S., Franssen, E.H., Auer, S.R. and Souren, L.E. (1999) 'Towards a science of Alzheimer's disease management: a model based upon current knowledge of retrogenesis', *Int. Psychogeriatr.* 11: 7–23.

Terry, R.D., Katzman, R., Bick, K.L. and Sisodia, S.S. (eds) (1999) *Alzheimer Disease*, New York: Lippincott Williams and Wilkins.

World Health Organization (1986) *Dementia in Later Life: Research and Action. Report of a WHO Scientific Group on Senile Dementia*, WHO Technical Report Series 730, Geneva: World Health Organization.

Chapter 2

All God's children[1]
The spiritual needs of people with dementia

Hilda Flint

Spirituality – the needs of people with dementia

Throughout the ages there has been a sense that there can only be one origin – one creator, that ultimately there is some kind of unity. If we can see ourselves as being part of that unity, we can feel safe. This is how we can find meaning in life. This is not simply understanding – it is feeling, 'being', and includes the whole created universe. Within that creation personal relationships are crucial to this feeling of belonging, normally lived out in some form of community, giving meaning even if not dependent on an external religious faith. Where cognitive abilities are undeveloped, impaired or even absent, for instance for the infant, those with learning difficulties, or for a person in dementia, companionship, support and reassurance from others are paramount, and evidence that ultimate 'meaning' has not been lost. The individual is not isolated in an ivory tower. Human beings are 'social animals', even if some choose to withdraw from 'the world' and find their identity in seclusion, for whom 'God' or nature may offer their needed sense of significance within the cosmos.

Malcolm Goldsmith explores this in his analysis of concepts of God.[2] Not only is the relationship between the created and the creator not dependent on understanding, faith, or remembrance of tradition and dogma, for him it relies on the initiative of the creator. While our response may be of understanding, or intuitive, of feeling and emotion, for Goldsmith the key to our search for meaning is that God, the creator, the 'origin' takes full responsibility for the well-being and ultimately for the significance of his/her/its creation. Goldsmith's insight of 'being remembered by God', rather than having to access God through faith or understanding, avoids the demand for response by the created being to the creator. Humanity may but is not obliged to return awareness, appreciation, gratitude, or ultimately, love. This view offers meaning which is unconditional; especially appropriate, not simply for a human race which is endlessly creating its own suffering, but for those in dementia who no longer have the cognitive powers to plan the present, remember the past or foresee the future coherently.

God's concern for the whole of creation

The situation over the last half of the twentieth century has changed fundamentally from, for instance, Austin Farrer's pity for the 'imbecile' unable to respond to God's initiative.[3] For him the theological problem was that 'we do not know how we should relate to the mercy of God beings who never enjoy a glimmer of reason'. But if 'God' is only in relationship with those with cognitive ability, this would disqualify all but an elite of mankind. There is no biblical justification for this view. From Genesis and throughout the Judaic/Christian tradition, God is concerned for the whole of creation. When Jonah protests at God's concern for the wicked city of Nineveh, God's response is clear; 'Should not I spare Nineveh, that great city, wherein are more than sixscore thousand persons that cannot discern between their right hand and their left hand; and also much cattle?'[4]

New Testament teaching continues this comprehensive understanding: the kingdom of heaven is to be entered as 'little children'; God is concerned for every sparrow; the lilies of the field; and every hair on the head is counted. In the epistle to the Corinthians, St Paul is unequivocal – nothing matters unless it is grounded in love.[5] It is not enough to think through these issues; intelligence is a very late development. For the infant, meaning relates to being kept safe, warm, fed. It is only as the child develops that the sense of otherness develops, and the absence of the secure 'other' may create panic. The expression 'spirituality' – the need for meaning – must be appropriate to any human being, and at any stage of their life.

Over 100 years ago William James, offering a strictly psychological view in keeping with nineteenth-century 'scientific' thinking, wrote of religious experience as the 'ideal power with which we feel ourselves in connection, the 'God' of ordinary men'. He cautiously commented: The only thing that it unequivocally testifies to is that we can experience union with *something* larger than ourselves and in that union find our greatest peace.' On a practical note James suggested:

> The practical needs and experiences of religion seem to me sufficiently met by the belief that beyond each man and in a fashion continuous with him there exists a larger power which is friendly to him and his ideals. All that the facts require is that the power should be both other and larger than our conscious selves.[6]

Where the search for the sense of belonging in the creation is expressed in a variety of faiths, followers are expected to commit themselves to the dogmas and beliefs of that tradition. While leaders may profess an understanding of the philosophy underlying their beliefs, for the great majority of followers it is as much in tradition, culture and the safety of their community that they find security, and a sense of meaning in their lives. For them actions speak louder than words. It is important for a faith community to maintain contact with the person developing or already suffering dementia, and to share the stress of the carers, especially when the patient is still at home; a directive strongly expressed by the Roman Catholic Bishops to their parishes in 2001.[7]

In similar vein, Bishop John Taylor in the opening chapter of *The Go-Between God* presented his understanding of the work of the Holy Spirit as that which enables people to open themselves up in relationship to one another which can serve to affirm identity: 'In these days more and more people are sick and lost because they do not know with any certainty who they are or what they are. They can find their identity and their role only when someone else sees them with love.'[8] This recognition occurs at a deeper level than normal understanding. Taylor suggests that it is the awareness of a deep fellowship that creates the communion which is of God. It is unexpected, not consciously thought about, but in openness to God there is space for the fellowship to happen. It is even more about 'being' than about 'doing'.

Towards implicit religion

If a person-centred approach to spirituality is adopted, it is important to be able to discover and empathize with whatever may give meaning to the individual, recognizing that in a multifaith, multicultural society this may be infinitely variable. An established religious practice may offer a way to maintain and nurture the person's sense of meaning, and should not be side-stepped as 'private', or insignificant as a relevant component of a care plan. Where there is no obvious religious interest, it is as important to maintain a high level of personal communication to maintain a sense of identity, relationship with others, and familiarity of environment.[9]

In an article on the effects of multisensory stimulation,[10] Colin MacDonald writes that the most important aspect of maintaining well-being for people with dementia is 'the attitude or approach adopted by staff'. Taking MacDonald's comments further, where sensory experiences are so important in maintaining a person's awareness of the world and of people outside themselves, spirituality, the sense of being part of a world which has some meaning outside oneself, will rely on the quality of relationships, analogous to the spirituality others enjoy in their conceptual understanding of 'God'.

What derives from MacDonald's work is a recognition of the non-cognitive ways in which we can relate to each other and to the created universe: to revalue the arts, the emotions and sensory expressions of relatedness as significant in the spiritual development of people, especially those for whom understanding is limited – no longer 'imbeciles' but 'children of God'. MacDonald comments that in residential institutions there is a danger that the 'personal' care plan is determined by the institution's resources, rather than by the person's own life experience.

MacDonald's overall comment on a research project using multisensory intervention was that it was appreciated by residents when in use, but without much effect on their moods on return to their normal environment. Personal relationships and attitudes in day-to-day activities can be more significant than separate specialist provision.[11] In these relationships and attitudes implicit spiritual values can be recognized and validated.

MacDonald's challenge is in his question: 'Does training in the art of sensory stimulation have to be so intensive and complicated, or is all that is required simply a positive, creative response to a basic human need for sensuality?' An interesting comment comes from Ashley Montague's study of the importance of touching,[12] especially for the elderly: 'It is especially in the ageing that we see touching at its best as an act of spiritual grace and a continuing human sacrament.' The power of touching needs to be recognized, and not abused, since the sense of personal respect can easily be lost, and trespassing on personal space may accompany care which is concerned with physical needs, and oblivious to the deeper significance of touching.

Implicit religion

This leads into another concept – 'implicit religion' – suggested by Edward Bailey, where 'moments of heightened consciousness, whether they are understood in terms of transcendence, values or religion [occur]'. He does not restrict the occurrence of 'implicit' religion to particular moments of awareness, but suggests that the less obvious times when community and relationships are allowed to develop may be even more important.[13] Such developments can be viewed as examples of human responses to God's initiative, and the mutuality of the relationship between God and humanity. While this may be one sided for people with dementia, that also supports Goldsmith's faith in God's initiative and ultimate self-offering, which does not require explicit response. Whether a theology informing practice is consciously identified or not, it is the interaction between concepts and praxis that gives meaning to practice, and which may determine the quality of relationships between carers and those being cared for. Where such relationships can be nurtured, they can reflect and demonstrate humanity's dependence upon God, and affirm God's initiative in 'remembering' his creation.

Over the last 50 years, for Jean Vanier in L'Arche and others who have set up small community homes for people with learning difficulties, there has been great satisfaction in developing a spiritually vibrant life. They have demonstrated that those who would in the past have been institutionalized and dismissed as 'imbeciles' – regarded as little more than animals – have lives which can be rich in emotional response. In reciprocal relationships with each other and with those caring for them, they can find meaning for themselves, and for others who are able to relate to them, setting aside the 'normal' cognitive expectations of understanding and intelligent development. The lack of inhibition characteristic of their residents is in many ways similar to that of people in the middle stages of dementia, and confirms Goldsmith's comment that there is a rich seam of spirituality to be explored.

In the 1970s an Asian priest, Kosuke Koyama, wrote several books[14] emphasizing the importance of communicating with people appropriately. If their normal pace was behind a buffalo cart at three miles an hour, it was no good presenting a gospel packaged in Western style: 'Jesus Christ does not carry his cross as a business man carries his briefcase.'[15] So it is with dementia. Presenting concepts about a God of love are irrelevant to someone who has lost the capacity to think conceptually. To practise loving relationships – the love of God – will deliver the message that they still have meaning in life, that they are still respected, cared for, loved, and are 'real persons'.

Loveday and Kitwood comment that 'people with dementia generally have rich and powerful inner lives, in the realm of feeling and emotion'.[16] Where feelings or emotions are expressed more violently than we are accustomed to in everyday life, this may be written off as troublesome behaviour and met by overstressed care staff with medication, or by exhausted spouses or family members with anger and misunderstanding, which can increase the person's sense of isolation, bewilderment and exclusion. An example of such exasperation occurs in the film *Iris*, when John Bayley reacts with anger at his wife's tearful cry for comfort.[17] As there is less inhibition or control in the expression of the feelings and emotions of people with dementia, so it is important for these feelings to be acknowledged and validated rather than suppressed or rejected. In so doing we give the message that not only are the feelings real, but the person expressing them is also real.[18] Such feelings may be identified as 'spiritual' if they are giving a sense of being 'at one with' others, beyond the immediate relationship or experience of isolation and fear. Spiritual well-being is cared for, or neglected, in the 'present moment' when past and future have little or no apparent meaning, and *concepts* of 'God' are irrelevant. The manager of a care home commented that a succession of such moments were of great value in building up a feeling of safety and well-being in a resident, regardless of whether each moment was apparently soon forgotten.[19]

In a study of non-verbal communication, Cook and Hubbard commented: 'Our findings show that people with dementia are very good at using non-verbal communication to convey a wide range of meanings.'[20] Their observations covered communication between people with dementia and care staff, and also interactions between people with dementia themselves. Body language, touch, facial expressions, eye contact, smiles, outbursts of anger, or laughter, can convey feelings and emotion without having to be verbalized. For carers, whether family or institutional, to be able to interact positively can enhance the encounter, making it significant as a validation of reality in the relationship. That this is of spiritual value in bringing at least a moment of good meaning into their lives is an instance of 'grace' – of the link between the human and the divine, even if only for the transitory moment.

Negative social and medical attitudes to dementia

Tom Kitwood graphically illustrated that the prevailing negative social and medical attitudes to dementia were as much part of the problem as the physical deterioration being suffered: 'In every case societal and social-psychological aspects are involved in some way, and I have suggested that they should be regarded as integral to the process of decline.'[21] He is careful not to take any one aspect of dementia and dementia care on its own, and offers four main criteria by which development can be assessed: moral, psychological focusing on 'experience, action and spirituality', care practice, and neuroscience. The interaction between these needs to be taken into account, to present a more holistic view of the situation of those suffering from dementia and their carers.

Change of attitude amongst staff

Well-being and ill-being profiles were used in one home to assess the effect of a careful introduction of person-centred care, written up by Chrissie Hosking.[22] The aim of the project was to introduce a change of attitude amongst the staff, and the improvement of quality of life for the dementia patients. Training for the staff, the introduction of a 'multisensory environment' – a snoezelen room, and the auditing of the patients' well-being and ill-being to measure changes were steps taken to implement the project. At one point staff were trained to provide hand massage to relieve tension. As staff became more aware of the value of person-centred care plans, tailored to previous life experiences and present needs, so the general well-being scores improved. Hosking commented that a year later staff attitudes were still changing, and that 'what was once considered an unpopular job is now increasingly about enabling people to get the best out of their remaining days'. As an exercise in spiritual development through increased personal attention, the project appears to have shown positive results, even if no one mentioned the word 'spirituality'. The most significant aspect of the project was the development of the person-centred care plans for patients which served to recall and affirm their sense of well-being.

Physical and general psycho-social issues, which would help to keep the person safe in a future routine, were noted. Patients were monitored for any effect that changes in their care plans achieved, but in personalizing care plans for the patients there was no mention of the value of identifying any religious or spiritual activities. These might well have come from much earlier even childhood commitments, since given up and not necessarily obvious to the carers of a later time, but could have helped in giving a more holistic view of each patient. As the personality regresses back through the physical stages of development, so the introduction of early religious or spiritual practice might be helpful in confirming a meaningful life routine. My mother, not much of a churchgoer during her adult life, seemed to enjoy attending Sunday services in her last few months when she was losing her full faculties, and singing hymns with us in her last days in hospital, a reversion to early practice.

Use of the arts

People in dementia cannot be expected to *understand* whether or how they belong to the world outside themselves, or matter to other people, but there are other ways of understanding than reason, through the senses – sight, hearing, kinaesthetic, taste, smell. In Building Community through Arts (BCA)[23] training workshops in which I have been involved, such simple arts media are used to encourage the development of interpersonal relationships, a sense of safety, of being loved, and maybe of loving and belonging. As occasions of 'implicit religion', such experiential work seems to be an unspoken affirmation of spirituality while caring for people in dementia. It also witnesses to the importance of activities which give opportunities for one-to-one or small group interactions.

On one occasion at a tea dance organized in the home, an elderly resident was dancing with his daughter. Their mutual affection was obvious in their physical closeness, their palpable pleasure in the present moment. Whether the resident 'knew' that he was dancing with his daughter, or maybe had memories of being with his wife, seemed irrelevant. For those few minutes he was being held in a safe relationship of loving, being loved and belonging, which seemed to me to be deeply 'spiritual'. Was this, I wondered, another instance of a spirituality which affirmed his place in the wider company, a sense of 'being', and of being held safe in a situation beyond his own self?

The encounter between human beings and God

The moment of belonging in a personal relationship contrasted with services held in the home where residents come together to share in a more traditional service. For those who were brought to join in the services which I attended, it was obvious that for some the familiarity of the words and actions were significant. Memories were evoked and words which were familiar, such as the Lord's Prayer, repeated. Whether the reading of a passage from scripture was 'understood' was not clear, but it seemed that the act of having it read by the minister was itself significant.[24] There was a familiarity in the ritual which appeared reassuring, and the atmosphere at the end of the service was peaceful and relaxed. How far this was 'meaningful' to residents with dementia of any other faith, or to those for whom no previous religious activity had been of any significance, is not obvious, but the importance of ritual, especially where it is part of earlier experience, is generally accepted.

Leonardo Boff describes the grace of God as 'the supreme reality that envelops (human beings) insofar as it signifies encounter, limitless openness, and communion'.[25] The encounter between human beings and God is profoundly creative. It adds possibilities of 'being something more'. An astonishing affirmation of this thought came in a review of a BCA programme in a residential home, when a care assistant said: 'Thank you for teaching us we can be more – Thank you for showing us we can be more – And we will be more, I promise you.'[26] This can be taken as another example of 'implicit religion', where a 'moment of heightened consciousness' was expressed. The question is whether this can be sustained in ordinary day-to-day living, when 'it could be argued that it is more important'.[27] It then becomes even more crucial to maintain the quality of the encounters between carers and cared for, and between each other, which can reflect the communion between them and God.

As people become increasingly dependent on their carers, the quality of their relationships will mirror the value we place on the relationship between God and his creation. To maintain this relationship gives meaning to existence, and to recognize it in those who have lost their cognitive – and eventually apparent sensory – faculties is to affirm a corporate spirituality, in which dependency on God and on each other gives value to each component individual.

The importance of context is underlined by Patrick Bracken in his contribution to the Bishop John Robinson Conference 2000, 'Social Truth and Reality'.[28] His comment that psychiatry has been over-influenced by the scientific assumptions of the Enlightenment leads him to write: 'This analysis goes some way towards explaining why psychiatry has been blind to the importance of context.' Bracken comes from experience with the home treatment service for mental health patients in Bradford, where listening to the service users has resulted in significant changes in the way medical intervention, drugs and medication have been used. Greater attention to the development of relationships and less on sedation or basic physical needs, would help to maintain meaning for patients, affirming their value both for themselves and in the experience of their carers along with their place in their communities.

The borderline between madness and spiritual crises

Psychic struggles throughout life, if not met and resolved, may at any time precipitate crises which psychiatry is apt to diagnose as psychotic, leading to further suppression, rather than the resolution of the crisis. This realization led Anton Boisen to his life work in setting up the Pastoral Counselling movement, and to the researches of Stanislav Grof, showing that a psychic rather than a medical approach could offer healing and peace of mind. Following Jung on the influence of the unconscious on psychic development, Grof commented on the ineffectiveness of traditional psychotherapy in accessing the unconscious, where problems and conflicts are apt to arise. His own practice, using holotropic therapy and, in his early years, psychedelic drugs, were he claimed better ways of uncovering the psychic disturbances so often diagnosed as psychotic illness. He pointed out that through this therapy 'the spiritual search and philosophical quest then become important new dimensions of life'.[29] Whether this can be achieved once a person has lost their ability to understand their problems, or whether the close support and care which is offered by Grof through such crises can resolve the distress of a person in dementia does not appear to have been tested. For Grof, as controls slip the way is laid open for negative archetypes and the shadow side of the unconscious to emerge, to distress the person suffering psychic crisis. Is it possible, even probable, that for the person in dementia caring support is more likely to resolve an underlying disorder than medication? The borderline between psychosis, psychic disturbance and mystical experience is not clear, and perhaps it can only be understood by the close cooperation of practitioners from each field.

The many different ways in which people in dementia behave – their moods and emotions, their strategies in the early stages which often include a denial colluded with by their families, their angers and frustrations – present a confusing and apparently illogical picture. To find meaning in this chaos is a challenge both to theology and further research in the medical field. Medical intervention has commonly been to suppress disturbing symptoms rather than to understand them. However, a broader view which takes psychic disturbance seriously may help to clarify deeper spiritual causes – unresolved conflicts from the past or 'spiritual emergencies', as described by Grof. He does not appear to have explored the effect of unconscious forces on the lives of people with dementia, which could uncover more of these 'important new dimensions of life'.

In the Bishop John Robinson *Newsletter*, John Rowan introduces the image of the ox-herding pictures by Suzuki,[30] demonstrating that it is not enough to achieve the highest level of spiritual enlightenment: 'there is a second journey back down the levels with the realisations that have been achieved'.[31] That this return to 'normal' life is significant is also emphasized by other writers on the spiritual journey. For instance, Harry Moody and David Carroll identify the 'return' as the final stage of spiritual journeying.[32] When people are in dementia, it is not possible to tell what their last stage of spiritual development may be. However, it cannot be assumed that it is into oblivion.

All this assumes a certain degree of self-awareness and consciousness. If the mental faculties have faded, then people may have got stuck in one stage or another. As faculties deteriorate, there may be a regression through the various stages, with the result that the person with dementia reverts to the prepersonal stage. If this is the process of dementia, then for carers and professionals it is essential that they should have some concept of what may have been experienced, and what may remain in the subconscious, to stabilize or disturb the person's peace, and not assume that the regression is to a blank sheet. If the deterioration is uneven, some parts of the person's life remaining more significant than others, then knowledge of their life history and care in maintaining appropriate stimuli become important, but in our experience in some homes, issues of confidentiality inhibit the sharing of this knowledge.

Respect for the natural cycles of life

Jack Kornfield, in *A Path with Heart*, comments on the cycles of ageing: 'Old age is seen as a defeat to be resisted and feared.'[33] However, he suggests that when we respect the natural cycles of life, we find that each of life's stages has a spiritual dimension and holds the seeds for spiritual growth. For example, one of the major sources of our spiritual consciousness is found in our earliest life – the benevolent oneness of existence in our mother's womb. Our consciousness holds this memory in its depths, and the possibility of oneness which remains in nearly all traditions as an ultimate goal of union with the divine. Throughout life there are many cycles of endings which challenge us with the spiritual tasks of grieving, of letting go gracefully, of releasing control, of finding equanimity and openhearted compassion in the face of loss. Distress in dementia may well reflect our failures to face these issues earlier in life. To understand this and work with the unresolved grieving and frustrations may offer a way forward in more successful caring for those in dementia in later life, as suggested by Grof, than is achieved by medication and suppression of disturbing symptoms.

Integration of a spiritual dimension into nursing care

So that these encounters can be fully valued and repeated, the integration of a spiritual dimension into nursing care is recommended by Lynn Rew.[34] She speaks of intuition as a 'way of knowing without having concrete data to confirm the truth, [which] is evidence of the spiritual dimension and connection between persons'. She describes ways in which intuition or sensitivity to subtle cues can add to the 'normally' observed data used to assess a patient's condition and needs. To develop spirituality in the care of people with dementia also means developing the carer's own sense of having meaning in life. To develop her ability to use and develop her intuition effectively, the nurse needs to become aware of her own spirituality, and be able to express this in her caring activities. Rew points out that to become 'receptive to spiritual and intuitive truths a person must first clear a pathway or channel for these truths to travel into conscious awareness'.

That many nurses still do not acknowledge that spirituality is really part of their nursing practice is also an observation made by Elizabeth MacKinlay. She believes that training is needed to develop an holistic understanding of the spiritual needs of older adults, not only those with dementia – training that goes across the board to all who are involved in the care of the elderly.[35] Such a demand opens up the need for support and training for home carers, nurses and local groups. Community programmes and support are also needed to provide for carers, who are the first to face the physical, emotional and spiritual challenges of caring for those with dementia in the community.

Deborah McLeod, a doctoral candidate with the Faculty of Nursing at the University of Calgary,[36] is examining how health care professionals address the spiritual concerns of families who live with serious illness:

> Although we know spiritual beliefs are powerful influences on how well families deal with serious illness, we don't know very much about the nursing practices that help families draw on those beliefs. Nurses often find themselves being confronted by spiritual questions that emerge in the face of life, death, and the suffering of the people to whom they provide care. Other researchers have found many of these patients and families need help with overcoming their fears, finding hope or meaning in life, or someone to talk to to find peace of mind. As a health care system, we provide very little in this area.

Drawing the physical, psychic and spiritual areas of human experience together offers a better way forward than the disparate medical, psychiatric, or basic physical containment practices typical of the care offered at the time when Farrer expressed his bewilderment. Nevertheless, as MacKinlay and Macleod suggest, the past spiritual story of a person in dementia may offer a more perceptive understanding of their present needs for being kept safe, not only in their physical care, but in their deeper need still to be in touch with some sense of *being in relation* to their surroundings – their families, carers, and the professionals responsible for their well-being.

Conclusion

All God's children

The strength and spirituality of the whole community is reflected in the care given to those who are least able to care for themselves. In 2001 the Social Welfare Committee of the (Roman) Catholic Bishops' Conference of England and Wales issued guidelines for the information of parishes throughout the country.[37] They affirmed: 'People with Alzheimer's Disease and other dementias are fully members of the Church. Consequently they have a right to enjoy the benefits of the pastoral care and teaching of the Church.' Further they asserted: 'The Catholic Church is not simply concerned with the needs of people who are its own members, but of everyone.' The needs of carers as well as patients are addressed, and the role of local faith groups contributing to the support of people with dementia and their carers in their local communities. While they are particularly concerned to maintain familiar practice and to encourage memories of ritual and liturgies, they are alive to the broader needs of people to be cared for and supported through all aspects of their lives. Formal practice is important, but it is not the only sphere of spiritual care:

> *It is important to remember the value of what we do each day.* If we are aware of this then we escape from the trap of seeing some activities as spiritually worthwhile (such as attendance in church or prayer), and other as entirely secular with no relationship to God, save to avoid displeasing him with sin.
>
> (Social Welfare Committee 2001, my emphasis)

It would be interesting to know how far these words have filtered down into the consciousness of local parishes, and how far dialogue with specialist support groups or the medical professions has developed. The bishops also recognize that through working with people with dementia all may discover in their presence something vital about acceptance, presence and love, a view also put forward by Goldsmith. This is not simply an act of 'charity' for their benefit, but, crucially, a widening of our whole communities' perspective into the spiritual dimension of human life. As the Social Committee points out: 'They may help us reconnect ourselves with what is basically and most profoundly human.'

As the numbers of older people increase, and the number of people with dementia keeps pace, to understand and work for their spiritual needs is increasingly urgent if large numbers of people are to be included rather than excluded from our community, giving them – *and ourselves* – a better sense of meaning in existence, and a more positive, less frightening approach to death.

Notes

1 M. Goldsmith, 'Dementia', in A. Jewell (ed.) *Spirituality and Ageing*, London, Jessica Kingsley, 1999, Chapter 14.
2 Ibid.
3 A. Farrer, *Love Almighty and Ills Unlimited*, London, Fontana, 1966, p. 189.
4 Jonah 4. 11.
5 1 Corinthians 13.
6 W. James, *The Varieties of Religious Experience*, Harmondsworth, Penguin, 1902/ 1985, p. 525.

7 Social Welfare Committee of the Bishops' Conference of England and Wales, *Spiritual Needs of People with Dementia*, 2001.

8 J.V. Taylor, *The Go-Between God*, London, SCM Press, 1972.

9 L. Rew, 'Intuition: Nursing knowledge and the spiritual dimension of persons', *Journal of Holistic Nursing Practice*, 2001, May: 56–68.

10 C. MacDonald, 'Back to the real sensory world our "care" has taken away,' *Journal of Dementia Care*, 2002, Jan–Feb, p. 33.

11 C. Hosking, 'Looking after well-being: a tool for clinical audit', *Dementia Care*, 2002, April, pp. 18–20.

12 A. Montague, *Touching: The Human Significance of the Skin*, New York, Harper & Row, 1986, p. 396.

13 E. Bailey, *Implicit Religion*, London, Middlesex University Press, p. 12.

14 K. Koyama, *Water Buffalo Theology*, 1974; *No Handle on the Cross*, 1976; *Three Mile an Hour God*, 1979, London, SCM Press.

15 K. Koyama, *No Handle on the Cross*, London, SCM Press, 1976, p. 1.

16 B. Loveday and T. Kitwood, *Improving Dementia Care*, London, Hawker Publications, 1998, p. 15.

17 *Iris*, 2002 film version of *Memoir of Iris Murdoch*, John Bayley.

18 B. Loveday and T. Kitwood, op. cit., p. 15.

19 John Gray, Manager, Craig House, reviewing with BCA trainers, 8 February 2000.

20 A. Cook and G. Hubbard 'Beyond words', *Dementia Services Development*, 2000, Sept/Oct, no. 7.

21 T. Kitwood *Dementia Reconsidered*, Buckingham, Open University Press, 1997, chapter 3.

22 C. Hosking, op. cit., pp. 18–20.

23 Building Community through Arts (BCA) is the outreach programme of Kew Studio, a community-based studio. BCA has pioneered training programmes for staff in residential homes, using simple arts media to encourage a sense of community through all levels in the home and with relatives and the wider community.

24 M. Goodall, '*Memory and spiritual life – the important role of ritual*', workshop in Dementia Care Conference, London, 2002.

25 L. Boff, *Liberating Grace*, Maryknoll, NY, Orbis Books, 1993, p. 4.

26 Craig House Report of BCA Training Programme, July 2000.

27 E. Bailey, op. cit., p. 12.

28 P.J. Bracken, 'Social truth and reality', Bishop John Robinson Conference papers, 2000, pp. 16–19.

29 C. Grof and S. Grof, *The Stormy Search for the Self*, London, Thorsons, 1991, pp. 1–9.

30 D.T. Suzuki, *Zen Mind Beginner's Mind*, New York, Wetherill, 1950.

31 J. Rowan, 'Spiritual truth and reality', *Bp John Robinson Newsletter*, conference edition, 2001, p. 9.

32 H. Moody and D. Carroll, *The Five Stages of the Soul*, New York, Doubleday, Rider, 1997, Chapter 8, pp. 310–53.

33 J. Kornfield, *A Path with Heart*, New York, Bantam Books, 1993, p. 175.

34 Rew, op. cit., pp. 60–61.

35 E. MacKinlay, *The Spiritual Dimension of Ageing*, London, Jessica Kingsley, 2001, pp. 246–7.

36 D. Mcleod, *Notice of New Research*, University of Calgary, Canada, unpublished.

37 Social Welfare Committee of the Bishops' Conference of England and Wales, *Spiritual Needs of People with Dementia*, 2001.

References

Bailey, E. (1998) *Implicit Religion*, London: Middlesex University Press.

Boff, L. (1993) *Liberating Grace*, Maryknoll, NY: Orbis Books, p. 4.

Bracken, P.J. (2000) 'Social truth and reality', Bishop John Robinson Conference papers, pp. 16–19.

Cook, A. and Hubbard, G. (2000) 'Beyond words', *Dementia Services Development*, Sept/Oct, 7.

Farrer, A. (1966) *Love Almighty and Ills Unlimited*, London: Fontana, p. 189.

Goldsmith, M. (1999) 'Dementia', in A. Jewell (ed.) *Spirituality and Ageing*, London: Jessica Kingsley.

—— (2002) 'Through a glass darkly' in E. Mackinlay, J. Ellor and S. Pickard (eds) *Aging, Spirituality and Pastoral Care: A Multi-national Perspective*, New York: Hawarth.

Goodall, M. (2002) 'Memory and spiritual life – the important role of ritual', workshop in Dementia Care Conference, London.

Grof, C. and Grof, S. (1991) *The Stormy Search for the Self*, London: Thorsons.

Hosking, C. (2002) 'Looking after well-being: a tool for clinical audit', *Dementia Care Journal*, March/April: 18–20.

Iris (2002) film version of *Memoir of Iris Murdoch*, John Bayley.

James, W. (1902/1985) *The Varieties of Religious Experience*, Harmondsworth: Penguin.

Jones, G.M.M. and Miesen, B.M.L. (eds) (1992) *Care-giving in Dementia: Research and Applications*, vol. 1, London: Routledge.

Kitwood, T. (1997) *Dementia Reconsidered*, Buckingham: Open University Press, Chapter 3.

Kornfield, J. (1993) *A Path with Heart*, New York: Bantam Books.

Koyama, K. (1974) *Water Buffalo Theology*, London: SCM Press.

—— (1976) *No Handle on the Cross*, London: SCM Press.

—— (1979) *Three Mile an Hour God*, London: SCM Press.

Lash, N. (1988) *Easter in Ordinary*, London: SCM Press.

Loveday, B. and Kitwood, T. (1998) *Improving Dementia Care*, London: Hawker Publications.

MacDonald, C. (2002) 'Back to the real sensory world our "care" has taken away', *Journal of Dementia Care*. Jan/Feb: 33.

MacKinlay, E. (2001) *The Spiritual Dimension of Ageing*, London: Jessica Kingsley.

Miesen, B.M.L. and Jones, G.M.M. (eds) (1997) *Care-giving in Dementia: Research and Applications*, vol. 2, London: Routledge.

Montague, A. (1986) *Touching: The Human Significance of the Skin*, New York: Harper & Row.

Moody, H. and Carroll, D. (1997) *The Five Stages of the Soul*, New York: Doubleday.

Rew, L. (1989) 'Intuition: nursing knowledge and the spiritual dimension of persons', *Holistic Nursing Practice*, May: 60–61.

Rowan, J. (2001) 'Spiritual truth and reality', *Bishop John Robinson Newsletter*, conference edition: 9.

Suzuki, D.T. (1950) *Zen Mind Beginner's Mind*, New York: Wetherill.

Taylor, J.V. (1972) *The Go-Between God*, London, SCM Press.

Social Welfare Committee of the Bishops' Conference of England and Wales (2001) *Spiritual Needs of People with Dementia*.

Appendix

13 August 2002
Coping mechanisms for serious illness: spiritual health care in need of more attention

A doctoral candidate with the Faculty of Nursing at the University of Calgary is examining how health care professionals address the spiritual concerns of families who live with serious illness.

'Although we know spiritual beliefs are powerful influences on how well families deal with serious illness, we don't know very much about the nursing practices that help families draw on those beliefs,' says Deborah McLeod, whose research is funded by the Social Sciences and Humanities Research Council. 'Nurses often find themselves being confronted by spiritual questions that emerge in the face of life, death, and the suffering of the people to whom they provide care. Other researchers have found many of these patients and families need help with overcoming their fears, finding hope or meaning in life, or someone to talk to to find peace of mind. As a health care system, we provide very little in this area.'

As part of her research, McLeod is studying 15 videotapes of therapeutic work conducted with families at the Family Nursing Unit at the University of Calgary. Her thesis builds on previous research which concluded that therapeutic conversations helped family members gain new perspectives, improve communication, share the burden of illness and strengthen family and personal resources. Both studies draw on the Illness Beliefs Model, which highlights the importance of beliefs in healing and suffering and was developed by Dr Lorraine Wright and her colleagues in the Faculty of Nursing at the University of Calgary.

'Concerns that affect families and patients include a variety of issues such as dealing with the grief caused by the loss of a career following a stroke; devastation from loss of sexual function due to prostate cancer; or a break-down in parenting from fatigue and irritability caused by the many demands of multiple sclerosis,' says McLeod.

Addressing the beliefs people hold is key to how they cope with such concerns. 'We need to help patients draw on those beliefs in a way that contributes to their healing,' McLeod says. 'Understanding more about spiritual care practices has the potential to humanize health care and to strengthen families' ability to cope.'

McLeod, an assistant professor at the Department of Nursing at Dalhousie University, currently works as a clinician scientist with the Capital Health Cancer Program in Halifax, Nova Scotia. To speak with Deborah McLeod, phone (902) 473-2964, or contact Barbara Balfour, media relations, phone (403) 220-2920. e-mail bbalfour@ucalgary.ca. fax: (403) 282-8413.

Chapter 3

Metaphors for teaching about changing memory and cognition in Alzheimer's disease

Bookcases in a library

Gemma M.M. Jones

Summary overview

This chapter draws together the concepts of behavioural staging, neuropathological staging and a metaphor of memory changes in dementia. The 'bookcases in a library' metaphor (in which specific bookcases have 'restricted use' or become 'inaccessible' over time) is a dynamic teaching tool for explaining what happens to memory and cognitive ability in Alzheimer type dementia (AD). Such teaching is intended to increase understanding of how cognitive functions change over time, how anomalies in memory functioning can be understood, and also to have a direct impact on day-to-day interactions and communication with persons with AD. This metaphor is simple and easily remembered, unlike some of the current academic models.

This bookcase teaching metaphor has been successfully used for over 20 years in Canada, the Netherlands and the UK, and adapted as part of the content of the course 'Communication and Care-giving in Dementia: A Positive Vision'. The response to this metaphor, and subsequent feedback on how practical and readily teachable it is to others, by health care professional and family member course participants themselves, has prompted its inclusion in this book. This material was first presented in this form at the European Alzheimer's Congress in London, 1999.

Introducing the problem faced by educators

How is it that many persons with dementia can remember and seek out their favourite caregiving staff, although they cannot learn new nouns and names, or where they are in 'time' or 'spatial setting'?

Imagine you will be teaching a roomful of health care professionals, or family carers. The subject is how memory and thinking ability (cognition) change over the course of AD. Many family carers and professional caregivers will not even have heard of the term cognitive psychology, current models of memory and even their understanding of short and long-term memory will be highly variable. How then does one try to explain what can happen over the course of an illness that may go on for 20 years in such a way as to offer practical understanding of ongoing changes and handles for communication? How would you do it? How difficult is it to teach these things in a clear and simple way, which is helpful to care-giving and does not compromise accuracy? Some educators have tried to explain changes in cognitive ability by discussing the memory aspects of cognitive psychology models. However, they quickly noticed that when a phrase such as 'information processing ability' is used, lay eyes in the audience 'glaze over'. The overall problems in dementia are related to changes in a combination of attentional, memory, logical thinking, visual/perceptual and language abilities which do link up within the concept of 'information processing' ability. How can this best be taught?

Clinicians also wrestle at length with this problem, especially when they are involved in relating a diagnosis and offering an explanation and ongoing support afterwards. Many 'carer support workers' say they struggle most in trying to explain to family members the difference between 'cannot' versus 'will not'. There is an enormous difference in trying to care for a person with AD who is 'not being able to' versus 'appears to be unwilling to'. What is also difficult to explain is how a person's abilities may vary from day to day.

This chapter will focus primarily on what happens in Alzheimer type dementia (AD). It also describes reasonably well what happens to persons experiencing progressive multi-infarct dementia. It is not as easy to describe what is happening in other types of dementing illness, which can have some-what similar but nonetheless unique patterns of change. (Much is starting to be learnt about the unique patterns and progression of damage in illnesses such as frontal lobe dementias, dementia in conjunction with Parkinson's disease, Korsakov's syndrome, and combinations of dementias, or when a dementia co-exists with a particular type of physical or mental illness.)

This chapter presents several metaphors: a rubber stamp, blackboard, and primarily, specific bookcases within a library. Eventually, the first book-case will become increasingly difficult to access; later the second one also, leaving persons with AD only the others to use. The bookcase model will be briefly linked to the current understanding of the neuropathological stages of Alzheimer's disease (Braak and Braak 1998), and the brain circuitry underlying emotions (Le Doux 1986, 1992, 1993, 1994; Zola-Morgan *et al.* 1991), and the associated behavioural stages of dementia (Feil 1992, 1993; Jones and Burns 1992; Jones 1997). The overall concepts linked in this chapter are summarized in Table 3.1.

What models/metaphors need changing or replacing?

Everyone has a model of memory, whether they are consciously aware of it or not. Not all models are equally useful though. Some models are too simple and lead to dangerous assumptions and conclusions. The first thing

Table 3.1 Summary comparison of the staging models and the bookcase metaphor

	0 I wonder if anything is happening …?	1 Mal-orientation	2 Time confusion	3 Repeated motion/ speech	4 End-stage withdrawal (vegetation)
Behavioural Stage (Feil 1992; Jones 1997)	Usually recognized in retrospect; not detectable by behaviour alone	Mistakes start to be noticeable and more frequent	Obvious disorientation and disinhibition. Emotionally honest responses	Phrases, words, whistles, hums and key movements repeated for self-stimulation	Little response except to clear sensory input
Key behaviour/s in each stage	Often person appears to become a little quieter and may detach from key hobbies and activities. Small errors such as misplacing and forgetting things appear to be normal for age still	Struggle to maintain normal functioning. Often appear defensive and blaming. Tense coping with mistakes, at least for a while. Visuo-perceptual errors start. Noun finding ability is impaired. Simpler noun substitutes used	Obviously lost in time and space. Trouble with persons' names and recognizing persons. May think grown children are young, still working, and deceased parents still alive. Often frightened unless others are present in visual field	Visual field is very restricted. Difficult to get and maintain eye contact. Responses noticeably slowed. Swear words, calls for help and expletives persist longest. Perseveration in movements and speech. Can often still feed self if 'finger food' meals provided	Persons can still engage visually with their surroundings, though briefly. Words replaced mostly by sounds. Appear to close eyes and withdraw often though not asleep
Neuropathological or Braak stages of AD (Braak and Braak, 1998; Braak et al. 1998)	1 and 2. Ten-year duration. Asymptomatic, despite damage near the entorhinal and trans-entorhinal area	3. Hippocampal area damage	4. More damage to temporal lobe surrounding hippocampus; amygdala still spared	5. Damage spreads posteriorally, upwards and forwards towards frontal lobe of cortex	6. Auditory part of temporal lobe and motor cortex most spared
Bookcase stage	Micro-wobble in factual/time bookcase. Some errors occurring, but they still appear to be within the expected norm mostly. The person with AD will be noticing and becoming more uncertain in themselves	Micro-wobble in factual/time Bookcase. Errors now become more noticeable. It is very confrontational to argue about 'the facts', which are not fully being taken in or linked to other information	Factual/time bookcase collapses. No top shelf on which to store new memories. Unique new problem solving using emotional bookcase primarily	Emotional bookcase gets micro-wobble. Use of the sensory bookcases aids communication and interaction. Music, singing, familiar poems prose and prayers often strongly responded to	Emotional bookcase gets larger wobble. Use of the sensory bookcases, especially touch, music and nurturing voice tones get strongest responses

Note: The author has adapted, expanded and linked the bookcase metaphor to other staging models over the past 20 years. The first reference heard to it was in Canada in 1982 by Naomi Feil, though its original source is unknown.

that needs replacing is the notion that memory is the only ability which is affected in dementia. For simplicity's sake, this chapter will speak in terms of persons with AD as experiencing difficulties with attention, certain types of memory, logical thinking ability and language ability. (Other types of functioning are also affected, in addition to age-related and pathological changes in sensory functioning, but for our purposes here the above are sufficient.)

Why focus on attention, memory and logical thinking ability? Because they have direct implications for understanding how communication and interaction need adapting as the dementia process progresses. If one isn't aware that persons with dementia can experience difficulties beyond 'memory troubles', one is unlikely to try to adapt the one's own speech or the environment in such a way as to help a person concentrate. Communication moves towards using simpler language, which emphasizes the most important words. Communication also gradually moves to using other senses. The basic message that needs communicating when persons are frightened, which is more often than we have known in the past, is 'You're not alone, I'm here and I'm staying with you for a while'. This message can be conveyed through all of the senses, by touch and nurturing voice tones especially, even if the language is not understood.

The next thing that needs replacing is this 'all or none' concept of memory. Memory isn't one thing that someone either 'has' or 'hasn't' got. Yet, how often have you heard someone say 'She's lost her memory?' 'He's got no memory?' And, even more sadly, 'There's no point in visiting anymore, he can't remember my name, doesn't know me, doesn't even know I come in.' 'She tells everyone I never visit and I come in every day . . . she can't remember anything.' When persons use such expressions, whether they realize it or not, they are using a model of memory which assumes that it is only one discrete thing, either you have it and can use it or you don't.

Some psychologists suggest that there may be 30 or more types of memory. Some of these become fragile and damaged. In the past five years much has become known about the particular order in which this happens in AD (Miller and Morris 1993; Braak and Braak 1998; Braak et al. 1998). The progression of difficulties that such damage causes will be the focus of this chapter (see also Chapter 12 this volume).

From a care-giving point of view, it is important to know some basic information about what types of memory will become difficult/impossible for a person to use and also what types remain more 'intact'. This leads to the care-giving strategy or maxim of 'Support what is weak; optimize and use what is spared'. In other words, accurate models or metaphors need to guide our best efforts to care for a person with dementia so that we do not lose sight of the person, what they are struggling with, and above all what perceptions and feelings can arise from their difficulties and frustrations. Such care requires specific knowledge of the illness in addition to motivation on the part of professional caregivers and family carers. Motivation comes from desire to help and accompany a person through the course of their illness whilst trying to understand what happens during this process. Without understanding care, dementia can be an experience of increasing fear, disconnection and extreme isolation. Fear, not dementia precludes happiness.

The important question for the purpose of this chapter then is how best to explain what happens to 'thinking ability' in dementia, in a simple way to help guide care practices, without being inaccurate.

Some limitations of previous metaphors

The difficulties with a number of previous attempts to do this are given below. Skip over these if you wish to go straight to the Rubber Stamp, Blackboard and Bookcase metaphors. Table 3.2 lists various attempts to explain memory changes in dementia over the past 25 years. These are a start, but inadequately explain what is currently known about the process of AD. (The original authorship of these metaphors is unknown to me.)

In the models shown in Table 3.2, largely there is the assumption that the memories themselves are the units or objects that are damaged or 'lost'. (Note that no one can yet locate/take a piece of tissue from the brain and say 'these particular protein/genetic codes, or whatever structural units comprise 'physical memory' are your memories of what happened on your fifth birthday.') As already stated, the problems in AD are known to be much more extensive than the notion of 'losing memories'. Memory difficulties can involve damage to the formation and storage of new information and access to stored memories. Abilities such as attention and logical thinking need to be accounted for, as well as changed to visuo-spatial, perceptual awareness and language, which are also gradually affected and linked with memory difficulties.

The models in Table 3.2 do not explain the paradoxes about memory which carers are most troubled and puzzled by. How is it, for example, that a person with AD may not remember getting married, or even recall that they had children, let alone their names, and yet when the favourite granddaughter comes in to visit they recognize and know her by name? One gentleman could say his dog's name until a few days before his death, but had not spoken his wife's name in the previous three years.

When asked one evening whether she 'had done anything special that day', a lady could not remember having gone out on a special outing. This puzzled the family and caregivers since she had had a wonderful time and had not wanted to return to the residence. However, later while sitting in the lounge she saw a news story on TV about where she had been that day. Suddenly, she remembered and related some specific details about the outing.

Table 3.2 Some metaphors used in past decades to explain memory changes in dementia

Metaphor or model	Normal functioning	Explanation for the problem in dementia
Memory as a film projector	The projector plays all the frames at the correct speed, reflecting what really happened, and was recorded.	The projector doesn't project all the frames anymore, and/or the film becomes damaged so that some frames are skipped, thus the projected film is no longer an accurate representation of what happened and can distort in strange ways.
Memory as a brick wall	Each brick represents a unit of stored memory. The bricks stay in place and can be located as needed.	Some bricks become loose, eventually fall out of the wall. The wall stands with gaps where the lost memories are.
Memory as a filing cabinet	Files equal memories. They are stored according to time or category.	Some say that files just get lost. Others, that dementia is like a poor secretary who forgets to refile the files, or files them incorrectly, so that they are no longer there for use.
Memory as a Persian carpet	The various coloured woollen strands represent different types of memories. The carpet grows in size and pattern during life, but in essence remains a stable, useful object.	Brain damage in dementia is like a moth that starts eating away at the carpet; where the holes are, memories are lost forever.
Memory as a deck of cards	Most people 'think' with a full set of cards, memories and abilities.	Losing cards in one's deck, assumes memories and abilities are lost. Note this analogy is also used pejoratively for some types of mental illness or disability.
Memory as one old bookcase	Books/memories are collected over time, filling it from the bottom shelf upwards.	In dementia, the bookcase starts to be emptied from the top (most recently acquired), downwards, hence leaving old memories intact the longest, with no memories on recent top shelves.
Memory as a computer	Ram memory, disc memory, software and hardware allow the system to store and retrieve information and execute desired operations.	Various explanations: reduced Ram, hard disc memory, limited access to memory, various software and hardware problems.

Paying attention

Selecting and imprinting impressions on a rubber stamp which makes imprints into memory

In AD attentional ability is affected as well as memory. Many mistakes made by persons with AD are attentional errors, not memory errors (Jones *et al.* 1992; Miller and Morris 1993). Since the ability to pay attention precedes the ability to store an experience or impression into memory, or retrieve it from memory, let's start with a simple diagram of this process of events leading up to memory retrieval. Figure 3.1 illustrates this in a simple way. Note that of the many signals our senses note, not all of them are stored into memory. Our senses are the first filters to information. Our ability to pay attention and select out things of importance, novelty or interest, is the second line of filtration. A nice way to think of this process is to think of a rubber stamp, which has a changeable under-surface. Whatever information is placed onto this rubber stamp constitutes our 'impression'. This impression can be imprinted onto a temporary blackboard working space, and then into memory in several places. Note that there are several imprints made in the brain of any given impression. Later on, these different storage sites of the 'impressions' will be synonymous with memories stored on different types of bookcases that will be referred to.

Attention is a very complex function to describe (Parasuraman 2000). Overall, psychologists refer to two key modes or types of attention. There is 'divided or split attention' (like when you are 'multitasking' or paying attention to several things at once), and 'undivided or sustained attention' (like when you are focusing on one thing to the exclusion of other things). Attentional functioning is linked in special ways to sensory and memory functioning. For our purposes, let's say that all persons have both modes of attention. Depending on what task is being done or what state a person is in, at a given time, one type of attention is more suitable than the other. Overall, persons usually seem to be better at one type of attention than another because it is less 'effortful' for them.

Attention is linked to memory formation. As Figure 3.1 shows, if you cannot pay attention, an impression is not formed onto the undersurface of the 'rubber stamp' and imprints do not get stamped/stored onto the temporary blackboard space or into more permanent memory. Notice that our senses are our first filters for what we eventually store into memory.

No one can remember everything. When someone has not been able to pay attention to something, it doesn't become a memory. Therefore it is not a question of a person 'forgetting' or 'not remembering' since no impression was made or memories imprinted to be forgotten. Real memory problems are a consequence of having stored the bit of information, but not being able to locate, access or use it again.

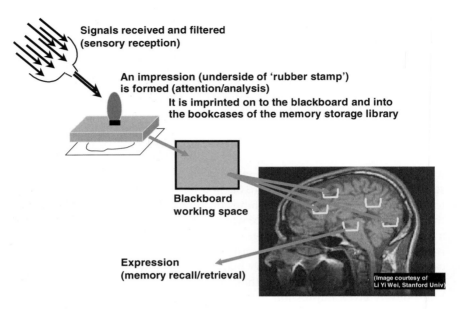

Signals received and filtered
(sensory reception)

An impression (underside of 'rubber stamp')
is formed (attention/analysis)

It is imprinted on to the blackboard and into
the bookcases of the memory storage library

Blackboard
working space

Expression
(memory recall/retrieval)

(Image courtesy of
Li Yi Wei, Stanford Univ)

Figure 3.1 The sequence of events leading up to memory storage and recall. Think of
each place of imprint as a bookcase.

There is also another sense in which the term memory linked to attention
is used. This will be of most direct use to our thinking about dementia. This
is the sense in which attention allows us to keep a focus on the many daily
things that need to be done. This is a type of 'quick reference' or 'memo-
type memory', to which you need quick access, but which is also usually
forgotten quickly. Some refer to this as 'working memory (Baddley *et al.*
1991). For our purposes let's think of this type of ability as a kind of
blackboard in one's head.

The blackboard model of memory/attentional ability difficulties in dementia

Imagine that each of us has a blackboard in our head. Each of us has a
different sized blackboard. The size of the blackboard determines how many
memos or reminders about daily tasks and messages that we can write will
fit on it. Let's assume that 50 memos at one time is about the capacity of the
average sized blackboard (see Figure 3.2). (Yes, there are rare individuals
who seem to have blackboards that can keep track of and manage 500
memos!) However, the size of our own blackboard is not totally fixed. It can
expand and shrink somewhat, depending on our circumstances (it is likely

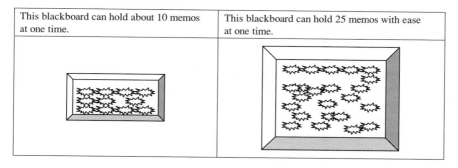

This blackboard can hold about 10 memos at one time.	This blackboard can hold 25 memos with ease at one time.

Figure 3.2 Attentional errors are linked to memory difficulties. The rule governing these blackboards is the same, 'full is full'. Having AD shrinks the size of a person's blackboard, thereby decreasing the capacity of a person to work with many bits of information at the same time, and to form imprints, which in turn record memories.

that the under-surface of the rubber stamp also changes in size, or the clarity of the print face of the information it is recording).

Unusual circumstances such as being tired, ill, stressed or distracted can temporarily shrink the size of the blackboard. You also know that there are circumstances in which the blackboard in your head seems to be able to hold more information than normal. Have you ever noticed this after holidays, or a nice break, or personal success of some kind? What happens if your blackboard can only deal with 50 memos or items of information and you try to cram on 51 or more items anyhow? The one rule seems to be: 'full is full', regardless of the size of the blackboard. If you try to overfill your blackboard, something gets lost or forgotten, mixed up or exchanged or replaced, and you start to make mistakes in what you're doing or were intending to do. Have you ever noticed how this often happens when you're multitasking in a rush? Have you ever gone upstairs or into a room and not known what you were doing in there until you retraced your steps?

AD can be thought of as a process that gradually and permanently reduces the size of the blackboard in a person's brain. In the end, perhaps only one memo, a few key words or one phrase can fit onto it, and be worked with (or processed) at one time. This is why carer communication constantly needs to be simplified and adapted, to fit with what the person's blackboard size is, what they can comprehend.

If AD causes someone's blackboard to become smaller, and the person experiences greater difficulty in paying attention (i.e. it becomes increasingly effortful to work with even small amounts of information), then it stands to reason that increasingly less information will be formed (into impressions) and imprinted (onto the blackboard) and stored into memory as dementia progresses. That's where the key metaphor about memory comes in.

A new metaphor of memory change in Alzheimer type dementia: different types of bookcases in a library

Let's think of different types of bookcases in a library. Each type of bookcase stores memories, but differently. It is not yet known exactly how many kinds of different bookcases or memory storage systems exist within the brain. There is evidence for different storage locations for 'factual/time memory', 'emotional memory' and 'sensory memories' (sight, sound, smell, touch, taste and kinesthetic sense, that is your body awareness of balance and movement). Cognitive psychologists speak of other types of memory: echoic memory, short-term memory, long-term memory, working memory, spatial memory, procedural memory, and others. We do not yet know if these are separate types of memory or special linkages of attentional ability with specific types of memory, in various combinations. Let's now turn to building up the bookcases in a library metaphor, one bookcase at a time.

The normal memory bookcase (facts storage by chronological time)

Think of memories or impressions somehow being stored or categorized with reference to chronological time portions. Now think of these memories being placed on some sort of shelving: early memories on the bottom, later ones higher up. If you imagine that each shelf holds five years of memories, you might think of something like Figure 3.3.

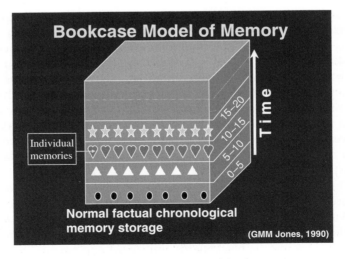

Figure 3.3 Hypothetical 'normal factual/time memory' bookcase.

Using this metaphor, and such hypothetical time categories, by the time one reached age 80, there would be 20 shelves, all loaded full of memories, and a new 'top shelf' just starting to be filled. Under normal circumstances, this storage or filing system works reasonably well, in that we can skip around from memory to memory (spanning considerable time periods) without becoming stuck in one particular place, and without becoming disoriented in time. (You can prove this to yourself by trying to think of an early school memory, then switching to a memory of your first bicycle or scooter, and then to a memory of your first job interview, and then going back to memories of early school days.)

If someone were to call you, or the phone were to ring, or a fire alarm sound, regardless of where you were on your bookcase, you could return to what is happening, to answering the phone (to our present reality) without any difficulty. By and large, we can move from shelf to shelf, back and forth, as often as we like without disrupting the location of the memories. (Such orientation and reminiscing disorientation is discussed in detail in Jones and Burns (1992). In the absence of brain damage this system stands us in reasonably good stead throughout life. (This is not to deny that perceptions and memories cannot change somewhat over time, as is well described in the psychological literature.) Overall, Figure 3.3 summarizes normal memory functioning in a simple way so that we can move on to what happens in AD.

Overview: What happens to the factual/chronological time bookcase in AD?

To start with, think of some sort of a process which weakens the structure of the bookcase. A micro-wobble becomes a serious wobble, and eventually the bookcase collapses. (Think perhaps of the screws rusting, the pegs loosening, or the wood deteriorating.) When the bookcase collapses, some memories will become squashed under the weight of the structure; some of the memories on the top bookshelf will be displaced and lost, eventually leaving no top bookshelf on which to place new memories. What happens when there is no top bookshelf left? What other types of bookcases or memory storage systems remain? What are their limitations? These are the questions to be answered next.

The factual/time bookcase has a micro–wobble: Behavioural Stage 0

In Alzheimer's type dementia, the first signs of memory difficulties are very difficult to pinpoint; that's because they are small and intermittent to begin with. They gradually increase and are definitely noticed by the person who experiences them, though not always by others. This is frustrating and

---

Box 3.1   Have you ever made one of these slips?

Common daily mistakes we can all make include:

- misplacing things in daily use, such as glasses, keys, handbags, wallets
- forgetting familiar names when the pressure is on suddenly to use them
- going upstairs or into a room and not being able to remember what you went in there for (and needing to retrace one's steps to capture the intention/thought again)
- making cross-over type errors, where you put the teapot in the fridge and the milk on the table (there are loads of variations on this one!)
- not being able to focus and take in the key point of a conversation or a written article
- having difficulty finding someone's name when caught off guard or 'out of context'

---

frightening. The reason why such mistakes and difficulties are so invisible in the earliest stages of the illness is because they are extensions of the types of difficulties everyone has when they're tired, ill, stressed, overloaded, distracted, not concentrating fully on what's happening. Box 3.1 lists examples of some of these types of mistakes. In the same way that you notice when you make a mistake (for different reasons), a person with AD will also notice that things are 'going wrong'. He or she will probably not have any idea why things are increasingly going wrong though. Many persons are frightened of 'going crazy', or being seen as 'incompetent'. Often they try to compensate or cover up their slips and mistakes. Denying and blaming are among the most common ways of doing this initially. Coping styles are discussed briefly later.

Imagine that, at some point, something starts to happen to the structure of the actual bookcase, rather than to the individual memories stored on it. Imagine that the screws or pegs are loosening even more. First, a micro-wobble starts, as is shown in Figure 3.4. Eventually it becomes a major wobble.

It is impossible to put an exact time frame on this, but family carers often report that, in retrospect, they started noticing the tiny errors and the first unusual occurrences about five to ten years before a diagnosis of AD. The neuropathological research of Braak and Braak (1998), similarly suggests that such damage starts occurring up to ten years before errors are clearly visible and a diagnosis is made. Furthermore, they confirm that their first and second 'neuropathological' stages occur without obvious symptoms. This means that the first types of damage occur in the near-hippocampal (the entorhinal and transentorhinal) areas of the brain (shown later in the chapter). While this is happening the brain is finding ways to compensate

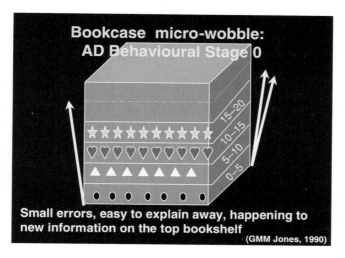

Figure 3.4 The first signs of errors as the bookcase gets a micro-wobble.

and errors and behaviour change are not yet readily apparent (see also Chapter 1 about brain plasticity).

When a 'micro-wobble' starts, think about what is happening to the stored memories on the uppermost bookshelf. They are jiggling out of position a little and returning more or less into position, though some will be bumped off the shelf. This is the time when difficulties are starting, but are largely invisible to the outside world. Often, through great extra effort and motivation on the part of the person with AD to do things correctly, the brain compensates the best it can. This might mean that a person takes more time to complete something, or has to check it several times, or has to use lists extra carefully, but they continue to function much as normal to outside observers.

If the mistakes are small, no cause is yet sought. Furthermore, such difficulties are often intermittent. They can be attributed to things such as normal aging, too much stress at work, becoming a little deaf and not hearing things properly, having difficulty with pending/retirement, role changes and other health concerns.

More serious wobble: Behavioural Stage I

The bookcase wobble continues and will eventually worsen in AD. Note that if a person has multi-infarct dementia and the infarcts, or transient ischaemic attacks (TIAs), stop now, then the wobble will not necessarily worsen. Imagine that the bookcase veers over to the right, then to the left

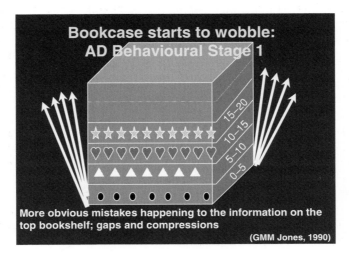

Figure 3.5 Errors are more frequent and noticeable as the wobble worsens.

suddenly. What happens to the memories on the top bookshelf? Some will be displaced, others compressed together and some may slip off the top shelf, leaving micro-gaps. As the wobbles continue, that results in additional disruption and loss of the stored information (Figure 3.5).

This explains how someone can get only some of the facts, or only part of the information, and hence the 'wrong end of the stick' entirely, even though the things remembered are in themselves accurate. For example, one lady in a residential home complained that the staff members were whispering and plotting together to do things to make her look inept when she wasn't. In reality, she had heard staff whispering behind her door nearly every morning. The trouble was that no one liked to bring the breakfast tray into this lady's room, and there was often a long discussion between them as to who was going to do it on a given morning. Why? Because when 'something didn't suit her' this lady was known to grab the hot drink from the tray and throw it at staff. So there was a general reluctance to help her and much discussion and stalling for time. The old lady picked up on the whispers behind her door, but attributed wrong motives to it. No doubt even after staff entered the room, thinking about their own safety uppermost, they will not have stayed long or been very polite with her, thus reinforcing her perception of things.

What happens to new information placed on the top shelf of a wobbly bookcase? It is sometimes unreliable as a result of the effects of compression and decompression and mix-ups of information on the top shelf. This is seen as tiny memory gaps and information mix-ups, and filling in the gaps 'on the spot' or confabulating, as they are detected.

As the wobble worsens, most family members and friends become aware that 'something is wrong', but they do not know what to do. If the person with the wobbly bookcase is defensive, blaming, denying, covering up the difficulties, it can be very difficult to remain in easy, comfortable, normal contact with them. Some family members and friends have said, in retrospect, that they felt as if they were being rebuffed, or pushed away, as if the person wanted more privacy.

This is potentially the most difficult time of all. Persons in the early part of a dementia process are aware that something is 'not right', but do not understand what is happening, and often try 'harder' to no avail. For family and friends, it is difficult because offers of support and suggestions to go to the doctor are often not welcomed and sometimes provoke outright hostility. What we often fail to notice (because misunderstandings are happening, feelings are becoming very hurt, and the person with dementia is becoming frightened and angry) is how much effort a person with dementia is putting into trying to do things, especially important things, 'correctly'.

Different responses to noticing mistakes caused by the wobble

There are many different coping styles for dealing with such changes. Most persons, at least for a while, struggle greatly. Some persons can become almost intolerable to live with. They cannot accept (or sometimes believe) that they themselves are making such errors, never having made them before in their adulthood, and having always prided themselves on their own high standards at performing tasks. This is particularly true of persons who have had work and jobs of great responsibility formerly. (Obviously personality type, life experience, knowledge about aging and dementia, and many other factors will play a role in how an individual responds.) More 'easy-going' persons are not usually as hard on themselves for making mistakes. Whatever the variables, there are individuals for whom the awareness of making errors is devastating to their ability to function, as well as their self-image and self-worth. Three examples follow.

Examples

A gentleman who had long been a highly competent designer in a highly competitive advertising firm was increasingly struggling to keep his own paperwork in order at home. He could no longer use his filing cabinets effectively, and at one point had converted the entire living-room floor to be a substitute large-scale filing cabinet. All the contents of his files were carefully spread out on the floor. The first thing one noticed when standing in the doorway of the living room, for there was no place to walk across it anymore, was the hundreds of yellow post-it notes on the array of papers. He was up till late every night trying to check everything against lists he was making to try to keep things under control. Sometimes he fell asleep on a chair and slept in his clothes all night. Piles of unopened correspondence had started to accumulate in the kitchen. He seemed increasingly unaware of these, so great was his concentration on managing the paperwork on the living-room floor.

Another lady did not struggle with her mistakes so much. She did not try to hide them from her friends and family. She laughed them off casually, blaming them on normal aging memory problems. 'Look at that. Can you believe I put the teapot in the fridge when I was getting the milk for the tea? I must be losing it, but what do you expect at my age? I like cold tea too fortunately.'

One gentleman was aware he was having difficulties reversing his car out of the driveway in the past months. He did not want his wife to see him struggle, and had taken to calling her to sit in the car only after it was parked safely on the road. She became worried when this process was taking over 30 minutes and many attempts, with increasing numbers of bumps and scratches to the car. This is when she sought help, much to the fury of her husband, who denied anything was unusual other than that the car was becoming older, wearing, and becoming less manoeuverable: he could not bear to think that it might have something to do with a change in his own abilities and remained defensive for a long while.

Remember that visual-spatial ability is simultaneously becoming impaired and that this affects perception at this time also. Perhaps the clearest way of seeing this is from the drawings that persons in this first behavioural stage of AD try to copy from a model. The errors in Figure 3.6 are not a result of

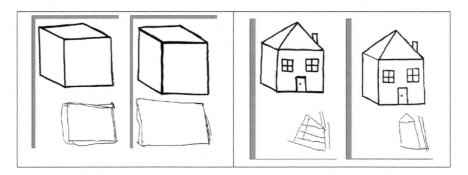

Figure 3.6 These drawings were copied by a person with AD, several months apart. Notice that the starts and stops are not well controlled, although the person knows what they are supposed to do, and also that their own drawings are not turning out well. Some of the lines have been completed 'by memory', not from looking at the model. Note particularly the first cube copying attempt, which has been 'doctored' to give the appearance of a three-dimensional cube by adding lines which are not in the model.
The bookcase collapses (Behavioural Stage 2, loss of time/space perception)

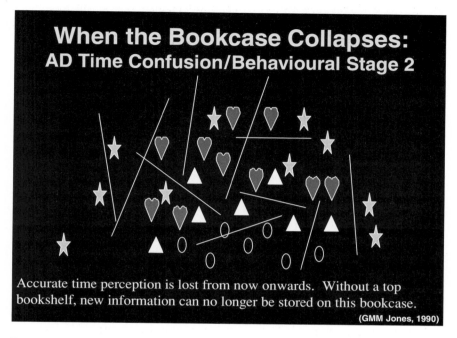

When the Bookcase Collapses:
AD Time Confusion/Behavioural Stage 2

Accurate time perception is lost from now onwards. Without a top
bookshelf, new information can no longer be stored on this bookcase.

(GMM Jones, 1990)

Figure 3.7 The factual/time storage bookcase collapses with many subsequent adaptations
and changes in behaviour.

someone not knowing what they are supposed to do. They are a result of
not being able to coordinate many eye movements as they are performing a
task, and losing track of what they are doing.

What happens when the bookcase finally collapses, after perhaps becoming
increasingly wobbly for over five years? What we observe in reality fits in
well with thinking of the bookshelving as beginning to sag, and eventually
collapsing. When this happens, some memories are more difficult to access
than others. Which stay in place the best? The ones at the bottom are
compressed nearly exactly into their normal place. Which memories are
spread around and dislodged most? Recent memories, ones that were stored
on the uppermost shelves (Figure 3.7). The first information which becomes
difficult to access is the information on the current top shelf; the information which had been stored with increasing difficulty while the bookcase
was wobbling. Note that the bookcase does not collapse totally overnight.
This is a gradual process in the case of AD. However, with some types of
stroke damage (vascular dementia) this can happen very rapidly.

At some point when the bookshelf is collapsing, time perception becomes
increasingly disturbed. Persons have increasing difficulty knowing the correct
time, date, season and year. They may 'get stuck' in memories of places in

the past and find it increasingly difficult to manoeuvre their way through them, back to present reality. A person's conversation and behaviour will often correspond with where in time they think they are, and who they think to be alive then. They may have times of realizing they are old, but these do not remain. (Reality Orientation methods can help persons in stages 0 and 1, but when the factual/time bookcase has collapsed, since there is no top shelf on which to place newly learned information, a person cannot remember 'the facts' that others are trying to tell them. Emotional details and information can often be remembered because they are stored in a different location, i.e. on a different bookcase, as we'll see later on.)

We observe that different types of errors will be made now, and that much of the defensiveness about such errors has gone. Such errors do not just involve 'missing and forgotten, incorrectly synthesized or stored facts'. They start to involve perception, mostly notably time and location perception, and also visual-spatial perception.

These new mistakes usually start slowly and increase in frequency. Someone might make occasional mistakes when they are tired or at certain times of the day. Initially, it is not unusual for a person to suddenly catch the mistake they are making (such as referring to a parent who is long dead in present tense) and then correct it (by explaining that the parent is dead). Later however, such errors start to occur more often throughout the day and are not corrected. They can range from the person with dementia becoming unaware of the current year, through to eventually thinking that they are at work again, back at home with their own young children, or that they are young again, and living with their own parents. Increasingly, during this collapsing process persons will have difficulty with information in past time extending from days to months, years and decades.

Since the information from the distant past is relatively secured into place under the collapsed bookshelf, distant memories are often possible to access and talk about, though not necessarily with any sense of time accuracy. Using reminiscence in conversation is often a good way to communicate. It is also possible to reminisce with someone and see how far forward in time they can come. Sometimes it helps to bring the person to a brief but clear awareness of present time. This is not a lasting awareness, however. 'Lucid moments' seem to become rarer as the dementia progresses, but have been reportedly seen in all stages of the illness.

What happens when there is no top bookshelf on which to put new memories?

While the 'factual/chronological time storage' bookshelf is collapsing and once it has collapsed, we cannot expect persons to be able to store any new information about what has/is happening to them. There is no top shelf on which to put new memories and information, although some past information is still accessible. This is why staff who ask about what a person did this morning, what they ate, whether or not they had visitors, what presents they got for their birthday, etc., often get such strange responses.

Have you ever heard some say that they never get fed or never have visitors when you have clearly seen that they have? This is a good time to mention that the feelings can be correct, even though the facts aren't. Persons with AD should be helped to enjoy present time, and can partake of it with as much pleasure as they possibly can out of every moment. However, caregivers should not expect a person to remember recent or ongoing events because this type of memory storage is now permanently damaged.

Example: Afternoon tea

Imagine that Mrs Evans, who has AD, is living in a residential home, and that you are a member of staff there. One afternoon, you are busy serving tea and a slice of cake for all the residents seated in the lounge. You pour Mrs Evans a cup of tea first. She is pleased and drinks it all, rather too quickly. (This is a good reason for being extra cautious about the temperature of drinks, and other things given to persons in this stage of dementia.) A few minutes later, Mrs Evans observes that the ladies sitting next to her are drinking tea, and that her cup is empty. With her poor perceptual ability and other difficulties, her experience of reality might be that she is feeling forgotten and left out. Without a top bookshelf, she cannot remember having had any tea, and protests loudly to you, 'I haven't had any tea and would like a cup please.' It is only minutes since you just served her. Do you see how innocent this error is, if indeed her top shelf has collapsed and she cannot place into memory things that are happening now?

All that some staff see though is that she was served first, that she's selfish for not waiting for others to be served, and that you are rushing around as fast as you can and have no desire to give in to the ego-centricities of a self-centred old lady. (How often do caregivers misinterpret such errors and sometimes go so far as to tell residents off. When caregiving staff haven't been taught any equivalent about this top bookshelf collapsing, they do not understand why persons cannot remember/learn new/recent information, even briefly. They are apt to think, and sometimes say, 'She can remember what she wants to remember all right.' This attributes deliberate ill-will to a person with AD and can cause a resentful attitude, which is not helpful to either the staff member or the person with AD.)

What next? Other bookcases in the memory library

Fortunately, the brain has multiple storage systems. Taken together, these different types of memory storage can be thought of as different bookcases in the brain's library. Of course, normally when we remember we are accessing

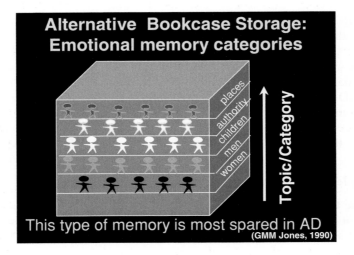

Figure 3.8 The second bookcase for emotional memory storage.

information from the many bookcases simultaneously. This happens so automatically that we have no perception of the brain accessing different places to locate and retrieve our memories for us.

It seems though that the factual/time storage is our primary bookcase. We saw that the 'factual/time storage' bookcase is the site of primary damage in AD. It will become increasingly difficult to access and eventually impossible, like the 'restricted access' section of a library. How does a person continue to live and problem solve their world when this first major restriction upon memory retrieval is imposed? What other bookcase becomes most important now? It is the emotional storage bookcase. It is accurate in its own way, but is not 'factually' accurate in terms of providing information about time, names, and descriptive details.

Figure 3.8 shows this second type of bookcase, the emotional storage system. The categories or shelves are no longer units of time, but clusters of similar 'topical, emotional' categories. (Thanks to the work of le Doux, Selemon and many others, we now know much more about the location and brain circuitry of this emotional system.)

About the emotional memory bookcase

On this totally separate bookcase, imagine that memories are stored by topical/emotional categories. For the purpose of our metaphor, imagine it is arranged something as follows. On the first, bottom shelf, are memories of all of the women in your life who loved and cared for you, with whom you had a close relationship (mother, sister, aunts, granny, girlfriends, cousins, wife).

On the next shelf are memories of all of the men in your life who loved and cared for you, with whom you had a close relationship (dad, brothers, uncles, granddad, boyfriends, cousins, husband).

Somewhere is a shelf where memories are stored of people who 'got up your nose in life', or perhaps people who 'pushed your buttons'. Perhaps they are people with whom you didn't have close relationship; the authority figures in your life, memories of unjust interactions. (Perhaps you, like many others, have a memory of a teacher who didn't judge your work fairly, or of a friend who betrayed your confidence, or of a boss who withheld a promotion when you deserved one.)

In AD, this 'emotional memory' bookcase remains 'intact' much longer than the 'chronological time memory' bookcase (Braak and Braak 1998; Braak *et al.* 1998). Its location is called the amygdala, and is shown at the end of the chapter. The enduring functioning of this emotional bookcase explains why persons can often remember (and learn about) things with a deep emotional impact (things, people and events), but not everyday facts. The emotional flavour of events and impressions can be stored and recalled much longer than the exact factual details. In AD this emotional type of memory usually continues to work, though someone may be totally disoriented in time. (It appears that in the frontal lobe dementing illnesses, with some large strokes, and in other types of frontal lobe damage such as those caused by brain tumours, the emotional bookcase can be damaged first, leaving access to the chronological time memory intact, but emotional memories and responses flattened, inappropriate or difficult to access. When this happens we can speak of apparent personality change and atypical dementia behaviour patterns.)

The kind of problem solving and remembering that can be done, with access only to emotional memory, is very limited. It is as if persons with dementia can only ask a limited number of questions, pertaining to emotions, to figure out what is happening around them. (Note that when we try to problem solve without brain damage, seeking information about 'facts', primarily we use the first type of bookshelf. We can access and figure out answers to many particular factual questions such as who, where, what, when, why, if, did, how?)

The 'why' question is most important since it involves an understanding of cause and effect, causality and consequences. Such thinking is necessary in order to be able to plan effectively. The ability to answer 'why' involves our higher logical thinking functions, and is one of the first things to become damaged and weakened when the bookcase develops a wobble. It is also one of the first questions we should stop asking persons in Behavioural Stage 1 of dementia, as their insight and logical thinking ability is becoming damaged and they cannot explain why. Have you heard persons asking someone 'Why do you think someone stole you handbag?' 'Why do you think that lady is talking about you?' 'Why do you think that someone has poisoned your food?'

The limitations of using the emotional bookcase to problem solve

This emotional bookcase, operating on its own instead of in tandem with the factual/time bookcase, is limited in the information it can provide. It gives information about stored feelings, not facts in a time context. When a person with AD is trying to figure out what is happening around them (such as who someone is, where they are, and what is happening), it seems as if they can only use a limited number of 'emotional', non-factual questions to solve their problems and understand situations. The key kinds of questions asked seem to be: 'Who does this person *feel* like or remind me of?' 'Where does this place *feel* like?' 'What does it *feel* like is going on around here?' The answers to such questions may not be wholly (or at all) factually correct, but the feelings will be.

For example, a resident in a nursing home who was once a nurse may *feel* that she cannot go to bed at night because all the other staff members are still up and working hard. She may think she is also working still. Another resident who has been wandering restlessly and has not been able to secure the positive attention of anyone may feel so frightened that the only place they want to go is 'home', to feelings of safety. (Home is, in the first instance, a feeling of 'being at home'. Home is also a literal place memory, but that is of secondary importance in this stage of AD.)

This helps to explain how some settings and events in present time seem to trigger particular memories of events, which *felt* the same way in past time, leaving a person with dementia speaking about the present in terms of past memories and feelings. It helps to explain how experienced fear and anger in the present can cause a person to relive vulnerable circumstances from former times in their life (Miesen and Jones 1997). Health care professionals often benefit enormously from the kinds of 'answers' that this emotional type of memory recall provides. A kind of closeness to persons with dementia (that has not been earned) is often present because the feeling of the caregiver reminds the person with dementia of others who have left indelible memories of feeling loved and cared for on the emotional bookcase. The person with dementia then treats the caregiver 'as if' they are that person, or wants to introduce them to each other. Have you ever had a person with AD tell you that they were sure their mother would like you and suggest you should have tea together?

The ability to find nouns and names and use them correctly is also usually damaged in parallel with the collapse of the first bookcase (this language area of the brain is next to the site of first damage and is also shown at the end of the chapter). In order to problem solve 'who' a caregiver is, a person with dementia will often resort to using names of persons who felt similar somehow, from the emotional bookcase.

Let me illustrate with a story from my own work. One day I worked a 12-hour shift although normally shifts were only eight hours. It was the first time that I had seen some residents from morning right through to evening. I helped one lady with dementia to get out of bed in the morning. She spoke to me as if I was her sister. In the afternoon, I helped this lady to bed for a 'cat-nap'. She spoke to me as if I was her mother. After dinner, I helped to get her ready for bed and she called me 'grandmother'. At the time I was in my twenties and didn't know about these bookcases. I wasn't pleased with her mistakes. I thought, 'Even on a long shift I don't turn from Jekyll into Hyde, from sister into granny.' What I didn't know then was that I had been 'on the right feeling shelf' with this lady all day. I ought to have been very pleased. Something about me felt similar to those persons who were in the category of 'all the women in her life who had been close to this lady'. She had been trying to figure out, in the only way she was able to, who I was. Factually incorrect, but without the ability to learn staff names, emotionally correct. I had been caring for her and helping her. She accessed her memories of others who had given her this feeling, and called me by their names, which is the very best she could manage to do at the stage of her illness.

This also explains why sons are often called by their brother's, father's or uncle's names, and why daughters are often called by sister's, mother's or aunt's name. (Someone once told me that her mother always called her by their pet cat's name. Luckily the daughter knew the mother was besotted with the cat, and so she was also on a good feeling bookshelf too.)

Later on, the ability to name names is further reduced; names are substituted and simplified. For example, you might observe that a person with AD calls all females 'Maggie', or even refers to them all as 'she'.

In summary then, a person who is disoriented in time is operating with the bookshelf combination shown in Figure 3.9. This shows that a person continues to struggle with their dementia by having to problem solve life with a damaged primary bookshelf, and reduced language ability to relate what they are able to retrieve from the emotional bookcase.

Mistaken identities that are not positive

Incidentally, sometimes through no fault of our own, not through anything we have done or said, we remind someone of one of the persons on their emotional bookshelf labelled 'people who got up my nose in life'. The cues can be so varied that they are almost impossible to figure out. Sometimes it is one's size, hair colour, the location of a mole, the way one laughs, or even the colour nail polish one wears. In those instances, it is wise to accept that you may not be the best member of staff to work with a given individual. They will likely continue to mistake you for someone else in their memory, and can no

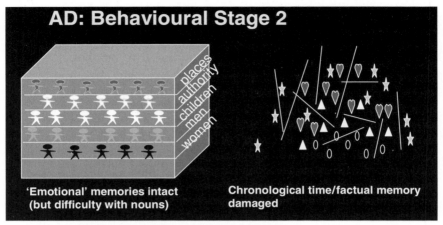

Figure 3.9 Summary of the state of the primary and secondary bookcases when a person with AD becomes disoriented in time and place (Behavioural Stage 2).

longer learn that you are not that person. (See Miesen 1998, chapter on transference and counter-transference problems, for a more detailed discussion of this topic.)

Helping someone move from one emotional memory shelf to another in Stage 2

It is also possible, if a person in Behavioural Stage 2 is 'stuck' on a shelf with unpleasant feelings, to try to get them to a different memory shelf. This is only possible if you have some life history information and can provide prompts such as: 'Remember the story you told me about your brother, when you skived off school and went fishing and your mother caught you?' Obviously the more details you know about key stories that bring back good memories for a person, the better. You can try to use words that the person can no longer use fluidly, to direct their thoughts to happier times.

Yet more bookcases (Behavioural Stages 3 and 4)

It has only been in the past five years or so, with new information about the neuropathological stages of AD, that it has been possible to extend the bookcase metaphor to later stages of the illness. It is the existence of these extra, sensory bookcases that allows us to extend the concept of bookcases to a library setting.

It is difficult to say exactly when, but it seems that when language ability is damaged to the point where even phrases do not come out accurately, the emotional bookshelf also starts to get a micro-wobble. All caregivers will know that at this point sensory memories still seem to stimulate limited verbal and behavioural responses. This pertains especially to the use of the senses that work at close range: smell, taste, touch, and kinesthesia. (Note that vision and hearing can operate at both near and far range. Recall that perceptual ability already starts to become impaired much earlier in the course of the illness. At this point you will often need to notice where and how large a person's field of vision is, and place yourself within it and look directly at a person to try to get direct eye contact.) Figure 3.10 shows the micro-wobble starting in the emotional bookcase, and progressing on to a wobble in Behavioural Stage 4.

How does one make extra use of sensory information to help a person in this stage of AD? One lady, for example, could not respond to the question 'Do you need to use the toilet?' However, she was still able to realize she

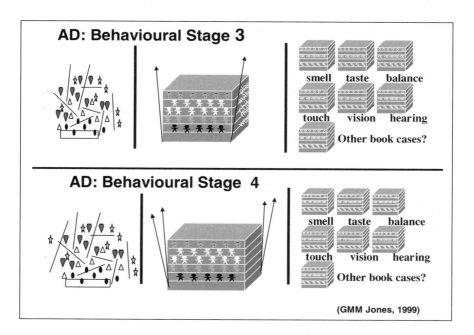

Figure 3.10 Sensory bookcases become increasingly important to utilize in aiding communication and memory stimulation during Behavioural Stages 3 and 4, as the
emotional bookcase also starts to get a micro-wobble.

needed the toilet if you walked with her and she saw the toilet (because the door was purposefully left open with the lights on). She was no longer able to see or comprehend the signs on the toilet door, but she could recognize the smell of bathroom freshener or disinfectant as you helped to steer her towards the open toilet door. She also needed help to raise her skirt and find the top seam of her panties, and also to position herself correctly in front of the toilet so she could feel the toilet ledge against the back of her legs, but then she was fine. (Note that the latter three aspects of help have to do with visuo-spatial difficulties.)

Here's another example. If you were to ask Mr Wilson whether he liked cats, he could not give a response. However, if you showed him a photo of a cat or placed a real cat on his lap, you would see immediately that he was crazy about cats by watching his reaction to these direct sensory triggers or prompts.

Bookcase metaphor summary

The primary factual/time bookshelf is the site of first and major damage in AD. This gradual damage translates into attentional, memory and logical thinking difficulties. Eventually the bookcase collapses, leaving the oldest memories in place. However, once this structure has collapsed, there is no top bookshelf left on which to place new memories. From this point onwards, a person with AD cannot learn and remember new 'factual' information. A second bookcase, that stores emotional memories still functions well, but is limited as to what information it can provide. With the concurrent language and visuo-spatial and perceptual difficulties, a person will encounter the world as an increasingly frightening place, particularly if they cannot continuously see persons and familiar objects around them (Table 3.3).

Where are the biological controllers for these bookcases?

We've spoken about the main ways the brain has for storing and accessing information: factually with 'regard to time', and emotionally by 'like experience' categorization. Where are the controllers for these abilities? The locations for the hippocampus and amygdala, referred to earlier in this chapter are shown in Figures 3.11 and 3.12. They are on the side areas of the head called the temporal lobes. The hippocampus (Latin for seahorse) has many functions, but it is the control centre for factual memory. It is also the control centre for memory and logical thinking ability. The amygdala (Latin for almond) is the control centre for the emotional tone that is remembered about things. Normally, they do not operate in isolation of each other.

Table 3.3 Summary of the bookshelf metaphor throughout the course of AD

Factual	Emotional	Sensory

Normal memory uses all but mostly the factual/time bookcase

Behavioural Stage 0 Micro-wobble starts in the factual/time bookcase

Behavioural Stage 1 Wobble leading to noticeable errors in factual/time bookcase

Behavioural Stage 2 Factual time bookcase collapse, emotional bookcase intact

Behavioural Stage 3 Emotional bookcase micro-wobble, sensory bookcases intact

Behavioural Stage 4 Wobble in the emotional bookcase, other bookcases intact

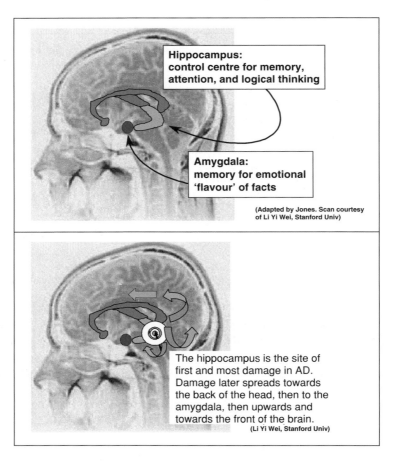

Hippocampus:
control centre for memory,
attention, and logical thinking

Amygdala:
memory for emotional
'flavour' of facts

(Adapted by Jones. Scan courtesy
of Li Yi Wei, Stanford Univ)

The hippocampus is the site of
first and most damage in AD.
Damage later spreads towards
the back of the head, then to the
amygdala, then upwards and
towards the front of the brain.
(Li Yi Wei, Stanford Univ)

Figure 3.11 The areas around the hippocampus roughly correspond to the functions shown in Figure 3.12. This shows that memory, visuo-spatial ability and language functioning are all affected in Behavioural Stages 1 and 2 of the illness.

Conclusion

Linking the behavioural and neuropathological stage models is a significant help to educators because it confirms that, although brain damage to particular areas does affect ability and behaviour, it is not the sole determinant of behaviour in dementia. It enable us to think in terms of reaching the person with dementia beyond the difficulties and barriers caused by the brain damage. It provides scope for understanding the importance of caring in the context of being familiar with a person's life history, and supports observations that lucid moments are possible and do exist in all stages of the

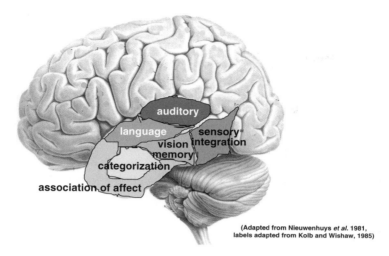

(Adapted from Nieuwenhuys *et al.* 1981,
labels adapted from Kolb and Wishaw, 1985)

Figure 3.12 The functions governed by different areas of the temporal lobe. The memory area corresponds to the location of the hippocampus, which lies deeper within the temporal lobe.

illness. Individual bookcases may wobble and collapse, but memories can be stimulated and retrieved through many other bookcases and routes over the entire course of the illness. This gives hope for humane care and keeps the person with dementia our focus, as a person, complete with memories and life experience and their own inner reality.

Note

Some of the material in this chapter is contained in the notes and syllabus for the course 'Communication and Caregiving in Dementia' developed and taught by the author.

References

Baddeley, A.D., Bressi, S., Della Salla, S., Logie, R. and Spinnler, H. (1991) 'The decline of working memory in Alzheimer's disease', *Brain* 114: 2521–42.

Braak, H. and Braak, E. (1998) 'Evolution of neuronal changes in the course of Alzheimer's disease', *J. Neural Transmission* (suppl.): 53.

Braak, H., Vos, R.A.I. *et al.* (1998) 'Neuropathological hallmarks of Alzheimer's and Parkinson's diseases', *Pro Progress in Brain Research* 117: 801–19.

Feil, N. (1982) *Validation, The Feil Method*. Cleveland, OH: Feil Productions, 4614 Prospect Ave., Cleveland, OH 44103, USA.

—— (1992) 'Validation therapy with late onset dementia populations', in G.M.M. Jones and B. Miesen (eds) *Care-giving in Dementia*, vol. 1, London: Routledge, pp. 199–218.

—— (1993) *The Validation Breakthrough*, London: Health Professions Press.

Jones, G.M.M. (1997) 'A review of Feil's validation method', *Current Opinion in Psychiatry* 10: 326–32.

Jones, G.M.M. and Burns, A. (1992) 'Reminiscing disorientation theory', in G.M.M. Jones and B. Miesen (eds) *Care-giving in Dementia: Research and Applications*, vol. 1, London: Routledge, pp. 57–76.

Jones, G.M.M., Sahakian, B.J., Levy, R., Warturton, D.M. and Gray, J.A. (1992) 'Effects of acute subcutaneous nicotine on attention, information processing and short-term memory in Alzheimer's disease', *Psychopharmacology* 108: 485–94.

Kolb, B. and Wishaw, I.Q. (1987) *Fundamentals of Human Neuropsychology*, New York: Freeman.

Le Doux, J. (1986) 'Sensory systems and emotion', *Integrative Psychiatry* 4: 237–43.

—— (1992) 'Emotion and the limbic system concept', *Concepts in Neuroscience* 2: 169–99.

—— (1993) 'Emotional memory systems in the brain', *Behavioural Brain Research* 58(1–2): 69–79.

—— (1994) 'Emotion, memory and the brain', *Scientific American* June 270(6): 50–7.

Miesen, B. (1998) *Dementia in Close Up*, trans. G.M.M. Jones, London: Routledge.

Miesen, B. and Jones, G.M.M. (1997) 'Psychic pain resurfacing in dementia: from new to past trauma', in L. Hunt, M. Marshall and C. Rowlings (eds) *Past Trauma in Late Life*, London: Jessica Kingsley.

Miller, E. and Morris, R. (1993) *The Psychology of Dementia*, Chichester: Wiley.

Parasuraman, R. (ed.) (2000) *The Attentive Brain*, London: MIT Press.

Selemon, L.D. *et al.* (1995) 'Prefrontal cortex [and working memory]', *American J. of Psychiatry* 152: 805–18.

Zola-Morgan, S., Squire, L.R. *et al.* (1991) 'Independence of memory functions and emotional behavior: separate contributions of the hippocampal formation and the amygdala', *Hippocampus* l, 2: 207–20.

Chapter 4

Personal Construct Psychology and person-centred care

Clare Morris

Introduction

This chapter seeks to elaborate the contribution of Personal Construct Psychology (PCP, Kelly 1955: 91), not only to understanding the experience of dementia from the point of view of the person diagnosed, the family caregiver, health professionals, you and me, but also as a framework for describing the process of person-centred care that is seen to be central to good practice for this client group.

There is a great deal of discussion in the literature about person-centred care, which is widely recognized as the critical shift in philosophy required in the development of the 'new culture of dementia care'. The range of creative approaches to communicating, working with and designing appropriate environments for people with dementia is ever increasing: Naomi Feil's Validation Therapy (1982); Goudie and Stokes' Resolution Therapy (1999); Charles Murphy's Life Story Work (1994); Tom Kitwood's concept of 'personhood' and 'well-being' (2001); Gary Prouty's Pre-Therapy (1999); and Yale's group therapy for early stage Alzheimer's (1995), to name but a few. But there is also a great deal of criticism about the practicality of achieving this 'ideal' in the 'real world' (Packer 2000).

Working with people with dementia at all stages of the disease, but perhaps particularly so in the more advanced stages, is stressful. Staff recruitment and retention problems are pervasive, and low morale and burn-out are the norm in many of the care facilities, both in the UK and across the world. The recognition of the economic benefits of nurturing your staff that is commonplace in business settings has yet to have the same influence in the public and health service sectors.

It is not uncommon to come across creative and well-motivated staff who return from inspiring courses only to find they are 'unable' to put into practice what they have learnt because of pressures of time. The 'new culture of dementia care' has been elaborated in relation to the client group and the responsibility lies with the formal caregivers to put this into practice, but without reference to the organizations within which they work. Change is difficult at the best of times, but it seems to me that it is an empty gesture to invest money in training individuals unless all members, at all levels of the organization, have made a commitment to the goal of person-centred care.

Part of the story, but by no means the only answer to the problem of facilitating a change in the culture of an organization, is the issue of non-managerial clinical supervision. It is recognized that family caregivers benefit from sharing their experiences in support groups, and yet formal caregivers are often expected to work long hours and provide quality care for people with a disease that has enormous social stigma, can induce terrible suffering, and for which there is no cure, only an inevitable death – a tall order by any standards.

Time out from the tasks of work in order to reflect on interventions made, how these could be done differently, and to problem solve situations that seem insurmountable, not only improves practice but makes staff feel of value and promotes a sense of being able to make a difference, despite the relentlessly progressive nature of the syndrome of dementia. A personal sense of 'making a difference' is one of the crucial elements in averting low morale and burn-out in formal and informal caregivers; something that will be illustrated in the elaboration of the experience of dementia for all those involved.

The need for a theory

Many of the creative interventions for this client group have their own philosophies and rationales and are often seen as distinct approaches. Killick and Allan (2001) point out that what all these approaches have in common is a 'person-centred focus'. They argue that communication is central to all approaches to dementia care, and in elaborating ways to communicate with people at all stages of dementia, they stress the importance of caregivers seeking to understand themselves and the way their own processes impact on their caring role.

Tom Kitwood coined the term 'personhood', the concepts of which are 'complex ideas, slippery and intangible as soon as you start to think about them' (Killick and Allan 2001). Kitwood's theory of personhood is rooted in philosophy, elaborating ways of being and relating, and maintains that no one can flourish in isolation. The need to connect with another is inherent in human nature, and therefore a 'normal' need of any person, including people with dementia. Care-giving without this 'meeting' is felt to lead to dehumanization, and this is elaborated in his account of 'malignant social psychology'. Malignant social psychology refers to the ways caregivers may interact with people with dementia and contribute to the secondary handicaps associated with dementia. Essentially his writing puts the emphasis on the *person* with dementia, as opposed to the stereotypic view of the person with *dementia*.

Bère Miesen (1999) advocates that 'first, we need to understand what is happening to them', and to do this we need to understand the nature of cognitive impairment in order to help the person experiencing those symptoms 'find a handhold'. Gemma Jones's 'Reminiscing Disorientation Theory' (1997) elaborates this notion by describing the problem of disorientation as one of the transit between 'reminiscing disorientation' and reality, whether voluntarily or automatically. Fundamentally, she sees the person with dementia trying to make sense of, or find meaning in their environment, under the circumstances of increasingly threatening cognitive and emotional chaos. Miesen (1999) has applied Bowlby's Attachment Theory to the experience of dementia. He points out that 'attachment behaviours' (proximity and closeness seeking behaviour) exist in people at all stages of their lives, particularly when they feel unsafe and insecure. The 'awareness context' describes the observation that people with dementia continue to feel that strange things are happening to them at all stages of the disease. He also relates this to the experience of the caregiver. There is an interdependence of closeness-giving behaviour and the need to 'maintain enough distance'. In order to recognize potential signs of 'over involvement, meddling, or a sense of total helplessness', it is important for caregivers to reflect on their own feelings about their work.

Ian Morton (1999) traces the undoubtedly important influence that Carl Rogers and person-centred counselling have had on the development of a variety of approaches in the 'new culture of dementia care'. He is concerned that not all so-called 'person-centred' approaches conform to their origins in Rogerian theory and practice. He feels there is a danger of the term 'person-centred' becoming 'synonymous with good quality', and seeks to clarify the principles of client-centred therapy and their implications for person-centred care in dementia. Whilst theory and techniques are important, he talks of Rogers's stress on the attitude of the therapist, and ways to create a 'helping relationship'.

The experience of dementia has been elaborated in various ways, therefore, from a more abstract and philosophical perspective to practical ways to communicate and intervene, and each has an important role. At the heart of all of these theories and approaches is the person. However, it seems that a satisfactory definition and theory of person-centred care has yet to emerge. What is this 'thing' that so many people have identified, but which is so elusive to description? Does it matter? We can all intuitively tell when a particular intervention is working, or not as the case may be. Why do we need a theory?

Everyone needs a theory in order to give meaning to their actions and develop personally and professionally. For example, formal caregivers will all have a theory about the nature of the syndrome of dementia, and some may be more informed than others. The belief that a particular resident of a care home cannot communicate may mean that the carer does not talk to him or her, and may carry out intimate nursing tasks whilst talking to a colleague. I have witnessed how a formal caregiver, after attending a validation group with a resident such as this, completely changed her perception of what this person could and could not do, subsequently changing her approach. The way we individually make sense of events (our personal theory) guides our actions.

Furthermore, all services are funded on the basis of efficacious intervention that is an economically viable way to deal with the problem of dementia, rather than an altruistic motive to keep everyone as happy as possible. We still need to show that person-centred care makes economic sense, that it is achievable on a restricted budget, and that it keeps staff happier, healthier and wanting to come to work.

A meta-theory that can make sense of and provide us with a way of describing how people interact with the world in any situation, at any level of awareness, with or without symptoms of dementia, may well be a way of describing the nature of person-centred care, and indeed the lack of it. At the heart of good and not so good practice are people, each with their own theory of events that informs and determines their behaviour.

Personal Construct Psychology (PCP) is one such meta-theory, an individual psychology that can capture the experience of people in the task of living, which can be applied equally to the person with dementia at all stages of the disease, family and formal caregivers, you and me. It is a framework that can describe the process of therapy from the individual's perspective in any situation, and consequently can integrate the eclectic influences of the cultural revolution in dementia care. Morris (2000d) and Bender (2002) also promote PCP as a useful 'overarching theoretical approach' for describing person-centred care for people with dementia.

Importantly, PCP is an approach to understanding the experience of people generally. Any approach that can make sense of the way anyone behaves and the choices which are made, including the behaviour and choices of people with symptoms of cognitive impairment, has to be a very respectful way to attempt to understand the experience of dementia. Whatever chronic illness may befall someone, the threat of becoming 'a patient and nothing but a patient' seems to be paramount for many people. This issue is fuelled by society's view of disability generally, and in particular diminishing cognitive ability.

In this same vein, PCP is not an *alternative* therapy for people with dementia, something that should be seen as in competition or in any way negating or detracting from other therapies. On the contrary, PCP is more of an 'umbrella' theory or meta-theory that makes sense of why these approaches work in many situations and why they might not work in others. It is a framework that could go a long way towards describing the *process* of therapy, the process of person-centred care and how 'personhood' is achieved in people generally.

Rehabilitation, learning and motivation

Central to all theories of therapy is an appreciation of what is known about the way people learn, how we account for motivation and the therapeutic relationship. Issues of transference or in medical and research contexts what is often termed the 'placebo effect', have always entered the debate as to what is actually taking place in effective therapy. It is beyond the scope of this chapter to give a historical outline of the long and unresolved disputes in neurological rehabilitation, but it appears to me that these issues are the very same as those that are being addressed in the person-centred approaches to working with people with progressive cognitive impairment. Medical 'rehabilitation' is usually provided only for those who have a stable condition, and directed towards improving a particular skill. The process of rehabilitation, psychotherapy, and communicating with people with a diagnosis of dementia all have one thing in common: the person with their own theory of what is happening to them and what might be done about it.

When a specific programme, technique, or therapeutic approach is ineffective, there are numerous ways this 'resistance' is explained, and the issue of motivation on the part of the patient is often raised. In medical research design, particular attention is paid to eliminating the effect of 'placebo'. In neuropsychological research an attempt is made to control for the effect of the therapeutic relationship. These are issues known to have an important influence in bringing about change, but so far have proved elusive to description.

Attempting to 'control' or cancel out the unique and powerful influence in therapy of what it means to be human is difficult. This process may always defy measurement, but with advances in the understanding of behaviour from the study of neuroscience, and a theory which can elaborate the role of the person in all these situations, we can evaluate in greater detail the nature of people's responses to our interventions, whether they are successful, or whether we meet with 'resistance'. In this way the scientific method is applied to designing more and more effective intervention for the *individual*, rather than pursuing the expectation that a particular approach will be effective in all those with a particular condition. In neuropsychological rehabilitation, advances in understanding of the unique way language, memory and perception can break down in individuals have given credence to the value of single case design in therapeutic research (Howard 1986).

Personal Construct Psychology (PCP)

George Kelly's theory of personal constructs (1991) is a comprehensive theory about how people go about the process of living. Its starting point is a philosophy coined 'Constructive Alternativism', which makes the assumption that there is a real world out there, but people can only construct a version of that reality. Our construction of the world is constantly under review and change, hopefully improved upon, but the *truth* is never attained in any absolute sense. Importantly, however, the way in which a given person makes sense represents the truth for them at that particular time. Constructing reality is seen as 'man and woman's nature', the very fact of being alive is a continual striving to make sense of the world around him or her.

This premise has important implications for people with dementia, people whose nature it is to construct a version of reality at any given moment in time, but whose perceptual, memory and language impairments might well mean their experience of events is very different from those who do not have such impairments. The vastly different ways two people might, and frequently do, construe an event in everyday life are hugely magnified by these highly debilitating, progressive, and often fluctuating cognitive changes.

PCP and motivation

Fransella (1984) describes PCP as 'starting from the premise that we, each one of us, is a process. We are alive. One feature of living matter is that it inherently changes. There is therefore no need for a theoretical concept of energy to explain what "motivates" the person to act'. Making sense of events is seen to be a fundamental property of being human. The comprehensive theory captures and accounts for all those instances where people fail to demonstrate this natural tendency, and lack motivation or 'resist' our attempts to help them, however well planned and appropriate we feel our therapy to be, and however much from the outside we may consider it to be against that person's interest. Instead of feeling demoralized (invalidated) by our futile attempts to help a given person who 'lacks motivation', this theory can help us to make sense of their 'choice', and in some but maybe not all cases design an intervention that does 'make a difference'.

The person as scientist

The metaphor of 'person the scientist' underpins the PCP approach to describing how people go about the task of living. People are seen to construct their own personal theory of people, objects and events, test this theory through their actions, and modify it according to the 'results' of their 'experiment'. The results of this experiment are either *validated*, confirming our personal theory, or *invalidated*, suggesting that our theory is wrong and requires revision. Revision of our theory of events is what is involved in the process of change.

This idea is a simple and practical one, and fully elaborated in the body of the theory itself, some important parts of which I will try to share with you in this chapter. George Kelly's theory of personal constructs is, however, very comprehensive, and it would be inadvisable to try to condense his two volumes into one short chapter. Therefore I will limit my discussion to that which helps to illustrate some important issues, in the hope that it will whet the reader's appetite to explore the richness of this approach to understanding people further. The essence of the theory is an abstract framework in which it is possible to understand a person's behaviour by attempting to see the world through their eyes, whether this is deemed 'normal' or 'deviant'. All behaviour is seen to make sense in light of the way the individual perceives events, and as such we ask the question: 'To what problem is this behaviour the solution?' The notion that all behaviour is meaningful is likewise crucial to all the person-centred approaches to working with people with a diagnosis of dementia.

Reflexivity

Reflexivity refers to the property that this theory of the *person* applies to everyone: practitioner and client; child and adult; each and every one of us as we go about our business. It is not a pathological model, but applies equally to you and me, people with severe and enduring mental health problems, people with learning disabilities, as well as people with a diagnosis of dementia and those attempting to care for them. This brings respect and humanity to the experience of dementia that the stigma of this disease erodes, and has an important influence to bear on the nature of the therapeutic relationship.

Angela Cotter (2001) describes the dominant perspective of our society as being individualism, independence, and an overvaluing of cognitive skills over creativity and understanding, in terms of Jung's 'Shadow'. This is a Jungian concept which stands for 'those rejected aspects of ourselves that are cast in darkness: repressed because individuals or societies feel they are not acceptable'. To look in the light where it is easy to see, as opposed to stepping into the shadow and 'an ill-defined world', is likened to the problem of caring for people with dementia; a need to dare explore the unknown, our shadows. PCP can help to give structure to this venture, something to help guide our intervention in what seems like uncharted territory. The same framework describes the processes in ourselves as caregivers, and the importance of doing this is advocated by other leading authors (Miesen 1999; Killick and Allen 2001).

The metaphor for therapy advocated by George Kelly is one of partnership, similar to that between a research student and their supervisor. The person in therapy is the expert on himself or herself, and the therapist is the expert on the nature of change. This starting point in therapy has proved to be an empowering one, particularly so for people with enduring mental illness or progressive cognitive impairment, in stark contrast to the way society would construe their situation. This stance allows the practitioner to feel more comfortable with not having the answer, handing the responsibility for change to the 'client' or 'patient', and creating a platform from which to 'elaborate the complaint' (Kelly 1991); a strategy with which to dare to look in Jung's Shadow for the context of behaviour that is outside our immediate understanding. An example of this can be found in Rose, my first referral in a new job in psychiatry, one year post graduation as a speech and language therapist. The analogy of looking in the shadow described by Angela Cotter has great resonance in trying to formulate a plan to intervene with a woman of nearly 60, referred for an 'agonizing stammer', who presented without any verbal communication, rocking, moaning and attempting unsuccessfully to vomit in her lap. 'Looking in the light' would have probably prompted an attempt to apply usual strategies for the assessment of her stammer, with the conclusion that it would be impossible to work with this woman until she was able to discuss her complaint. Looking in the 'shadow' involved working non-verbally, in a similar way as one would with someone with advanced dementia, in order to make contact and develop a therapeutic relationship. What followed is a very long story. However, after some 20 years of regular readmissions to hospital, Rose has now been well for in excess of eight years, with no sign of relapse.

Behaviour is an experiment

As 'personal scientists', in every action and interaction we are making predictions and testing them out, as I am in writing this chapter. The results of our experiment, or the outcome of our behaviour, either validates or invalidates our theory of events. Our responses to the evidence derived from our experiments determine whether, and how, we adapt and change in relation to events.

Validation

If we are right in our prediction, then we are validated, and will repeat our 'experiment', continue with the behaviour, and even make more elaborate experiments along the same theme to develop our understanding of the world. This in 'Kellyan' terms is known as *aggression*. Aggression to Kelly means the active elaboration of our personal theory of the world, and in most cases would be seen as a desirable state of affairs.

The elaboration of PCP in relation to the experience of dementia has been a long process with 'experiments' to test an evolving personal theory in a variety of contexts; some more 'validating' than others, but all contributing important 'evidence' in order to refine and develop a more comprehensive understanding of the process of therapeutic work with people with dementia and their families. Writing this chapter represents further testing of the prediction that this approach will make sense of something for you.

Some of the important sources of validation for a person with dementia are successful communication, feeling understood, and exercising choice. These are areas of validation for all of us, and seriously compromised by the experience of dementia. The experience of validation in therapy at the time is by no means to be underestimated in terms of its significance. However, the extent to which it can be transferred into that person's everyday life is the true yardstick. Helping families, residential staff members, as well as the general public, to understand the nature of neurological disabilities, and how to help compensate for them, will assist to increase the experience of validation for the individual with dementia in daily life.

Invalidation

Should our prediction turn out to be wrong, then we are invalidated; as I would be if I found that what I am trying to express is meaningless to you. Life is full of ups and downs for everyone. We experience invalidation at regular intervals, but when we are coping well this is balanced by validation in other ways, and we can always change the way we do things.

Invalidation is not always a bad thing, but a vital part of the process of change and our own personal evolution. An example of this for people with dementia is the notion that if you have difficulty remembering things you are stupid, something that it is important to invalidate. This is society's construct internalized in many of us. Perhaps only by coming to know a person with dementia well, and by having an understanding of the nature of cognitive disabilities, can one begin to appreciate the intelligence and creativity with which people manage their disabilities.

A younger person with dementia will be invalidated in their sense of competence much of the time through having to give up work and finding 'busybodies' interfering in their life by providing 'help'. Care staff are invalidated by not being able to provide person-centred care through resource constraints, or because people do not respond to their interventions. So what can we do in the face of invalidation? Most situations can be accounted for by the following alternatives. Each response is seen to be adaptive, and serves to help us to maintain control in the face of invalidation. People are not seen to be passively reactive, but actively engaged in the process of making sense, whether at a conscious level or at a lower level of awareness (see Figure 4.1).

1   We can try again (see Box 4.1).
2   We can re-evaluate our theory, generate an alternative hypothesis, and so conduct a different experiment by behaving differently (see Box 4.2).

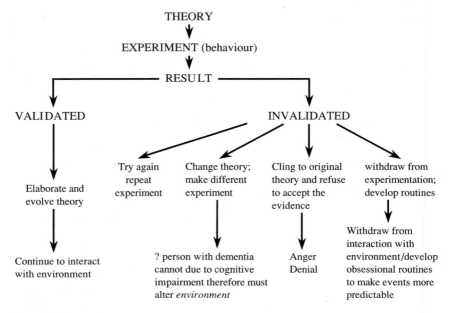

THEORY

EXPERIMENT (behaviour)

RESULT

VALIDATED

INVALIDATED

Elaborate and
evolve theory

Try again
repeat
experiment

Change theory;
make different
experiment

Cling to original
theory and refuse
to accept the
evidence

withdraw from
experimentation;
develop routines

Continue to interact
with environment

? person with dementia
cannot due to cognitive
impairment therefore must
alter *environment*

Anger
Denial

Withdraw from
interaction with
environment/develop
obsessional routines
to make events more
predictable

Figure 4.1 Personal scientist

Box 4.1   Making the same experiment again

We do not throw aside our personal theory of an event lightly. Maybe there is
something 'in the weather', or we are having an 'off day'. We can dissociate
ourselves from the possibility that our theory is faulty, put the invalidating
evidence down to freak chance and repeat our behaviour. This strategy is seen
in people with dementia too. An example of this is Albert (Packer 2000) who
eventually lost his temper after repeated invalidated attempts to discover his
circumstances on admission to hospital. As caregivers we are all likely to have
been in the position of deciding to try a particular strategy again. Maybe we
are unsure of what else to do at the time.

3   We can refuse to accept the outcome of our 'experiment' and cling to
     our original prediction (see Box 4.3).
4   We may choose to withdraw from 'experimentation' in order to avoid
     putting our 'faulty' theory to the test (see Box 4.4).

Box 4.2   Reconstruction

We do, however, get things wrong and need to revise our personal theory. In light of the invalidating evidence from talks in the early years of my career, I reconstrued the way I presented the material and gave a great deal more thought to the likely expectations of those in the audience. It could be argued that the person with brain injury may be limited in their ability to re-evaluate their theory because of the nature of cognitive disability. However, I have witnessed *reconstruction* in some of my clients.

Gina reconstrued Alzheimer's disease, as did her husband. This was achieved through giving her time to talk in a confidential environment, and helping her to 'put her cards on the table' in order to problem solve the issues arising as a result of her condition. She discovered that by being more open about her disability with family, friends and some, but not all, acquaintances, the task of living with AD was less of a burden. When others understood more about the nature of her experience and how they could make things easier (they have a more detailed theory on which to base their predictions), many people responded more often in a way that was validating for Gina. For example, when she explained about her word-finding problems and how it helped to be given time, people were less embarrassed and more likely to tolerate the long silences in the pursuit of meaning. Gina came to describe her condition as 'not the end of the world'.

Change is difficult at the best of times, and with neurological deficits that affect flexibility and organization of your thinking, it could be expected to be much more difficult. Whilst people in the earlier stages of dementia can and do reconstrue their circumstances, the onus is likely to be on the caregiver to change *their* behaviour to accommodate the neurological deficits of the person with dementia in order to enable *reconstruction*, or possibly in many cases we are attempting to compensate for deficits in order to facilitate the ability to make sense and therefore encourage 'appropriate' behaviour. This has been demonstrated by various approaches to caring for people with dementia, including building design, communication strategies and activities that help the person with dementia to better predict and feel safe in their environment. Attention to altering the environment or context in which our client is living is not confined to people with dementia but all client groups, and indeed ourselves in our own lives. We change and evolve with new experiences, changes in circumstances, and with each new person we come to know. Our theory of the world needs updating, and this is a very significant part of the picture when working psychotherapeutically with anyone using this framework. In the earlier example of Rose, almost all interventions were directed towards altering her environment. While there was significant, profound and lasting change, she never volunteered what she thought had changed, except in a very concrete way.

Box 4.3   Refusing to accept the outcome of our experiment

Theories very dear to a person's heart are very resistant to change. If we don't like the evidence, we can choose to interfere with it. 'Denial' may manifest itself in anger, aggression and the tendency to blame others or find excuses, because to acknowledge the 'truth' is untenable. A family caregiver may be unable to appreciate the nature of language disorder in neurological disease, and is likely to be protecting themselves from the awareness that the person they love and care for is losing the ability to express themselves as before. A common reaction is to insist the person with aphasia access the 'right' word, e.g. 'meat' is wrong when you mean 'beef', possibly fuelled by the widespread belief that 'if you do not use it, you lose it'. The importance of the pursuit of meaning can be lost when we are faced with communicating with people whose language is affected (Morris 2000b). We can feel the influence of society's construing of linguistic competence in this example. *Hostility*, as it is known in PCP terms, is the continued effort to extort validational evidence, or in other words 'cook the books' to maintain a particular way of seeing things, and is a label that requires caution. Does the person actually *know* they are wrong? There is always a very good reason for hostility, and it plays an important part in protecting the core of our being. It is frequently seen in the early stages of dementia, perhaps because acknowledging that your faculties are slipping is likely to be very threatening to one's sense of being a person, and has been described as worse than death itself.

For Rebecca (Morris 1999b) and many other people with dementia it is just too threatening to face up to what she *knows* is happening. Despite being in an advanced stage of an inherited dementia, where her speech and language, memory, and mobility among other things were all affected in a similar way to her mother, and despite having both her young children in full-time nursery care, Rebecca talked of returning to work once her children were older. Shortly after this conversation, she handed her purse to the cashier in her local store for her to take the right money for her shopping. Her refusal to accept professional input could be better understood in terms of her own personal goal to ignore validational evidence and insist that life was going according to plan, but she was certainly not unaware of her difficulties.

'Confabulation', angry or aggressive behaviour, refusing to cooperate and blaming others, are all possible signs of *hostility* in a person who *needs* to distort the 'evidence' in order to maintain some degree of control and composure in everyday life. It is important to respect denial rather than try to orientate people to the 'error of their ways'. This is not a recommendation to collude with denial, but to try to validate the person's life experience. Rebecca had a great deal to contribute about the nature of her work as a make-up consultant, without it being necessary to go along with her claim that she would ever be returning to work. Trying to provide support for people with dementia and their families can be a very frustrating business and often health care professionals are 'forced' into confronting denial in order to carry out their remit. The experience of caring for your son or daughter who is dying from the human form of BSE in cattle, known as variant CJD (Creutzfeldt Jacob Disease) must represent every parent's nightmare. Some people have only been able to cope with caring for their relative by believing that their son or daughter will get better, which in their heart of hearts they know will not be the case. The advent of a possible treatment has fuelled this response. Discussion and decisions about alternative feeding, ignoring recommendations that the affected person is fed upright and fluids thickened, refusing to use hoists or any other symbol of 'disability' or incapacity are common, causing no end of difficulty for health care professionals who need to adhere to standards and policies. There is no set answer to these situations. However, listening to families, focusing on the affected person's needs and quality of life, demonstrating validating strategies, activities and interventions, coming to know them as a person and not just a patient – and above all being flexible – helps to maintain a therapeutic and supportive relationship where the appropriate decisions are made as they arise and can no longer be ignored. Health professionals need to anticipate deterioration in planning service provision. However, families often cannot.

Box 4.4   Withdrawing from experimentation

This can manifest itself either passively or actively, as in physical withdrawal from the environment, or obsessive compulsive behaviour which attempts to increase predictability of the person's world. *Constriction* (the term given to this withdrawal from experimentation) is enforced to a great extent in neurological disease. Difficulty expressing yourself will tend to restrict conversation. Visual and perceptual deficits will mean you miss out on information or it is distorted. Further constriction takes place with repeated invalidation, illustrated by the way people with Alzheimer's gradually withdraw from interaction with their environment: people may often take to their bed for very long periods; people with frontal lobe degeneration such as Pick's disease often develop 'obsessional' routines to cope with their anxiety. One gentleman, when he attended clinic, would at regular intervals leave the interview and march out of the hospital, up to a lamp-post, touch it and march back. When asked why he did this, he said because it made him 'feel lucky, unlike this Pick's thing'. Perhaps it was a way of creating a small island of validation for himself, as the lamp-post was always there to be touched. Likewise, Bill (Packer 2000), who created a 'no-go' area around himself, was perhaps constricting in response to the perceptual problems common in some forms of dementia. If events fail to make sense and people's actions do not appear as they are intended, but are frightening and unpredictable, or if you are responding to hallucinations, then creating a 'no-go' zone is a practical solution to the problem (Morris 1999c, 2000a).

Levels of awareness

Our 'theory' of the world is built up of *constructs*, which are discriminations of similarity and difference about events around us. These constructs are built up over a lifetime, possibly from the moment of conception, but more easily recognizable after we are born. A baby quickly learns to recognize 'mother' from 'not mother', hunger versus satisfied, warmth versus feeling cold. Infants learn how to effect a change in their environment, gradually building up a more and more elaborate, non-verbal theory of the world around them. This theory is elaborated in the mother–child relationship: 'an exchange, par excellence, of people making people' (Shotter 1970). As language develops, children learn to express their discriminations through language, and our theories of the world continue to be elaborated with the help of language. It is important, however, to stress that constructs are *not* the verbal labels we use to communicate our construing.

So construing is developing very early in life, before the development of language, and is not purely a cognitive affair. Those parts of our construing we are actually able to verbalize are probably only the 'tip of the iceberg'. How many times do you get a 'gut' feeling about something you cannot or have difficulty in putting words to? Have you ever met someone for the first time and had a strong sense of whether you liked or disliked them, which you could only put an explanation to several meetings later? Preverbal and non-verbal construing is related to the very essence of our being, the spiritual dimension that has an enormous impact in the field of dementia care.

In the same way as our theories of events do not exist purely in conscious awareness, our 'experiments' or behaviour are not necessarily something we are consciously aware of formulating. We 'construe' or experiment and change with our whole bodies and we may never notice or articulate the process. An illustration of this is to be found in sitting down. We make a prediction as to how hard or soft a chair is by glancing at it. Then the whole of our body is tuned into the experiment of sitting in that chair without falling on the floor. The experience of invalidation is felt when it is harder or softer than expected, or when it breaks or wobbles. Our theory of sitting behaviour is very elaborate, built up over a lifetime. It requires the involvement and coordination of many different muscles, all finely tuned to enable us to sit down gracefully in a range of sitting contexts, simply by glancing at the seat. When it goes wrong we might be more cautious next time, but essentially our theory remains intact. If we break a leg, we have to reconstrue the whole process. If neurological disease interferes with our functioning, again we must reconstrue. A condition known affectionately as 'bottom apraxia' makes this explicit. If every time you try to sit down you are unable to coordinate your body successfully, your theory of sitting is going to be invalidated, and is likely to affect your behaviour and activity. Perhaps you might constrict and pace up and down, wander, or sit for long periods taking 'possession' of your favourite chair. Perhaps you might get very angry and irritable, 'blaming' people around you for interfering. If those trying to help you are unaware of the nature of your struggle, they may well try to encourage you to do things that frighten you.

If your condition is stable, you may 'reconstrue' and find ways of adapting to your disability. With a progressive condition affecting cognition and mobility, this is likely to be much more difficult. Certainly one of the most difficult things for people in this situation is trying to do 'two things at once': for example, listening to instructions and trying to coordinate limbs that won't do as they are willed; walking and having a conversation; using a knife and fork and following what others are saying.

'Gut' construing

Construing at lower levels of awareness could be described as 'gut' construing. How is it people with memory impairment can benefit from therapeutic work when they can't remember what has been said? Margaret has moderately severe vascular dementia and was part of a validation group for two years. It was a shock to the nurses to discover she could speak, although she was unable to contribute fully to the conversation in the group. However, she used to join in songs and make occasional comments such as: 'It is better to have loved and lost than never to have loved at all' and 'my brain is going up the wall'. After 18 months in the group, she was able to say what she liked about the group, whilst not actually in the group or the group room. She liked to 'see what everyone is wearing'. Once cued into the fact that it was time for the 'meeting', she could 'remember' the good feelings that had taken place over time. People with dementia often recognize and remember people who have very pleasant or very unpleasant associations. Oliver Sacks (1985) gives an account of an 'experiment' to shake hands with a man with amnesia when he had a drawing pin in his hand, demonstrating this 'gut memory'; he refused ever to shake hands with him again, but could not remember what had happened nor explain why.

Validation, invalidation, and all these alternative responses to invalidation take place at all levels of awareness, and at the level of 'gut' construing it would appear that memory may be relatively preserved in people with memory disorders. At this level of awareness, therefore, new experiences do have an influence on our construing of events. We are not totally dependent on a conscious and articulate evaluation in order to reconstrue, which has important implications for therapeutic intervention in neurological disease.

Core construing

It is important to account for the fact that some aspects of ourselves and the way we make sense of the world are more important than others. For example, if I were to burn the food at a dinner party, I would be far less traumatized by the experience than the chef, Delia Smith, might be. Some aspects of our being in the world are far more central than others. Core roles, such as being a woman, a parent, a good communicator, and someone who makes a difference to those around me, have a much greater bearing on my functioning than producing high quality cuisine. For Delia Smith this may be a different story, but there may be some commonality there too. The stereotyping and stigma of dementia represents society's construing of the symptoms of memory failure, intellectual decline, dependence on others, and odd behaviour. These constructs form part of our own core construing too, and have an important influence on the way we respond to the appearance of these symptoms in ourselves. Preverbal and non-verbal construing is part of our 'core', and the closer a construction is to our core, the more resistant it will be to change. Choice, competence and independence are 'core' for most people. However, culinary expertise and constructions of cleanliness or tidiness may have a good deal more variability in terms of their importance for different people. We see the influence of core construing in the behaviour of people with dementia, an example of which can be found in the management of continence. Some people are far more tolerant of the standard ways of managing incontinence than others: regular toileting, wearing pads, and being cleaned up. Many a placid person kicks and hits out when this particular nursing intervention is carried out. Maureen, with advanced dementia, was causing considerable management difficulties for nursing staff, who needed to hold her down in order to change her due to being doubly incontinent. She was in denial, barging out of the toilet with 'bloody cheek', and lashing out when being changed. Her background as a school matron, a conscientious mother and housewife who set a lot of store by cleanliness, her comment when attempts were made to toilet her regularly (perhaps she associated this with being treated like a toddler) all pointed towards core construing, something that would be highly resistant to change. By approaching her and inviting her to come for her morning wash, she was fully cooperative, becoming upset and distressed when she discovered her incontinence, but never violent. It became possible to validate her feelings about her incontinence in private, and it became unnecessary to restrain her.

To achieve meaning, to make contact, is validation at a core level. This can be achieved in many different ways. Whilst cooking may not be a core issue for everybody, eating is. Some people enjoy eating more than others, and some people are eating disordered, but food is an issue central to all of us and crucial to survival. It is also often the one activity that can still be pleasurable (and therefore validating) for people with advanced dementia. Newton and Stewart (1997) describe an approach to nutrition that seeks to tap into tacit memories of eating, and invites us to make every day a party. Dr Stewart's background in Personal Construct Psychology is evident but unstated in the way he roots nutritional and physical disability issues in the culture and context of people's eating behaviour. The need for both professionals and family caregivers to 'make a difference' to the person they are caring for is also seen as paramount.

Sociality

People require social interaction for their well-being, but it is through trying to predict the way *others* make sense of events that we enter into a relationship. Our predictions and therefore theory may be wrong, but the attempt to do so is what, in PCP terms, is termed *sociality*. The attempt to stand in the shoes of another is the way we achieve relationship, and therefore psychological contact. It feels good when someone accurately subsumes your experience; it feels less good when your needs and feelings are not understood, but it also helps when you can sense that the attempt is made. Furthermore: 'it is important to remember that any interaction between two people who are making attempts to understand each other's construction system (Sociality) leads to each playing a social role in relation to each other, and this may in turn lead to changes in both construct systems' (Dalton and Dunnet 1992: 65). The mother–child relationship described by Shotter (1970) as 'people making people' highlights this. It is not just the baby who is changing and learning, the mother (father, other siblings, extended family, and so on) are all undergoing change as a result of construing the baby's needs. Furthermore, this transcends language. Discrimination, anticipation and validation are at the heart of any relationship, and it is this we need to promote in those whose relationships are compromised through cognitive disability.

In PCP, any prediction made about another's experience is *propositional* (tentative and seeking clarification). This is a very useful platform from which to plan person-centred dementia care, as it frees us to try things out, evaluate their benefit and change or develop the approach. In the case of the person with dementia who is 'unaware' of our presence, are they really unaware, or so *constricted* that they are unable or unwilling to respond? Is response delayed so long that we are already involved in something else? It is always important (but not necessarily easy) to assume the person is aware. To reconstrue 'unaware of my presence' is to free yourself from the invalidation of caring for someone who does not acknowledge your existence. Careful observation of the person's behaviour may provide clues to a way to make contact sometimes. If we don't have training and, most importantly, supervision, reconstruing situations such as these is far more difficult. Add to this the time-pressured reality of continuing care, and we might be tempted to constrict by withdrawing and focusing on other residents, or we might be hostile and punitive. This stance provides us with a more validating path to follow, a hopeful one in which we might be able to make a difference.

Steven Wey (personal communication 2001) works therapeutically with people with dementia, using a variety of techniques and frameworks, and is influenced by PCP. He uses the technique of 'mirroring' a great deal, where an apparently meaningless or undirected action is mirrored in order to facilitate social exchange. This does not have to involve words. In fact some powerful examples involve no speech at all: throwing and catching a ball, or round object involves predicting the response of others. This is sociality, and where the exchange is successful the experience will be validating.

Bipolar nature of construing

In PCP terms, one of the most important properties of a construct (our theory is made up of many linked constructs) is that it is bipolar. We only know exactly what someone means when we know what they *don't* mean. Bill's construing of mealtimes (Packer 2000) was very different to other aspects of his day, as this was the only time he would allow anyone near him. The hypothesis of Box 4.5 emerges.

Box 4.5   Bipolar nature of construing

Validated	Invalidated
Eating	Creates no-go zone
Permits interaction	? all other situations – no trust

By observing his behaviour it is possible to build up a profile of situations where Albert permits interaction and allows proximity and where he does not. In what circumstances would this behaviour make sense? To what problem is a given behaviour the solution (Morris 1999a)? By creating a 'no-go' zone, Bill is constricting his world to make it more manageable in light of the way *he perceives events*. Predictions could be made about how he is seeing, hearing, remembering and feeling in relation to our theories of how this could be distorted from our perception of events. With these predictions we can plan intervention and try alternative strategies. The more elaborate the theory we have of his likely perceptual difficulties, the more specifically we can design intervention strategies that compensate for them (Morris 1999c, 2000a). There will always be times when we are unable to find ways to validate, but there is therapeutic value in the stance we take towards it.

Anxiety, threat and guilt

Anxiety, threat and guilt are terms used in everyday conversation, but have very specific meaning in Personal Construct Psychology. *Anxiety* is defined as the awareness that events are outside the range of convenience of your construct system. You literally don't have an adequate theory with which to make sense of events. *Threat* is the awareness that there is going to be a comprehensive change in your core construing, such as Delia Smith might experience if she burnt the dinner. The most extreme form of threat is death. *Guilt* is dislodgement from your core, as was experienced by Maureen when she became aware of her incontinence.

In Killick and Allan (2001), John Killick describes his feelings when first left in a room with people with advanced dementia. He was unable to understand what they were trying to say or do, what might be motivating them. This represents Kellyan anxiety and, whilst this is a very powerful example, perhaps we can all recognize similar feelings in our experience. He experienced fear of harm and contamination, and found his expectations of 'normality' were completely overturned. He could sense no reason, no empathy and no love. He describes the basic part of being human as the belief that we all share something that is recognizable and communicable. Without this belief we are threatened to the core.

By living for a week with the residents he found that 'every person was unique and responded to a different approach', and that there was a need in people with advanced dementia to 'continue in relationship despite the difficulties encountered'. It was through communication and successful exchange that personhood became a reality. He comments that this is where the crucial issues in the care of people with dementia lie. Through spending time with the residents, John Killick discovered it was possible to find ways to relate to each individual. Anxiety in this situation gave rise to elaboration of his personal theory of the world and reconstruction, as it did for me when faced with Rose's behaviour. Once validated in his attempts to make contact with the residents, the threat of harm and contamination dissipated.

Anxiety and threat do not always lead to elaboration and reconstruction. We may well choose to constrict and withdraw, such is the threat to our core construing. As caregivers, anxiety and threat will certainly raise their heads from time to time, but it is possible to use them constructively. The more we become aware of our own construing, the more we can anticipate these situations. For the person with dementia and, among other disabilities, a failing memory, anxiety and threat are going to be daily, if not hourly or constant states.

If intervention strategies induce threat, such as will occur when denial is confronted, we can expect a rough ride. Dealing with Maureen's incontinence in the context of helping with her daily washing routine validated her core sense of herself as a person who washes regularly and avoided the

threat induced by needing to be 'cleaned up'. Restraint was no longer necessary, and it became possible to comfort her in the unavoidable realization
that she had been dislodged from her core perception of herself as clean,
hygienic, and in control of her body (guilt).

Allistair, an elderly gentleman, diagnosed with Alzheimer's disease, was
referred for an assessment of his aphasia. Unable to cope with the threat
and invalidation experienced in being brought face to face with the elaboration of his disability, Allistair chose to withdraw and refused language testing.
A change in approach to the use of pictures to facilitate communication about
his likes and dislikes brought about a very different response in Allistair.
He enjoyed being able to communicate important things about his life, and
ways to facilitate communication were fed back to other members of the
multidisciplinary team. A year later, long after sessions to facilitate communication had ceased, Allistair was very distressed and conveyed that he would
like to sit down and discuss recent events with his wife. He had begun to
experience hallucinations, for which he had been prescribed melleril, which
unfortunately had not prevented hallucinations, but had caused postural problems so that he was unable to walk very far and could no longer accompany
his wife to the supermarket. She would have to lock him in their flat and poke
his fingers back through the gap in the door, as he struggled not to be left
behind. It appears that the validating experience of successful communication was in some way 'remembered', despite his severe memory impairment.

Allistair deteriorated and died within three months, but only after communicating his love for his wife and his sorrow at the distress he was causing
her. He conveyed at this time that it was not dying he was frightened of, but
living with these symptoms.

In working with people who are asymptomatic but at risk of a familial
dementia, the choices at stake in pursuing genetic counselling will be between
the anxiety of not knowing whether or not you carry the mutation, or the
threat of discovering you do carry the gene for the disease in your family.
Each time you forget what you went upstairs for, each time you lose something you know you put in a safe place, these feelings will be brought to the
fore. Threat and guilt are often experienced by those discovering that they
have escaped inheriting the mutant gene.

Relevance of PCP to other approaches to care-giving in dementia

The crucial feature of PCP is that all behaviour is defined in terms of the
experience of the *person* doing the behaving. This comprehensive and abstract
framework has resonance in many approaches to care-giving for this reason,
and a brief review of some of these in relation to PCP follows.

In elaborating a model for communication, Jones (1992) studied the interactions between nursing staff and residents of a nursing home. The study

concluded that low-quality interactions arise in part due to the limited use of case history information, a limited understanding of the pathology, and little notion of the meaning of the experience of dementia to the resident themselves. In Kellyan terms this amounts to *anxiety*. Caregivers who do not have an elaborated theory of what it means to have dementia, from a theoretical, practical or personal perspective, have little to inform their behaviour (the experiment to test out their theory of the situation at hand). In the absence of any other information, it is not surprising that the caregiver falls back on society's construing of the person with dementia as a helpless, dependent person who is unaware, unable to communicate, and doesn't remember anything you say: a lost cause to be cared for in the physical and custodial sense. *Sociality* is likewise relevant here. By coming to understand something of a person's history and the nature of their disabilities, it is possible to try to stand in the shoes of the person with dementia, and therefore begin to play a social process in relation to them, in contrast to custodial care.

Validation Therapy (Feil 1982) has been an important influence in the development of my work with people with dementia and their families, providing a set of techniques that fits with the abstract philosophy and framework of PCP. The construct *validation-invalidation* provides a more elaborated concept of what we might be trying to achieve in caring for and communicating with people with dementia. By subsuming the unique construing of each individual, we are able to identify both what is personally validating, in addition to those areas that are likely to be validating for all of us, which in this analysis Validation Therapy techniques seek to achieve. Feeling listened to, feeling understood, sharing an experience, and being given time are all stances that validate 'personhood', and in PCP terms represent commonality in the core construing of the majority of people.

The guidelines for communicating with people at different stages of dementia have been a vital platform from which to elaborate my own construing of how to interact with my clients. For example, a handshake forms a very important part of my assessment when meeting someone with dementia for the first time, giving an instant sense of that person's personal space. The use of formal conventions is respectful and therefore validating. This, along with an approach to therapy which sees the client as an equal partner, is powerfully validating in stark contrast to the person with dementia's experience in the big wide world. It is significant that for many of my clients in Behavioural Stage 1, within a short space of time I am greeted with a hug and a kiss in the middle of outpatients, much to the surprise of other patients and staff. For others there will always be a more formal relationship. Perhaps some of these differences are as much related to the personal construction systems of the individual, and therefore the unique experience of the syndrome of dementia for each person.

Reminiscing Disorientation Theory (RDT, Jones 1992), mentioned at the beginning of this chapter, provides in my view a good alternative explanation for those behaviours which are commonly diagnosed as 'delusions' or 'psychosis'. The fundamental assumption that people are striving to make sense of their environment whilst in 'emotional and cognitive chaos' is compatible with the notion of a personal scientist: people construct their own version of reality, and as a result what you see is true for you. RDT reduces Kellyan anxiety for the caregiver who is confronted with bizarre communications that bear no resemblance to their view of 'reality', and facilitates sociality by helping the caregiver to subsume the experience of cognitive disorder which distorts the person with dementia's interpretation of their environment. The more we consider the personal experience of neurological symptoms, the more the secondary symptoms of 'challenging', 'dangerous', 'problematic', or merely 'annoying' behaviour can be understood as arising from that individual's 'reality'.

Loss and attachment are discussed a good deal in the literature (Miesen 1992, 1997, 1999). Any framework that develops understanding of the difficult behaviours associated with dementia promotes sociality. If we can recognize these behaviours as appropriate reactions to loss, we can begin to play a social role in relation to that person, that is have a meaningful relationship, 'make contact'. The terms 'living bereavement', 'loss of self', and 'loss of role' all have pertinence for people with dementia, and their families and caregivers. Loss in PCP terms involves any or all of the constructs of transition (anxiety, threat, guilt and hostility), as would arise in any form of change, whether forced upon you suddenly, gradually, or whether it is what you choose to do. Miesen has elaborated the concept of 'awareness-context' which relates to the person with dementia being aware that strange things are happening. This is anxiety: the world doesn't add up any more, the person can't make sense of what is happening to them, in contrast to there being nothing to construe, as would be the case if the person was truly unaware of there being anything wrong. This state of anxiety is in itself threatening to most people, as it is likely to involve the 'awareness of an imminent and comprehensive change in core role structure' (Kelly 1991) to find that you are unable to make sense. Your 'competence' and *commonality* with other people is in question. It would appear that threat is far greater for the person who cannot make sense (and is perhaps in fear of going crazy?) than for the person who is aware that there is potentially something very serious wrong with them. For example, a young girl diagnosed with variant CJD was told by her family that her symptoms were due to a virus in her brain, after some months of living with the belief that her symptoms were psychiatric, and therefore 'all in her head'. She heaved a sigh of relief and commented, 'I knew there was something wrong with me.'

Attachment behaviours that are expressed by all of us throughout life vary a great deal in their content, and their success in achieving their goal of reassurance and security. Demands for attention can frequently drive people away, and might in some instances be an expression of hostility in that person. Miesen (1999) suggests that attachment behaviours in a person with dementia follow the pattern demonstrated throughout their life, which in turn have their roots in early childhood. *Preverbal construing* and construing at low levels of awareness is the part of Personal Construct Theory that helps to make sense of what is happening for the individual. The experience must in some ways be similar to the experience of a young baby who knows only one person. Turning to or searching for something you know makes perfect sense in light of the experience of progressive and/or fluctuating cognitive impairment. Seeing that goal and only that goal is a form of constriction, in order to simplify the problem of making sense.

Human experience is bound to have commonality and as such generalizations and observations about the experience of dementia are likely to hold true for most situations, greatly improving the ability to intervene in a way that makes a difference. For those people who present an even more challenging picture, a PCP analysis can be used to problem solve what might be going on for the individual specifically, in order that the most appropriate approach for that person at that time in relation to a particular situation can be selected and tested out. Accurately subsuming someone's experience leads to our interventions being validated and working. It is also true to say that even if we are wrong, and have to stand back, revise our hypotheses and try something new, we are still exercising sociality, and it is this process that is of therapeutic value.

It is interesting to comment here that in providing psychotherapy for people with issues of guilt the need for frequent contact with the client and considerable issues concerning transference are discussed in the literature (Winter 1992). Again it is comforting to know that the experience of loss in dementia has resonance in terms of therapeutic intervention for *anyone* experiencing dislodgement from a core sense of themselves for whatever reason.

Conclusion

PCP does not represent an alternative approach for working with people with dementia, but a meta-theory of therapy and interpersonal processes that transcends all client groups and circumstances, and provides a unified rationale for the 'person-centred focus' of the wide range of creative approaches within the 'new culture of dementia care'. It has proved to be a very useful framework for understanding the experience of dementia from the perspective of the person with cognitive impairment, their family and formal caregivers, and can help to conceptualize and problem solve behavioural problems in people at any stage of the disease (see Table 4.1). Furthermore, it is an approach to understanding how people in general go about the task of living. I wonder how you and I would cope with living with the onset of progressive cognitive impairment?

Table 4.1 Glossary of PCP terminology

PCP terminology involves many words in common usage to describe constructs and psychological processes. However, they have been given very specific definitions. The words retain contact with their common meaning, but are subtly redefined 'to broaden the concept or lose some commonly held prejudicial associations' (Dalton and Dunnet 1992). Kelly *always* defines his terms on what is happening within the person, and *not* how someone else would experience this. Kellyan terminology used in this chapter has been summarized below.

Constructs	Discriminations of similarity and difference that make up our 'theory' of events and the world about us. Constructs are 'bipolar'; for example, some people are *kind*, as opposed to *cruel*, *warm* as opposed to *distant*, *controlled* as opposed to *goes with the flow*. Sometimes people are similar in terms of their **constructs**, others use constructs which have different 'poles'; for example, *controlled* versus *all over the place*. **Constructs** are the discrimination rather than the verbal labels, and these verbal labels may not be limited to a single word, but an entire phrase or explanation.
Construing	The collection of constructs used to make sense of a situation represents our **construing**. This is *not* the same as thinking: we construe as we look, listen, touch, feel, and move, in order to interpret the situation, event or action.
Core construing	**Core construing** represents those parts of our construct system that are very important, central to our sense of self. Our **core** represents our identity and maintenance of our core structures is vital to functioning.
Non-verbal construing	**Non-verbal construing** involves constructs at a low level of awareness, but which can become verbalized as they are discovered in therapy, for example. The non-verbal construing involved in sitting down is likely to involve both **preverbal** and **non-verbal constructs**.
Preverbal construing	**Preverbal constructs** develop before the onset of language, but continue to be important in everyday life despite not being available to conscious awareness. They are usually connected to love, warmth, feeding and so on.
Propositional constructs	Constructs are **propositional** when they are 'tried on for size'; a stance that is useful when making sense of new situations. This is in contrast to being pre-emptive, which sees something as being a certain quality and only that quality, for example prejudice may be based on pre-emptive constructs.
Reconstruction	Reconstruction refers to a change in a person's theory of events, and usually arises from invalidation.
Validation–invalidation	The outcome of our behaviour (an experiment to test out our personal theory) either validates or invalidates our view of events.
Constriction–dilation	**Constriction** is the narrowing of the perceptual field in order to minimize apparent incompatibilities in our theory of

Table 4.1   (continued)

	the world. We can choose to shut out what makes us uncertain, confused or invalidated. **Dilation**, on the other hand is the broadening of our perceptual field in order to take in more aspects of our environment.
Commonality and individuality	The extent to which people are similar or individual in their theory of the world.
Sociality	The extent to which we attempt to step into the shoes of another person in order to see the world as they do. This is the basis for relationship and a necessary part of the process of change, promoting the evolution of our personal theory of the world.
Constructs of transition	The dimensions in PCP which describe reactions to change from the individual's perspective.
Hostility	Hostility arises in people when core construing is threatened: it is the 'continued effort to extort validational evidence in favour of a type of social prediction which has already been recognized as a failure' (Kelly 1991). The person does not 'like' the outcome of their experiment, and so tries to 'cook the books' by manipulating people or events to fit their existing view of the world. Hostility is not necessarily a 'bad' thing, as it protects our 'core', and is not the same as not recognizing evidence. For a person to be hostile, at some level they need to *know* they are wrong.
Aggression	Aggressiveness is the 'active elaboration of one's perceptual field' (Kelly 1991). It is a person's nature to make sense of events, and aggression is seen in most situations to be a positive attribute where this is engaged in proactively. For example, a person might show aggression in the area of learning to play football (because this is validating), but never go swimming because they are not 'good at swimming', are frightened of water, and so on.
Anxiety	'The awareness that events with which one is confronted lie outside the range of convenience of his construct system' (Kelly 1991), or in plain English, the person simply does not know what to do, as his or her theory of the world is inadequate for the situation at hand. **Anxiety** is seen as the 'harbinger of change'. A certain level of **anxiety** is necessary to lead us to be **aggressive** in developing our theory to deal with more and more events.
Threat	'The awareness of an imminent comprehensive change in one's core structures' (Kelly 1991). Threat feels extremely uncomfortable and is often associated with outrage or panic. Often people respond to threat with the fight or flight reaction (hostility or constriction), which may be expressed physically or psychologically.
Guilt	'The awareness of dislodgement of the self from one's core role structure' (Kelly 1991) We become **guilty** when we find ourselves behaving in a way that goes against our **core**. **Guilt** can be very debilitating, and for any individual, the events that induce Kellyan guilt may be vastly different: what is trivial to one person may be of core importance to another.

References

Bender, M. (2002) *Exploration in Dementia*, London: Jessica Kingsley.

Cotter, A. (2001) 'Healing where light and shadows meet', *Journal of Dementia Care* 9, 1: 20–22.

Dalton, P. and Dunnet, G. (1992) *Psychology for Living: Personal Construct Theory for Professionals and Clients*, Chichester: Wiley.

Feil, N. (1982) *V/F Validation Therapy: The Feil Method*, 1st edn, Cleveland: Feil Productions.

Fransella, F. (1984) 'Resistance', unpublished paper, Centre for Personal Construct Psychology.

Goudie, F. and Stokes, G. (1999) 'Resolution Therapy 1', in I. Morton *Person-Centred Approaches to Dementia Care*, Bicester: Winslow Press.

Howard, D. (1986) 'Beyond randomised controlled trials: the case for effective case studies of the effects of treatment in aphasia', *British Journal of Disorders of Communication*, 21: 89–102.

Jones, G. (1992) 'A communication model for dementia', in G.M.M. Jones and B. Miesen (eds) *Care-giving in Dementia: Research and Applications*, vol. 1, London: Routledge.

Jones, G. and Burns, A. (1992) 'Reminiscing disorientation theory', in G.M.M. Jones and B. Miesen (eds) *Care-giving in Dementia: Research and Applications*, vol. 1, London: Routledge.

Jones, G.M.M. (1997) 'A review of Feil's validation method for communicating with and caring for dementia sufferers', *Current Opinion in Psychiatry* 10: 326–32.

Kelly, G. (1955) 'The Psychology of Personal Constructs', in G. Lindsay (ed.) *A History of Psychology in Autobiography*, vol. 1, New York: Norton.

—— (1991) *The Psychology of Personal Constructs*, New York: Norton.

Killick, J. and Allan, K. (2001) *Communication and the Care of People with Dementia*, Buckingham: Open University Press.

Kitwood, T. (2001) 'Personhood', in J. Killick and K. Allan *Communication and the Care of People with Dementia*, Buckingham: Open University Press.

Miesen, B. (1992) 'Attachment theory and dementia', in B. Miesen, and G. Jones (eds) *Care-giving in Dementia: Research and Applications*, vol. 1, London: Routledge.

—— (1997) 'The challenge of attachment', in B. Miesen and G.M.M. Jones (eds) *Care-giving in Dementia: Research and Applications*, vol. 2, London: Routledge.

—— (1999) *Dementia: A Close Up*, trans. G.M.M. Jones, London: Routledge.

Morris, C. (1999a) 'Building up a toolbox of strategies for communication', *Journal of Dementia Care* 7, 4: 28–30.

—— (1999b) 'How denial can lead to anger and aggression', *Journal of Dementia Care* 7, 5: 25–7.

—— (1999c) 'Visual impairments and problems with perception', *Journal of Dementia Care* 7, 6: 26–8.

—— (2000a) 'Hallucinations and delusions: what you see is real for you', *Journal of Dementia Care* 8, 1: 28–30.

—— (2000b) 'Understanding difficulties with speech and language', *Journal of Dementia Care* 8, 2: 24–6.

—— (2000c) 'Understanding specific memory disorders', *Journal of Dementia Care* 8, 3: 26–8.

—— (2000d) 'Working with people, making sense of dementia', *Journal of Dementia Care* 8, 4: 23–5.

Morton, I. (1999) *Person-Centred Approaches to Dementia Care*, Bicester: Winslow Press.

Murphy, C.J. (1994) ' "It started with a sea-shell". Life story work and people with dementia', University of Stirling.

Newton, L. and Stewart, A. (1997) *Finger Foods for Independence: For People with Alzheimer's Disease and Others Who Experience Eating Difficulties*, Adelaide: Creative State Pty Ltd.

Packer, T. (2000) 'Does person-centred care exist?', *Journal of Dementia Care* 8, 3: 19–21.

Prouty, G. (1999) 'The Relevance of Prouty's Pre-therapy to Dementia Care', in I. Morton, *Person-Centred Approaches to Dementia Care*, Bicester: Winslow Press.

Sacks, O. (1985) *The Man Who Mistook His Wife for a Hat*, London: Duckworth.

Shotter, J. (1970) 'Men, the man makers', in D. Bannister (ed.) *Perspectives in Personal Construct Theory*. New York: Academic Press.

Wey, S. (2001) Personal communication.

Winter, D.A. (1992) *PCP in Clinical Practice: Theory, Research and Applications*, London: Routledge.

Yale, R. (1995) *Developing Support Groups for Individuals with Early Stage Alzheimer's Disease*, Baltimore: Health Professions Press.

Part II

Interventions in care facilities

Chapter 5

Living in lifestyle groups in nursing homes

Changeover to a psychosocial model of care-giving in dementia

Anne-Marth Hogewoning-van der Vossen

Introduction

For many years, the main emphasis in a number of psychogeriatric nursing homes in the Netherlands has been on the 'medical model'. The objective of this model is to provide medical care and physical treatment. However, insight into the dementia shows us that older persons with dementia have a primary need for psychosocial support and assistance (Droës and Finnema 1999). To meet this need, we have to change from a medical to a psychosocial model for care in nursing homes. Such a changeover is no easy task as it involves changing the behaviour of all staff, not to mention completely restructuring the organization. Change, in this sense does not so much mean devising new concepts, but rather starting off a psychological process. Only by making a link with the daily work of staff will it be possible to instil this psychological process. To be successful, it is necessary to find out what originally inspired the care staff. The vast majority of them opted for a career in health care because they wanted to care for others. However, with the current system, many staff find themselves stuck in a clinical and routine way of giving care. This makes many of them constantly feel that they are falling short of the mark. By talking to care-giving staff about their ideas of good care, it is clear that many of them are inspired to change. What is more, because of their practical experience, they have the knowledge that is essential to come up with effective concepts.

So to bring about change, it is necessary to have an effective translation of words and images that are strongly identified with and can be recognized. It is also important to design the concept together with those professional caregiving staff members who actually work in the field. Only then will we be able to produce concepts that are useful, because they link in with the practical situation (Van Splunteren and Borselaar 1998). Tailored training and support programmes during the change process also play a vital role.

In this chapter, a single case study will be used to describe how the transformation was effected from a traditional medical model to a form of psychosocial model within a particular nursing home. The study was conducted from spring 1998 to spring 2001 at the De Strijp psychogeriatric nursing home, which is part of the AHS (general nursing and care foundation in The Hague). This nursing home deploys what we call a 'lifestyle concept' of care. This concept is a psychosocial model for nursing home care, based on the prime criterion of preserving the lifestyle of the resident as far as possible.

The crux of the process is to work out how the daily activities of staff have been affected during the transformation to the lifestyle concept. What resources and actions has the organization deployed to get the care staff behind the concept and in this way actually to change something for older persons with dementia?

To give us a better understanding of how the change process was carried out, the first section explains the actual contents of the lifestyle concept. By comparing the traditional model of nursing-home care with the lifestyle model, we can see how the overall organization has been upended. No structure has remained standing and above all a far-reaching change in culture has been put into effect. The second section gives an overview of three related principles of change. By implementing change on the basis of these principles, it is possible to influence the daily work of the staff. Following on from this theoretical overview, the third section translates the theory into practice, taking a single case study that describes the changeover from the traditional model for nursing home care to the lifestyle concept. As we look at the transformation to the lifestyle concept, we can see that the change process is based on the three principles of change referred to above. In addition to carrying out structural changes, a link is found with the daily work of staff.

Changeover to the lifestyle concept

The study started in 1998. Although the quality of care in the nursing home referred to was average at the time, a considerable amount of restlessness or passivity was apparent among the residents. The new management team drew the conclusion from this that the quality of life of the residents was not satisfactory. After an initial period of looking at other nursing homes, the management team opted for the lifestyle concept. (The lifestyle concept was developed in the early 1990s by the Hogewey nursing home in Weesp, the Netherlands.) This concept is built on the following two related visions:

1   A vision of care-giving based on residents being entitled to continue their own way of living as far as possible as soon as they enter the home. By making the lifestyle of the resident the focal point, we are moving away from the medical model towards a psychosocial one.
2   A vision of the organization based on the assumption that it is only possible to achieve the above vision of care if we go over to small-scale, decentralized organizational units, integrating living, care and welfare.

Changing over to the psychosocial model

Research has shown that with the decline of their cognitive functions persons with dementia are constantly living with the awareness that they no longer have any control over their own lives. This causes considerable fear and insecurity, which ultimately affects their self-respect. These feelings give rise to the need to seek the proximity of other people and be in a trusted environment. If persons with dementia are treated in the right way, it can give them a feeling of security and help them maintain their self-respect. The basic skills required of staff working in a nursing home are therefore the ability to watch out for fear, powerlessness and sorrow, or simply to be aware of a person's life story. Assistance is also needed to fill in the days, since it is no longer possible for persons with dementia to structure their own days and undertake activities. What is more, when their short-term memory starts to fail, they often revert to earlier periods in their life when their memory still worked well. Objects and activities from these periods of their lives should form a part of the environment within the nursing home, as they offer them something to hold on to (Miesen 1999).

In many respects, the medical model disregards the above needs (Vink and Hoosemans 2000). In fact the environment in many nursing homes which operate on the basis of the medical model is fairly stark and clinical, with staff walking around in white uniforms. Instead of building on recollections of residents' earlier lives, this environment evokes associations with a stay in hospital. If the right support and assistance are not given, situations arise that can rightly be described as horror scenarios; for instance, sitting still in a chair for hours due to boredom or aggressive behaviour as a reaction to being treated wrongly. It is possible to prevent this sort of situation by moving away from the medical model towards a psychosocial model. The main differences between the two models are shown in Table 5.1.

It is interesting to point out the changes that were necessary to produce the psychosocial model. Changing over the structure so that residents are classified in lifestyle groups is a relatively simple process and can be achieved in a short space of time. A far more complex task is to achieve the cultural change necessary if professional caregivers are to treat residents in a different way. This concerns the relationship between the resident and the professional caregiver – in other words the crux of the change process.

Changing this relationship involves changing a psychological process. It is no longer a question of introducing different methods and techniques, but involves changing people's own behaviour. How this change in behaviour was brought about is described later in this chapter. It is a long-term process that can be divided into a number of phases. The first phase of this process is to let go of the routine clinical work – in other words, staff providing care without much involvement of their feelings. In the next phase, staff become more emotionally involved with the residents and give care almost intuitively

Table 5.1 The medical model and the psychosocial model

Medical model	Psychosocial model
• Older persons with dementia are categorized according to the level of care they need, i.e. during their time at the nursing home they are moved to departments corresponding to the stage of dementia they have reached.	• Older persons with dementia are admitted to the nursing home in their preferred lifestyle group and carry on living there to the end.
• Older persons with dementia are treated as patients suffering from the disease dementia.	• Older persons with dementia are treated as people who need to continue their own lives as far as possible once they have been admitted to the nursing home.
• Emphasis is placed on the physical aspects of care. Staff are trained to carry out nursing work and to help people wash, dress, eat and go to the toilet.	• Emphasis is placed on the psychosocial aspects of giving care. Staff are not only trained on how to provide physical care, but also learn how to deal with older persons with dementia.
• The focus is on the restrictions that the disease dementia brings about.	• The focus is on activating the skills of the older persons with dementia. For instance, residents can become members of associations or can cook meals in the lounge areas.
• The (para)medical caregivers are the key players in the multidisciplinary team.	• Multidisciplinary teams also exist, but the key players are the caregivers who work in the direct environment of the residents.
• The environment is clinical and the departments are closed off.	• The environment is homelike and the residents can move around freely within the building.

on the basis of their feelings. The last phase is the most difficult. It involves enabling staff to deal with these emotions on a professional level. Giving care to persons with dementia is a matter of striking the right balance between professional distance and emotional involvement.

Changing over to small-scale, results-driven teams

The care vision of the lifestyle concept means totally restructuring the organization. We can only achieve our aim of enabling older persons with dementia in nursing homes to lead their own lives as far as possible if the staff working directly with the residents have a feel for their needs. This is only possible if the entire organizational structure and related style of management are changed. Table 5.2 shows the main differences between the old and new organizational model.

Table 5.2 The main differences between the old and new organizational models

Old organizational model	New organizational model
• The organizational principle is based on what is offered by the services.	• The organizational principle is based on the questions originating from the lifestyle groups.
• The care teams are responsible for coordinating and carrying out the provision of care.	• The care teams have overall responsibility for coordinating and carrying out care, living arrangements and personnel policy.
• Control is centralized, involving more than one interface between the management team and the direct caregivers.	• Responsibilities are held low down in the organization and there are no interfaces between the management team and managers of the lifestyle groups (what we call section managers).
• Facilities management and P&O department are supporting services. Any questions arising from the care service are directed to the head of the care service.	• The management team comprises three line managers responsible for the fields of care, living arrangements and personnel. There is a direct line between these three managers and the section managers.
• Departments are large with 30 residents.	• Lifestyle groups are small scale with ten residents (in future this figure will be six) supervised by small teams of around ten members of staff.
• The manager is responsible for coordinating care and giving team leaders instructions for carrying out their daily work.	• The manager is tasked with offering the team the basic conditions necessary for them to perform their work independently. The manager's role is that of coach and entrepreneur.
• Teams are large and only a few members of staff are entrusted with the necessary powers.	• Teams are small and self-steering, with all members of the team having their own responsibilities.
• Policy is developed by policy-makers.	• Policy is developed in policy teams made up of members of staff holding different positions.
• General policy documents are drawn up with general objectives, which say little to the staff carrying out the policy.	• Work is results driven. The teams draw up annual plans stating their own objectives, which relate to the objectives of the organization. Staff are supported by means of development phases in which individual objectives are worked out.
• Evaluations are carried out by staff employed in general services or by external consultants.	• Evaluations are carried out at all levels of the organization. Not only the people carrying out the work but also the users are involved in the evaluation process.

When changing over to a new organizational vision, it is also a relatively simple process to introduce a different structure. The hard part is to change over to a new style of management (Goossens 1994). Decentralization means handing out the necessary powers. This calls for trust in other people's abilities and letting go of a position of power, which in turn means giving people the opportunity to experiment and make mistakes (Hendry 1996). Here too, the daily work of staff will only really change if a change in behaviour is brought about. Managers have to let go of more and become process supporters, while staff take on more responsibility. Before we describe how the lifestyle concept was introduced, the following section provides a theoretical basis for the approach adopted in change processes.

Three principles of change

The development of an organization involves a cyclical process of unfreezing, changing and then refreezing (Lewin 1952). Bringing about successful change is more than just getting rid of one thing and replacing it with another. You can only truly bring about change if these new arrangements actually become a part of the routine activities of the organization. Many organizational changes seem to get stuck halfway through this cycle (Gast and Kloek 2000). This section describes three related theoretical principles with which change processes must comply. Leaving out any of these principles may explain why the change process gets stuck.

Change under a common agenda

Following on from Hegel and Marx, an organization can be described as a systematic complex or whole made up of values and norms (Habermas 1968). This complex is formed by the interaction between the top and bottom layers of the organization. The top layer is created by translating the values and norms into structured ideas, for instance, care visions, annual plans and reports. The bottom layer is created by the daily work of the employees. This work is generally characterized by routines, in which values and norms are translated into formal and informal agreements between members of groups in the organization (Korthals and Kunneman 1979). For instance, a routine could be first knocking on the door before entering the bedroom of a resident.

A typical healthy organization is one in which the top and bottom layers are motivated by the same values and norms. There is a common agenda, as it were. Many organizational changes become stifled if there is no common agenda. For instance, there is an objective in the care vision stating that the process of giving care must be driven by questions. In practice, however, residents may be handed out a cheese sandwich wrapped in cellophane day in day out. This shows that there is a gap between the bottom and top layers. The top layer is based on the norm that there has to be scope for individual choice. The bottom layer exercises the norm that work has to be carried out efficiently, so that as many residents as possible can be cared for within a specific period of time. The message from the top layer has not

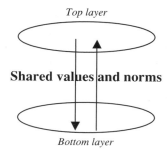

Figure 5.1 Change under a common agenda

been incorporated into the daily work. The above example makes it clear that it is important to take time during the process of change to develop common values and norms. In doing so, it is important to use words and images that connect with the experiences of the staff. Only those values and norms that staff themselves recognize as being 'right' will be adopted as routine by them in their daily work. In short, we can state that organizational changes have the chance of succeeding if they are motivated by shared values and norms or a common agenda (Figure 5.1).

Change via socialization

Following on from the above, we have to find out how to form this common agenda. Sharing values and norms within an organization calls for a process of socialization. Socialization means that members of a group internalize the prevailing values and norms of the group so that they can belong to it (Argyris and Schön 1978). This feeling of belonging enhances self-respect and security. In the health care sector in particular, it is important to take this group process into account. Care-giving is not a technical product, but is brought about by people. Another reason for the failure of certain change processes is the fact that systems are changed without taking their social context into consideration. Change managers have to associate changes with the values and norms that exist within the group (Bruel and Colsen 1998). For instance, an important value for many care staff is that you should take good care of your fellow human beings. The group will more readily accept a change that clearly associates with this value. Conversely, this means that changes arising from values that differ from the prevailing norms will encounter considerable resistance. For instance, in many teams in the health care sector, there is a prevailing norm that hard work means a lot of physical work. The caregiver who has already got eight people out of bed by ten o'clock in the morning often gets a lot of appreciation from the other members of the team. The new norm that 'drinking coffee with the residents in the lounge

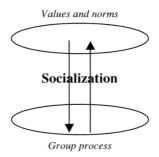

Figure 5.2 Change via socialization

is just as important' conflicts with the old norm. So to make sure that this norm becomes a part of the group process, it first has to be discussed with the group. The trick is to find a link with the other values within the group. Drinking coffee with a resident could be justified, for instance, on the basis of the value that you 'have to take good care of your fellow human beings'.

A typical feature of socialization processes is that certain figures in the group play a pioneering role. They are greatly respected by the group because their behaviour is perfectly in line with the group's values and norms. To introduce changes, it is a good idea to use these pioneers as role models because they are in a position to win over the rest of the group. They are therefore often referred to in the literature as 'change agents' (Schein 1985).

Existing relationships within the group sometimes form the very obstacle to change. Over the course of time, a specific group culture has developed that is difficult to break through. The only way of influencing the behaviour of the members of such a group is to change the social context, for instance by splitting the group up. In short, we can state that a second condition for organizational changes to succeed is that these changes are linked to the group processes within the organization (Figure 5.2).

Change via learning from experience

A third approach to describing successful change is by reflecting on how organizations learn. In his experimental learning theory, Kolb states that organizations develop by *learning from experience*. Learning does not mean changing behaviour, but creating knowledge through the transformation of experience (Kolb 1984). While people are at work, they form part of a group and through experience this group has adopted specific roles and working methods. As long as these roles and working methods are distributed effectively, there is hidden dialogue or tacit knowledge. It is only when problems arise that this dialogue comes to the fore. The members of the group exchange ideas about their work and experiment with new methods and roles. If the problems are resolved as a result of these experiments, the experiments then take on the form of a routine again and dialogue disappears into the background (Mastenbroek 1995). Learning in this sense means combining action with reflection.

This learning theory gives important pointers for managing change. The emphasis of change management should be on ensuring that the groups within the organization learn from experience, and this learning can be stimulated by focusing on dialogue (Senge 1990). Getting a dialogue under way does not just mean that the members of the group involved discuss issues together, they also experiment. During a change process, staff must have the opportunity to find out for themselves whether a new method works or not. For instance, one of the objectives of the lifestyle model is to get persons with dementia to lead their own lives as far as possible within the nursing home. To meet this objective, the organization has to adopt the daily rhythm of the residents as much as possible, which calls for flexible working hours for the staff and care teams. However, it is often not possible to change existing work schedules in one go from top to bottom due to individual circumstances. A much better way of doing it is to get the team itself to experiment and find out what is possible. The organization has to make time for dialogue as well as ensure a feeling of security. In other words, new ideas should be rewarded and any mistakes made must not be punished. Time and money should also be invested in supporting staff in the process of adopting new skills. Management is also expected to be flexible. Progressive insight gained by experimenting with new ideas will inevitably lead to change.

Organizational change often gets stifled if there is no opportunity for learning from experience. For instance, if a new concept is developed without there being any dialogue within the group required to work with this concept, it will frequently encounter resistance. The group will not see the concept as a solution but as a threat to the existing order within the group. It is also important for staff to perceive concrete change at an early stage in the change process. If they see change in the context in which they are working, they will feel that something is actually happening. For instance, getting rid of white uniforms has an enormous impact, because this is a visible sign that a new vision is now being adopted.

In short, we can state that a third condition for organizational changes to succeed is that change comes about through learning from experience. The groups within the organization learn how to adopt a problem-solving approach via cyclical action and reflection (Figure 5.3).

The above principles make it clear that changes will not come about if they are presented on a silver platter. Change is a psychological process that can only come about if there are shared values and norms and if the changes are implemented via socialization and learning from experience. The following

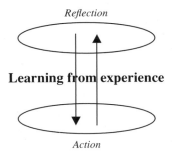

Figure 5.3 Change via learning from experience

section describes how the three principles of change can be applied in practice. An account is given of an actual process of changing over from the traditional model for nursing home care to the lifestyle concept.

Change in practice

The old situation

In the spring of 1998, the management team of the De Strijp nursing home opted for the introduction of the lifestyle model. Because no one within the management team had any experience of 'change management', an external advisor was called in. The advisor made an initial assessment of the situation, concluding that the potential for change was slim because the level of training of staff was on average low. What is more, change calls for managers who work in a process-oriented way and manage through coaching. However, the home's managers at that time were really busy managing with the focus on content, as they were themselves involved in implementation. Despite this slim potential, the assessment nevertheless revealed willingness to change on the part of the staff.

This willingness was due to dissatisfaction with how people worked together within the home, rather than the idea that the care provided was not good. Communication within the organization was poor. Coordination between the various services was not satisfactory and work was based on a supply basis. Family members were also dissatisfied. A survey carried out as part of the assessment showed that they were mostly dissatisfied with the admission procedure. On the day of admission, they and the person being admitted were suddenly confronted with a totally unknown world. Far too much information was thrown at them and little time was given to their feelings and emotions. Once their loved one had been admitted, many family members felt as if they had literally handed them over, whereas they wanted to stay involved in the lives of their loved ones. Many were not happy with the way in which their partner or relative passed the day. There was far too little to do and dissatisfaction within the departments was evident. Finally, families indicated that it was difficult to find a contact person in the departments. There were 5 departments of 30 residents with teams of 25 staff on average. Family members with questions were often sent from pillar to post. It was striking that most staff did not realize that the residents' next of kin were dissatisfied. Many of them had already been working for years in line with the medical model and physical care was for them the key criterion of care-giving.

It was clear from the assessment that introducing the lifestyle concept would be a radical change. But how could you make sure staff would be prepared to accept a completely different way of working? An account is given of the changeover to the lifestyle concept based on the three principles of change described in the previous section.

How was a common agenda created?

It is important to create a common agenda in a process of change. The assessment revealed that there was no shared vision of care-giving and cooperation at the home. Creating a shared vision would first of all mean undergoing a process of awareness. 'What is good for older persons with dementia?' and 'How do we want to work together?' were the key questions to be answered to work out a shared vision or common agenda.

The management team realized that this process of awareness would only work if the new vision was developed step by step together with the staff (Whyte 1991). A project team was set up with representatives from all levels of the organization and works council. In autumn 1998, a new care and organization vision was developed via workshops attended by the key figures from the organization. All staff and family members were given an overview of the new vision in the form of a hard placemat (Figure 5.4).

The 'action team approach' was adopted to work out the vision. (The action team approach was designed by Arthur Andersen Business Consulting) (King and Andersen 1990). Over a period of three months, specific topics were tackled by seven small teams, each with its own remit. The teams were diverse, made up of staff with different positions from all levels of the organization. Family members were also represented in the action teams. Topics were tackled from different viewpoints and input was derived from theory and practice. The end reports produced by the action teams were integrated, distributed to all departments and discussed at progress meetings. A central information meeting was then organized to explain what the coming year was going to look like. The second part of the meeting took the form of a quiz, with staff being asked fun as well as serious questions to test their knowledge of the vision. One of the action teams produced a code of conduct, containing a number of important behavioural codes based on the experiences

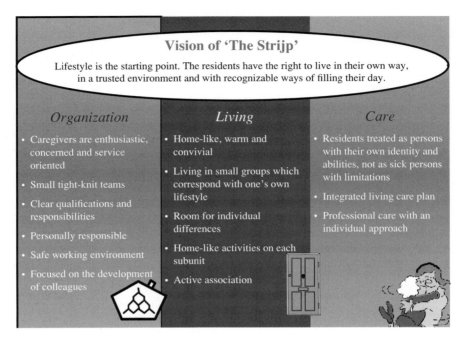

Figure 5.4 Place mat setting out the new vision of De Strijp nursing home

of a resident. To get the staff to embrace this code of conduct, a special game was designed. This game was played in teams with real people, and the various scenarios evoked discussion about basic behavioural ethics. Using the same action team approach, the vision was translated into plans that could actually be implemented. Seven implementation teams were set up, tasked with turning the end reports of the above action teams into concrete plans.

Because not all staff could take part in the action teams, eight 'vision roll-out' evenings were organized. During these evenings, all teams were given the opportunity to give interactive presentations to show what they consciously wanted to maintain or improve from their daily work with the residents (Box 5.1).

How was the socialization process initiated?

Changes within organizations have to be embedded within a social context. People within an organization form part of a group and are guided by the group culture (Weick 1979). To bring about change, you have to exploit these group processes as this is the way in which values and norms are incorporated

---

Box 5.1 Topics of the action and implementation teams

Topics of the action teams:

1. What are the key features of the new ways of care-giving?
2. What lifestyles are there among our residents?
3. What positions and staff training are needed?
4. How are we going to communicate with staff and families?
5. How can we integrate facilities services in the care process?
6. Draw up a code of conduct for staff.
7. What changes are needed to the building?

Topics of the implementation teams:

1. New care dossier and resident monitoring system.
2. New consultation structure with representatives.
3. New admission procedure.
4. Classify lifestyle groups in consultation with families.
5. Set up structure of associations.
6. Set up an à la carte restaurant for residents and family members.
7. Change the shop into a supermarket.

Box 5.2 Kick-off day

To make it clear to staff that the lifestyles project was starting, a kick-off day was organized. Every department performed a cabaret turn and song, and the logo and slogan of the project were introduced. Staff were asked what sort of associations were brought to mind by the slogan and logo. A first milestone was clearly reached with the kick-off, and preliminary discussions were initiated.

---

into the daily work. Use is sometimes made of prevailing norms and values and vehicles of culture, because they can affect the process of bringing about change. However, sometimes it is necessary to change the social context itself, as otherwise change will never permeate through to the members of the group.

It is interesting that the changeover to the lifestyle model was implemented by a totally new management team. The relatively young and inexperienced managers were 100 per cent behind the lifestyle concept. Instead of a hierarchical, centralized style of leadership, short, open communication lines were established with the aim of encouraging responsibility to be held low down in the organization (De Jager 1994). The introduction of the lifestyle concept called for completely different skills from middle management. The focus of their work shifted from coordinating care to coaching staff, managing budgets and developing policies. More than half the middle managers were changed during the change process, as they had difficulties with this shift in their work.

Various new communication tools were introduced with the aim of encouraging dialogue with staff. For instance, a large information board was put up in the foyer with information about the project. Part of the board was reserved for feedback or questions from people. An ideas box was set up next to the board. The best idea submitted was awarded a prize each quarter. Besides the usual house news, a fortnightly newsletter was introduced. This provided a mouthpiece for family members, relatives and staff to express their views about the change process from their point of view.

Instead of debating 'policies' behind closed doors, the new management team worked alongside the staff and family members/relatives to implement the new concept. As discussed above, the action team approach was the method adopted to implement the vision. This approach also had a significant impact on the process of socialization. The diverse composition of the teams meant that discussion was encouraged at many different points in the organization and support gained for change, because it was felt that the department of a specific action team had itself contributed to the change. Above all, the mixed composition of the teams helped to break through the old island culture and people from different departments would pop in and see each other.

During the transformation to the lifestyle model, three relatively minor changes were carried out that nevertheless had a major impact on the group process. The changes in question probably had this much impact because they involved removing three recognizable symbols of the medical model. The first change was to open up the nurses' stations. The windows were taken out and doors removed. By opening up the stations in this way, it was impossible for the care staff to retire to the nurses' station after their morning round (Figure 5.5). This meant that they were available to residents and their families throughout the day and made it clear that their function involved more than just physical care (Figure 5.6). A year later, the nurses' stations had been completely removed and made into seating areas for residents.

The second change was opening up the doors within the nursing home, so that residents could move about freely throughout the home. Previously, their living area was restricted to their own department, as there were coded locks on the doors. This change not only presented greater opportunities for residents, but also had a significant impact on staff. Residents, and therefore staff too, were taught about other lifestyle groups. Staff from general departments such as the secretary's office and personnel department also came into more direct contact with the residents (and therefore also the care-giving staff), as they would often receive regular visits from residents.

Figure 5.5 Old-style nursing station

Figure 5.6 New-style nursing station

The third change was the abolition of white uniforms. By coincidence this also had a positive impact on the group processes. Anticipating the agreement of the works council, the project team decided to make the wearing of uniforms optional. Seventy per cent of staff immediately took up this opportunity. In the four months leading to the official abolition of uniforms, those for and against debated the issue in the departments. By the time the abolition of uniforms was officially announced, there was only a very small group of staff remaining who had not been convinced.

By changing over to the lifestyle model, a conscious decision was made to break up all care teams. Small groups that had been together for a long time with their own rules of behaviour were split up. Staff were given the opportunity to write down two different lifestyle groups with which they felt an affinity. Without the involvement of anyone else, three managers then divided up staff on the basis of distributing quality and availability as evenly as possible. The expected protest failed to materialize. This was probably because everyone had been involved in the change process for months now – they were basically in the same boat. What's more, the teams were announced in a novel way rather than via a list on a noticeboard somewhere in the building. When announcing the new teams, each team member was given 100 guilders to go out and have some fun with their future team.

Nearly every member of staff was given a new position. Building on the end report drawn up by the action team staff, a social plan was drawn up in consultation with the trade union and works council and a social support committee was set up. Part of the role of the care staff was to be responsible for both caring and living. This meant that lounge and mealtime assistants also had to be trained in care tasks. In anticipation of the decentralization of cooking meals, several members of staff from facilities services were re-trained to take up care positions. In a later phase, all care staff would be trained in one of the key living tasks, i.e. cookery. Activity assistants were removed from the care teams and given the role of association leaders. The introduction of the lifestyle concept gave physiotherapists, psychologists, social workers and spiritual counsellors different roles. They started working on a consultancy basis and were no longer automatically present in consultations with representatives. On the other hand, these professionals took on a coaching role in the process of increasing the quality of care. For instance, a contact consultation was set up between the psychologist and the teams.

Finally, in the course of the change process, the role of the family was visibly changed. First, they were asked to point out what they really wanted to change and their recommendations were actually incorporated in the implementation plans. Then they completed surveys which were used to work out the various lifestyles. Apart from this, a few members of families played an active role in the action and implementation teams. What is more, each team drew up a plan together with the families on how to decorate and furnish the lounge of the individual lifestyle groups.

Box 5.3   Alzheimer Café and waiting list care

To ensure that a resident's life in the nursing home continued as closely as possible to how it was before admission, the nursing home launched two initiatives in 2000 together with the regional organization for mental health care, Parnassia. First of all, an **Alzheimer Café** was introduced at a café in the centre of town based on the concept of Bère Miesen. Every month, persons with dementia, their carers and other relatives and professionals meet in this café. Besides giving information, these sessions provide an important opportunity to mix with fellow sufferers and reduce the burden on those who care for persons with dementia.

The meetings also provide an opportunity for **waiting list care** in the months prior to admission. Depending on the needs of the client on the list and his/her carer(s), it is possible to receive home support from a multidisciplinary team comprising a case manager, nursing home doctor, psychologist, physiotherapist and psychotherapist. Waiting list care also offers the opportunity to spend a few mornings or afternoons within the future lifestyle group and become a member of one or more associations. This means that admission to the nursing home is a gradual process and carers are given support at an earlier stage.

After the first year of the change process, the centrally held family evenings were replaced with family evenings organized within the respective lifestyle groups. This improved contact between the families and teams and meant that information could be exchanged more directly. The point of most interest is that by organizing residents into small lifestyle groups living in recognizable homelike surroundings, their families also seemed to feel more at home in the residents' living environment. Previously, when families came to visit the residents, they would always leave the department. Now many family members stay in the lounge or use one of the many seating areas within the section.

How can people learn from experience?

The last principle of change described in the previous section highlights the fact that successful change requires learning from experience. Learning means combining action with reflection. The opportunity to combine the two must be provided during the process of change. This means devoting a certain amount of time to reflecting on what is to be done. Similarly, it must be possible to try things out and actually learn from practice. It is also important to develop skills in order to work in line with the new approach. Staff learn through action, but extra support and training are also needed. How were people able to learn from experience in the process of changing over to the lifestyle model?

One of the key instruments for learning from experience is evaluation. Throughout the process of change, it was necessary to evaluate the situation with one another on a constant basis. In practice, things sometimes turned out differently from what was expected during the preparatory phases. For instance, in the second half of the year after the changeover, staff pointed out that work had become harder, even though the reorganization meant there were more hands on board. There was evidently a feeling that the change process had 'dipped'. The matter was evaluated by the works council and management team, and reasons for the perceived increased workload were identified. By introducing a system of working on a smaller scale and integrated positions, staff had come to be much closer to the residents. Staff were now far more emotionally involved with the residents, but they were not sufficiently equipped to see this involvement as part of their professional work. The psychological workload therefore became much greater. Furthermore, the difficulties staff faced doing their daily work in the lounge were underestimated. People often felt these tasks were fairly tedious and no longer experienced the satisfaction they used to feel when carrying out routine physical work. Staff also felt a far greater burden of responsibility on their shoulders because more often than not they were there on their own due to the small size of the teams. The evaluation was so enlightening that the management team decided to carry out evaluations with all the teams on the same basis. Through the evaluations, staff were able to see for themselves what lay at the root of their perceived work pressure. Measures to be taken to reduce the workload were discussed at evaluation meetings. By recognizing the cause of the work pressure, part of the problem was already resolved. In addition, through these evaluations, many members of staff realized how much had already been achieved.

Another key instrument for learning from experience is creating a temporary experimental setting. In 2001, based on the results of the above evaluations, it was decided to introduce three new concepts through experimentation. The first concept was to change over to a guidance and cooperation model within the section. Instead of having one group manager per lifestyle group, one manager would give guidance to three lifestyle groups within one section. To reduce the feeling of vulnerability when working in small teams, the concept of cooperation between three teams was experimented with, without detracting from the idea of having a specific team for each lifestyle group. The experimental setting was also used to develop and introduce the concept of autonomous teams. Together with the three teams from the pilot department and the 'staff development' policy team, the section manager devised a number of instruments to develop autonomy. These were achieved in each case through the process of experimentation and evaluation.

Box 5.4   Examples of instruments for autonomous teams

1   A matrix for distributing team tasks.
2   A schedule to show the stage of autonomy reached by each team.
3   A form for assigning learning objectives.
4   A contract between the section manager and care manager on the management team, laying down agreements on budgets, basic conditions and quality tests.
5   Personal development profiles for each position.
6   A self-diagnosis instrument, which can be used to test the extent to which a team has met its objectives.

The third concept introduced in the pilot department is cooking within the lifestyle group. It was decided to build up gradually from two to five days. One of the cooks and the food advisor would give a couple of hours of their time on the days on which meals would be cooked, to give support. The food advisor taught how to apply a set of legal provisions (specially adapted by this official) in the field of hygiene in small-scale catering.

As pointed out earlier, in addition to learning through experimentation and evaluation, staff also have to learn skills via training and courses. Besides the usual courses for nursing skills and professional care-giving, other training courses were organized as part of introducing the lifestyle model and the training budget was increased fivefold.

One of the most important tasks in changing over to the lifestyle model is to ensure the professional approach of staff in their dealings with persons with dementia. It's all very well if the building is furnished in a homelike way and the teams are autonomous, but the very core of the lifestyle concept centres on the residents being treated properly. This requires specific knowledge and expertise. To familiarize everyone with the same basic concept of dementia, all staff (from receptionists to care staff), volunteers and, for instance, client advisors were divided into mixed groups and put on a course on dealing with dementia. This took place over four mornings or afternoons and was based on the book *Dementia in Close-up: Understanding and Caring for Persons with Dementia* (Miesen 1999). In addition to gaining a greater understanding of the disease itself and what goes on with older persons with dementia and those directly involved, people are given a handle on how to treat it. Families are also presented with a copy of the course book, based on the idea that it is important for everyone to have the same vision of dementia. In addition to the course on dealing with dementia, the following four training courses were also organized as part of changing over to the lifestyle concept:

1   A course on how to give feedback for all staff working in teams. To prepare for this course, staff are given homework. The course includes exercises on giving feedback via role playing on the basis of case histories.

2   A course on communication during change for the members of the management team. The course contains exercises based on role playing, for instance, on how to encourage active contribution by asking open questions.

3   A course on coaching leadership for all middle managers. They also received individual support via supervision meetings with an external supervisor.

4   A course on cooking in lifestyle groups for all care staff. This course gives information on recipes, dietary requirements, the organization of cooking and rules concerning hygiene. The course was run by the cook and food advisor who assisted in the process of introducing cooking in lifestyle groups.

First results

In the evaluations after the first year of the new lifestyle groups, practically all staff stated that they did not want to go back to the old situation. The key reason indicated was that they saw that residents were doing better on a daily basis. The feeling of peace within the home was particularly noticeable. In addition, residents were taking part in daily activities for a longer period of time. This feedback was also confirmed through statistics. For instance, the overall number of incidents over a six-month period had halved, as the number of incidents of aggression had decreased by two-thirds compared to the years before changing over to the lifestyle concept. The decrease in aggressive incidents was primarily apparent in the afternoons, between 16.00 and 18.00 hrs. Before, many residents felt the need to go home at this time, because it was the time for them to cook for their family, for instance. Others used to become distressed because there was nothing for them to do in the nursing home in the afternoons. Even the introduction of cooking in the lounges was a way for residents to fill their days.

In a benchmark study carried out by a major national firm of consultants on five nursing homes in the region, the De Strijp nursing home came out on top in 2001. This study into the quality of care examined both the living environment and the care systems adopted and surveyed all users in and around the nursing home. During work visits by staff from other nursing homes, the observation was often made that the home seemed to have a far easier target group of residents. There were far fewer wheelchairs and residents seemed so peaceful. However, it was clear from the care insurer's statistics that the home had admitted many residents with urgent problems just like the other nursing homes in the region.

Looking back at the change process, it was hard work and often a case of trial and error. However, the visible improvement for residents and the feeling that everyone within the nursing home had contributed to this made it a truly inspiring time for the majority of those involved. After three years of intensive change, the time has now come for ensuring implementation. The coming years will be a time for doing what we have promised and further integrating the lifestyle concept. It seems as if the time for learning and change is now over, but nothing could be further from the truth. The very way in which the nursing home introduced the lifestyle model means it has become an organization that will never stop learning. The three principles of change as described in this chapter form an integral part of the usual organizational process. Policy is still being developed via the action team approach, experiments are conducted and evaluations made. What is more, it can be stated that due to its learning experience, the organization now has learning needs at a higher level. For instance, by placing the lives and welfare of residents at centre stage, new demands were placed upon facilities services and personnel policy. As already stated earlier, the core of the lifestyle concept is the proper treatment of each individual resident. This places high demands on the professional approach of staff and in turn high demands on the support they are offered by the organization. Arranging training and courses is a support, but it is not enough.

Because of this, the De Strijp nursing home, where this study took place, has introduced a new position, a full-time advisor in psychogeriatrics. This position has since been filled by a psychologist with extensive experience in treating, supporting and caring for older people (with dementia) and their families. His prime task is (emotionally) to support all staff – from top to bottom – in their work and help them to (continue to) professionalize. He must ensure that all available multidisciplinary expertise is cascaded down to the shop floor as it were, so that adequate treatment of persons with dementia and their families can be assured on an individual basis. The time for intensive change may well be over, but there is still plenty to be learned.

References

Argyris, C. and Schön, P. (1978) *Organisational Learning: A Theory of Action Perspective*, Reading Mass: Addison Wesley.

Bruel, M. and Colsen, C. (1998) *De geluksfabriek. Over het binden en boeien van mensen in organisaties*, Schiedam: Scriptum.

Droës, R.M., Finnema, E.J. *et al.* (1999) *Geïntegreerde belevingsgerichte zorg versus gangbare zorg voor dementerende ouderen in het home; een klinisch experimenteel onderzoek naar de effecten en kosten*. Amsterdam/Utrecht: Vrije Universiteit, Trimbisinstituut, Nzi.

Gast, Ter E. and Kloek, M. (2000) 'Dilemma's van de flexibele organisatie', *Gids voor personeelsmanagement* 79, 10: 77–81.

Goossens, W. (1994) 'Strategische managementontwikkeling. Werken aan het succes van een organisatie', *Leidinggeven en Organiseren* 44, 6: 179–83.

Jager, de P. (1994) 'Communicating in times of change', *Journal of Systems Management* 6267/3, June: 28–30.

Habermas, J. (1968) *Erkenntnis und interesse*, Frankfurt: Suhrkamp.

Hendry, C. (1996) 'Understanding and creating whole organizational change through learning theory', *Human Relations* 49, 5: 621–41.

King, N. and Andersen, N. (1990) 'Innovation and creativity in working groups', in M.A. West and J.L. Farr *Innovation and Creativity at Work*, Chichester: Wiley, pp. 81–100.

Kolb, D.A. (1984) *Experiental Learning: Experience as the Source of Learning and Development*, Englewood Cliffs, NJ: Prentice-Hall.

Korthals, M. and Kunneman, H. (1979) *Arbeid en interaktie*, Muiderberg: Coutinho.

Lewin, K. (1952) *Field Theory in Social Science*, London: Tavistock.

Mastenbroek, W. (1995) 'Hoe goed veranderingsmanagement verbetering om zeep brengt', *Leidinggeven en Organiseren* 45, 1: 15–16.

Miesen, B. (1992) 'Dement: zo gek nog niet', *Kleine psychologie van de dementie*, Houtem: Bohn Stafleu Van Loghum.

—— (1999) *Dementia in Close-up: Understanding and Caring for Persons with Dementia*. London: Routledge.

—— (2000) *Mijn leed, mijn lief*, Houtem/Diegem: Bohn Stafleu Van Loghum.

Schein, E.H. (1985) *Organizational Culture and Leadership*. London and San Francisco: Jossey-Bass.

Senge, P.M. (1990) *De vijfde discipline. De kunst en praktijk van de lerende organisatie*, Schiedam: Scriptum Books.

Splunteren, P.T. van, Borselaar, H. *et al.* (1998) *Werken aan vernieuwing. Handreikingen voor ontwikkeling en implementatie van vernieuwingen in de ouderenzorg*, Houtem/Diegem: Bohn Stafleu Van Loghum.

Vink, M.T. and Hoosemans, A.E.M. (2000) 'Gevoelens zijn tijdloos. Belevingsgerichte interventies bij ouderen', *Psychologie en ouderen 4*, Houtem/Diegem: Bohn Stafleu Van Loghum.

Weick, K.E. (1979) *The Social Psychology of Organizing*, 2nd edn, Reading, MA: Addison-Wesley.

Whyte, W.F. (1991) *Participatory Action Research*, Newbury Park: Sage.

Chapter 6

Sonas aPc

Activating the potential for communication through multisensory stimulation

Rosemary Hamill and Terry Connors

Quality of life has become a predominant issue in the care of older people in hospitals and homes. Shifts in health care philosophy in the past 50 years have placed the issue firmly in the centre of health care delivery and the development of the health care environment. While previous models of care management focused strongly on the physical, medical and functional dimensions of care, quality of life management also focuses on social and psychological dimensions of well-being. Consequently, maintaining and developing quality of life for older people – their social and psychological functioning – will increasingly shape the agenda in health care delivery in the coming years.

In Ireland, the health care environment is a substantial one. Over 20,000 older people currently reside in long-stay care in Ireland: 5000 in health board hospitals; 1500 in welfare homes; 1500 in district hospitals; 6000 in private nursing homes; 3000 in voluntary nursing homes or hospitals; 3000 in psychiatric care. A large proportion of these residents suffer from dementia, varying from 10 per cent in health board welfare homes, to 20 per cent in health board hospitals, to between 25 per cent and 60 per cent in private and voluntary homes and hospitals. As attitudes to care have changed in recent years, so too has our understanding of caring for those with debilitating illnesses such as the dementias. Contemporary research and writing have focused very strongly on the 'presences' rather than the 'absences' of those with dementia and other communicative illnesses (Kitwood 1993). In support of this, rehabilitative approaches have been very successful in enabling people who had heretofore not been considered candidates for rehabilitative intervention. Others have shown that the care environment can indeed act to debilitate people, through care practices which prevent development and rehabilitation and which act to further cut off people from resources within themselves, within others and within the environment (Connors 1997). In particular, care staff play a key role in determining whether or not the environment is enabling or disabling. Recent research has shown that staff who are trained in person-centred dementia care choose more person-centred strategies, and fewer disease-focused strategies when dealing with patients with dementia (Lintern and Woods 2000). Through training, staff in that study became more aware of patients' needs for independence, occupation, understanding and self-worth, improving the quality of care they were able to deliver to patients in the programme.

A second important implication of quality of life and psychosocial interventions is their consequences from a care management perspective. Many behavioural problems, such as emotional instability, resistance to care and physical and verbal attacks, arise from sensory deprivation, unskilful caregiver –patient interactions, and patient anxiety, fear and loneliness (Leverett 1991). Fogel (1994) has identified two important patient-related factors producing problem behaviours which are amenable to modification through intervention (a) the patient's perception of the current situation; (b) alternative outlets for self-expression. Given this evidence, it is apparent that quality of life and psychosocial interventions can help reduce behavioural problems by increasing enjoyable contact between patients and staff, increasing sensory stimulation, reducing patient anxiety and loneliness; providing opportunities for the patients to express and enjoy themselves; and by facilitating social interaction and group activities.

A third area in which quality of life and psychosocial interventions can have an important effect is communication. Communication is essential to healthy cognitive, emotional and social functioning, and this is particularly true in the case of dementia where changes in communicative abilities and challenging behaviours cut people off from others and from their own identity. It is probably best to consider communication and relationship as sides of the same coin. Improved communication helps to build relationship with others and maintain relationship with self, and a better image of self and others improves communication. Given the impact of communication and relationship on quality of life, it is not surprising that each of the interventions discussed focuses in some way on these factors.

Interventions to improve the quality of life of older people in residential care focus on social and psychological functioning and on identifying and reducing disability introduced by the care environment. Such strategies include:

- minimizing medication
- maintaining self-esteem
- developing meaningful activities
- enhancing activities of daily living
- introducing specific interventions (Lubinski 1995).

Unifocal interventions have been used to improve both verbal and non-verbal communication skills including: Problem-solving for Behavioural Management (Gallagher-Thompson 1994); Sensory Stimulation and Exercise

(Rader 1987); Ways of Coping (Morris *et al.* 1992). It is noteworthy that the target factor common to all of these management approaches is communication capacity, and that all of these interventions recognize its primacy. Unifocal interventions such as work therapy, communication training, music therapy, reminiscence work and reality orientation also appear to have significant positive effects on patient functioning and quality of life (Penhale *et al.* 1998). However, multisensory interventions, such as Sonas aPc, entail the best of these elements.

The basis of this approach is epitomized by Lubinski:

> Communication becomes the crucial difference between isolation and social connectedness, between dependence and independence and between withdrawal and fulfilment.
>
> (Lubinski 1981: 339)

Like many interventions, the activities involved in Sonas provide opportunities for the caregiver and the person with dementia to enjoy positive experiences together which are inherently relationship building. However, this programme goes further, aiming to activate the potential for communication. The intervention is particularly beneficial as it taps into the important psychological domains of self-esteem and agency (through task completion and acting on the environment), increasing interpersonal and social contact, providing practice through memory exercises, and achieving this in a nonthreatening way. Sonas is designed to meet the needs of older people with dementia (including Alzheimer's, Parkinson's disease and stroke). This approach has been adapted to create a second programme called Anam, which is specific to older people with intellectual disabilities.

Sensory stimulation

The theory behind the use of sensory stimulation incorporates aspects of meeting needs (Ellis and Thorn 2000), avoiding sensory deprivation (Hilgarde *et al.* 1979), the possibility that stimulation can produce actual change in the brain (Ellis and Thorn 2000), and the contribution of unstimulating environments to the dementing process (Bower 1967). In the latter study the author suggests that both organic and psychogenic factors are involved in the advance of dementia – an idea that resonates with more recent work (Kitwood 1990). Benefits of sensory stimulation activities resulting in improvement in activities of daily living; memory function; cognitive ability; verbalization; socialization; decreased depression and medication have been noted (Witucki and Twibell 1997), although these authors recognize that it is not easy to separate responses to sensory stimulation from responses to human interaction.

Although there are differing views surrounding the amount and delivery of sensory stimulation (Ellis and Thorn 2000), and the need for sensory regulation to ensure maintenance of vigilance and to rule out habituation (Wood 1991), there is a growing body of literature that indicates its positive effects (Kovach 2000). Work over the past few years has taken an important step in looking at how stimulation can be taken out of the 'white room' situation into more accessible locations (McNamara and Kempenaar 1998; Wareing 2000; MacDonald 2002).

Memory impairment is a major feature of dementia, and it is suggested that increasing awareness through attention to the senses in the situation where memories are laid down may help later recall in the same situation (Killick and Allan 2001). These authors also suggest a link between emotion and memory in that emotional disturbance such as anxiety or depression may affect encoding and retrieval.

Background to Sonas aPc

The word Sonas is Irish and means well-being, joy or happiness and the initials aPc stand for 'activating potential for communication'. It is therefore not a system that sets out to cure the communication problems experienced in dementia, but rather to assist people to realize whatever potential they have. Sonas is a needs-led approach arising from the observed need for interaction between older people and their environment – the environment consisting of both physical surroundings and people. It was the paucity of interaction that made Sister Mary Threadgold, a speech and language therapist and Sister of Charity, aware of the need for some kind of intervention that would engage people in long-stay facilities, many of whom had dementia, in such a way that it would promote interaction.

It is not possible to interact with our fellow human beings unless we communicate with them, even if our communication is not of the verbal kind. Indeed, a large proportion of natural human communication takes place through non-verbal channels including facial expression, body language, gesture and tone of voice or vocalization. As well as lack of communication in many of the residential facilities Sr Mary visited, there was also lack of stimulation in the environment. She felt that the non-verbal communication she observed appeared to communicate sadness and dejection. Sr Mary had worked for a number of years with people who had profound intellectual disability, and had found that the use of music and touch provided a successful means of interacting with them and tapping their resources. Recognizing the link of cognitive impairment between dementia and intellectual disability, she considered that a similar approach might help people with dementia to realize their communicative potential, and she devised a method of multi-sensory stimulation aimed at activating whatever potential for communication is retained.

Ideology

The idea behind this method was that an environment would be created within a group session that would provide both sensory stimulation and communicative partners. The structured format of the group session comprises the following:

- a signature tune
- opening and closing songs
- relaxing and dance music
- exercises
- opportunity for use of percussion instruments
- stimulation of the senses of smell, taste and touch
- proverbs and poetry
- time for participants who chose to make a contribution of their own.

Each section of the session has a special significance. The role of the signature tune is to alert people through a musical trigger of memory. The opening and closing songs address each person by name, emphasizing individuality, and greeting is made through eye contact and handshake. The purpose of the singalongs is to trigger memory and to facilitate expression through singing. The exercise component of the session gives opportunity to take part in gentle exercise to instruction and demonstration. The association of words and actions in this section assists in promoting understanding. It is thought that interactive exercise promotes awareness of others (Dinan 1998), and this will accentuate the social and communicative environment that the group session provides.

Touch is introduced through gentle massage on the shoulders and back, accompanied by relaxing music, and there is opportunity for further expression through dancing or the use of percussion instruments. Group members are given a chance to complete proverbs, which are well learned early in life, often repeated and well laid down in memory. It is suggested that well-learned material can be drawn from what has been accumulated over the years without necessarily having to relearn (Woods 1992). Poetry is incorporated in the session and this can be listened to or joined in with, according to the preference and ability of the participants. During the session the senses of taste and smell are also stimulated.

Repetition of the same structure is a strong point of the Sonas approach and this is facilitated by the fact that the programme is packaged on audiotape/CD along with an instruction manual. This does not mean, however, that variety cannot be introduced. There are points in the programme where different stimuli can be introduced, and this allows practitioners to use their skills and judgement as facilitators, and to respond to the needs and abilities of the members of the group. The packaging of the approach has two further advantages:

1   It assists carers in their interactions – the programme guides them and they are then able to focus fully on their clients.

2   The taped format also means that the clients will receive the same input regardless of who is delivering the session. This adds to continuity for older people in a culture where staff changes may be frequent.

The Sonas group session has been described above and it is the main thrust of the approach. It is, however, acknowledged that a group is not necessarily appropriate for every individual. This may be because of the individual's preference. Some people do not function well in a group or the behaviour of someone may detract from the experience of others. With this in mind, Sonas aPc also offers an individual session based on music and touch. This is carried out on a one-to-one basis by a facilitator, again following a set format with certain pieces of music being associated with gentle massage on the shoulders, back, hands and head. The aim of this session is also to activate the potential for communication, but it does this in a different way. The session is designed to promote relaxation and calmness, to communicate through music and touch, and to provide a communicative partner who will respond to any spontaneous communication that comes from the older person.

Communication is at the centre of Sonas and the reason for using sensory stimulation in its aim to activate communicative potential is that there is a very definite link between the senses and communication: 'If the loop of communication has any beginning, it starts with our senses' (O'Connor and Seymour 1990). A brief consideration of how a sensory experience can lead to communication will help to clarify this.

Using the visual sense as an example, the experience of seeing trees covered with yellow, gold and red leaves will communicate the season of the year. This immediate level of communication can be taken a step further with memories being triggered by the association between sensory stimulation and what it represents. The strength of long-term memory may then be a source of support for communication. This sense also brings a wealth of information through the observation of facial expression, body language and gesture.

Looking at the other senses in turn it is possible to see how each can make its own contribution to the communication process. Hearing has its obvious function of receiving verbal communication – the words and sentences that we use. It also picks up the vocal tone that is a hugely important part of any verbal message, and a part that is often heavily relied on by people who may no longer be able to interpret the meaning of the words they hear. As well as the interpersonal aspects of communication that are received through the sense of hearing, there are environmental sounds that convey information, for example, passing traffic, domestic duties being carried out or weather conditions.

The olfactory sense may receive the smell of cut grass and this will communicate that somewhere in close proximity a lawn is being mowed. The familiarity of a perfume may indicate someone's presence, or the smell of food preparation may indicate an imminent meal. The sense of taste can tell the nature of what is being eaten, whether it is liked or disliked and if it is fresh or stale. Touch can be thought of in two ways, tactile and interpersonal. The tactile way brings information about texture, temperature, shape and humidity, and the interpersonal way can inform of the intent behind the touch. Through the way in which touch is used, infants know whether or not they are cared for (Montagu 1978). There is no reason to assume that this is only the case with infants and that it does not also apply to adults and older people.

It is known that the natural ageing process has an effect on the senses, and in the older population there can be specific sensory loss. Where this is the case, stimulation of all the senses can help to compensate. It is easy, for example, to imagine that people who have visual loss will rely more heavily on their sense of hearing for information regarding their surroundings. There is also the suggestion that the olfactory sense is diminished in Alzheimer's disease (Vance 1999). This fact is recognized by the multisensory approach of Sonas. Music is extensively used throughout the session, not just because it acts as an auditory stimulus, but also because it is seen to have wider benefits. Music is thought to have effects which calm people, diminish wandering, help to access memories and improve self-esteem and social cohesion (Pickles 1997).

Whilst the main aim of Sonas aPc is to activate potential for communication, it also aims to train and support carers in the use of this approach, to encourage a communicative environment and to have stimulation of communication seen as an essential part of care planning. Sonas is an approach devised in response to the need to address communication difficulty, an approach that uses creativity, imagination and experience. The philosophy on which it is based recognizes unmet communication need; the right to realize potential; the importance of preventing social isolation, promoting integration, quality of life and personal dignity.

Sonas aPc Training

The whole Sonas approach, whether group or individual, is delivered by trained practitioners. These practitioners do not need to have a professional qualification but rather are people who possess certain personal qualities. Desirable qualities are sensitivity to older people, energy, enthusiasm, openness to the broader aspects of communication and sincerity in their interactions with people. The training itself is given at a two-day workshop over a period of six weeks and focuses on communication and how it can change under certain circumstances (e.g. in dementia), the influence that the environment can have on communication and how to implement the Sonas approach. Sonas and Anam training workshops are delivered by a panel of tutors who have themselves undergone an intensive four-day training course and carried out supervised workshops.

Sonas aPc is a not-for-profit organization which has charitable status and receives funding from the Irish government on an annual basis. Approximately 5000 people in Ireland, USA, UK, Channel Islands and Australia have been trained in the Sonas approach, with the result that many thousands of older people are currently receiving its benefits.

Some of the benefits reported by staff who use the system are:

- increased interaction
- improved concentration
- emotional interchange
- reminiscing
- increased awareness among staff of abilities rather than disabilities
- catharsis
- lightened atmosphere.

Since its inception in 1990, Sonas has received many reports from people who use it as to its effectiveness, but as with any intervention this needs to be supported by evidence.

Qualitative evidence for the efficacy of Sonas

The credibility of any intervention lies partly in a theoretical base and partly in empirical evidence of its efficacy. In 1996 a study was carried out by Linehan and Birkbeck and this unpublished work suggested that the Sonas method was indeed effective in increasing the levels of purposeful activity, social interaction and verbal communication. There was also an associated improvement in spatial orientation, independent functioning and use of initiative over the study period, together with a reduction in the occurrence of inappropriate behaviour. The improvements in behaviour noted during the session were observed to carry over into the post-session period.

In 1998, Sonas aPc entered into a pilot project with four residential units of care, training members of staff who then provided 20 Sonas group sessions bi-weekly for some of their residents (Hamill 1998). This was a fact-finding exercise to see how the approach was being used in the units and to gauge its benefits for residents, staff and relatives. The result of this was a considerable amount of positive feedback and a lot of anecdotal evidence suggesting that Sonas had indeed been of benefit. There were comments from staff such as: 'Sonas I have found to be of immense value in observing levels of communication' and 'During the time of Sonas there were noticeable positive improvements in the residents' communication skills and a general increase in their self-confidence.' Relatives' comments such as 'Shows some signs of taking initiative in conversation and in asking the odd question' and 'He grips cardigan buttons to indicate that he doesn't want to go to bed. See a huge change in him – he is much more bubbly now' indicated that they had seen some positive change.

The following is a description which highlights the change that occurred in one person who took part in the study and the new information gained by members of staff. A brief profile of the lady supplied by staff stated: 'Likes company, seeks attention, likes radio/TV, no verbal communication.'

Reports from the Sonas session facilitators stated: 'Some words' after session one; 'Words used appropriately' after session four; 'Responds well to proverbs' after session eleven. The intervention of Sonas was able to bring to light that someone who had previously been thought to have no verbal communication was, in fact, able to use speech appropriately.

Quantitative evidence for the efficacy of Sonas

Following this pilot study a research protocol was developed to determine the benefits of Sonas using objective measures, operationalizing the aim of Sonas (to activate the potential for communication) in terms of standardized measures of cognitive functioning, mood, behaviour disturbance, communication and physical self-maintenance. Two studies, known as Model Unit Projects 1 and 2, were carried out using this protocol. In each study, staff from participating units (hospitals/nursing homes) were trained in the delivery of Sonas, and patients with dementia who had the functional capacity to complete cognitive and other assessments were selected to participate. In the first study, Model Unit Project 1, the initial cohort consisted of 32 residents, 24 who would receive Sonas and 8 others acting as a control group (at the time of the first analysis there were 18 remaining in the experimental group). In the second study, Model Unit Project 2, 64 residents took part. In the first phase, 48 received Sonas and 16 acted as a control group, while in the second phase all of the residents remaining in the study (the experimental group and the former control group) received Sonas. In both studies, experimental and control groups were matched by gender, age and cognitive functioning after initial assessment. Details were also recorded of main diagnosis; time since diagnosis; time since admission; coexisting conditions; time since last medical examination; and psychoactive medication. The outcome measures used were as follows: cognition (Mini Mental State Examination; Folstein *et al.* 1975); mood (Geriatric Depression Rating Scale; Shelk and Yesavage 1986); behaviour disturbance (Baumgarten Dementia Rating Scale; Baumgarten *et al.* 1990); disturbance in activities of daily living (Blessed-Roth Scale; Roth *et al.* 1988); communication disturbance (Holden 5-point Scale). After initial assessments were complete, residents assigned to the experimental condition participated in Sonas sessions on a bi-weekly basis. Control groups

Table 6.1 Model Unit Project 1 sample characteristics at Time 2

	Experimental group			Control group		
Gender	12 Women	6 Men		5 Women	3 Men	
Diagnosis	13 Dementia	5 Parkinson's		8 Dementia		
Age	Mean	SD	Range	Mean	SD	Range
	78.86	7.01	60–94	81.25	6.2	64–90

were brought together for the same duration and with the same frequency for an informal chat but no other activities were introduced. The findings of the two studies are now described.

Model Unit Project 1

The sample for Model Unit Project 1 as analysed at Time 2 is described in Table 6.1, and indicates a proportionate balance between experimental and control groups on key variables such as gender, diagnosis and age.

The analysis indicated that those who had received Sonas had improved cognitive scores, reduced depression scores, reduced ADL disturbance scores and reduced communication disturbance scores compared to baseline. There was no significant change in the functioning of the control group on any of these variables except mood: the control group also had reduced depression scores (see Table 6.2). While the observed changes in functioning in the experimental group could be attributed to the intervention, the improved mood in the control group is likely to have been a function of the increased social contact experienced by the group, as this was the only change in their activities during the period.

As the sample size in Model Unit Project 1 was small, a further study with a larger sample was conducted that included people with other communication difficulties besides dementia, e.g. stroke, Parkinson's (Connors 2001a).

Model Unit Project 2

In Model Unit Project 2, the experimental group consisted of 48 residents initially. The control group (initially n = 16) received no intervention for the first three months, then received Sonas for a three-month period, allowing for the effects with the combined sample to be examined. Demographic variables of the sample are described in Table 6.3.

Due to illness and death, a number of residents were lost from the study, and attrition rates for the experimental and control groups are described in Table 6.4.

After residents in the experimental condition had received Sonas for three months (T1 to T2) there were significant increases in cognitive scores, and

Table 6.2 Means and significance levels: experimental and control groups at 2 assessment times (N = 26)

	Experimental (n = 18) Mean	SD	Control (n = 8) Mean	SD	Significance
Cognition TI	12.00	4.97	14.37	4.43	NS
Cognition T2	14.94	6.30	14.87	5.59	NS
Difference TI, T2	p = 0.01		NS		
Mood disturbance TI	4.11	3.32	3.87	4.01	NS
Mood disturbance T2	2.61	2.83	1.62	2.55	NS
Difference TI, T2	p = 0.02		p = 0.01		
ADL disturbance TI	11.02	3.26	7.12	3.48	0.011
ADL disturbance T2	9.00	3.37	6.50	4.26	NS
Difference TI, T2	p = 0.001		NS		
Communication disturbance TI	13.05	6.61	7.50	7.32	0.023
Communication disturbance T2	10.05	3.55	9.00	5.96	NS
Difference TI, T2	p = 0.03		NS		
Behaviour disturbance TI	25.16	9.14	15.12	8.45	0.010
Behaviour disturbance T2	24.38	10.57	23.75	17.51	NS
Difference TI, T2	NS		NS		

Table 6.3 Model Unit Project 2 sample characteristics

	Experimental group (n = 48)			Control group (n = 16)		
Gender	43 Women	5 Men		16 Women		
Diagnosis	27 Alzheimer	21 Parkinson's		10 Alzheimer	6 Other	
Age	Mean	SD	Range	Mean	SD	Range
	81	8.06	66–98	81.25	6.6	64–92

Table 6.4 Sample sizes and attrition from the study at Time 1, Time 2 and Time 3

	Time 1	Time 2 (3 months)	Time 3 (6 months)
Experimental group	48	43	37
Control group	16	14	12
Total	64	57	49
Attrition		7	15

Table 6.5 Means, SDs and significance levels: experimental and control groups

	Experimental Mean	SD	Control Mean	SD	Significance
Cognition T1	10.13	4.81	11.58	4.42	NS
Cognition T2	12.83	5.56	11.66	4.69	NS
Cognition T3	13.00	7.45	14.83	6.13	NS
Difference T1, T2	p = 0.000		NS		
Difference T2, T3	NS		0.01		
Difference T1, T3	p = 0.002		NS		
ADL disturbance T1	11.02	10.59	13.66	8.27	0.011
ADL disturbance T2	9.00	8.97	14.83	8.27	NS
ADL disturbance T3	10.37	9.32	13.83	10.06	0.005
Difference T1, T2	NS		NS		
Difference T2, T3	p = 0.02		NS		
Difference T1, T3	NS		NS		
Behaviour disturbance T1	4.89	4.13	4.90	6.14	0.010
Behaviour disturbance T2	4.81	3.62	6.00	6.80	NS
Behaviour disturbance T3	3.89	4.01	2.60	3.30	NS
Difference T1, T2	NS		NS		
Difference T2, T3	0.01		0.053		
Difference T1, T3	0.07 (NS)		NS		
Communication disturbance T1	10.59	7.74	11.90	8.05	NS
Communication disturbance T2	8.97	5.60	11.91	6.86	NS
Communication disturbance T3	9.32	6.65	8.25	6.01	NS
Difference T1, T2	0.08 (NS)		NS		
Difference T2, T3	NS		0.03		
Difference T1, T3	NS		NS		

at six month follow-up (T2 to T3), there were significant reductions in mean ADL disturbance and behaviour disturbance scores also (Table 6.5).

There were no significant changes in the control group during Time 1 to Time 2. Having acted as controls to the experimental group during this time, the control group then began receiving Sonas. After three months (Time 2 to Time 3), mean cognitive scores had increased significantly and mean behaviour disturbance scores had fallen significantly for this group. The results support a positive effect of Sonas on resident functioning, improving cognition and reducing behaviour disturbance.

In the experimental group with diagnoses of dementia only (n = 20), there were significant increases in mean cognitive scores from Time 1 to Time 2

Table 6.6 Means and SDs of experimental group with dementia vs. other diagnoses

	Experimental group – dementia		Experimental group – other diagnoses		
	Mean	SD	Mean	SD	
Cognition T1	8.15	3.78	12.47	4.93	0.005
Cognition T2	10.00	3.09	16.17	6.03	0.000
Cognition T3	9.10	4.41	17.58	7.77	0.000
Difference T1, T2	0.01		0.001		
Difference T2, T3	NS		0.063 (NS)		
Difference T1, T3	NS		0.003		
ADL disturbance T1	19.80	7.74	13.76	10.78	0.054
ADL disturbance T2	20.55	8.24	13.88	10.29	0.035
ADL disturbance T3	18.00	9.48	13.11	10.78	NS
Difference T1, T2	NS		NS		
Difference T2, T3	0.048		NS		
Difference T1, T3	NS		NS		
Communication disturbance T1	14.95	7.35	5.47	4.37	0.000
Communication disturbance T2	11.60	5.28	5.88	4.32	0.001
Communication disturbance T3	12.15	6.83	6.00	4.73	0.004
Difference T1, T2	0.01		NS		
Difference T2, T3	NS		NS		
Difference T1, T3	0.07 (NS)		NS		

and reductions in mean ADL disturbance scores from Time 2 to Time 3 (Table 6.6). In the experimental group with diagnoses other than dementia (n = 17) there were significant increases only in mean cognitive scores from Time 1 to 2 and Time 1 to 3.

A further analysis looked at the entire group of residents (original experimental and control groups together) when all were receiving Sonas in the final three months of the study. For the entire group (n = 49), there were significant reductions in mean behaviour disturbance scores and activities of daily living (ADL) disturbance scores (Table 6.7). For those with dementia only in this group (n = 28), there were significant reductions in mean behaviour disturbance scores (t = 2.71, df = 27, p < 0.01) and ADL disturbance scores (t = 2.29, df = 27, p < 0.03). For those with diagnoses other than dementia in the combined group (n = 21) there were significant increases in mean cognitive scores only (t = 2.67, df = 20, p < .014).

Together, the MUP studies suggest that Sonas does help to improve a number of behaviours essential to communicating (and to quality of life) such as cognition, mood, self-maintenance and communicative capacity itself. In this sense, it achieves its aim of 'activating the potential for communication'.

Table 6.7 Means and SDs: combined group receiving Sonas from T2 to T3 (n = 49)

| | Cognition | | ADL disturbance | | Behaviour disturbance | |
	Mean	SD	Mean	SD	Mean	SD
Time 2	12.55	5.34	16.83	9.37	5.10	4.57
Time 3	13.44	7.13	15.28	10.26	3.59	3.87
Difference T2, T3	0.074 (NS)		0.030		0.003	

The approach appears therefore to be particularly useful in working with those who are withdrawn or whose ability to communicate has been diminished by illness and/or institutionalization. Older people with dementia in residential care are particularly vulnerable in this respect.

Sonas in the community

Sonas is not an approach limited to residential care and there is also scope for its application in the community. One such application which we have examined in our research is with carers of people with dementia who face the deterioration of the communicative abilities of the person with dementia and deterioration in the relationship between caregiver and patient. To evaluate the efficacy of Sonas as a community intervention, measures of carer well-being, quality of life, interaction with their relative, and functioning of the person with dementia were taken before carers were trained in using aspects of the Sonas approach with their relatives, and again after 6 weeks and 12 weeks (Connors 2001b).

The study found that communication ability of the person with dementia and the level of interaction between the person with dementia and the carer were the strongest predictors of carer well-being. Communication ability of the person with dementia was significantly associated with carer quality of life ($p = 0.003$), psychological health as measured by the GHQ12 ($p = 0.03$) and stress ($p = 0.03$). Interaction between the carer and the person with dementia was significantly associated with carer quality of life ($p = 0.002$), stress ($p = 0.004$), psychological health as measured by the GHQ12 ($p = 0.01$), and willingness to institutionalize the person with dementia ($p = 0.004$). The results emphasize the primacy of interaction and communication as variables affecting carer health and well-being.

With regard to the effect of Sonas, carers who completed the training had significantly higher *interaction* scores than those who did not ($p = 0.003$). While there was no difference between the training and non-training groups at baseline, the training group had significantly improved in interaction with the person with dementia ($p = 0.041$), carer psychological health ($p = 0.034$), and carer quality of life ($p = 0.041$).

While the results show some benefit to participants in the short term, the effects had dissipated by the week 12 follow-up. Unless integrated into an overall strategy of supported home care, the benefits of activities such as Sonas are unlikely alone to overcome the many other burdens carers shoulder: the grinding routine of around-the-clock care; the ongoing loss and impending institutionalization and death of a loved one; inadequate social support; and inappropriate or inadequate social and medical support. The findings stress the huge importance to carer health and well-being of communication and interaction between the carer and the person with dementia. Consequently, it is not surprising that carers were very positive about the Sonas programme, especially the opportunity it provided for contact with other carers, and the professional support it gave. To respond to the needs identified in the study, Sonas has developed a communication and stress management training course for carers, and is currently training three groups of carers in a pilot intervention.

The way forward

A lot of the past for Sonas aPc has been devoted to training people in its implementation, developing the approach in both residential and community settings and establishing its credibility as an evidence-based practice. The future holds many challenges in carrying this approach forward. These challenges lie in forming a foundation which will allow Sonas to be a sustainable and accessible method of intervention.

In order for any intervention to be sustained, certain factors are necessary. First, it must continue to have effective application. This means that continual review of the approach is needed, and that it keeps pace with changes in the nature of the older population and with the advancing knowledge about conditions like dementia. It also means that there is a need for continued research. Second, there must be a level of committed support from people who are in a position to empower and enable the care practitioners who actually carry out the programme. The required support can be divided into three categories:

1   Provision of training.
2   Provision of resources by way of staff, time and facilities.
3   Listening to the voices of those who are carrying out the sessions so that the intervention can influence the total care of people with communication difficulty.

There are aspects other than training that are needed to ensure that there is a positive change in the delivery of care: 'an increase in perceived confidence and competence among staff may well lead to innovation, but innovation must be encouraged by managers if enthusiasm is not to be dampened.

Training alone then is unlikely to be enough' (Nolan and Keady 1996). Trying to facilitate this need for a committed approach to the care of the whole person with dementia and other communication difficulties is one of the main challenges that Sonas aPc now faces. In pursuit of this it has recently developed more structured modular programmes which are designed to assist health care professionals, their teams and family carers in better implementing the Sonas approach beyond the session into the care environment of the older person. These programmes involve all the stakeholders, including staff, management and families. These initiatives, together with training for family carers, will occupy Sonas aPc for some time to come, and it is hoped lead to a better climate of care.

As well as providing a way of addressing communication in dementia that is both sustainable and credible, there is a need for accessibility of the programme. Its accessibility depends first on the support of those who manage the service and their recognition of the importance of addressing psychosocial, emotional and spiritual needs as well as physical needs. Second, it depends on the ability of the small Sonas organization to make this intervention available in a wider geographical way.

Whether or not we believe that dementia is an illness, a disability, or a different way of 'becoming', we need to accept the fact that people with dementia do not seem to be able to alter their path. So whilst the challenges are considerable, it is incumbent on those of us who do not have dementia to find ways of keeping company and maintaining interaction, communication and relationships with those of us who do. The dynamics of Sonas at the level of process are opaque, but the benefits at the level of behaviour are quite tangible. At a process level, the Sonas aPc method appears to work because it taps into latent general abilities such as thinking and acting that prefigure, give rise to and enable communication. This reawakening of the potential to communicate is an extremely profound occurrence because it brings people back into communion with themselves, with others and with their environment. Communication is central, and as one person with dementia has put it:

You see, you are words. Words can make or break you.

(Killick 1997)

Sonas works because, unlike much of the rest of society, it embodies a real optimism about illness and about old age. In contrast, health care that proceeds from a pessimistic view of ageing is unlikely to appreciate the importance of, or provide opportunities for, communication. Apart from the direct benefit to patient quality of life, improvements in care-relevant behaviours are inevitably passed on to frontline staff. Improvements in behaviour and activities of daily living (ADL) make caring for people easier, reduce the workload, may lead to greater job satisfaction and ultimately improve overall quality of care.

The prevalence of dementia, and Alzheimer's disease in particular, continues to grow in the Western world and the effects on families worldwide are devastating. In the absence of medications that might slow, stop or reverse the progress of the disease, improving quality of life and quality of care through interventions such as Sonas is the essence of contemporary dementia care. To date, Sonas has been shown to significantly improve patient quality of life and quality of care in residential and day care settings. As an intervention in community dementia care, it has been very well received by carers. Apart from the immediate practical benefit, interventions such as Sonas demonstrate that health care is most effective in meeting deeply human needs only when the principles it applies are themselves deeply human.

References

Baumgarten, M., Becker, R. and Gauthier, S. (1990) 'Validity and reliability of the Dementia Disturbance Scale', *J. Am. Geriatric Society* 38: 221–6.

Bower, H.M. (1967) 'Sensory stimulation and the treatment of senile dementia', *Medical Journal of Australia* 1, 22: 1113–19.

Butin, D.N. (1991) 'Helping those with dementia to live at home: an educational series for caregivers', *Physical and Occupational Therapy in Geriatrics* 9, 3/4: 69–82.

Connors, T.C. (1997) 'Caregiving to a family member with Alzheimer's disease: psychological, social and socio-cultural factors', unpublished doctoral dissertation, Department of Psychology, National University of Ireland, Galway.

—— (2000) *Activating the Potential for Communication in People with Dementia in Residential Care: Sonas Model Unit Project 1*, Dublin: Sonas aPc.

—— (2001a) *Activating the Potential for Communication in People with Dementia in Residential Care: Sonas Model Unit Project 2*, Dublin: Sonas aPc.

—— (2001b) *Sonas aPc for Family Carers of People with Dementia: A Community Study*, Dublin: Sonas aPc.

Dinan, S. (1998) 'Fit for life: why exercise is vital for everyone', *Journal of Dementia Care* 6, 3: 22–5.

Ellis, J. and Thorn, T. (2000) 'Sensory stimulation: where do we go from here?', *Journal of Dementia Care* 8, 1: 33–7.

Fogel, B. (1994) 'Quality care for the nursing home patient', in J.N. Morris (ed.) *The HRCA Manual*, Natick, MA: Hebrew Rehabilitation Center for the Aged, Eliot Press.

Folstein, M.F., Folstein, E. and McHugh, P.R. (1975) 'Mini mental state: a practical method for grading the cognitive state of patients for the clinician', *Journal of Psychiatric Research* 12: 189–98.

Gallagher-Thompson, D. (1994) 'Clinical intervention strategies for distressed caregivers: rationale and development of psychoeducational approaches', in E. Light, G. Niederehe and B. Lebowitz (eds) *Stress Effects on Family Caregivers of Alzheimer's Patients*, New York: Springer.

Hamill, R. (1998) 'Caring for older people with communication difficulty: report on the implementation of Sonas aPc', unpublished report, Duhlin: Sonas aPc.

Helwick, L.D. (1994) 'Stimulation programs for coma patients', *Critical Care Nurse* August: 47–52.

Hilgarde, E.R., Atkinson, R.L. and Atkinson, R.C. (1979) *Introduction to Psychology*, San Diego: Harcourt, Brace, Janovich.

Keane-Hagarty, E., Farran, C.J. and Salloway, S. (1990) *Caregiver Educational Support Group Manual and Instructor's Manual, Chicago*, IL: Rush Alzheimer's Disease Center.

Killick, J. (1997) *You are Words*, London: Hawker.

Killick, J. and Allan, K. (2001) *Communication and the Care of People with Dementia*, Buckingham: Open University Press.

Kitwood, T. (1990) 'The Dialectics of dementia: with particular reference to Alzheimer's disease', *Ageing and Society* 10: 177–96.

—— (1993) 'Towards a theory of dementia care: the interpersonal process', *Ageing and Society* 13: 51–67.

Kovach, C.R. (2000) 'Sensoristasis and imbalance in persons with dementia', *Journal of Nursing Scholarship* 32, 4: 379–84.

Leverett, M. (1991) 'Approaches to problem behaviours in dementia', in E.D. Taira (ed.) *The Mentally Impaired: Strategies and Interventions to Maintain Functioning. Physical and Occupational Therapy in Geriatrics* 9, 3/4: 93–106.

Linehan, C. and Birkbeck, G. (1996) 'An Evaluation of Sonas aPc: a multisensorial approach to activate the potential for communication in the elderly', unpublished report.

Lintern, T. and Woods, B. (2000) 'Before and after training: a case study of intervention', *Journal of Dementia Care* 8, 1: 15–17.

Lubinski, R. (1981) 'Speech, language and audiology programs in home health care agencies and nursing homes', in D.S. Beasley and A.G. Davis (eds) *Aging, Communication Processes and Disorders*, New York: Grune and Straton.

—— (1995) 'Environmental considerations for elderly patients', *Dementia and Communication*, San Diego, CA: Singular.

MacDonald, C. (2002) 'Back to the real sensory world our "care" has taken away', *Journal of Dementia Care* 10, 1: 33–6.

McNamara, C. and Kempenaar, L. (1998) 'The benefits of specific sensory stimulation', *Journal of Dementia Care* 6, 6: 14–15.

Miller, E. and Morris, R. (1993) *The Psychology of Dementia*, Chichester: Wiley.

Mittelman, M.S., Ferris, S.H., Shulman, E., Steinberg, G., Ambinder, A. and Mackell, J. (1997) 'Effects of a multicomponent support program on spouse–caregivers of Alzheimer's disease patients: results of a treatment/control study', in L.L. Heston (ed.) *Progress in Alzheimer's Disease and Similar Conditions*, Washington, DC: American Psychiatric Press.

Montagu, A. (1978) *Touching – the Human Significance of the Skin*, New York: Harper & Row.

Morris, R.G., Woods, R.T., Davies, K.S., Berry, J. and Morris, L.W. (1992) 'The use of a coping strategy focused support group for carers of dementia sufferers', *Counselling Psychology Quarterly* 5: 337–48.

Nolan, M. and Keady, J. (1996) 'Training together: a challenge for the future', *Journal of Dementia Care* 4, 5: 10–12.

O'Connor, J. and Seymour, J. (1990) *Introducing Neuro-Linguistic Programming*, London: Thorsons.

Penhale, B., Bradley, G., Parker, J.R., Manthorpe, J., Gynnerstedt, K., Schartau, M., Pierrot, L., Quinio, Y. and Zingraff, J. (1998) *The Equal Project: Enhancing the Quality of Life of People with Alzheimer's Disease*, Hull: University of Hull.

Pickles, V. (1997) 'Music's power, purpose and potential', *Journal of Dementia Care* 5, 3: 20–21.

Pynoos, J. and Ohta, R.J. (1991) 'In-home interventions for persons with Alzheimer's disease and their caregivers', *Physical and Occupational Therapy in Geriatrics* 9, 3/4: 84–92.

Rabins, P.V. (1997) 'Caring for persons with dementing illnesses: a current perspective', in L.L. Heston (ed.) *Progress in Alzheimer's Disease and Similar Conditions*, Washington, DC: American Psychiatric Press.

Rader, J. (1987) 'A comprehensive staff approach to problem wandering', *The Gerontologist* 27, 6: 756–60.

Review of Community Care Services (1987) *Community Care Services: An Overview*, Dublin: National Economic and Social Council.

Roth, M., Huppert, F.A., Tym, E. and Mountjoy, C.Q. (1988) *CAMDEX: The Cambridge Examination for Mental Disorders in the Elderly*, Cambridge: Cambridge University Press.

Schulz, R., Williamson, G.M., Morycz, R.K. and Biegel, D.E. (1992) 'Costs and benefits of providing care to Alzheimer's patients', in S. Spacapan and S. Oskamp (eds) *Helping and Being Helped: Naturalistic Studies*, Newbury Park, CA: Sage.

Shelk, J. and Yesavage, J. (1986) 'Geriatric Depression Rating Scale (GDS): recent evidence and a shorter version', in T.L. Brink (ed.) *Clinical Gerontology*, New York: Haworth Press.

Sonas (1998) *Activating the Potential for Communication: A Report on the Implementation of Sonas Since 1990*, Dublin: Sonas.

Survey of the Workload of Public Health Nurses (1975) *Report of a Working Party on General Nursing*, Dublin: Stationary Office.

Teri, L. (1990) *Managing and Understanding Behavioural Problems in Alzheimer's Disease and Related Disorders*. Training program with videotapes and written manual. Seattle, Washington.

—— (1997) 'Behavioural techniques for treatment of patients with Alzheimer's disease', in R. Becker, and E. Giacobini (eds) *Alzheimer's Disease: From Molecular Biology to Therapy*, Boston: Birkhauser.

Vance, D. (1999) 'Considering olfactory stimulation for adults with age-related dementia', *Perceptual Motor Skills* 88: 398–400.

Wareing, L.A. (2000) 'Pathways through the senses to individualised care', *Journal of Dementia Care* 8, 1: 22–4.

Witucki, J.M. and Twibell, R.S. (1997) 'The effect of sensory stimulation activities on the psychological well being of patients with advanced Alzheimer's disease', *Americal Journal of Alzheimer's Disease* Jan./Feb.: 10–15.

Wood, R.L. (1991) 'Critical analysis of the concept of sensory stimulation for patients in vegetative states', *Brain Injury* 5, 4: 401–9.

Woods, B. (1997) 'The beginnings of a new culture in care', in T. Kitwood and S. Benson (eds) *The New Culture in Dementia Care*, London: Hawker Publications.

Woods, R. (1992) *Care-Giving in Dementia*, vol. 1, London: Routledge.

Working Party on Services for the Elderly (1988) *The Years Ahead: A Policy for the Elderly*, Dublin: Government Publications.

Chapter 7

Memory groups

Facilitating open dialogue between persons with dementia

Neil Mapes

Introduction

This chapter will take a reflective look at my involvement in the setting up, running and evaluation of memory groups for people with dementia in a day-care setting. I was involved in three different groups over an 18-month period. The experiences during this time will be partly reported here and will form the basis for this chapter's argument that memory groups are an effective therapy tool for those working with people who have dementia. My experience comes from running memory groups in a day-care setting, but the idea of running memory groups in the community, hospital, long-stay care or other settings is perfectly feasible and worthwhile pursuing. This chapter will concentrate on practical issues such as: setting up a memory group, running a memory group, and the role of the facilitator(s). In addition, time will be spent reflecting on the relative strengths, weaknesses and criticisms of memory groups as a tool and of the work highlighted.

Memory groups have been in existence for some years and yet have received little academic attention. Memory groups are clearly distinct from memory clinics. Memory clinics, by nature of their medical basis have been the subject of numerous studies. For example, Logiudice *et al.* (1999) argued that memory clinics improve the quality of life for carers of those attending a memory clinic. Luce *et al.* (2001) concluded that memory clinics are identifying cases of dementia earlier than traditional old age psychiatry services. In balance, Bender (1996) outlined some of the main concerns with memory clinics. In my experience memory groups tend to be found in non-medical locations. Although often conducted in a more informal manner, they do not lack professionalism. Often the group has been set up by an inspired individual with drive to help others.

Memory groups have many similarities with the recent prominence and success of patient support groups. Support groups for caregivers are a long-established and proven effective therapy. Internet-based groups are now available for caregivers (White and Dorman 2000). Many practitioners have opened up this therapy to people with dementia. These support groups have a growing body of evidence that establishes their effectiveness. Back in 1995 supportive seminar groups were conducted for individuals with the illness and caregivers that lent support to the feasibility of a group approach for early stage dementia patients (Snyder *et al.* 1995). They have since been recognized as a therapy that assists early stage individuals with dementia to build coping strategies and reduce distress (Kasl-Godley and Gatz 2000). They have also grown partly as a result of the increase in early diagnosis of dementia, with more people having insight and awareness of their problems. Many practitioners are setting up support groups in response to this growing need (Goldsilver and Gruneir 2001). These support groups have been recognized as a valuable psychosocial intervention for people in the early stage of dementia (Petry 1999) as they have their focus on education, sharing of experiences and coping strategy development. The memory groups that will be discussed here are similar in that the focus is on these key areas with the more explicit emphasis on memory, its workings, and how it can be helped. The patient support groups, in various guises, have become widespread, with many having web access and promotion, both in the UK and further afield. For example, the dementia services development centre for the south west (England) is evaluating the efficacy of support groups for people with early stage dementia (information available at www.dementia-voice.org.uk). Further afield in New South Wales, Australia, the Alzheimer's Association has secured funding to run an early stage dementia programme until the end of 2004 called 'Living with Memory Loss' (information available at www.alznsw.asn.au).

The UK memory groups hope to add to the variety of patient-focused groups that have proven to be effective and are being set up around the globe. The work here has similarities with the support groups mentioned yet is something separate, as will be detailed in this chapter. It is important that these groups are formalized and conducted in many more areas, disciplines and settings. If run, evaluated and published, these groups can become more than just a good idea; they can develop into a body of knowledge of how memory groups can be effective in enhancing the well-being of those with dementia and how they can best be used.

A grounding

This chapter is based within social constructionism theory. For readers unfamiliar with this approach Burr's (1995) book is recommended by way of introduction. Within social constructionism it is important to examine language use: what and how language constructs different understandings, which then become socially validated. Thus, it is important to examine the social context of language or conversations and how these conversations help us to understand people and processes. As Edwards and Potter put it: 'Versions and explanations can be treated therefore as windows upon thought, pictures of cognitive representations or descriptions of the world' (1992: 179).

By looking closely at the conversations we have with people with dementia and what the individuals themselves say, we can come to understand their worlds more closely. A social constructionist approach is believed to present a natural fit for group therapy, its theory and practice (O'Leary 2001).

The argument put forward in this chapter is that historically people have not talked openly about dementia, particularly *with* those who have dementia. This is in line with a recent Mental Health Foundation report that is urging professionals to tell people the truth about their dementia (more information can be found at www.mentalhealth.org.uk). It is the lack of talking with people with dementia that has led to certain (mis)understandings and things being taken for granted about the condition, which have become socially validated: for example, 'there is no point in asking him as he's lost it'. These and other kinds of statements, thankfully less common these days, contribute en masse to society's assumption that these people are mad, while we are okay. These misunderstandings have lots of other taken-for-granteds attached to them; for example, mad people cannot make decisions for themselves, are dangerous, and so on. Furthermore, based on these misunderstandings, treatment work with these individuals has focused on 'what can be done for them'. Therefore, the way in which we talk to each other and what we say have great relevance in constructing how we understand others and ourselves.

This chapter will focus on how memory groups enable open dialoguing of how it feels to live with dementia. It is this dialoguing, taking place between individuals with dementia and the individuals working with them, that is beneficial in changing understandings of the illness and essentially enhances the well-being of those with the illness. Thus the theme throughout this chapter will be the importance of analysing the subject being dialogued or how dementia is talked about, and therefore understood. Specific attention will be drawn to key issues that arose within the memory groups reported. These include: knowledge and power, ownership, belonging and relating. These key issues are some of the strengths of running memory groups with people with dementia.

Memory groups are but one practice of many in which we can encourage people to talk openly about their illness. I will draw on my own experiences of setting up, facilitating and evaluating memory groups to highlight how people with dementia are capable of supporting each other. This is enabled by allowing these individuals to talk to each other in a supportive and trusting environment about what is important to them, about their feelings and about their dementia. In taking the time to talk openly with people with dementia we can truly discover what it is like for them to have the illness. By challenging outdated beliefs and replacing them with more realistic understandings through conversations, the way our society understands and treats people with dementia can be changed. This chapter is not a requisite for conducting good treatment. However, it will be one example of how to gain something worthwhile in working with people who have dementia.

Setting up a memory group

In order to set up a successful memory group there will be a lot of work to carry out before it actually starts. This work is best shared by two people who will then go on to joint-facilitate the sessions. It is important that at least one facilitator is a 'professional'. I feel this is important for many reasons, including the practical assessment of individuals and the difficult task of facilitating and evaluating group sessions. Often a psychologist acts as the professional, but it could easily be any other professional involved in the care of people with dementia who has a high degree of understanding of how the memory works, group dynamics and communication, assessment and evaluation. The second facilitator can be a lay person or caregiver (although not someone who has close emotional ties with a member of the group). The second facilitator can strengthen their own communication skills as well as gaining useful insights into dementia. This dual role often strengthens the relationship between professional and caregiver, which in some settings is very valuable and needed.

Once there are two people eager and capable to start, there needs to be some thought given to the aims of the memory group. In the groups in which I have been involved we had the following primary and secondary aims:

1   *Primary aim*: to create a supportive environment in which members of the memory group could feel comfortable sharing their feelings and experiences relating to their memory problems.
2   *Secondary aim*: to provide members with a basic understanding of how the memory is understood to work. Where possible, help to enable members to adopt the use of memory aids as part of their everyday routines.

Essentially the aims of the memory groups were based around encouraging people to take a more active part in the society to which they have belonged for so long; to allow them to be someone who has value and who has something worthwhile to offer another. However your aims are worded, this central theme is key. The aims are not fixed in stone, and of course you may feel that they may not be wholly appropriate for a group you are considering. Therefore it is important to spend some time thinking about your aims for the group. This is of course partly dependent on the members themselves.

The group members

You do of course need ready access to a reasonably large number of people who have dementia (this is often where the professional comes in). It is helpful to aim for a group with a minimum of four and maximum of eight people. A group that is any larger or smaller with two facilitators can lose its cohesion, balance and effectiveness. A group of six members seemed to work best in my experience. Suitable members for the groups I was involved in were chosen from the attendees of the day service in the first instance. There are of course other ways of accessing your potential group members in a community, hospital or long-stay care setting. Some careful consideration needs to be made about who will benefit most from such a group and how these people will be selected. You also need to consider what alternative therapies those individuals that are not deemed to be suitable for the group will receive. Suitable members were screened and needed to fulfil certain criteria:

1   Members who, following an assessment with the Clifton Assessment Procedure for the Elderly (CAPE) assessment tool (Pattie and Gilleard 1979), achieved a score which categorized them as Grade A (minimal impairment) or Grade B (mild impairment).
2   Members who had memory difficulties that were causing problems in their everyday lives.
3   Members who had some degree of insight into their memory problems.

First, based on initial experiences and from the groups as they developed, it appeared that individuals with the least cognitive impairment were most able to benefit from the group.

This does not rule out people with more severe impairment from being included in memory groups and indeed they need to be considered when drawing up such groups. As Perrin (1997) showed, there is a dearth of occupational provision for those with severe dementia, with most spending the greater part of their day unoccupied. She also highlighted the conditions of minimum well-being experienced by most residents in the study for most of the time. For the interested reader, there are many relevant approaches and therapies for people with more severe dementia. For example, O'Donovan (1996) explores a validation approach from a nursing perspective in working with severely demented clients. Bleathman and Morton (1992) examined validation groups. Gibb et al. (1997) highlighted the benefits of Tai chi and reminiscence with individuals with moderately advanced dementia. However, more thought is needed in conducting group work with this client group. A memory group with this client group would be different to the work outlined in this chapter.

There are other assessment tools that could be used in assessing suitability other than the CAPE. These include: the Mini Mental State Examination (MMSE, Folstein et al. 1975); the Middlesex Elderly Assessment of Mental State (MEAMS, Golding 1989). This chapter will not spend time on the strengths and weaknesses of these assessments. Whichever assessment tool you use, you do need to use one so that you have a very good idea of your potential members' abilities as this tends to limit problems you may have in the sessions. Numerous sources in the psychiatric literature provide guidelines for conducting a mental status examination (Taylor 1981; Othmer and Othmer 1994), but it should always be carried out by a competent practitioner.

Second, members who had memory difficulties that were causing problems in their everyday lives and had insight into these problems were deemed to be people who might benefit most from attending such a group. Often in the lives of people with dementia these two topics are painfully linked; for example, a man who cannot remember the name of the company where his son works and who is aware of how embarrassing this is.

The ages of those who took part in the group ranged from 68 to 83 years old. Both males and females took part in all groups. The age range and gender appeared to have no detrimental effect on the group. There are however individuals who may prefer and benefit from being in a group with those of the same gender or of a similar age, for example, a group for younger people with dementia.

Running a memory group

On a practical level all of the potential members need to be in the same location every week. This sounds obvious but in a day-care setting people may only attend on certain days and a community group would need one location that all could safely reach. You also need to consider people's availability and willingness to take part in such groups every week. It is wise to obtain written agreement from the person with dementia and their carer, if there is one. I have been involved in groups that ran for five weeks, six weeks and nineteen weeks. Some thought needs to be given to the length of the group and how effective this is. A six-week programme may be the most appropriate for this particular group and will be outlined. Longer groups have obvious problems associated with them such as having to stop a member attending due to cognitive decline or having to introduce a new member into an already cohesive group. A shorter programme limits these problems and allows more people to take part in the group over time. People also enjoy and gain from attending more than one series of groups.

What follows is a rough outline of a six-week programme memory group. The emphasis here continues to be the social constructionist approach, in that truths regarding whether memories are accurate or not are not important. What is important is how memory (and dementia) is talked about and its effects on the hearers. The session content follows a set pattern so that the person with dementia is slowly guided and orientated to being in the group each time. The focus is always on talking openly about difficulties with remembering and forgetting. This is promoted in each session in a way that normalizes these experiences and allows discussion of why they happen and how they can be helped.

This six-week programme is one example of a programme structure for a memory group. There is a lot of scope for changing certain topics discussed, but certain variables are best left fixed. For example, it helps if your group can be on the same day, time and location each week so that orientation problems are limited. It also helps if your members and facilitators sit in the same chairs each week (which is easier said than done at times). In the work carried out, each session lasted for approximately one hour, including a very informal time (15 mins) for drinks and conversation at the end. Again this is open to experimentation and some may feel the need to run a group of longer duration. In this six-week example, each week has central aims and a set pattern with games to elicit discussion of topics.

Kim's Game and the Name Game are referred to here: the former is well known and documented; the latter is the name given to the common game used with people with dementia to assist in remembering people's names by talking about a 'favourite'. This is used with different topics every week for variety; for example, favourite pets, holidays, sports, meals, etc. The use of both these games is not for memory training or learning 'facts' but to draw out and expand the experiences of the group members. For example, Kim's Game can be used to open discussion on how things are easier to find if they are kept in the same place.

Week one

The general intentions are to explain the purpose and aims of the group, to promote group cohesion and to encourage group members to feel comfortable to share their experiences:

- Welcome to the memory group.
- Each person to introduce themselves to the group (including facilitators) and to spend a few minutes talking to the group about some of their life experiences which they feel they can say a little about: for example, who they are; where they live and with whom; where they were born; what jobs they have done, etc.
- Describe the purpose of the memory group.
- Clarify the rules of the group: i.e. all discussions are confidential, turn taking, the right to speak and be heard, or to remain quiet.
- The Name Game to be used as an ice-breaking exercise and to prompt discussion relating to common memory difficulties experienced by the group.

Week two

The general aims are to 'normalize' the experience of memory difficulties, to emphasize the different types of memory and how people may have difficulties with some parts of their memory whilst other areas remain intact:

- Welcome to the memory group.
- Members to introduce themselves to the group (names only).
- Brief recap of the aims of the group and the content of the last session.
- Emphasize the importance of sitting in the same seats.
- The Name Game: used to illustrate effects of depth processing (Craik and Lockhart 1972) and suggestions for ways to improve memory for names.
- Kim's Game used to illustrate the different types of memory processes such as encoding, storage and retrieval.
- Introduce the cupboard analogy of memory and the idea of memory aids.

Week three

The general aims are to offer suggestions regarding how to make the best of your memory, to continue to introduce the idea of memory aids and promote their use in everyday life:

- Welcome to the memory group.
- Members to introduce themselves (names only).
- Brief recap of the aims of the group and the content of the last session.
- Emphasize the importance of sitting in the same seats.
- The Name Game and Kim's Game to illustrate making the best of your memory.
- Offer suggestions for the use of memory aids.
- Encourage discussion regarding the use of memory aids, individual experiences and their pros and cons.

Week four

The general aims are to introduce the idea of cued recall and to offer suggestions regarding how to prompt one's memory where there is doubt (e.g. 'What did I come upstairs for?'):

- Welcome to the group.
- Members to introduce themselves to the group (names only).
- Brief recap of the aims of the group and the content of the last session.
- Introduce the idea of cued recall and offer suggestions as to what to do when you are unsure, e.g. whether or not you have done something.
- Discuss factors that affect concentration such as noise, distraction, depression, worry, embarrassment, etc.
- Encourage members to talk of their experiences with their memories.

Week five

The general aims are to enable the group members to feel safe to discuss their feelings relating to their memory difficulties and to encourage peer support:

- Welcome to the memory group.
- Members to introduce themselves to the group (names only).
- Brief recap of the aims of the group and content of the last session.
- Name Game.
- Encourage discussion about feelings and experiences relating to their memory difficulties: for example, the taboo nature of memory difficulties, embarrassment, anxiety, depression and frustration.

Week six

The general aims are to draw the group to a close and allow time to discuss finishing the group and emphasize the benefits of memory aids:

- Welcome to the memory group.
- Members to introduce themselves to the group (names only).
- Brief recap of the aims of the group and the content of the last session.
- Name Game and Kim's Game used to illustrate the effect of deeper processing and that the memory can be helped by using internal and external memory aids.
- Draw the group to a close and allow informal time for discussion.

It is helpful to have a rough agenda of items to discuss such as the six-week programme outlined above, but there will of course be things that the group members will want to talk about and need to be given space and time to do so. In the groups reported here, members would often talk of the embarrassment they felt when they couldn't remember someone's name. This was compounded by the fact that so many people at the day centre knew their names. People in the group often wanted to give advice to one another about how to manage a problem. For example, one man told another how he kept a diary in his top jacket pocket and wrote everything important down in it. (Sometimes the advice was not always this constructive.) People also wanted to talk about their favourite memories and important events in their lives. This is where the boundary between a memory group and a reminiscence group becomes blurred because it is often helpful for the person to tell this story as it gives the group a sense of who this person is and empowers the teller. These conversations do need to be kept in balance by the facilitator. Therefore not only do you need a direction for each session, but also a certain amount of flexibility to ensure that it has some degree of success.

This six-week programme is flexible. When a longer group was conducted that ran for 19 weeks, more time was devoted in each session to specific emotional issues. There is of course a lot of scope for experimentation with variables such as group numbers, group time length, number of weeks, location, and so on. Much more can be gleaned from how effective these groups are for helping people with dementia.

Evaluating a memory group

There are various ways of evaluating such a memory group. It is important that this evaluation takes into consideration the way in which people have talked about and therefore understood their problems. The memory groups have benefits that are tangible to the facilitators who spend time with the people with dementia in the groups that perhaps are not easily reflected in statistical measurement. But these benefits are clearly and powerfully portrayed in quotes from the members of the groups themselves. In the groups that I was involved with, the members were interviewed two weeks before attending the group and two weeks after. There were four questions concerning forgetting and remembering and how much concern this caused them. The following is a selection of real examples of members' comments taken from the pre-group and post-group interviews.

In the pre-group interview one lady said:

'Yes I have a memory problem. I've lost a life, it is a very difficult problem.' In the post-group interview the same lady said: 'Yes, I have a memory problem for recent things. I feel a shade better within myself. It is a manageable problem.'

Two other members said pre-group that they did worry about remembering things and post-group said they did not worry about remembering things; for example, 'No, I write things down and when I've done them I cross them off.'

Another member said: 'It's nice to know other people accept you even though you've got memory problems. I like the company and the jokes.'

Yet another member said the group was 'very satisfying, especially when I can remember people's names'.

The strengths of the memory groups

The powerful quotes above indicate to the reader over and above any strict measurement that the members did enjoy the supportive nature of the group and found it good to talk about their memory. The common thread amongst the members was that they found it reassuring to know that they were not the only ones with memory difficulties. This is interesting as the memory group reported here was conducted in a quiet room at a day centre where all attendees have similar problems with their memory associated with dementia, but none of the members knew this before the group. They did however have this awareness after the group. Returning to social constructionism, it can be argued that the experience of the memory group led to members reconstructing their problems and their situations.

The members benefited from someone else describing their problems and fears, which were often very close to their own. Often as professionals we hear the same problems being described by many patients and many common fears go unsaid. One of the great advantages of the memory group is that it enables people with dementia to come together so that they can hear how others have similar problems and then have some discussion as to how to help these problems.

After the memory group it became clear that members had developed bonds with each other as a result of their time together and that these bonds helped to make their usual time at the day centre more enjoyable and so enhance their well-being. The strengths of the memory groups can be examined in more detail by looking at the key issues arising from the group.

Key issues

The people who attended the groups did enjoy the sessions and subjectively were perceived to benefit from their attendance. There are certain key issues that arose within the groups that are worth expanding upon for the benefit of the reader.

Knowledge and power

Power is, arguably, based on the control of valuable resources, in this case knowledge. Throughout our lives we are aware of the importance of knowledge and of knowing, and that this is closely linked to power. The reverse is also true in that if you do not know (or lack knowledge) then it is likely that you will not be in a position of power. The members of the group were clearly empowered by having the knowledge that they were not alone with their problems ('I am glad I am not the only one'). This clearly has a powerful effect and is one of the benefits of most group therapies. They also felt empowered just by attending the group, since the chosen members would leave the day centre population as a whole and go together into a quiet room for 'their group'. The group then allowed time to talk about how the memory works and how it can help people. This being repeated allowed people to take on some knowledge that essentially empowered them. How the memory works was very much a new topic for all members as it is rarely studied in general education and in professions.

Life in relationship

As individuals we spend our whole lives in relation to others. As Tajfel and Turner (1986) argue: 'a significant part of our individual identity is derived from group membership'. We have the tags of mother, son, friend, work colleague, and many others, to help us define who we are and who the other people are with whom we spend our time. The dementing process can remove these tags and make it less clear who people are and how we relate to them, making the world a far more worrying place. This is particularly the case with unfamiliar or new places like a day centre, hospital ward or nursing home. The interesting development that came out of the memory group conducted at the day centre is that it gave back that sense of relating. Taft *et al.* (1997) argued that relating is an essential component of dementia care and is about building a sense of family or interconnectedness. This was seen with members, who over time knew who else was in in the group with them and that they shared things together as close friends. This extended to time outside the group, with members helping one another with daily tasks and sitting near one another. Previously they would not have known this person or been able to relate to them in any way. As more people from the centre took part in the memory groups, it became much more than a place where 16 people with dementia spent their day.

Ownership and belonging

As people we belong to many different groups throughout our lives. These groups can include family, school, swimming team, work colleagues, and numerous other groups. This belonging to groups gives us a sense of who we are and that we are valuable. The dementia process disrupts this awareness of group membership. The memory group seemed to go some distance to restore that important feeling of 'I belong'. The group developed a tangible cohesiveness. Cartwright (1968) argued that cohesiveness contributes to a group's potency and vitality and increases the significance of members for those who belong to the group. At times members had an almost elitist attitude to other day centre attendees in that they were going off to 'their group', where they were liked and valued by others. This gave the members a real sense of ownership at a time when possibly many other things in their lives were becoming owned by others, or were being done for them. This returns us to the earlier discussion about our taken-for-granteds concerning people with dementia and what they can and cannot do. Being able to tackle their problems themselves, with the help of others, gave people ownership of their problems in a way that made them feel less overwhelming and, in the words of one of the members, 'manageable'.

Thus, if we consider the original aims of the memory groups at the outset, they can be deemed to have been largely met. The group succeeded in creating a supportive environment in which people could discuss their problems. People appeared to understand a little more about how their memory works and to feel part of society again. The group also provided members with time and space to discuss how the memory is understood to work, although it is arguable how much of this information was retained. This leads us on to discussion of the weaknesses of such an approach.

The weaknesses of the memory groups

First, we discuss some of the weaknesses of the work, partly reported here, and then move on to a more general discussion. The last section of the secondary aims was not met. It was hoped that the group would enable members to adopt the use of memory aids as part of their everyday routines. However, it is very hard for group members to carry specific ideas from the group into everyday life. Community support would be needed for specific learning to take place effectively in the relevant situation.

It is possible to point out that an outdated assessment tool was used for screening purposes, that too much weight was attached to this tool and that a more comprehensive screening process should have taken place. This is valid and individuals and organizations are encouraged to invest the time and resources necessary in conducting comprehensive screening. However, this will not eliminate all possible future group difficulties and should not deter groups from being run.

Also there can be criticism of the use of Kim's Game if the following, from Alan Baddeley, is considered relevant: 'It is not uncommon for speech therapists to try to help patients with memory problems by giving them practice at Kim's game. Well meaning though this may be, the chances of it actually helping the patient are slight' (Baddeley 1996: 352). Whilst this may be unfair to speech therapists, it also does not allow for the context in using such a game. Concerns over game playing were not found in the groups concerned and people did benefit from the use of Kim's Game as a way of stimulating discussion about how memory works. If used inappropriately, the games could produce and emphasize failure. The work here is rightly open to criticism and is by no means prescriptive. It is hoped that it could be taken as a guide and a pointer towards what can be achieved.

More generally memory groups can be criticized for being an approach that encourages people to engage in therapy that they are not qualified to conduct. This returns us to the earlier discussion of the importance of one of the facilitators being a professional. Second, the groups could be criticized for being nothing more than a redefined reminiscence group. This is one of the problems in conducting such a group, as individuals will often want to reminisce. The role of the facilitator is to balance this out, among the many other difficult tasks within the group.

The role of the facilitator(s)

The facilitator has a very difficult role to fulfil. Managing the different personalities in such a group and directing the conversation can be very taxing, and indeed some experience of counselling is helpful. The tasks of facilitating are made much easier if the facilitator knows each of the members very well. Thus it is advisable for at least one of the facilitators to work regularly with or spend time with the potential members. Each group presents different problems that the facilitator must learn from. For example, in the groups conducted there were many difficult instances. One week Mrs A said 'I don't have a problem with my memory' and Mrs B said 'Nor do I'. The conversation took a downward turn from how we wanted it to be directed, with the more open members then not wanting to talk about their problems. The following week we encouraged a more open member to start off the discussion and we received different results. Mr C said 'My memory is not too good' and his comment was then backed up by Mrs A and then by Mrs B who agreed with him by saying 'My memory is terrible' and 'Mine too.' Knowing how to press the right buttons at the right time can be difficult, and it is impossible to get it right all the time in such groups. There will be episodes within groups when people may not admit or wish to discuss their problems as a result of something said or some other variable. This is why discussion between facilitators is advisable directly after the group to talk about what happened, why it wasn't helpful and how it can be changed for the next session.

The facilitator also has to manage the 'banter' within the group, which helps to bond individuals but can be very cutting and hurtful at times. In the groups reported here there were often light-hearted times when memory failures were looked back on by members as amusing. However, it is one thing to laugh at oneself and another to laugh at someone else. One member in one of the long-running groups was clearly deteriorating over a number of weeks and started to be 'picked on' by other members who felt they were better than this lady. In this instance the difficult decision was made to stop this lady's attendance and offer her an alternative group. Decisions like these are extremely difficult to take and are one of the challenges of such group work. Shorter groups help to limit these sorts of problems, but it is the responsibility of the facilitator to ensure 'banter' does not become bullying.

The facilitator needs to ensure everyone starts off by sitting in the same seats to aid orientation and recall from past groups and to direct conversation. There is the difficult decision to make about how long to let a member talk about an experience, which may start to become general reminiscence and the theme of a different group, straying away from the original purpose of telling the story. It can be difficult to stop that person without cutting them off. It is important that time is allowed after each session for members who do have a topic or concern not related to the group that they wish to talk about. As was found with the memory groups, many of the members had been given their first real chance to talk to someone who was willingly ready to listen and people can get very talkative once this realization is made. This needs careful management. Groups and group dynamics are complex and the subject of countless studies, Johnson and Johnson's (1997) book is a helpful starting point for the interested reader. As a facilitator you will learn how to effectively manage these dynamics at an exponential rate; in the words of Aristotle: 'For things we have to learn before we can do them, we learn by doing them.'

For the facilitator it can also be a very rewarding and enjoyable time. The group gives a focus to the conversations and often elicits thoughts and memories that may never have been aired before. So in that way you have a real sense of making a difference to the lives of the people with this illness. Facilitating such a group also helps a person to continue to understand and remind themselves of the difficulties people with dementia face every minute of the day. Often it is easy to attribute a higher functioning level to a person who is socially very presentable and displays good social etiquette. But this person may be able to remember very little and actually be very worried about where they are. The memory group allows the explicit stating of people's day-to-day problems, which are sometimes masked by good social etiquette, good presentation and other automatic techniques, in order to help people's true difficulties.

By the very nature of this kind of group work, it can be very demanding emotionally on the facilitator. It is important that the facilitators have time together after each group for many reasons: first to note how successful and effective that session has been, and also to learn from one another about their skills and to support one another. It is advisable to have regular supervision with a more experienced colleague when facilitating such groups as often you are having the discussions with people with dementia that most people are afraid to have and avoid. Taking this step and talking about these problems is where I feel the difference is made, but this step is not always taken easily.

Conclusions

The memory groups, partly reported here, have very much been trials to discover what is helpful and effective in running them. Many patient-focused support groups are now in existence and this work hopes to contribute to the variety of such groups. There are many considerations involved in setting up and running such groups and there are many pitfalls to try and avoid. In sharing the experiences here and the pitfalls already found, it is hoped that these groups will become more defined and recognized as valuable ways of working as more groups are replicated. This therapeutic tool needs developing and refining. There is large scope for running the groups in a variety of settings, which would foster multi-agency working and bring professionals closer. These could include both private and public day centres, hospital wards, a community setting, e.g. in a GP surgery and in a variety of long-stay care settings. There is also scope for all-male or all-female groups, as well as groups targeted at specific age cohorts. The session content has enormous scope, with time being available to focus on specific concerns or on specific helpful memory aids, and so on. Groups could be run with individuals with more severe impairment. There are many possibilities for how the work outlined here may be taken forward.

Ultimately this chapter has aimed to encourage people to engage in talking about the important issues in the lives of people with dementia, with people who have dementia (and others). The work in this chapter reflects how this can be done in a group setting. As professionals we must have the courage to extend beyond our fears and reach out to those with dementia, support them and allow them to support each other. In doing so, other people will unconsciously be given permission to do the same. As individuals it is our responsibility to challenge outdated assumptions that are commonly held in society and to replace these assumptions with explanations and talk of what it may be like to have such an illness. The goal of this chapter is to get people talking/dialoguing dementia so that a more helpful understanding of the illness emerges and is recognized. Big shifts in understanding stem from each and every conversation about a particular subject.

Acknowledgements

The memory groups that are discussed in this chapter were carried out whilst the author was employed by the Rugby Psychology Department in Warwickshire for Rugby NHS Trust. The author would like to extend his thanks to Jane Muers, clinical psychologist, for her support and to Rugby MIND, Services for Elderly People, where the groups met.

References

Baddeley, A. (1996) *Your Memory – A User's Guide*, London: Prion.
Bender, M.P. (1996) 'Memory clinics: locked doors on the gravy train?', *PSIGE Newsletter* 58: 63. (PSIGE is a Special Interest Group of the Division of Clinical Psychology of the British Psychological Society.)
Bleathman, C. and Morton, I. (1992) 'Validation therapy: extracts from 20 groups with dementia sufferers', *Journal of Advanced Nursing* 17, 6: 658–66.
Burr, V. (1995) *An Introduction to Social Constructionism*, London: Routledge.
Cartwright, D. (1968) 'The premise for groupwork', in D. Cartwright and A. Zander, *Group Dynamics: Research and Theory*, 3rd edn, London: Tavistock.
Craik, F.I.M. and Lockhart, R.S. (1972) 'Levels of processing: a framework for memory research', *Journal of Verbal Learning and Verbal Behaviour* 11: 671–84.
Edwards, D. and Potter, J. (1992) *Discussive Psychology*, London: Sage.

Folstein, M.F., Folstein, S.E. and McHugh, P.R. (1975) 'Mini-mental state', *Journal of Psychiatric Research* 12: 189–98.

Gibb, H., Morris, C.T. and Gleisberg, J. (1997) 'A therapeutic programme for people with dementia', *International Journal of Nursing Practice* 3, 3: 191–9.

Golding, E. (1989) *Middlesex Elderly Assessment of Mental State*, Thames Valley Test Company.

Goldsilver, P.M. and Gruneir, M.R. (2001) 'Early stage dementia group: an innovative model of support for individuals in the early stages of dementia', *American Journal of Alzheimer's Disease and Other Dementias* 16, 2: 109–14.

Johnson, D.W. and Johnson, F.P. (1997) *Joining together Group Theory and Group Skills*, 6th edn, New York: Allyn and Bacon.

Kasl-Godley, J. and Gatz, M. (2000) 'Psychosocial interventions for individuals with dementia: an integration of theory, therapy and a clinical understanding of dementia', *Clinical Psychology Review* 20, 6: 755–82.

Logiudice, D., Waltrowicz, N., Brown, K., Burrows, C., Ames, D. and Flicker, L. (1999) 'Do memory clinics improve the quality of life of carers? A randomised pilot trial', *International Journal of Geriatric Psychiatry* 14, 8: 626–32.

Luce, A., McKeith, I., Swann, A., Daniel, S. and O'Brien, J. (2001) 'How do memory clinics compare with traditional old age psychiatry services?', *International Journal of Geriatric Psychiatry* 16, 9: 837–45.

O'Donovan, S. (1996) 'A validation approach to severely demented clients', *Nursing Standard* 11, 13/14: 48–52.

O'Leary, J.V. (2001) 'The postmodern turn in group therapy', *International Journal of Group Psychotherapy* 51, 4: 473–87.

Othmer, E. and Othmer, S.C. (1994) *The Clinical Interview Using DSM-IV, Vol. 1 Fundamentals*, Washington, DC: American Psychiatric Press.

Pattie, A.H. and Gilleard, C.J. (1979) *The Clifton Assessment Procedures for the Elderly (CAPE)*, Sevenoaks: Hodder and Stoughton.

Perrin, T. (1997) 'Occupational need in severe dementia: a descriptive study', *Journal of Advanced Nursing* 25: 934–41.

Petry, H. (1999) [Support groups for patients in the early stages of dementia – usefulness and experiences], article in German. *Therapeutische Umschau. Revue therapeutique* 56, 2: 109–13.

Snyder, L., Quayhagen, M.P., Shepherd, S. and Bower, D. (1995) 'Supportive seminar groups: an intervention for early stage dementia patients', *The Gerontologist* 35, 5: 691–5.

Taft, L.B., Fazio, S., Seman, D. and Stansell, J. (1997) 'A psychosocial model of dementia care: theoretical and empirical support', *Archives of Psychiatric Nursing* 11, 1: 13–20.

Tajfel, H. and Turner, J.C. (1986) 'The social identity theory of intergroup behaviour', in W.G. Austin and S. Worchel (eds) *The Psychology of Intergroup Relations*, Chicago: USA.

Taylor, M.A. (1981) *The Neuropsychiatric Mental Status Examination*, Jamaica, NY: Spectrum.

White, M.H. and Dorman, S.M. (2000) 'On line support for caregivers. Analysis of an internet Alzheimer's mailgroup', *Computers in Nursing* 18, 4: 168–76.

Chapter 8

Music therapy for persons with dementia

Mariëtte Broersen and
Niek van Nieuwenhuijzen

Introduction

This chapter aims to give an impression of the value of music therapy for persons with dementia. It describes the character of the therapeutic process and the therapeutic relationship, and it shows tools and methods used by music therapists, illustrated by case descriptions. It also indicates which role the music therapist should take in between the other disciplines in the field. Further, it describes theories, results of research and perspectives for the future.

Music therapy is a form of psychotherapy that is used in the treatment of different kinds of clients. The main fields in which music therapists work are psychiatry, care for mentally challenged, (physical) rehabilitation, juvenile care, elderly care and old age psychiatry settings. Music therapy differs from verbal psychotherapy for its specific use of qualities of music. Music therapy is suited to emotional and interactional problems, and is used actively (the client plays music, mostly together with the therapist), receptively (the client listens to music), or combined.

In the last decade, the number of music therapists working with persons with dementia has increased remarkably. Research brought music therapy to the attention of doctors, psychologists and other workers in this area.

It is important to mention that the chapter is written from the Dutch point of view on music therapy and dementia. Music therapists there work mainly eclectically. Overall it is similar to the West-European way of treating clients. We will not go in detail about how different musical therapeutic approaches fit with different kinds of dementia.

Music therapy and dementia

Music therapy and quality of life of persons with dementia

Smeijsters (2000) discerns five approaches in music therapy: orthopsychiatric (stimulating the development), supportive, palliative (supporting how to deal with and learning how to cope with problems), re-educative, and reconstructive (working through problems).

Each of these approaches we can find in music therapy for persons with dementia. Some examples of goals in this field are: increase the concentration span (orthopsychiatric), decrease of wandering behaviour (orthopsychiatric), decrease fear of failure or learn how to cope with it (supportive), finding a new emotional balance after experience of loss (supportive), softening psychic pain (palliative), decrease depressed feelings (re-educative or reconstructive), increase social interaction (supportive, re-educative or reconstructive), decrease anger (supportive, re-educative or reconstructive). The approach to the goals differs, depending on the depth in which the underlying problems are addressed.

Besides an organic cerebral illness (DSM-IV), dementia can be seen as a 'chronic psycho-trauma' (Miesen 1999): the person with dementia is continuously confronted with loss, powerlessness and disruption of daily life. The whole situation can be seen as a slow process of dying, as Dehm (1997) states. According to Miesen, there is evidence that persons with dementia are much more and much longer conscious of their situation than was previously supposed. Several kinds of behaviour in dementia can be seen as normal reactions to, for example, being lost or being lonely. Coping strategies include searching for support, denial and withdrawal. The 'awareness' of the person with dementia has implications for how to approach, and how to involve him/her in the process of dementia. It is important for everyone in his environment to see the person with dementia as someone struggling with their trauma, contact them as a serious partner and to avoid taking away their identity. This awareness also implies that the person with dementia, although limited by declining cognitive skills, offers diverse points of contact in therapy (see e.g. Miesen 1999).

A music therapist is, in the broadest sense, someone who can help the person with dementia in the chronic trauma he is going through. The music therapist can play an important role in coping with it, for example, by helping the person to grieve, manage fear and loneliness, or to find new ways of making contact. The overall goal of the music therapist can best be described as to increase the quality of the demented person's life.

Aldridge (2000), referring among others to Bonder (1994), mentions that until the mid-1980s psychotherapy and counselling techniques had rarely been used with persons with dementia. He notes a trend towards a 'person-centered' and 'non-pharmacological' approach and a growing interest in the use of music therapy and counselling techniques.

In the literature as well as in daily practice nevertheless the question returns as to whether one can speak of psychotherapy for persons with dementia. This question derives from the underlying questions: 'Can a person with dementia actually change?' 'Can a person with dementia reach some kind of insight into his problems?' It is such a crucial question that we will elaborate on it in the next sections.

Before elaborating, it is necessary to give a more detailed description of what happens during music therapy. The therapist aims to set a process of change in motion. The specific qualities of music, used systematically, are the tools of the music therapist. The experiences of the client through the music and the relations created through these experiences, are the dynamic forces behind the process of change (Bruscia, in Smeijsters 2000).

Can a person with dementia actually change?

When we reflect upon the daily practice of music therapy for persons with dementia, we can find all the elements of the process described above. Daily practice of music therapy indeed shows that many clients with dementia can go through a process of change, although it takes more time, more repetition, shorter and more frequent sessions than in other fields of work. Hausman (1992) describes these modifications in frequency and duration of sessions. Further, the possibility of change depends upon the degree to which the disease has progressed and the point in the progression of the disease at which the person with dementia and the therapist begin the therapy (Hausman 1992). The last major aspect for possibilities of change is the factor of the pre-morbid degree of psychological sophistication of the person with dementia. This last point does not seem to count for music therapy, which turns out to be a very easy, accessible form of therapy for most persons with dementia. (This will be described in more detail later in this chapter.)

Another characteristic of the work with patients with a degenerative illness is that their situation frequently changes because of new factors, such as a stroke or rapid deterioration. This demands a largely adaptive quality of the therapist during their work. For example, in a week's time the therapist may have to change from working through a problem to softening psychic pain. Again, the advantage of music therapy is that it can be very accessible to people at different stages of dementia. In the case of stroke or rapid deterioration, the musical experience is mostly preserved. A change in the situation of the person does not have to end the therapy. This indicates that music therapy can be helpful in giving a person with dementia as much quality of life as possible through all the stages of dementia. It means, however, that the music therapist has to observe the client very closely before deciding on a certain approach. It makes no sense to start working through a problem (re-educative or reconstructive) with a person with dementia who very rapidly passes through the stages of dementia.

Can a person with dementia reach some kind of insight?

Dehm (1997) and Smeijsters (2000) help in answering this question. Dehm points to the importance of looking at transference and countertransference and the changes in these, to recognize what process of change is going on.

Smeijsters (2000) points to the possibility of passing through the process only within the music; Aldridge (2000) also points in this direction.

The specific characteristics of music therapy (i.e. how client and therapist use structure in music, and expression through music in the here-and-now situation) offer the advantage that the therapeutic process is made audible and visible in music. The experiences of the client through the music and the relations (between therapist and client and clients among themselves) created through these experiences, are the dynamic forces behind the process of change. One doesn't have to verbalize the feelings and relations these dynamic forces bring about – although the therapist certainly does use verbalization if possible – but one can express oneself musically, actively, or more passively by choosing certain music to be played.

Another nonverbal aspect of the question 'Do persons with dementia attain some insight in their problems?' follows. The insight often leans more strongly on what could be called 'emotional knowledge' rather than 'rational knowledge'. Of course, this situation exists in all fields of work, but here it has a more prominent place because of the cognitive deterioration. Insight in the classical sense of the word doesn't often exist in this field of work. The therapist has to find out, within the therapeutic relationship, the degree and character of the insight of the client (see Pavlicevic 1997). Consequently, the therapist in this field, more than in others, has to use and sharpen his intuition.

Moreover, the therapist must look closely at the problems and life history of the person with dementia. Often, he has to contact relatives of the person to gain a better understanding of his client. Members of the multidisciplinary team often give each other important additional information about the life history of a client.

Hausman (1992) mentions two more things regarding the question of the insight. Transference often develops very rapidly in clients with dementia, and they can be reached affectively long after they cease to be reached cognitively. The affective responses in the limbic system seem to be the last to vanish (Hausman 1992, taken from Verwoerdt 1981). Slaets underlines this observation by adding that music can influence the limbic system even before the musical signal has reached the cortex (Slaets, in Adriaansz *et al.* 1994).

Specific qualities of music

Music has a number of very different aspects which the music therapist can use whenever necessary. Music has a physical aspect: it has a direct influence on, for example, heartbeat, skin, and other vegetative functions in the body (Harrer 1982 and Frank 1982, in Smeijsters 1996). It also has a primitive aspect: phylogenetically music is often seen as the fundament out of which language has developed. The fact that music directly touches the affects in the limbic system also points in this direction. Furthermore, music has a ritual aspect: for instance, it is used in a lot of rituals in life in all cultures. Apparently, this is a deep necessity of human beings.

Pavlicevic (1997), as one of many, describes the inherent musicality of our communicative acts as well as the communicative emotion in music therapy improvisation of therapist and client. There is a significant amount of literature about the emotional influence of music. There are also a number of theories on this topic. For the sake of clarity we only mention three kinds of emotional responses to music that are important in working with clients with dementia:

1   Emotion aroused by music,
2   Emotional character attributed to music,
3   Emotional appreciation of music (Jansma and De Vries 1995).

The philosopher Langer (1978) describes the resemblance between aspects of inner life – physical and mental – and aspects of music, for example, patterns of movement and standing still or tension and relaxation. According to Langer, because of this resemblance music is most appropriate in communicating emotions.

The music therapist regards these specific characteristics of music as his tools. These characteristics define why music therapy is indicated for a certain problem, instead of another sort of therapy. A music therapist must always be able to link a certain problem to a certain specific quality of music. For example, the problem fear of failure can be connected with the characteristic of music that it is volatile. The fact that there is no tangible result can be very important in working on problems of fear of failure. We will present a limited number of characteristics of music, connected to a limited number of problems (taken from Smeijsters 1995, 2000; Van Nieuwenhuijzen and Broersen 1998; Jansma and De Vries 1995; Clair 1996a).

Box 8.1   Characteristics of music

• A musical form is easily connected with something outside the music. This way, music can be a symbol for an endless number of things, events and relations outside music (Smeijsters 1995, 2000; Van Nieuwenhuijzen and Broersen 1998). This offers opportunities to work symbolically through emotional problems with people who (still) have trouble recognizing or verbalizing certain events or relations.

• Music evokes an association with an event, thing or relation (Smeijsters 1995, 2000; Van Nieuwenhuijzen and Broersen 1998). This happens very easily in music. It offers the same opportunities as described in the previous characteristic.

- Musical parameters reflect different states of mind (Smeijsters 1995, 2000), for example, a slow tempo and low dynamics often express sadness. During music therapy clients are offered a way to express themselves and give an impression of their feelings. It is assumed that changes in musical forms can be transferred to bring about changes in someone's emotional life. This analogy can be applied on behavioural problems as well.
- Music is not the reality of daily life. Negative emotions of a certain event, problem or relation can be recalled with greater distance and might therefore be more appreciated than in reality (Jansma and De Vries 1995; Smeijsters 1995). It can come to the client in an easier manner, which can be necessary for people who need this kind of safety to work on a problem.
- Music is intertwined to movement. It activates the body as well as the mind. Therefore it can set in motion the mind or emotions of someone who has got stuck in certain problems.
- Music moves in time (Smeijsters 1995, 2000). This has different implications. Because of this characteristic, for example, music has a kind of predictability (Smeijsters 1995, 2000), which offers safety and support. It appeals to ordination and collecting one's thoughts (Smeijsters 1995, 2000). This offers possibilities to work with people who are restless and chaotic in their minds. Further, it implies that music can be stopped when necessary (Jansma and De Vries 1995). This possibility gives a feeling of control and safety. This opens prospects to work with persons having problems such as anxiety and panic. Another implication of the characteristic of music moving in time (especially when combined with factors such as tonality) is that a feeling of rounding off and completion can be reached easily (Clair 1996a). This can be important in working on problems related to parting and mourning.
- Music can be varied from being very structured to being chaotic. This offers an environment to work with problems in the areas of structure and control. It also creates opportunities to give someone a feeling of a firm grip upon a situation, for example, in problems of fear of failure.
- Music touches very basic feelings of inter and intrapersonal relations (Van Nieuwenhuijzen and Broersen 1998). In a music therapy situation, interaction matters can be addressed that otherwise would be very difficult to raise; for example, matters in connection with the preverbal stage.
- Music often takes place at a half-conscious level (Van Nieuwenhuijzen and Broersen 1998). This offers opportunities in working with people having trouble recognizing problems.
- Making music simultaneously is functional, contrary to simultaneous speech (Van Nieuwenhuijzen and Broersen 1998). This can, for example, be important in working with people who find a verbal conversation too confronting or start talking to cover their problems.
- Music is flexible. The music therapist can always adapt the skill level through slowing down the tempo, making the ambits smaller, lowering the amount of instruments, and so on. This can make music therapy an easily accessible form of therapy. An experience of success is easily reached. For people with fear of failure or very quickly changing capabilities, this is very important.

Dementia and music

From the description above, we note that many of the characteristics of music can be helpful in the treatment of persons with dementia. Besides we draw your attention to the following studies. As concluded in different studies (i.e. Aldridge and Aldridge 1992; Swartz *et al.* 1989), on the process of dementia, the musical part of the brain is preserved much longer than the verbal part. This means, for example, that someone can play the piano as he did all his life until a late stage of dementia. Also, a person with dementia may be able to sing although not able to speak well anymore. The experience of being able to sing can be important in the therapeutic process; for example, because someone discovers they are able to do something instead of being unable to do anything. An advantage of music therapy for people whose verbal capacities are fading is that music therapy mostly doesn't require much instruction. As mentioned earlier, next to the preservation of musical skills, the affective responses in the limbic system seem to be active the longest. The combination of these two areas implicates that music therapy can have a strong effect on the self-awareness and ability to communicate of the person with dementia.

Another feature of the music/dementia relationship is that speech assumes more and more musical characteristics, like rhythm and melody. For example, we can find repetition of words, non-words or parts of words, connected melodically (Broersen *et al.* 1995). Music therapy fits very well with this kind of speech (Feil: stage 3 speech or 'word salad'). Still functioning at the end of the process of deterioration is the so-called 'analogue language' (Watzlawick *et al.* 1967). This body language forms the core in the communication through improvisational music in music therapy.

Methods

Introduction

The importance of a good diagnosis by the music therapist while observing interactions, as well as life history information about the client with dementia, is mentioned above. There are a number of issues that need continuous monitoring preceding the therapy, during the period of the observation and during the actual treatment period. We present the most important ones below.

The stage of dementia of the client

After determining, to the extent possible, the degree and speed of the progression of different aspects of the dementia, the therapist examines the implications of undertaking music therapy. From the literature, a few general remarks can be made about music in connection with different stages of dementia:

- Mostly somewhere late in the second behavioural stage of dementia (see Chapter 13) singing in the usual sense of the word stops (Clair 1996a). This doesn't mean that singing isn't important anymore. The therapist who sings for the person with dementia or singing together can still be of great value. In the latter, the person with dementia can use his voice by humming or using vocalizations.
- In progressing dementia, the range of musical memories of the person with dementia becomes smaller and moves towards the beginning of his life (Aldridge and Aldridge 1992; Clair 1996a). This is important to enable the therapist to choose appropriate musical assignments or to understand why the person with dementia is or is not reacting.
- In the beginning stages of dementia it can sometimes be important to use instruments that the client has played (although it is definitely not necessary for a successful treatment with music therapy to have ever laid a hand on an instrument). It can give one a feeling of grip and being proud of oneself. As the dementia progresses it is advised to omit these instruments because they can cause a lot of frustration (Clair 1996a). It is better to choose an instrument that has some of the characteristics of the original one, for example, a xylophone when the original instrument was a piano.
- The more the process of dementia progresses, the more important vibro-tactile sensations (the sensation of vibration through holding an instrument in the hands, the lap or another part of the body) become (Clair and Bernstein 1990).

The therapist examines the stage of dementia not only through reading files, speaking with other disciplines and observing the person with dementia, but also by analysing the client's responses to the music. The music therapist can contribute to the diagnosis of the person with dementia by observing musical reactions. Certain aspects can be assessed that otherwise are more difficult or not at all possible to be analysed.

Aldridge and Aldridge (1992), among others, point out that music improvisation can determine a number of things: motor coordination, persistence in a certain task, anticipation of changes, small disturbances in language, episodic memory and the capacity of interpersonal communication. Raijmaekers (1993), using a 'music observation program', mentions the possibilities to specify diagnoses for the aspects of understanding instruction, memory, capability to choose, explore, combine, musical language, musical contact and interaction, reaction to both simple and more complex situations, social functioning, assessment of music making, multiple choice and free associating. She emphasizes the importance of comparing the data with those of other members of the multidisciplinary team.

Problems for which the person with dementia is referred to music therapy

What is the character of the problem? Is it an actual problem of the present or is it a problem of the past that is exposed because the dementia lowered a client's capacities of coping? Is it a problem experienced by the person with dementia himself or witnessed by the people surrounding him? In this situation too the musical observation can contribute to the diagnosis. In the musical situation the problem can be explored. The music therapist can assess the aspects mentioned by Aldridge and Aldridge (1992) and Raijmaekers (1993). In addition, he can focus on emotional aspects. An example with respect to people with a depression might clarify this. Often these clients show a strong resistance to actively playing music. In that case the therapist has to choose a receptive method. The observation of someone not being able to play could contribute to the multidisciplinary discussion on the topic of whether a client is depressed or not.

The music–language relationship in the present and past

When we combine the things mentioned above in 'dementia and music', we can conclude that during the process of dementia music comes more and more into prominence, while linguistic skills are slowly declining. It is important for the therapist to be aware of the deterioration process in the continuum language–music of the client. To find out more about the relationship between music–language of the person with dementia in the past, the therapist seeks answers to the following questions: Was the person verbally orientated? Was verbalization of feelings or problems important/usual for him? Was his relationship with music spontaneous, professional, sophisticated, religious, helpful while working, and so on? Were there special positive or negative musical events in his past? It is important to notice that for music therapy it is not necessary that someone is musically educated.

Character of the person

One can ask a number of questions on this issue, in regard to events during music therapy. It helps the therapist to decide how to work or how to relate to the client. How can the emotional and interactional capacity of the person with dementia in the present and past be described? How did the client cope with problems of loss during his life? Were there important losses in his life? Was he dominant or compliant? Did he like to be alone or with others, etcetera?

The issue of indication

Can the therapist see a possible link between the client's problem and the musical characteristics? Does he encounter a counter-indication? Of course,

---

Box 8.2   Indications for music therapy

- Continuous gloominess or depression
- Not being able to express any feelings
- Having strong emotions (like sadness, fear, shame) and difficulties coping with them
- Strong and frequent changes in emotions
- Fear of failure, low self-esteem, insecurity
- Making no contact with other people
- Having problems connecting with other people
- Restlessness, agitation, compulsiveness, aggression and other problems of this kind
- Problems that can be brought back to preverbal stages of life

---

Box 8.3   Counter-indications to music therapy

- Hearing music is physically painful or irritating, hyperacuity
- Dissociation through music
- Deafness
- Acoustic hallucinations
- Musicogenic epilepsy
- Medication that badly influences experiencing music

---

these questions have to be assessed in the actual music therapy situation. This is one of the specific tasks to be performed in observation. One can never be sure of an indication or counter-indication beforehand. In general, in this field of music therapy, the indications for music therapy shown in Boxes 8.2 and 8.3 are used (taken from Van Nieuwenhuijzen and Broersen 1998).

The indication must be determined in response to the following questions (Van Nieuwenhuijzen and Broersen 1998):

- Can the person with dementia connect with his feelings, needs and problems through music?
- Does the musical expression, the 'musical language', of the client offer a possibility to communicate with the therapist or other music therapy participants?
- Is it plausible that music therapy will contribute in helping to solve, decrease, manage the problem? During the treatment period, the therapist assesses whether the original indication is still appropriate.

Individual or group

The therapist has to decide whether to place the client in an individual or group therapy. In this field of music therapy, groups are mostly small, for example, two to five people. A group therapy adds therapeutic aspects. Yalom (1975) mentions arousal of hope by seeing each other's progression; creating a feeling of universality through recognizing one's problem in another person; giving each other information; discovering being able to mean something for someone else; reliving the original family situation; development of social skills and finally, imitating behaviour.

In music therapy it is possible for people of very different cognitive levels and backgrounds to form a group. In improvisation, it is not difficult to combine these differences. This can result in a feeling of solidarity. The therapist can direct the improvisation by supporting one or more people, often without being noticed. Different needs, problems and capacities can be addressed in the same improvisation (Van Nieuwenhuijzen and Broersen 1998).

The indication for group therapy depends on the desirability of the group aspects with regard to the client's problem, his behaviour and his character. Often, working individually offers more safety and support. This can be necessary in order to be able to interact with the client at all. The behaviour of the person with dementia can be too disturbing for the other members of the group, therefore requiring individual therapy.

Goals

After the phase of observation and assessment, the therapist sets his goal(s) and subgoal(s) before starting the actual treatment. During the treatment period and the progression of the dementia, the therapist adapts the goals. The designation 'goal' and 'subgoal' is always relative and the goals are always intertwined. For example, 'using preserved skills' can be a subgoal of 'decreasing feelings of fear', which can be a subgoal of 'improving social interaction'. The goals and subgoals that appear most often in this field of music therapy are shown in Box 8.4.

Box 8.4 Possible goals of music therapy

- Increase acceptance
- Solve, decrease, manage depressed feelings
- Solve, decrease, manage fear, sadness, anger, etc.
- Achieve comfort, soften psychical pain
- Increase self-esteem and initiative, strengthen identity
- Increase social interaction, break through isolation
- Solve, decrease, manage a behavioural problem
- Increase or maintain capabilities of memory, orientation, language

---

Observation

In addition to what has already been said about observation, we stipulate some more aspects. During observation, the therapist guides the clients with dementia through different musical pathways: playing, singing and listening. Of course different music therapists use different standard programmes, adapted to the needs and capabilities of the clients. During observation, the therapist can use any music therapy method he will use during the actual treatment process. A number of these are described below.

Methods

The following methods can be combined, and in reality are not so easily separated from each other. The methods will be elucidated in the case descriptions below.

Improvising

Improvisation can create different experiences and relationships between therapist and group members. One can improvise together on one instrument, or each on a different one. It can be done vocally, mixed vocal and instrumental, individual, everyone together, or the therapist playing a solo. The person with dementia can contribute, even when he is only able to make the most basic sounds, such as tapping a drum with hand(s) or sticks, or humming one or two notes. The therapist can use different musical techniques to stimulate the client(s). Bruscia (1987) mentions 64 improvisational techniques, divided into 9 categories. Many of them are used in music therapy with persons with dementia (Box 8.5).

Bruscia stipulates that every technique has myriad applications when used alone, and even more when used in conjunction with others. In regard to persons with dementia it is important to notice that the more verbal techniques are used in earlier stages of dementia and often in more implicit ways.

Box 8.5   Examples of improvisational techniques

1 *Techniques of empathy* (four of six):
   - *imitating*: therapist plays the same thing as the client, after the client
   - *synchronizing*: therapist plays the same thing together with the client
   - *incorporating*: therapist uses a motive of the client
   - *reflecting*: therapist plays the mood the client is in.
2 *Structuring techniques* (two of three):
   - *rhythmic grounding*: keeping a rhythmic foundation for the client's improvising

- *shaping*: helping the client define the length of a phrase and give it an expressive shape.
3 *Techniques of intimacy* (three of four):
    - *sharing instruments*: using the same instrument as the client, or playing it cooperatively
    - *giving*: presenting the client a musical gift
    - *bonding*: developing a short piece or song, based on the client's responses, using it as a theme for the relationship.
4 *Elicitation techniques* (three of five):
    - *making spaces*: therapist leaves spaces within his improvisation for the client to interject
    - *interjecting*: waiting for a space in the client's music to fill in the gap
    - *completing*: answering or completing the client's musical question or antecedent phrase.
5 *Redirection techniques* (two of eight)
    - *intensifying or calming*: increasing or reducing the dynamics, tempo, rhythmic tension, and/or melodic tension
    - *intervening*: interrupting, destabilizing or redirecting fixations, perseverations or stereotypes of the client.
6 *Procedural techniques* (two of ten)
    - *receding*: taking a less active or controlling role, and allowing the client to direct the experience
    - *reporting*: after an improvisation having the client report on his experience while improvising.
7 *Referential techniques* (three of seven)
    - *symbolizing*: having the client use something musical to stand for or represent an event or person
    - *projecting*: having the client improvise music that depicts a real situation, feeling, event, etc.
    - *storytelling*: improvising music and stimulating the client to make up a story.
8 *Emotional exploration techniques* (seven of ten)
    - *holding*: therapist is supporting while the client is exploring
    - *doubling*: therapist expresses feelings the client finds difficult to cope with
    - *contrasting*: therapist makes the client play the contrary
    - *integrating*: finding a balance between contrasting elements
    - *sequencing*: helping the client to find the right order
    - *splitting*: improvising two conflicting aspects of the life of the client
    - *role taking*: therapist and client change roles while improvising.
9 *Discussion techniques* (four of ten)
    - *connecting*: therapist asks the client how musical experiences relate to other experiences
    - *clarifying*: therapist asks the client to clarify or verify information that has already been offered
    - *summarizing*: verbally recapitulating events in therapy
    - *interpreting*: offering possible explanations for the client's experiences.

More recognizable forms of making music together

Since for most people improvising is a new way of interacting, it can sometimes make them anxious or insecure. Therefore, it can be important to create a more recognizable situation, for example, through singing a song (with or without words) together and accompanying it. The therapist can choose which role (leading or accompaniment) the client will take and whether they change roles or not. In this musical assignment some of the techniques described by Bruscia are more difficult to achieve.

Using symbols

Different musical elements might become a symbol, such as a melodic tune, a song, a rhythmic motive, a musical turning point, an instrument, a certain piece of music, the relation between therapist and the person(s) with dementia. The session as a whole can even be experienced as a symbol for the whole of life, for example: meeting, making contact, conflicting, humour and, in the end, leaving. A song, or pieces of music of welcome and farewell are often important in this respect. Once the therapist has discovered the symbolic meaning of a musical element for a particular client, he will use it systematically.

Using music as an intermediary or transitional object

These concepts in music therapy originate from Benenzon (1983, in Smeijsters 1995) and Winnicott (1971, in Smeijsters 2000). The 'intermediary object' of Benenzon is a mediating object between therapist and client. It is very safe and fits in with the prenatal experience of the relation between mother and child. The therapist chooses safe and warm sounds, like the sounds of the uterus. From this point of regression to this early stage of life, in which therapist and client make contact, introducing new sounds and musical forms expands communication. In the end, the client actively makes contact. The therapist reacts at this contact by imitating the client.

The 'transitional object' of Winnicott is a space in which objectivity and subjectivity or fantasy and reality are intertwined: the child goes through a phase of transition, in which it learns to tune to each of these two worlds. A transitional object, such as a piece of cloth, helps the child. The object is filled with a subjective meaning. It gives comfort and safety when, for instance, the mother is not there. In music therapy, music can be used as a transitional object. It means that the therapist and the person with dementia find a way in music that can give the latter the comfort and protection that otherwise would be given by a person who had an important role in the life of the person with dementia.

Forming Gestalts

A Gestalt refers to an experience of 'wholeness' and balance. According to F. Perls, the goal in therapy is to form a good Gestalt (Smeijsters 1995), in the sense of closing a non-closed situation. Certainly for persons with dementia, the concept of Gestalt is important. It helps them to bring sense to their problems of parting life, acceptance and their often 'crumbling' perception and memory.

Creating a continuously sounding tone or a repeated chord underneath a musical form or body movement of the person with dementia can, for example, shape a Gestalt and give the client an experience of closing. Other examples of Gestalt are: assigning the client to play different aspects of himself or the therapist playing these for him; a group playing music subsequently after one another, creating one rhythm, form a Gestalt as well. Another assignment that can be used in music therapy with clients with dementia is 'give and take': one person chooses a song for another one; after that the other chooses, for example, a song for the first person, making the circle round. The therapist can help in choosing, for example, by giving two alternatives. Next to the experience of a Gestalt, it can be very important to experience the ability to be significant for another person and being worth receiving attention from another person. The latter actually belongs to the next method.

Bring into prominence things that the person with dementia is still capable of

This is an important aspect in finding a new balance in a situation of losing capacities, which might cause fear of failure and strong emotions. Besides the example mentioned above, illustrations of this method include the use of functions that are still more or less intact, such as other types of memory, motor capacities, singing a song by someone who can hardly speak; making use of imprinting something in short-term or long-term memory. Repeating, in every session, a song composed by the therapist, can help increase the latter. After some time, the client has learned the song and associates it with the therapy, although most of the time he only knows it in the context of the music therapy situation. This can give a great experience of accomplishment next to one of belonging to each other and being able to make new contacts.

Evoke 'sets of values'

Music has the power to evoke specific sets of values (Smeijsters *et al.* 1995). A set of values can be described as 'anything', either positive or negative, that is of importance in a person's life; for example, a book, an experience, a dream, or a relationship. A set of values is a cognitive construct that is heavily burdened with emotions. There is an endless number of sets of values. The importance of these sets of values changes along with changes in the emotional meaning they have for a person.

The therapist can bring into prominence such a set of values by choosing an instrument, a certain song or piece of music that expresses this area. Wijzenbeek (1996) developed a method for severely depressed patients in which sets of values are used. The therapist asks the client to imagine while listening to preselected fragments of music. This way the therapist creates an image of the relationship of the client with this particular set of values. In discussing these values with the client and working through different fragments of music, the client goes through the therapeutic process.

While working with clients with dementia, one has to adapt this method by helping the client to exhibit his images by using pictures of different atmospheres or, for example, by letting the person react by playing, or by choosing between two or three words offered by the therapist.

Musical history of life

A method that can be very helpful is creating a musical history of a client's life. The person with dementia must have some verbal capacities to be able to fulfil this assignment. Improvising, for example, on a guitar, the therapist asks the client things about different stages in his life. In little steps, he composes a song. This can be done individually or in a group. The therapist colours the song by the sound of his voice, melody, harmonics and rhythm. It is important to give the client time to rest or relax while singing a refrain or humming for a while. A variation on the making of a 'musical history of life', in case a client cannot speak any more, is to do so with the help of family and friends. The method gives a satisfying feeling of being validated and accepted and feeling that one's life has been valuable (Weghorst 2000).

The role of the music therapist

The case studies give a description of some of the specific roles of a music therapist working in elderly care. First, the therapist closely follows the person with dementia and adjusts his goals and methods to the situation of the client. The therapist helps the client to regain as much quality of life as possible. Second, the music therapist contributes to diagnosis as a member of the disciplinary team. He might advise the staff and family of the client about the approach of the person or his problems. Through music, he can assess matters that are sometimes more difficult to be touched verbally. Thus, he can get an insight into a client's inner world. If desired, he can also give advice about musical choice for the funeral of a client he has worked with for a longer period of time.

There are two more remarks to be made about the characteristics of the therapeutic process and the therapeutic relation in music therapy for persons with dementia. The attitude of the therapist is strongly empathic and client centred. He uses a strong unconditional positive regard. It is very important to make the therapeutic relation safe and sincere. In therapy the most important roles of transference and countertransference, besides several other forms, are the relations of parent–child or grandparent–grandchild. Dehm (1997) points at the reverse relation of child–parent, in which the person with dementia is the little child who seeks the warmth and peace of his mother.

Two short cases

Two music therapy treatment sessions are described hereafter, to provide an impression of how the focus is on the client. Aspects such as reference, observation, indications, methods and objectives are not prominent in this description.

Case history one

Mr K has lived in a nursing home for a couple of months. In the beginning, he looked quite satisfied, but he is getting more and more gloomy and from time to time he can be very angry. When asked how he feels, he invariably says that he is doing great, that he has a great time here, and that everyone is so nice to him. His gloominess and anger become worse and more frequent. Mr K is referred to music therapy, because the specific qualities of music make it possible to trigger all sorts of emotions, and in music therapy these emotions can be worked through to a certain level.

During observation, Mr K shows the same disguising and denying behaviour. He feels fantastic, he says. He is interested in music and in the instruments, but he avoids being involved in any activity during the first two sessions. He tells me that the piano is very important to him, although he never played the instrument himself. He has always liked it, because it is such a dignified instrument. In the third session he gets involved by choosing a song that I have to play on the piano.

My objectives are to discover and express together his underlying emotions and after that, to work through and accept, to a certain extent, the life events that are responsible for these fierce feelings.

During the subsequent sessions, the piano remains the main instrument for Mr K. He wants to sit at the piano next to me. It takes quite some time before he dares to touch the keyboard and risks playing one or two notes. He doesn't seem to realize that playing something that is not a pre-composed piece of music is good enough for the piano. This idea can cause resistance to playing anything at all. I ask him to repeat the two notes he played, which he accomplishes after a couple of sessions. I copy what he is playing and tell him that these are a nice couple of notes. He gives no reaction whatsoever. Some sessions later, Mr K has managed to play more notes after each other and is starting to enjoy his musicmaking on the piano. I play along with him, making variations to his musical expressions.

After a while I ask him if he can play as if we are in a hurry to catch a train. He likes this assignment very much. Little by little, he is able to play more themes, for example, walking like a cat, and a thunderstorm. We have built a trustworthy contact while making music and there is a lot of laughter from time to time. However, he is still trying to disguise his true emotions. He says that everything is fine and in a way I adapt to this because his true emotions will appear when I accept this behaviour.

Then we reach a period in which I ask him to play on the piano as someone who is 'angry' or as someone who is 'sad'. He tries, although it is definitely not as easy as the things we played before. His attitude is getting far more serious. I decide not to reflect verbally yet on his improvisation. Sometime, after playing 'anger', he tells me shortly that he has these feelings too. We talk about being angry for a while, after I have comforted him by playing a soothing song. In the subsequent sessions, we play sadness and anger again and Mr K tells me more about his hidden emotions. I have the feeling that losing his dignity is what is making him angry and sad. I play a very dignified piece of music on the piano. I expect to touch this specific set of values (losing dignity), to open and explore it with him.

After the piece he starts crying. He tells me he likes it so much and that he is grateful to me for playing it. We talk about dignity, although not directly connecting it to his problems, remaining within the limits of my approach until now.

After this session, we make a 'musical history' of life together, in which the area of dignity is a returning value (see the earlier description of Weghorst in methods). He is very happy with the result. I have to repeat it playing over and over again, accompanied by the piano. During this time, the anger and sadness of Mr K in daily life have decreased and become much milder and less frequent.

Case history two

Mrs T seems to be very unhappy in the nursing home. She is sitting in a corner of the living room and makes no contact with anybody whatsoever. She has major language problems that brought her into severe isolation. She is referred to music therapy because of its non-verbal communicative character. I want to observe her in the music therapy room, but that turns out to be impossible. When I come to collect her, she wants to join me in the music therapy room. But as soon as she is there, she starts screaming that she doesn't want to be there. I let her yell for a while, hoping that she will calm down, but it is not getting better. Then she suddenly stops, after mentioning something about her father. The second time the same thing happens.

I decide to read through her files again. I come across the information that she had a very dominant father. I formulate the hypothesis that she will scream and resist when things are forced upon her and she has the feeling that she has nothing to say about it. With this in mind, I try to take her to music therapy again. I decide to put myself in the role of a mother. When I come close to her in her corner, I hum for her like a mother would for her child. Without saying anything, she walks with me. In the music therapy room, I keep humming, accompanying myself on a zither. She sits at peace close to me, but doesn't make any verbal, musical or eye contact.

In the next period, first Mrs T very carefully makes a little eye contact while I play the zither. The contact is growing slowly but steadily. After a couple of sessions, I ask her if she wants to choose a song for the zither. I give her two alternatives. I have three reasons to do this: (1) Mrs T isn't capable any more of making a free choice; (2) I want her to experience the feeling of having an influence on the situation; (3) I want to avoid the therapy coming to a standstill. She chooses a song and hums with it when I play. Some time later, I ask her if she can strike a single bass string of the zither. I show her how to do it and so she does. As she strikes the tonic, I play one of the songs she likes most. She is surprised at the result and very satisfied.

Some sessions later, I present her with other instruments she might like to play. She very much likes the metallophone. When she plays on it, it has a soft, comforting sound. I see her self-esteem grow and she takes more and more time to explore it. She is playing more freely now on different instruments, and the quality of her making contact with me has improved. Therefore, one month later, I decide to try to let her join a group with two other, calm and nice ladies. I expect her to be able to make contact with these other two ladies, uplifting her self-esteem, by gaining credit for her musical skills.

She needs time to get used to this new situation, but after a while she takes up her role of the 'metallophone player'. The other ladies admire the nice sound she produces. The contact between the ladies in the music is getting stronger. After a couple of sessions they play 'give and take' (see methods) with my help and they play all around the little circle. In daily life, Mrs T also starts making some contact with a few people. She seems to be satisfied with these contacts.

After joining the music therapy group for a couple of months, Mrs T's health is deteriorating. She has broken a hip and her dementia is progressing quickly. She doesn't feel comfortable in the group any more, so we return to individual music therapy sessions, and the objectives connected with that previous stage. The deterioration of her motor skills forces me to replace the metallophone by great sonar bars. However, it appears that she is still able to play together with me, even if I have to use a far slower tempo.

Theory

Box 8.6   Theories, models and principles of music therapy

Music therapy builds upon psychological theories like psychoanalysis, phenomenology, behaviourism, communication and system theories. We limit ourselves to those aspects of theories, models and principles that a music therapist uses while working in elderly care (taken from Van Nieuwenhuijzen and Broersen 1998). These are summarized below.

1   *Psychoanalytical music therapy.* The unconscious can be explored by creating associations through listening or improvising. The relation of transference can give a client new insight and frees him from tensions. In this relation, the client can relive, deal with and integrate suppressed situations in a symbolic way.
2   *Behaviouristic music therapy.* Music can be used as a stimulus for relaxation as a counterbalance for fear. Further, music can be used to reinforce positive behaviour.
3   *Humanistic music therapy.* Through an unconditional positive regard, and a warm and sincere attitude towards the client, he might open up, discover his identity and be able to make more realistic choices for the future. Gestalt therapeutic music therapy can be seen as a form of this category.
4   *Communicative music therapy.* Through improvising, the therapist examines the interaction of the client and the way he verbalizes this interaction. Analogies in musical and extra-musical behaviour become apparent and the client gets the possibility to experiment with new interaction behaviour.
5   *Analogous process model.* Musical behaviour is seen as a reflection of behaviour in daily life. Through musical methods, it is possible to influence overall behaviour and experiences of clients.
6   *Creative process model.* Art forms, such as music, can free someone from rigid patterns in relation to his environment by searching, finding and experiencing his own composition, adjusted to his own needs.
7   *Iso principle.* The therapist connects to the feeling of the client.
8   *Level principle.* The therapist seeks a way to bend negative feelings to a more positive experience.

Scientific research

In the last decades, there has been a remarkable increase in research on music therapy and dementia. The present data are very valuable and can be used for future research. We must however mention that there is still much to be done. Most of the research in the last 40 years is actually about music in relation to psyche (and vice versa). Theories and results of research of neurological and physiological aspects of music include the subjects of the functioning of the hemispheres, the influence of music on, for example, the immune system, endocrine system, vegetative functions, and analogies between music and neurological processes (Smeijsters 1996).

A specific problem in the field of research in the Netherlands has to do with a semantic problem: the researchers are not music therapists and the music therapists are not researchers. This has to with the fact that the four-year, full-time courses for music therapy are more orientated towards practice and less towards research. At this very moment a discussion is going on between the different institutes for music therapy education about organizing one common national research centre.

Brotons (2000) has made a valuable overview of music therapy literature relating to elderly people. The topic of published research on music therapy and dementia can be divided into seven categories. The outcomes of each category are summarized in Box 8.7 (taken from Broersen 1993; Brotons 2000).

Box 8.7   Music therapy outcomes

1   *Behaviour.* This category has been researched most often and gives very clear outcomes. Results show that music activities/music therapy can be alternatives to medicines and restraints in case of agitation, wandering and disruptive behaviour (Lindenmuth *et al.* 1992; Brotons and Pickett-Cooper 1996). In using music to reduce agitation, it proves to be important to take into account the music styles, preferences of the subject and specific behaviours addressed (Ragneskog *et al.* 1996a, 1996b). In the Netherlands, A.Vink has started an extensive PhD research project about the influence of music therapy on agitation in persons with dementia.

2   *Social skills.* Several studies measure a significant positive effect of music activities/music therapy on social behaviour and interaction (Olderog-Millard and Smith 1989; Lord and Garner 1993). Research of Sambandham and Schirm (1995) and Clair (1991) suggest that music may be one form of communication that is preserved in persons with Alzheimer's disease and related disorders.

3   *Cognitive skills.* Until now this category has had little attention from re-searchers. Data suggest that music may enhance memory and language skills (Smith 1986; Prickett and Moore 1991; Carruth 1997). Moreover, the Prickett and Moore research shows that persons with dementia can learn new material in the context of a song. The Carruth research suggests that music can improve the ability to retain new information. All this must be seen within the context of a continuing process of deterioration.

4   *Preserved musical skills.* The preservation of musical skills observed in persons with dementia offers the music therapist a unique access to memories, feelings and knowledge that otherwise would be very difficult to reach (Brotons 2000). Substantial research has been done on this topic. Different explanations are given for the observation that musical skills are preserved in advanced stages of dementia:

- music is a part of the syntactical systems, which are preserved longer in persons with dementia (Swartz *et al.* 1989)
- music appeals to procedural memory and is therefore preserved until later stages of dementia (Beatty *et al.* 1988)
- music is the fundament out of which language has developed. Because the skills of persons with dementia seem to move towards their abilities during their childhood, music is preserved for a long time (Broersen 1993, Aldridge and Aldridge 1992).

5   *Music as an instrument of assessment.* Music can be used to measure several cognitive, behavioural and social skills that otherwise could not be measured or would be more difficult to measure. Aldridge and Aldridge (1992), Aldridge (1994) and Aldridge (1995) mention intentionality, attention, concentration, perseverance on a task and episodic memory.

6   *Preferences.* This category offers the general conclusion that persons with dementia enjoy music activities and can participate in different musical settings. Singing is a skill that may tend to decrease with progressing dementia (Clair and Bernstein 1990). Nevertheless, the human voice seems to be one of the most important stimuli (Clair 1996b). Fitzgerald-Cloutier (1992) observes most positive responses when singing without an accompanying instrument.

7   *Stimulating the senses.* Sensory stimulation through music can have a positive effect on the functioning and well-being of persons with dementia (Bower 1967). In practice, this kind of musical approach is being used in 'snoezelen'.

Future perspectives

We are very encouraged that music therapy is being more widely recognized as an important intra- and interpersonal intervention for both persons with dementia and their families, and that music therapists are increasingly playing an important part in the multidisciplinary team management of supportive long-term care. We want to close with some personal remarks about the future of music therapy in this field.

Including family in music therapy

There is a tendency to include family members or other important people in the life of the person with dementia in the music therapy situation. This can be of great value for both the client and the family members – who certainly have to cope with serious problems – in accepting the situation, coping with feelings such as being left alone, guilt, grief and powerlessness. The results in daily practice are very promising for the future. Research of Clair and others (Brotons 2000) indicates that through including family members in music therapy the person with dementia and their spouses, children, etc. discover new ways and perspectives to enhance their relationship. These aspects also are important in regard to the next subject.

Music therapy at the client's home

Another development that is closely related with the previous tendency, is that persons with dementia remain in their own homes as long as possible. Music therapy is increasingly done at the client's home. It can contribute to the client's feeling of well-being and enhance the relationship with relatives, as mentioned above. Through that, the period of living at home can be made longer.

Contribution to diagnostics in early stages of dementia

It is an important issue in care-giving in dementia to set a diagnosis as soon as possible, in order to be able to start a treatment programme at an early stage. This has advantages for the client as well as for relatives. Music therapy can make an important contribution to this early diagnosis because music therapy is actual, interactional and the communication between therapist and client is direct and quick. Moreover, people cannot mask themselves because improvisation is a totally unknown way of communication for them. Via the half-conscious and the emotional component of music, the therapist can trigger themes and sets of values that otherwise, in a verbal way, are difficult to reach (Consten 1986). Furthermore, the music therapy situation is easily accessible. The therapist can adjust to the motor and cognitive skills of the client. For most people music therapy is attractive and pleasant. All of these aspects suit with the needs and problems of people in an early stage of dementia.

Research

In our view, future research is needed, particularly to explore this last topic. Another important object for research is the relationship between the use of medicines and music therapy. This has two aspects: medicines can cause auditory and motor restrictions for music therapy; music therapy can reduce the medication a client needs, such as sleeping pills, antidepressants and medication against anxiety and panic. Further scientific research about the specific musical parameters responsible for evoking specific emotions and sets of values is of great importance, both to justify and stimulate increased use of music therapy with persons with dementia.

Acknowledgement

We want to thank Laurien Hakvoort for her advice on translation and contents.

References

Adriaansz, R., Schalkwijk, F. and Stijlen, L. (eds) (1994) *Methoden van muziektherapie. Een overzicht van muziektherapie in Nederland*, 2nd edn, Nijkerk: Intro.

Aldridge, A. (1995) 'Music therapy and the treatment of Alzheimer's disease', *Clinical Gerontologist* 16, 1: 41–57.

Aldridge, A. and Aldridge, G. (1992) 'Two epistemologies: music therapy and medicine in the treatment of dementia', *The Arts in Psychotherapy* 19: 243–55.

Aldridge, D. (1994) 'Alzheimer's disease: rhythm, timing and music as therapy', *Biomedical and Pharmocotherapy* 48, 7: 275–81.

—— (2000) *Music Therapy in Dementia Care*, London: Jessica Kingsley.

Beatty, W., Zavadil, K., Bailly, R., Rixen, G., Zavadil, L., Farnham, N. and Fisher, L. (1988) 'Preserved musical skill in a severely demented patient', *International Journal of Clinical Neuropsychology* 10, 4: 158–64.

Benenzon, R.O. (1983) *Einfuhrung in die Musiktherapie*, Munchen: Kösel Verlag.

Bonder, B. (1994) 'Psychotherapy for individuals with Alzheimer's disease', *Alzheimer's Disease and Associated Disorders* 8, 3: 75–81.

Bower, H.M. (1967) 'Sensory stimulation and the treatment of senile dementia', *Medical Journal of Australia* 1: 1113–9.

Broersen, M. (1993) 'Muziektherapie bij Alzheimerpatiënten. Een literatuurstudie', unpublished Master thesis, University of Amsterdam, The Netherlands.

Broersen, M., Groot, R. de and Jonker, C. (1995) 'Muziektherapie bij Alzheimerpatiënten. Enkele richtlijnen op basis van literatuur', *Tijdschrift voor Kreatieve Therapie* 4, 1: 9–14.

Brotons, M. (2000) 'Overview of the music therapy literature relating to elderly people', in D. Aldridge (ed.) *Music Therapy in Dementia Care*, London: Jessica Kingsley.

Brotons, M. and Pickett-Cooper, P. (1996) 'The effect of music therapy intervention on agitation behaviours of Alzheimer's disease patients', *Journal of Music Therapy* 33, 1: 2–18.

Bruscia, K.E. (1987) *Improvisational Models of Music Therapy*, Springfield, IL: Charles C. Thomas.

Carruth, E. (1997) 'The effects of singing and the spaced retrieval technique on improving face-name recognition in nursing home residents with memory loss', *Journal of Music Therapy* 34: 165–86.

Clair, A. (1991) 'Music therapy for a severely regressed person with a probable diagnosis of Alzheimer's disease', in K. Bruscia (ed.) *Case Studies in Music Therapy*, Phoenixville, PA: Barcelona Press.

—— (1996a) *Therapeutic Uses of Music with Older Adults*, Baltimore: Health Professions Press.

—— (1996b) 'The effect of singing on alert responses with late stage dementia', *Journal of Music Therapy* 333, 4: 234–47.

Clair, A.A. and Bernstein, B. (1990) 'A comparison of singing, vibrotactile and non-vibrotactile instrumental playing responses in severely regressed persons with dementia of the Alzheimer's type', *Journal of Music Therapy* 27, 3: 119–25.

Consten, J. (1986) *Muziek in gesprek. Een onderzoek naar het gebruik van muziektherapie als uitbreiding van de zelfconfrontatiemethode*, Nijmegen: Psychologisch Laboratorium Katholieke Universiteit Nijmegen.

Dehm, B. (1997) 'Übergänge'. Tod und Sterben in der Musiktherapie mit Dementen', *Musiktherapeutische Umschau* 2: 103–13.

Fitzgerald-Cloutier, M.L. (1992) *The Effects of Different Music Instruments Used for Accompaniment or Participation for Persons Diagnosed with Probable Alzheimer's Disease*, Canada: Heather Hill.

Hausman, C. (1992) 'Dynamic psychotherapy with elderly demented patients', in *Care-giving in Dementia*, vol. 1, London: Routledge.

Jansma, M. and Vries, B. de (1995) 'Muziek en emotie', in F. Evers, M. Jansma, P. Mak and B. de Vries (eds) *Muziekpsychologie*, Assen: Van Gorcum.

Langer, S.K. (1978) *Philosophy in a New Key. A Study of the Symbolism in Reason, Rite and Art*, 3rd edn, Cambridge, MA: Harvard University Press.

Lindenmuth, G., Patel, M. and Chang, P. (1992) 'Effects of music on sleep in healthy elderly and subjects with senile dementia of the Alzheimer's type', *American Journal of Alzheimer's Care and Related Disorders and Research* 2: 13–20.

Lord, T. and Garner, J. (1993) 'Effects of music on Alzheimer's patients', *Perceptual and Motor Skills* 76: 451–5.

Miesen, B. (1999) *Dementia in Close-up*, London: Routledge.

Nieuwenhuijzen, N. van and Broersen, M. (1998) 'Muziektherapie: waar woorden tekortschieten', *Leidraad Psychogeriatrie* B4: 80–103.

Olderog-Millard, K.A. and Smith, J.M. (1989) 'The influence of group singing on the behaviour of Alzheimer's disease patients', *Journal of Music Therapy* 26: 58–70.

Pavlicevic, M. (1997) *Music Therapy in Context. Music, Meaning and Relationship*, London: Jessica Kingsley.

Prickett, C. and Moore, R. (1991) 'The use of music to aid memory of Alzheimer's patients', *Journal of Music Therapy* 28, 2: 101–10.

Ragneskog, H., Brane, G., Karlsson, I. and Kihlgren, M. (1996a) 'Influence of dinner music on food intake and symptoms common in dementia', *Scandinavian Journal of Caring Science* 10: 11–17.

Ragneskog, H., Kihlgren, M., Karlsson, I. and Norberg, A. (1996b) 'Dinner music for demented patients: analysis of video-recorded observations', *Clinical Nursing Research* 5, 3: 262–82.

Raijmaekers, J. (1993) 'Music therapy's role in the diagnosis of psycho-geriatric patients in The Hague', in M. Heal and T. Wigram (eds) *Music Therapy in Health and Education*, London: Jessica Kingsley.

Sambandham, M. and Schirm, V. (1995) 'Music as a nursing intervention for residents with Alzheimer's disease in long-term care', *Geriatric Nursing* 16, 2: 79–82.

Smeijsters, H. (1995) *Handboek Muziektherapie*, Heerlen: Melos.

—— (1996) *Neurologische en fysiologische aspecten van muziektherapie*, Heerlen: Melos.

—— (2000) *Handboek Creatieve Therapie*, Bussum: Coutinho.

Smeijsters, H., Wijzenbeek, G.C.M. and Nieuwenhuijzen, N. van (1995), 'The evocation of values of depressed patients by excerpts of recorded music', *Journal of Music Therapy* 32, 3: 167–88.

Smith, G. (1986) 'A comparison of the effects of three treatment interventions on cognitive functioning of Alzheimer patients', *Music Therapy* 6a, 1: 41–56.

Swartz, K.P., Hantz, E.C., Crummer, G.C., Walton, J.P. and Frisina, R.D. (1989) 'Does the melody linger on? Music cognition in Alzheimer's disease', *Seminars in Neurology* 9, 2: 152–8.

Verwoerdt, A. (1981) 'Individual psychotherapy in senile dementia', in N.E. Miller and G.D. Cohen (eds) *Clinical Aspects of Alzheimer's Disease and Senile Dementia*, New York: Raven Press.

Watzlawick, P., Beavin, J.H. and Jackson, D.D. (1967) *Pragmatics of Human Communications*, New York: Norton.

Weghorst, N. (2000) 'Mijn leven is een lied. De toepassing van reminiscentie in een muziektherapeutische behandeling van dementerende patiënten,' unpublished paper, Conservatorium Hogeschool Enschede, The Netherlands.

Wijzenbeek, G. (1996) 'The use of composed music in the treatment of major depression', book of abstracts, Eighth World Congress of Music Therapy, Hamburg.

Winnicott, D.W. (1971) *Playing a Reality*, London: Tavistock.

Yalom, I.D. (1975) *The Theory and Practice of Group Psychotherapy*, New York: Basic Books.

Part III

Topics related to care-giving issues

Chapter 9

Towards a psychology of dementia care

Awareness and intangible loss

Bère Miesen

In memory of Ilse Warners (1930–1998), colleague and friend.

To really understand (older) people, it is important to have insight into how they actually perceive and value their lives.

(Nies, 1989)

Old age psychology (psychogerontology) is about understanding behavioural changes as persons grow older. Psychogerontology is multidisciplinary in nature: first, because it focuses on changes within a diversity of (behavioural) aspects related to growing old; second, because all these aspects relating to later life, especially when people have reached (an advanced) old age, should increasingly be studied in relation to each other. Psychogerontology adopts its own methodology, with emphasis on longitudinal research. It also frequently offers significant knowledge to supplement the earlier, overexclusive, unidisciplinary approach adopted by medical science and psychiatry when dealing with those psychologically disturbed in old age. But that is not all. Psychogerontology implicitly 'propagates' the idea that ageing and old age have their own psychological nature without this having to become 'problematic'. It is necessary to use the existing basic knowledge on ageing and old age when researching abnormal old age, whether clinical in nature or not, in order to be able to refute or correct current ways of thinking about dementia in the elderly. It is certainly true that psychogeriatrics as an area of work is now increasingly beginning to lose its exclusively 'in persons with dementia' character. The work of psychologists dealing with older persons with dementia is now no longer just confined to hospitals or homes.

Towards a psychology of dementia

Scientific knowledge in the field of dementia was initially primarily acquired using neuropsychological measuring instruments that charted the progress of cognitive loss via transverse research, often referring to the nature and location of cerebral impairment. To date, medical, psychological and multidisciplinary research have shed relatively little light on and paid scant attention to the affective responses of the person with dementia and the partner, the way in which these responses can be understood and the way in which various factors affect interaction between the two 'parties'. Even when such research has been done, for instance, under the heading of 'behavioural deficits', 'secondary symptoms' or even 'personality disorders', they are often mentioned in the same breath as cognitive deficits, and almost as a matter of course considered as the direct result of brain impairment.

The key features of dementia – impairment or progressive loss of all types of psychological function and cognitive skills such as memory, language, visuo-perceptual ability and planning – are the direct result of the disease, in other words, of cerebral abnormalities. This leads to decreasing independence and limitations in self-care. Persons with dementia become less and less able to function independently in their day-to-day life, at work and in their relationships and become increasingly reliant on help. This means that their dependence on third parties increases and their ability to maintain a level of autonomous functioning decreases. From the outset, the nature and gravity of the brain abnormalities as well as the speed at which the disease progresses and other interfering factors such as co-morbidity with heart and vascular disorders, all lead to tremendous individual differences in the course of the disease. Dementia is after all a syndrome for which a variety of cerebral abnormalities may be responsible.

To date, both clinical practice – diagnostics and treatment – and education and research have mainly been tackled from a bioneurological/medical and cognitive/practical perspective. Even the way in which support and care are organized is to a large extent based on this knowledge and insight. In short, it comes down to the following.

According to the DSM-IV criteria (which are the prevailing criteria for diagnosing mental difficulties and disorders), lists are used to rule out treatable causes of the cognitive deficits, so that the untreatable causes can then be differentiated. (see Box 9.1, p. 187). Depending on the diagnosed or suspected cause, the deficits are treated with a medicinal approach, sometimes as part of an experimental trial. Medication is also sometimes prescribed to combat the behavioural deficits.

In everyday practice, this knowledge not only appears one-sided, but also inadequate in terms of understanding what the individual person with dementia and their support system (their family and caregivers in care facilities or in the community) say, think, feel and do; and is inadequate in terms of helping them. The person with dementia and the family often find the support provided on the basis of this one-sided knowledge to be lacking. The main things they find lacking are continuity in the relationship with caregivers and consideration of awareness and perception aspects of the disease (Miesen and Kuypers 1998; Threels 2003).

Fortunately over the last few years, diagnostics in suspected dementia has begun to assume a more multidisciplinary character. What is more, greater consideration is given to early diagnosis and to the importance of (neuro)psychological research. The psychodynamic perspective of dementia has also increased in significance – in that greater consideration is given to the current perception of the disease. This has paved the way for a wide range of non-medical treatments, aimed at providing guidance and support in dealing with the disease (Jones and Miesen 1992; Droës 1997, 1998; Miesen and Jones 1997; Droës *et al.* 1999). A psychology of dementia is therefore easily attainable, essentially requiring an open approach to diagnosis and prognosis (Miesen 1990, 1998a; Flapper 1997; Miesen and Kuypers 1998). With emotionally open communication between partners, the emotional signals can be correctly and reliably translated, even if cognitive skills are impaired (Bretherton 1990).

Psychologists usually do not approach human behaviour from an implicitly medical or biological point of view. They have observed, from their many varied and intensive contacts with older person with dementia, that persons with dementia are more intensely affected by what is happening to them than has so far been assumed. It is becoming increasingly accepted that when diagnosing, treating and providing support for dementia, consideration should be given to the experiences of the person with dementia and the family. This not only involves explicit perception-based diagnostics and treatment, but also requires theoretical models firmly rooted in psychology.

It falls within the scope of psychogerontology to describe the catastrophic effect of dementia, how it develops, how the person with dementia and his family deal with it and how both 'parties' can be helped and supported. To be able to describe this, it is necessary to include a third perspective along with the usual bioneurological/medical and cognitive/practical perspectives, namely one based on perception/awareness (van Amelsvoort-Jones 1985; Jones 1988; Verdult 1993; Warners 1998). 'To obtain a valid impression of the overall gravity of dementia, it is important to give individual attention to cognitive decline, functional impairment, "behavioural deficits" and the burden experienced by carers' (Teunisse *et al.* 1994). In other words, the course of dementia can be followed by looking at:

- changes in cognitive function as a result of the disease
- the impact these have on the everyday life, work, relationships, etc. of the person with dementia and family
- the way in which both parties deal with the above.

The key features of each phase of dementia should therefore be described from a combined cognitive, practical/functional and psychological perspective in order to gain a complete overview of possible treatments.

Awareness

From a psychological point of view, dementia should be regarded as a chronic brain trauma that the person with dementia continuously confronts alongside the psychological trauma that continual feelings of powerlessness, disruption of normal everyday life and emotional upheaval bring. With a number of person with dementia (in my experience around 25 per cent), the phenomenon of unresolved conflicts also plays an important role. In other words, with the onset of dementia, a catastrophe occurs, usually gradually, in the life of the person with dementia, with all the inherent stress, without them being able to identify it. The full extent of the catastrophe only gradually dawns on them. It presents them with a whole load of practical as well as emotional and relationship problems, which they then have to work out how to deal with all over again (with only dwindling cerebral capacities at their disposal). So it is not possible to concretely identify the wrongdoer or stressor. Because the residual capacities are getting weaker and weaker – due to the progressive nature of the disease – the person with dementia is often 'fighting a losing battle'. A large proportion of the behaviour of a person with dementia can therefore be interpreted as normal behaviour in an abnormal or complicated situation. This also makes it clear that coping with the situation also depends on what this person has experienced and on his or her character. Every person with dementia will deal with their problems in their own unique way on the basis of their individual life history and personality structure. Box 9.1 shows the DSM-IV diagnostic criteria for both Alzheimer-type dementia and for post-traumatic stress disorder. Their significance is discussed hereafter.

If you compare the DSM-IV criteria for dementia of the Alzheimer's type (part 1 of the box) with the criteria for a post-traumatic stress disorder (part 2 of the box), there is an apparent difference in 'stressor or cause' for both clinical pictures. With one of them, the stressor is an organic cerebral disease and with the other the stressor is a shocking event. With dementia, there has been plenty of discussion about the consequences of the stressor, but none about how the consequences should be dealt with. The DSM-IV criteria do not take into account current evidence of the existence of a person's 'awareness'of what is happening to them (Miesen 1990; Droës 1991; Vernooij-Dassen 1993; van der Plaats 1994), and possible ways of dealing and coping with it. With post-traumatic stress disorder, it is a matter of identifying the disturbed way of dealing with the consequences of the stressor. This could be called an experience/perception-oriented approach. It is not difficult to recognize the various behavioural deficits belonging to dementia of reliving, avoidance/denial and hyper-vigilance:

> In the field of memory alone, there are at least three cognitive changes apparent in dementia: the ability to keep storing new information continues to deteriorate; it becomes increasingly difficult to call up recent

Box 9.1   DSM-IV diagnostic criteria for Alzheimer-type dementia and PTSD

DSM-IV diagnostic criteria for dementia of the Alzheimer's type (APA 1994)

A.   The development of multiple cognitive deficits manifested by both
  (1)   memory impairment (impaired ability to learn new information or to recall previously learned information)
  (2)   one (or more) of the following cognitive disturbances:
    (a)   aphasia (language disturbance)
    (b)   apraxia (impaired ability to carry out motor activities despite intact motor function)
    (c)   agnosia (failure to recognise or identify objects despite intact sensory function)
    (d)   disturbance in executive functioning (i.e., planning, organisation, sequencing, abstracting)
B.   The cognitive deficits in Criteria A1 and A2 each cause significant impairment in social or occupational functioning and represent a significant decline from a previous level of functioning.
C.   The course is characterised by gradual onset and continuing cognitive decline.
D.   The cognitive deficits in Criteria A1 and A2 are not due to any of the following:
  (1)   other central nervous system conditions that cause progressive deficits in memory and cognition (e.g., cerebrovascular disease, Parkinson's disease, Huntington's disease, subdural hematoma, normal-pressure hydrocephalus, brain tumour)
  (2)   systemic conditions that are known to cause dementia (e.g. hypo-thyroidism, vitamin B_{12} or folic acid deficiency, niacin deficiency, hypercalcemia, neurosyphilis, HIV infection)
  (3)   substance-induced conditions
E.   The deficits do not occur exclusively during the course of a delirium.
F.   The disturbance is not better accounted for by another Axis 1 disorder (e.g. Major Depressive Disorder, Schizophrenia).

DSM-IV diagnostic criteria for Posttraumatic Stress Disorder (APA 1994)

A.   The person has been exposed to a traumatic event in which both of the following were present:
  (1)   the person experienced, witnessed, or was confronted with an event or events that involved actual or threatened death or serious injury, or a threat to the physical integrity of self or others
  (2)   the person's response involved intense fear, helplessness, or horror. Note: In children, this may be expressed instead by disorganised or agitated behaviour.
B.   The traumatic event is persistently re-experienced in one (or more) of the following ways:
  (1)   recurrent and intrusive distressing recollections of the event, including images, thoughts, or perceptions. Note: In young children, repetitive

play may occur in which themes or aspects of the trauma are expressed

 (2) recurrent distressing dreams of the event. Note: In children, there may be frightening dreams without recognisable content.

 (3) acting or feeling as if the traumatic event were recurring (includes a sense of reliving the experience, illusions, hallucinations, and dissociative flashback episodes, including those that occur on awakening or when intoxicated). Note: In young children, trauma-specific re-enactment may occur.

 (4) intense psychological distress at exposure to internal or external cues that symbolise or resemble an aspect of the traumatic event

 (5) physiological reactivity on exposure to internal or external cues that symbolise or resemble an aspect of the traumatic event

C. Persistent avoidance of stimuli associated with the trauma and numbing of general responsiveness (not present before the trauma), as indicated by three (or more) of the following:

 (1) efforts to avoid thoughts, feelings or conversations associated with the trauma

 (2) efforts to avoid activities, places or people that arouse recollections of the trauma

 (3) inability to recall an important aspect of the trauma

 (4) markedly diminished interest or participation in significant activities

 (5) feeling of detachment or estrangement from others

 (6) restricted range of affect (e.g. unable to have loving feelings)

 (7) sense of a foreshortened future (e.g., does not expect to have a career, marriage, children, or a normal life span)

D. Persistent symptoms of increased arousal (not present before the trauma), as indicated by two (or more) of the following:

 (1) difficulty falling or staying asleep

 (2) irritability or outbursts of anger

 (3) difficulty concentrating

 (4) hyper-vigilance

 (5) exaggerated startle response

E. Duration of the disturbance (symptoms in Criteria B, C and D) is more than 1 month.

F. The disturbance causes clinically significant distress or impairment in social, occupational or other important areas of functioning.

events from one's memory; and, in the end, it even becomes difficult to recall early memories.

(Miesen and Jones 1999: 52)

If one realizes the problems faced continually by persons with dementia due to these memory deficits, and that they have to (learn how to) deal with them although their cerebral dysfunction is getting worse, then it is an understatement to say that the feeling of insecurity, trying to be normal and endeavouring to lead as normal a life as possible, are the points of most importance for the person with dementia (Phinney 1998).

With the onset of the disease, persons with dementia are mainly confronted with a sense of threat, which they resist. This fight gives the outside world the appearance of a façade, whereas inside the person feels powerlessness, insecurity and fear. Confrontation with failure is avoided where possible. After this, the perception of continuity is lost, and the person with dementia loses the ability to organize the past, present and future. Contact with the outside world becomes increasingly difficult. It is also no longer possible to keep up the façade. What the person with dementia is going through and (is) feeling, becomes obvious. Dialogue with the outside world is then lost. External stimuli are only interpreted within the scope of his/her own perception of the world. Finally, the persons with dementia cease to or barely respond to external stimuli, although they still respond to internal stimuli (Engelen and Peeters 1984; Ekkerink 1997).

Awareness context

Nearly 40 years ago, Glaser and Strauss (1965) introduced the concept of awareness context. They describe the awareness context of terminally ill persons with dementia, their relatives and the staff looking after them. From a sociological point of view, they stated that awareness of impending death could take on four different forms and that these affected the way in which the people involved interacted (see Box 9.2):

- closed awareness
- awareness based on assumption
- awareness based on mutual pretence
- open awareness.

The essence of the theory of Glaser and Strauss is that those who do not know they are going to die do not get round to grieving. Without information on (or awareness of) the approaching end, no process of dealing with or coping takes place. If this information is kept from person with dementia, one is taking the opportunity away from them to say goodbye and to complete their lives in their own way. It is only possible to effectively interpret what terminally ill persons with dementia are thinking, saying, feeling and doing (and hence look after them adequately), if one knows what they have been told or what they know about their disease. To have a good understanding of the behaviour of persons with dementia, one has to take their awareness context into consideration. Munnichs (1998) also refers to the importance of the awareness context: 'Apart from the gravity of the disease and the suspected lifespan, how does one know how dying people are doing, what

---

Box 9.2   Four forms of awareness of impending death (Glaser and Strauss 1965)

1   *Closed awareness.* The persons with dementia themselves cannot see their impending death, but those around them are well aware of it. Those close to them deploy all kinds of tactics to prevent this situation from changing. This involves diversion; superficial, brief and business-like communication; focus on the 'here and now'; and acting 'cheerfully' as if nothing is wrong.

2   *Awareness based on assumption.* Persons with dementia suspect that they are going to die, so on the one hand they try to test whether their assumption is correct and on the other relatives and staff try to prevent their efforts. The persons with dementia have restricted faculties at their disposal and are usually also restricted in their mobility. They can only use their eyes and ears, ask questions, provoke those around them to let information slip and possibly look at their medical records. The people around the person with dementia will try to glean how much they assume and then act accordingly, for instance, exaggeratedly acting as if nothing is wrong, hiding behind the doctor (or what the doctor says), or avoiding (direct contact with) the person with dementia as much as possible.

3   *Awareness based on mutual pretence.* This type of interaction between persons with dementia and those around them is very common. The people close to the person with dementia do not want to talk about the approaching end, nor does the person with dementia want to make an issue of it. Both avoid the truth. Both parties pay considerable attention to outward appearances and purposefully talk about 'safe subjects'. If one of the parties slips up, they usually carry on talking as if nothing has happened. For the person with dementia, this gives a sense of freedom and dignity, but also isolation. The necessary atmosphere of caution (constant vigilance) takes a lot out of the staff and family. They should always be on their guard and be careful of what they say. Sometimes this stage passes gradually or suddenly on to 'open awareness', if the pretence takes too much energy out of both parties and can no longer be kept up.

4   *Open awareness.* This is when persons with dementia and those close to them are aware of the impending death and act accordingly. This gives persons with dementia the opportunity to say goodbye to their family (and vice versa) and to bring a close to their life in line with their own ideas and wishes about how to die, how to prepare for death and any ceremonies to be held after their death.

---

they are feeling and thinking of their death? And do all the people around them know the same thing?'

Through clinical observations (e.g. van Loo 1988; Claus 1989) and research (e.g. Miesen 1990, 1993a; Weinstein *et al.* 1994), it has been shown that persons with dementia keep responding to their disease even a long time after they have lost 'understanding' of their disease. Awareness of a disease evidently lasts for longer than understanding of the disease. This fact is supported by the finding that psychodynamic psychotherapy is successful with persons in the early stages of Alzheimer's disease (Gabbard 1994; Goldstein 1952; Lewis 1986, 1991; Wragg and Jeste 1989; Weiner 1991; Haussman 1992; Solomon 1992; Solomon and Szwabo 1992), as well as through systematic research into what persons with dementia themselves say (Cotrell and Schultz 1993; Gorman 1993; Phinney 1998).

Explaining awareness

More than 20 years ago now, Verwoerdt (1981) tackled the issue of whether denial and avoidance on the part of the person with dementia can be explained organically or psychologically, or expressed in terms of 'awareness context'. Does awareness correlate with specific cerebral organic functioning? Can this explain why some persons (such as those with the onset of dementia due to isolated frontal lesions as with Pick's disease) do not seem to have any awareness of all the difficulties or problems in providing support that their condition entails (Hagberg 1997; Tainsh and Hinshelwood 1997)? Does this explain why most persons in the final stages of Alzheimer's disease, when the frontal lobes of the brain may also be affected, likewise no longer seem 'aware'?

According to Goldstein (1952), one of the first researchers into the psychological effects of brain damage, 'awareness' continues to exist for a long time and persons with dementia defend themselves 'against catastrophic anxiety by avoiding awareness (denying) of their defects'. They keep trying to gain control over the situation, even if it is only 'the illusion of control'. It is accepted in trauma theories that a sense of control has a positive effect on emotional well-being and is a way of dealing with a shocking event. DeBettignies et al. (1990) observed greater awareness in persons with vascular dementia than in people with Alzheimer's disease. On the other hand, Reed et al. (1993) claimed that it is not possible to prove whether the absence of awareness is related to the progression of the disease, because according to them awareness in people with Alzheimer's disease is highly variable and differs greatly from one person to the next. Sevush and Leve (1993) made a connection between denial or underestimation of the gravity of the memory deficits and general cognitive deficits. According to them, denial and avoidance were apparently the result of the disruption of the cognitive skills required to be aware that one is sick. Grattan et al. (1994) suggested that the frontal lobes in particular play a special role in this. Starkstein et al. (1995) also made a connection between the absence of awareness of disease (anosognosia) and blood circulation disorders of the right frontal lobe. Seltzer et al. (1995), however, are of the opinion that the absence of awareness is primarily a psychological development and for this very reason is not connected to memory deficits or the general decline itself. This brings us back to the issue raised by Verwoerdt (1981), also later very succinctly expressed by Gabbard (1994): 'Clinicians may struggle to differentiate between neurogenic and psychogenic denial.' His interpretation of denial and avoidance is otherwise totally clear: 'Persons with dementia in the early stages of Alzheimer's dementia may use denial to prevent the full impact of the illness from entering conscious awareness.'

Following on from this, Brugman and de Groot (1997: 51–52) described older persons with dementia in the Netherlands as people:

> whose use of adequate coping skills is impaired and yet still have to deal with a major life event [. . .]. Through the cognitive change and inherent consequences, persons with dementia experience stress, in that they undergo a loss of themselves – a disintegration in their personality, identity and physical perception. Secondly, they experience the consequences of (perceiving that they are or actually) losing roles, relationships, emotional support and work. The course of the disease includes impaired problem-solving skills, leading to impaired control over their environment and themselves, in turn leading to helplessness and dependence. All these stresses form part of the person's awareness context. [. . .] responses vary just as reaction to grieving may vary. [. . .] and these can be seen as a function of the awareness contexts. [. . .] Part of the behaviour of the person with dementia is a way of coping with the decline experienced. [. . .] Coping with one's own dementia is a process involving emotion-based, cognitive and behavioural strategies: looking for support from the attachment figure, avoiding acknowledgement of cognitive decline, denial or hiding from the truth, withdrawing to reduce the stress or literally 'going walkabout'. Persons with dementia will try to resist this shocking and traumatic event in an attempt to struggle against or hide their incompetence or to satisfy their need for security.

Beyond the growing stream of semi-autobiographical publications of (personal experiences with) Alzheimer's disease (Mahy 1987; Anifantakis and Tyler 1991; McGowin 1993; Sparks 1996) and first-hand accounts of dignitaries and political bigwigs (purposefully brought into the public eye), there is sufficient evidence that the concept of 'awareness context' introduced by Glaser and Strauss with respect to dying persons can also be applied to persons with dementia. They seem to be affected by their situation for a lot longer than researchers initially assumed; they seem to be really suffering. In the light of this, it is possible to see various symptoms of dementia – particularly those that used to be referred to as secondary phenomena – as normal responses to awareness and perception of powerlessness, discontinuity, feeling unsafe, lost and isolated. Denial and avoidance do not yet mean that awareness (of the pain) has gone – quite the contrary.

When we look at the basic literary, clinical and empirical components of awareness in persons with dementia, we see that they remain cognitively and emotionally affected by what is happening to them. In other words, they have to deal with an extremely stressful situation. In research conducted towards the end of the 1980s with persons in differing phases of dementia, a strong correlation was found between the phenomenon of parent fixation, attachment behaviour and the level of cognitive functioning (Miesen 1985a, 1990, 1993a). This led to the conclusion that persons with dementia would continue to have awareness of the effects of their condition. It is as if they are landed in a 'strange situation' in which they experience feeling unsafe for long periods of time, powerlessness and having no structures to hold on to. They are continually wrestling with feelings that they do not belong, that they do not feel at home and that there is a barrier between them and their nearest and dearest.

It is precisely this awareness context that leads persons with dementia to experience chronic trauma. They suddenly find themselves in a catastrophic situation. In the above-mentioned research into the meaning of parent fixation, Bowlby's attachment theory was introduced as an explanatory and theoretical framework for the origin of this phenomenon (Bowlby 1969, 1973, 1980). Dementia goes hand in hand with tremendous insecurity, and persons with dementia continue throughout the process to respond to it cognitively, emotionally and with specific behaviour. This behaviour can clearly be interpreted in part as a form of attachment behaviour, in the sense of proximity-seeking behaviour. The way in which persons with dementia respond to it depends on a number of factors, such as the remaining psychological functions and skills, personality and his or her life history.

If we assume that an awareness context exists, we see persons with dementia in a different light, namely as people experiencing chronic trauma and fighting against it. By looking at them in this way, we see them as persons with whom it is possible to talk about their situation and the consequences of their disease. If we acknowledge that persons with dementia have an awareness context, then our image and opinion of them change entirely. If this image and opinion are not shared by all those involved with persons with dementia, their primary carers, professional caregivers, researchers and the public, it will never be possible to fully accept the person's involvement in his or her process of dementia or to take them seriously. They are robbed of their identity; their lives are treated as commodities. Persons with dementia should therefore always be regarded as serious partners in every interaction or contact. If primary carers are convinced that they are aware of their situation and therefore have certain feelings, such as fear, this encourages the feeling of empathy. The process of grief becomes more bearable for both sides.

The concept of awareness context should enable clinicians and researchers alike to carefully differentiate between the real, primary symptoms of the disease on the one hand (in other words, behaviour and cognitive deficits relating directly to cerebral abnormalities) and responses triggered by the awareness and perception of these symptoms on the other. If the existence of the awareness context is not included in the diagnosis, part of the behaviour of a person with dementia will be wrongly attributed to brain impairment or the disease. Behaviour connected with dealing or coping with the condition will be disregarded. Earlier shocking events in the person's life, as well as personality structure and the attachment history between the person with dementia and his family, may complicate the process of coping with dementia and intensify the experience of the existing psychological pain (Miesen and Jones 1999). This may explain the stronger sense of denial and avoidance in about 25 per cent of the persons with dementia. If there is no intervention aimed at this exaggerated response, it is practically impossible for early diagnosis of cognitive change, because according to the person with dementia 'there is nothing wrong'.

The concept of awareness context paves the way for examining the various coping strategies. This requires research into the premorbid personality of the person with dementia, focusing on the following in particular: the impact of attachment patterns, the ways of dealing with disappointments and problems in life and life history. In the personality structure, explanations can be found for the differences in response to primary symptoms of dementia. Without this information, it is not possible to understand the differing reactions to the same primary symptoms, and without this understanding it is not possible to offer the right assistance or advice to carers about how to deal with someone (Miesen 1992b, 1997b). This information requires a detailed description of the individual life history, including traumatic events. If biographical details are not known, it will never be possible to understand why someone flies off the handle whenever they do not get the right answer or response – people 'lose their way', or from another point of view 'are faced with failure'.

By examining the correlation between awareness context, life history and personality, it is possible to predict a person's behaviour in the process of dementia. Irrespective of the causes of a dementia, the person undergoes a process of decline in his cognitive skills. To plan the care required, it is therefore necessary to prepare a phase model (Miesen 1992a). Because awareness is related to cognitive dysfunction, this will change from a more or less continuous awareness of one's own situation to unconnected moments of awareness. Faults can be made in planning the care required if attention is paid purely to the development of the disease and not to the individual differences in awareness context. Apart from changes in awareness, individual responses increasingly shift from being primarily cognitive to more affective.

We do not yet know whether the impact of the life history and personality structure is greater at the onset or end of the process of dementia. Given the progressive memory impairment with dementia, it would be worth while testing the theory of whether the impact of biographical variables gradually becomes less relevant compared to inherent personality factors. In this respect, it is possible to re-examine the discussion as to the effect of the disease on the personality of the person with dementia, this time using primarily psychological methods and measuring instruments. The point is simply to find out whether dementia always leads to deterioration in personality. Based on the opinion that dementia involves a psychological trauma, it is also possible to state that with people in need it is precisely the essential features of the person that come to the fore. It is surely clear that this raises extremely interesting points for research for psychologists (see Box 9.3).

Intangible loss

Dealing with loss is part of life. Sooner or later, everyone will have experienced loss or a shocking event. In general, the elderly will have seen their fair share of this. Professional caregivers and workers who are familiar with the grieving process will quickly be able to identify the related behaviour and feelings, such as: resistance, despair and detachment; or shock, denial, anger and sorrow; or the perplexity of the mourner, the long-lasting search for and strong longing for the lost person, the painful anguish and desperation when this person is not found; and finally finding a way to carry on living 'without' or 'with' the lost person (Bowlby 1980).

Many family members, especially the primary carers, find having to cope with their loved ones undergoing a dementing process a heavy burden and sooner or later a drain on their ability to bear it. A subjective assessment of this burden, however, may greatly differ from an objective one. Duijnstee (1992) uses three intervening factors to explain the individual differences in the 'strength required to bear' of primary carers. She identified variations in how people handle difficult situations, why they render care and how they deal emotionally with the situation. This is again influenced by factors such as health, knowledge of the course of the disease, the actual help provided by their own social network, financial circumstances, accommodation, the professional care received, the extent of insight into the behaviour of the person with dementia and emotional support. Their strength to bear mainly appears to depend on the mutual attachment of the couple and the way in which the primary carer deals with the loss of their loved one. This is no mean feat because throughout the entire course of the disease these people are themselves undergoing a grieving process, whether they are aware of it or not.

In his book *Rouw bij ouderen* [Grieving and the elderly], Buijssen (1998) devotes a short paragraph to 'loss through dementia': 'Already before the actual death of the elderly person with dementia, their partner is confronted with a radical change: The person is physically still there, but is becoming

Box 9.3   Relevant research questions with respect to coping with dementia

Working on the basic assumption that dementia is a chronic brain disease which causes considerable stress, problems in managing it and potential psychotrauma in the person with dementia and the partner, scientific research focuses on the vulnerability of both 'parties' in handling the disease, involving a psychology of coping with dementia. The following four research questions are relevant in this respect:

1   What impact do life history, personality structure and attachment history have on the way the person deals with the disease in the various phases of the process? What impact do negative life events, unresolved conflicts, shocking events or earlier psychotraumas have on the way the person deals with the disease?

2   Does the person's denial and avoidance of the disease have an organic cerebral and/or psychological explanation? To what extent does the awareness context of the person have a specific organic cerebral correlation? What does this mean for the deployment and potential success of specific interventions?

3   What significance do theories on stress, coping and psychotrauma have with respect to diagnosing the onset of the disease in good time? Can affective changes, in the sense of coping with stress, be detected earlier than cognitive changes, which are a direct consequence of the brain disease?

4   When the disease is actually diagnosed, what role do denial and avoidance of the disease play as part of a natural defence mechanism to combat the psychological pain of person and family? Does an earlier experience of (unresolved) psychological pain produce stronger denial and avoidance, making prompt diagnosis (and hence the commencement of interventions) almost an impossibility?

5   Is it possible to predict the way in which person and family cope with dementia from knowledge of their premorbid coping strategies and personality structure? If so, is it then possible to predict the course of the (expected) problems in dealing with dementia? And is it then possible to differentiate more closely between successful interventions? What impact does the way in which both 'parties' are (have been) attached in their relationship have on their contact and interaction?

6   What types of intervention are most adequate or successful with which family members experiencing the burden of bearing in which phase of the disease? For whom and in what stage of the disease do, for instance, practical help, emotional help, psychological education or a combination of these provide assistance? Does the success of combined support such as this change during the course of the disease?

increasingly mentally absent.' There is good reason for his referring to a 'process of bereavement' and to 'slowly saying goodbye'. This makes it quite clear that it is all about grieving behaviour. Buijssen quotes Kapust (1982) who describes this situation as a 'never-ending funeral'. In 1984, a book with a similar title was published by Ria van Boheemen-Walhain in the Netherlands: *Langzaam apcheid nemen. Het relaas van een verwerkingsproces* [Slowly saying goodbye. An account of dealing with it]. Buijssen also mentions a number of factors that make the grieving process with dementia particularly hard, including 'the lack of formalised rituals for saying goodbye'. He refers to Lezak (1978) who points out that 'although the person with dementia is changing beyond all recognition, the partner is not able to say goodbye properly as the changes are not recognised or identified by society as loss'. Cuijpers (1999) also states that 'carers often feel that they are already losing the person'. Because these feelings are very similar to what people go through when they have lost a loved one through death, they are often referred to as a form of 'anticipatory grieving' (van der Ven and Hectors 1983).

'Missing persons'

It has been shown from clinical experience as well as research that families of persons with dementia who do not receive practical assistance, support and guidance, remain both physically and psychologically vulnerable for a long time (van der Erf and de Jong 1993; Pot 1996). This is partly to do with the fact that the family is having to contend with a particularly complicated form of dealing with their loss, because the loss remained intangible for such a long time: as long as the person with dementia was still alive, the loss was not real. The loss of a partner or parent through dementia is usually a shocking event. It entails a grieving process in that the emotions felt are often very similar to those felt if a loved one goes missing indefinitely: without the proof of actual death, the loss is never finalized. At the very least, this gives rise to conflicting feelings. There is always hope, but feelings of fear and being unsafe continue to gnaw away. This increases the risk of pathology in handling the loss process and problems in dealing with the decline of the person with dementia (Miesen 1997a, 1998a).

The upshot of the above is that this is obviously a loss situation without identity and without status. This sheds a different light on the huge emotional burden experienced by family members caring for the person with dementia and on the fact that they sometimes may undergo a pathological grieving process. Primary carers not only have to contend with a continuous accumulation of all sorts of practical problems, but in particular, they also have to endure an emotional separation. If the person with dementia is then admitted to full-time care, the carers then also undergo a physical separation from the loved one. Only once the person with dementia has died will the emotional separation become concrete. Living together with a dementing partner means that you may well be 'together' under the same roof, but you are nevertheless separated from each other. It is evident that no matter how firmly attached the couple may be, they will grow apart from each other in such a situation. The likelihood that the couple will (be able to) express their feelings to each other is slim. In this respect, it can be seen that primary carers are often not only in a desperate situation for a long time, but also sooner or later start to long for the death of the person with dementia. This means the family situation is awash with chronic, vague, confusing and intimidating feelings.

It is no simple task for the healthy partner to respond to the attachment behaviour of the person with dementia. To preserve their 'emotional well-being', the partner has to keep their distance. They have to withdraw themselves emotionally as it were, whereas the person with dementia is increasingly often demanding the opposite of them – proximity. This means that the person with dementia is frequently less able to 'give back', which in turn upsets the balance in the relationship. In short, it involves dealing with a complicated process of grief caused by the intangible nature of the loss as the person with dementia is still living. The family has to retain its distance in order to meet the need for proximity. 'It can be seen from experience that the easier it is to keep a distance (you have to), the more the partner is able as it were to adopt another role for the person with dementia, i.e. as a person with dementia' (Miesen 1998a).

Pathological grief

When is a grieving process considered to be extremely problematic or pathological? In general, this applies in any of the following three conditions (Van den Bout and Kleber 1994):

1   If there is no grieving behaviour;
2   If grieving behaviour is delayed;
3   If grieving behaviour becomes chronic.

If someone acts as if nothing has happened, does not react until a later point in time or stays permanently grieving, one of the following factors is involved:

* the intensity of the emotional bond with the person before they become ill – in particular if there is ambivalence, too strong a dependence or exclusivity within the relationship
* the personality of the carer and his or her own individual style of care and coping (Ingebretsen and Solem 1997)
* the attachment history of both 'parties' (Ingebretsen and Solem 1998)
* the presence of old traumas or unresolved conflicts
* the perceptibility or concreteness of the loss.

This is also shown in an exploratory study of response to separation and coping strategies of partners of persons with dementia (de Groot 1996; de Groot *et al.* 1999). By comparing the feeling of missing to a specific circumstance of loss, it can be seen that pathological grief can occur when people are (continuously) living with a loved one who is suffering from dementia. While missing the person, the family is permanently looking for concrete proof or a sign that someone has actually died, however this may be. It seems to be emotionally unbearable to have to keep living with the uncertainty of not knowing what has happened. A proof of death or permanent separation offers at least some chance for the process of grieving to kick in. With dementia, there is no tangible reason for the feeling of loss. This is a problem often underestimated by other members of the family and professional caregivers. In practice, the fact that there is no tangible reason for grief leads to long-term feelings of hope and guilt, despite going against one's own better judgement. Letting go of the hope that the person with dementia will improve often feels like deceiving the other 'party', or trying to bury them alive. On many an occasion, the primary carer of a person with dementia wishes that this person would die. This wish is understandable given that death brings about an end to the suffering of the person with dementia or with the idea that death will bring about an end to one's own suffering. But this wish can mainly be understood from the point of view of wanting clarity in this incredible situation of loss, in which the family slowly has to say goodbye to a loved one who is still there. This not only makes it more difficult to accept the intangible loss of the partner, but also affects his or her ability to deal with the situation. If friends and acquaintances also do not see what is happening to the partner in such a situation, there tends to be an ongoing sense of emotional isolation, with all the respective consequences, such as depression, psychological and physical vulnerability, stress and burn-out.

In this respect, professional caregivers have the task of supporting the primary carers' ability to bear, by helping them slowly separate themselves from the person with dementia. This detachment process is all the more difficult given the point of view that the loss will remain indefinite for as long as the other one is still alive. The sorrow suffered by a family could be lessened if they learned to see that persons with dementia are indeed very much aware of their situation, that this makes them just as anxious or prompts other (normal) feelings and that they also feel increasingly isolated and have a need for safety. This would encourage empathy and understanding, as these feelings are 'familiar' to them. This realization can prevent a pathological grieving process or turn it into 'healthy' grief. By realizing that the person with dementia feels equally deserted and what is more has similar feelings, it is possible to keep the communication going for longer and encourage a more or less mutual grieving process.

To reach this goal, professional caregivers should always draw up three care plans: one for the person with dementia, one for the primary carer or partner and one for both parties. Other factors influencing the way in which grief is dealt with on both sides include skills in dealing with past problems, personality structure and unresolved conflicts. Knowledge about these factors will make it easier to prepare the care plans. Family members are generally fairly reticent about talking about their own experiences of loss and ways of dealing with problems if they are unable to see that they themselves require assistance in this respect. Professional caregivers should be trained to work out the stage of grief of the primary carers by looking at their behaviour. They should at any rate be able to identify the first contours of potential pathology and navigate a complicated grieving process along the right channel. They should be able to make the family aware of the complicated nature of their emotional situation and teach them not to underestimate this at any cost.

Implications for psychological interventions

Researchers are nowadays in agreement about the most suitable method for studying the significance of the behaviour of the elderly in general. In psychogerontology, longitudinal research is preferred to transverse research. In my opinion, this is also the case when studying and understanding the behaviour of older persons with dementia and their families. Longitudinal study in specific terms means continuity of the individual research or support situation. One consequence of this is, for example, that caregivers should have knowledge about the entire course of the disease and implications of this catastrophe for the person with dementia and his family. This knowledge is needed at the very onset of the process in order to be able to anticipate the next stage. It also means that later on in the process caregivers will have access to prior knowledge. This is of utmost importance in the final stages of the disease. Without this knowledge, it is particularly difficult to be able to interpret the behaviour of persons with dementia and their families and place it in the right context. In theory, once the diagnosis is made, one needs to strike the right balance between psychological education, counselling, medication and day care. As the latter two interventions fall outside the scope of this chapter, I would like to focus on psychological education and psychotherapy.

We know we can understand the experiences of the person with dementia and his family using psychological models, such as theories on attachment, psychological trauma, stress and coping. An important consequence of this is that all kinds of behaviour of the person, such as fear, restlessness, sorrow, aggression, inactivity, 'claiming' behaviour, shouting and screaming, can be regarded as a response to stress, awareness of loss or feeling unsafe, as attachment behaviour or as forms of coping. On this basis, they are more accessible to change and therapy. Therefore, treating and supporting persons with dementia and their families require continuity. The following points should therefore be applied, just as when dealing with trauma:

1 The catastrophe should be identified.
2 The nature and extent of this catastrophe should be charted.
3 Consideration should be given to the emotional handling or impact of the catastrophe.
4 Individual differences in withstanding the catastrophe should be analysed.
5 Information should be given about what help is available and where it can be sought.
6 Assistance should be given to get life back into order once the catastrophe is (definitively) over.

Translated into terms of dementia: What does dementia mean? What exactly is involved? What is the situation now? Why is it all too much for most of the persons? Who can be approached for assistance? How to proceed once the person with dementia has died (Van Erp *et al.* 1999)?

In general terms, the person and family are confronted with a number of the same tasks or problems in the course of the disease, but the way in which they deal with them differs (Droës 1991). In other words, the way in which each phase of dementia manifests itself is different for everyone. The same problems are encountered, but the way in which they become apparent to each person differs.

Persons with dementia, in particular with Alzheimer's disease, are usually aware that something is not right and that they are no longer functioning properly. This is because their reaction to the abnormal state of their brain is normal. It would be more unusual if they continued behaving as if nothing were wrong. The last is possible, as we have already seen, with frontal lesions or if old conflicts have not been resolved. In the latter case, the person with dementia will tend to either overreact or underreact if the unresolved conflict is triggered. This often leads to extreme avoidance or denial, with all the related practical consequences.

Rapid help and support are essential, especially given the phenomenon of the awareness of the person with dementia and the fact that for the family the loss is not definitive or concrete for a long period of time. Accounting for the person's awareness context means that they can be taken seriously as people who can and often want to be informed of their disease, how it will progress and the possible sources of help or intervention. Both phenomena also facilitate interventions beyond day care or admittance to a care home. The resulting impact is that both 'parties' – the person with dementia and his family – realize at an earlier stage where and when things are going wrong or what is threatening to undermine their 'ability to bear'. This means that they can ask for help at an earlier stage and call upon services such as day care or short-term admittance to a care facility.

A knock-on effect of these interventions is that communication between both 'parties' is stimulated – however difficult it may be – and that emotional isolation is put off for as long as possible. Partners who recognize the awareness and perception of a person with dementia will treat them more as an 'emotional equal' despite cognitive decline. They will therefore be more inclined to acknowledge the person's feelings and take them into consideration. This reduces the chance of the person with dementia feeling isolated at an early stage. Thus there is also less chance that partners will undergo a complicated grieving process. Expressed in terms of awareness, communication between the two 'parties' is better in an open awareness context than in a closed awareness context. With an open awareness context, it is possible for persons with dementia to discuss the fact that a sort of catastrophe has occurred in their lives with the advent of this disease, without them being (or having been) immediately aware of it – and the fact that the full extent of it is only gradually dawning on them – and the fact that the catastrophe is in the meantime presenting them with a host of practical, emotional and relationship problems that they have to relearn to manage, but with increasingly fewer cognitive skills. They are after all experiencing ongoing (psycho)trauma (i.e. powerlessness, upheaval and disruption) and they are perfectly aware of this, even without being able to point out or name the stressor.

The same more or less applies to the direct family members. But for them, the catastrophe remains indefinite for as long as the person with dementia is still alive. This makes it particularly difficult for families to deal with this disease. If, as stated before, unresolved conflicts again come to the surface in such a difficult situation, this draws heavily on the core personality structure of both parties.

Psychotherapy and psychological education

In a recent literature review of psychotherapy in dementia, Cheston (1998: 199–200) emphasized that: 'good dementia care must inevitably be psychotherapeutic in the sense of addressing emotional as well as physical needs', and he referred to three core aspects:

> helping the person with dementia to grieve for the multiple losses that they have suffered and which are yet to come; bearing witness to this process; and attending to the context of care. . . . Although formal psychotherapeutic work with individuals and in groups can be extremely useful, counselling skills can also be used as part of a general care plan. In many ways it is more important to think in terms of being psychotherapeutic in dementia care, rather than in terms of doing psychotherapy with dementia sufferers.

Cheston therefore places the disease in a realistic perspective in which the awareness and perception of the person with dementia are taken seriously. He also confirms the need for continuity in the care provided for person and family: 'There is a much greater need for the therapist to be visibly and reliably present on a long-term basis.' In passing, he releases the old age psychiatry (multidisciplinary) specialist from the restrictive bonds of the care facility, and declares that mediation therapy is an essential instrument with which to influence behaviour.

Despite the lack of scientific proof, there are numerous examples of successful psychotherapy and counselling with dementia sufferers from all the main psychotherapeutic schools of thought, according to Cheston (1998). He argues that 'each interaction between carer and dementia sufferer is a potential opportunity in which counselling techniques can be used to help the dementia sufferer to make sense of their experiences', and that 'dementia must be understood as a personal tragedy – it is unacceptable that its most immediate victims should so often have to struggle unheard and unheeded against personal disintegration and social isolation'. In the earlier words of Sutton and Cheston (1997): 'We cannot make this future "better" in the sense of taking this pain away – we can only try and listen and to help the person feel that they have been heard.'

From a psychosocial point of view, dementia involves the following aspects:

> helping the person to grieve, the need to listen or to bear witness, and managing the context of the work. . . . Incorporating psychotherapeutic ideas into dementia care involves listening to the process of having dementia, to the person's fears and their losses, and to their frustrations and fears about the future.
>
> (Cheston 1998: 206)

Before this, Gabbard (1994) was already convinced of the value of psycho-therapy for people with organic cerebral deficits. He argued in favour of having 'a feel' for and respecting the person with dementia's need to deny and avoid. He called this way of dealing with the reality of the deficit 'mourning' and found psychological education to be essential, especially at the beginning of therapy. He also emphasized the need for counselling couples together, as well as individual psychodynamic psychotherapy with the person with dementia.

Gabbard took the opposite of a nihilistic view of psychotherapy in treating dementia, as can be seen from his psychodynamic perspective that 'there is no such thing as an untreatable dementia. . . . much can be done to help these persons with dementia and their families deal with Alzheimer's on a daily basis'. He went on to formulate various useful principles or objectives which surprisingly are on very similar lines to the views of Verwoerdt (1981):

> Attend to self-esteem issues, assess characteristic defence mechanisms and help the person with dementia use them constructively, find ways to

replace defective ego functions and cognitive limitations, assist family members in developing new ways of relatedness that 'shore' up the person with dementia's self-esteem by decreasing negative interactions.

(Gabbard 1994: 712–13)

The awareness context of the 'parties' involved affects the way in which one copes with the situation of being terminally ill. The awareness context is also crucial for mutual communication. If, for whatever reason, there are contexts of awareness that do not mesh well with each other, then those involved become isolated, often with tragic consequences. For both the person with dementia and the family, psychological education appears to be an accepted and proven intervention for dealing with (chronic) diseases such as heart disease and cancer (Smith and Birchwood 1987; Abramowitz and Coursey 1989). Information on the disease and its effects impacts on the eventual process of dealing with it, for example, whether or not there is post-traumatic stress disorder (Solomon and Draine 1995). That is the very intention behind the Alzheimer café (Miesen 1998a; Miesen and Kuypers 1998; Threels 2003) and Alzheimer couple counselling (Huybrechtse and Kouwenhoven 2000), together with individual therapeutic sessions with persons with dementia. Whether or not this sort of intervention falls within the scope of formal psychotherapy is of lesser importance. 'In many ways it is more important to think in terms of being psychotherapeutic in dementia care, rather than in terms of doing (author: i.e. formal) psychotherapy with dementia sufferers' (Cheston 1998).

Psychosocial interventions in general

Psychological interventions in the field of dementia should always test against ongoing changes in the (residual) cognitive skills of the person with dementia. Whether it is (neuro)psychological or perception-oriented research (Diesfeldt 1995; Kok 1995; Sipsma 1995; Soudijn 1995; Derix 1996), the very fact of carrying out a study at all is regarded as an intervention: analysis of the ability to bear (*Zorgkompas* 1995); systems therapy (Engel 1998); psychodynamic psychotherapy (Jacobs 1995); structured lifereview (Smits 1996); behaviour therapy (van Grinsven 1996); psychological education or information (Threels 2003); couple counselling (Huybrechtse and Kouwenhoven 2000); psycho-motor therapy (Droës 1991); Pesso's psychomotor psychotherapy (Flapper 1998); family discussion groups (Cuijpers 1993, 1999); validation-related coping, reminiscence or individual and group reality orientation training (Verdult 1995; Ekkerink 1997); music therapy (van Nieuwenhuijzen and Broersen 1997); mediation therapy (Hamer 1997); guiding or structuring coping (Ekkerink 1997); Snoezelen sensory therapy (Kragt and Holtkamp 1996; Achterberg, Kok and Salentijn 1997); normalized living (Hoen 1998); warm care (Houweling 1987).

These interventions ensure that the world experienced by the person with dementia and his family is always understood. Although these interventions are defined differently, it is still possible to see general basic criteria: the essential aim is to maintain autonomy, control, confidence/familiarity, safety and individuality.

The view put forward by such authors as Wragg and Jeste (1989), Lewis (1991), Weiner (1991) and Gabbard (1994) shows a gradual development towards a more psychodynamic perspective that became generally accepted in the Netherlands at the end of the 1980s, also reflected in research carried out by Miesen (1990), Droës (1991), Vernooij-Dassen (1993) and Van der Plaats (1994). Such a perspective is also extremely important for recognizing the onset of dementia: before identifying cognitive changes, it is possible to diagnose (subtle) affective ones that may or may not have been perceived by the person with dementia. Once the cognitive changes can be observed and measured, the process may already have been going on for a while. Clarification is still required with respect to the crucial role of denial and avoidance as a natural defence mechanism to combat psychological distress, not just with the person with dementia but also the family; and above all, how this influences the actual timing of diagnosis. Because you can only take action once you know what is going on and how far it has gone, and make it clear that you need help and assistance. In this respect, it is an important challenge now for psychogerontologists 'to elaborate psychological and social psychological frameworks and apply them to three phenomena associated with dementia – depression, delusions and denial' (Bender and Cheston 1997). Only then can an important barrier to early diagnosis be removed, openness about the diagnosis can generally be beneficial, and there can be more continuity in the provision of psychosocial support. The psychologist is then more than amply resourced to provide support and assistance to deal with grief, reduce fear of separation of both parties and develop programmes to prevent the avoidance of mutual and social contacts. A precondition, however, is that psychologists take advantage of these resources, use their own expertise and do not let themselves be manipulated by erring towards a medical-biological perspective of dementia. Perception-oriented interventions with older persons with dementia belong firmly to the domain of the psychogerontologist (Cheston and Bender 1999; Miesen 2000).

Epilogue

I am now well over 50 years of age. I have lived and learned to leave most of my projections behind. I am well aware of what remains and have them reasonably under control. What I think, say, feel or do reflects primarily who I am (who I have become). Whether it is favourable or unfavourable, pleasant or unpleasant for others, makes little difference. For instance, events that once made an impression on me, but whose meaning I did not yet appreciate, now years later appear to have influenced my work as a clinical psychogerontologist, and especially how I relate to this as a person.

Thirty years ago, in 1969, I was working as an intern in a combined care facility. He was 75 and I was 22. I can still see him sitting in front of me, the other side of my desk. After undergoing an operation in hospital, he was temporarily admitted to a somatic ward. The psychologist at the care home, my supervisor, told me to assess him, so I duly arranged the session via the nursing staff. I can no longer remember whether I was meant to ask specific questions or whether the point was just to practise carrying out a psychological investigation.

At my request, the man in front of me immediately took the initiative himself. He wanted to talk to me and initially did not have the remotest interest in what my objectives were. I cannot remember his exact words, but I can remember the gist of what he said to me. The long and short of it was that he had no objection to cooperating with my investigation, provided I could satisfactorily explain to him why I wanted to assess him, what my personal views about it were and why exactly I wanted to (go on and) do this sort of work.

I found his questions at the time fairly shocking. Yes, what was the point of my knowledge and skills? What did I want from my profession and why? What were my views on life? Why did I want to become a psychogerontologist? Of course I gave him far from conclusive or definitive answers. After my initial confusion, I tried, I think, to answer his questions candidly. I floundered around for words and stammered my response – and he must have found this moving or charming. Perhaps it gave him a feeling of superiority or control. I don't know. In any case, he gave me permission in the end to investigate him. Talk about autonomy.

When I look back at this incident now, in retrospect, and interpret what it means, it is crystal clear to me that mastering the technology or skills and having the knowledge alone are not enough to be able to satisfactorily exercise the profession of a psychologist for the elderly. What is needed in the first place is purely, I would almost say 'primitively', perceiving what the clients themselves have to say, without immediately digging out all kinds of complex measuring instruments. In the second place, it is necessary to constantly keep in contact with yourself and work out what your motives are; and to have a clear message or vision, and to dare to face it and formulate it. You need to work out what fires and inspires you in the work you do. In other words, when working with persons with dementia, as a psychologist you should have a psychology of (or at least a psychological theory about) old age and dementia from which you derive your motivation for practising the profession and apply these to work out the various aspects of the issue you will be focusing on in your work, how you should do this and which (measuring) tools and methods you should use. Only then can you bear witness to and keep witnessing someone's life and struggle with existence while their brains are increasingly deserting them (Warners 1998). Feelings, after all, are ageless. And, last but not least, we can all bear witness to the distress that dementia causes.

References

Abramowitz, I. and Coursey, R. (1989) 'Impact of an educational support group on family participants who take care of their schizophrenic relatives', *Journal of Consulting and Clinical Psychology* 57: 232–6.

Achterberg, I., Kok, W. and Salentijn, C. (1997) ' "Snoezelen": a new way of communicating with the severely demented elderly', in B.M.L. Miesen and G.M.M. Jones (eds) *Care-giving in Dementia: Research and Applications*, vol. 2, London: Routledge, 119–26.

Amelsvoort-Jones, G.M.M. van (1985) 'Validation therapy: a companion to reality orientation', *The Canadian Nurse* March: 20–23.

American Psychiatric Association (APA) (1994) *Diagnostische Criteria van de DSM-IV. Beknopte handleiding*, trans. G.A.S. Koster van Groos, Lisse: Swetz and Zeitlinger.

Anifantakis, H. and Tyler, J. (1991) *The Diminished Mind*. New York: McGraw-Hill.

Bender, M. and Cheston, R. (1997) 'Inhabitants of a lost kingdom: a model of the subjective experiences of dementia', *Ageing and Society* 17: 513–32.

Boheemen-Walhain, R. van (1984) *Langzaam apcheid nemen. Het relaas van een verwer-kingsproces*, Deventer: Van Loghum Slaterus.

Bout, J. van den and Kleber, R. (1994) *Omgaan met verlies en geweld. Een leidraad voor rouw en traumaverwerking*, Utrecht/Antwerp: Kosmos-Z&K.

Bowlby, J. (1969) *Attachment and Loss. Vol. 1: Attachment*, London: Hogarth Press.

—— (1973) *Attachment and Loss. Vol. 2: Separation: Anxiety and Anger*, London: Hogarth Press.

—— (1980) *Attachment and Loss. Vol. 3: Loss: Sadness and Depression*, London: Hogarth Press/New York: Basic Books.

Bretherton, I. (1990) 'Open communication and internal working models: their role in the development of attachment relationships', in R.A. Thompson (ed.) *Socio-emotional Development. Nebraska Symposium of Motivation*. Lincoln: University Of Nebraska Press, pp. 57–113.

Brugman, G. and de Groot, F. (1997) 'Coping in levensloopperspectief. Buigen of barsten?', in M. Allewijn, F. de Groot, C. Hertogh, B. Miesen and I. Warners (eds) Houten: Bohn Stafleu van Loghum.

Buijssen, H. (1998) 'Rouw bij ouderen' in J. van den Bout (ed.) *Behandelings-strategieen bij gecompliceerde rouw en verliesverwerking*, Houten: Bohn Stafleu van Loghum, pp. 136–43.

Cheston, R. (1998) 'Psychotherapeutic work with dementia sufferers', *Journal of Social Work Practice* 12, 2: 199–207.

Cheston, R. and Bender, M. (1999) *Understanding Dementia. The Man with the Worried Eyes*, London: Jessica Kingsley.

Claus, H. (1989) 'Hoe kom ik nou aan zoiets? Een verkennend onderzoek naar de beleving van beginnende dementering', doctoral thesis, Leiden.

Cotrell, V. and Schultz, R. (1993) 'The perspective of the person with dementia with Alzheimer's disease: a neglected dimension of dementia research', *The Gerontologist* 33, 2: 205–11.

Cuijpers, P. (1993) 'De werking van ondersteuningsgroepen voor centraal verzorgenden van dementerende ouderen', thesis, KU Nijmegen.

Cuijpers, P. (1999) 'Familie en naasten. Verwantschap onder druk', in M. Allewijn, F. de Groot, C. Hertogh, B. Miesen and M. van Wetten (eds) *Leidraad Psychogeriatrie A5*, Houten: Bohn Stafleu van Loghum.

DeBettignies, B.M., Mahurin, R.K. and Pirozzolo, F.J. (1990) 'Insight for impairment in independent living skills in Alzheimer's disease and multi-infarct dementia', *J. of Clin. and Exp. Neuropsychiatry* 12: 355–63.

Derix, M. (1996) 'Onderzoek naar geheugenstoornissen. Even vergeten of niet meer weten', in M. Allewijn, C. Hertogh, B. Miesen and I. Warners (eds) *Leidraad Psychogeriatrie B3*, Houten: Bohn Stafleu Van Loghum.

Diesfeldt, H. (1995) 'Onderzoek van taalstoornissen. Een goed verstaander', in M. Allewijn, F. Gilson, H. Houweling, B. Miesen and I. Warners (eds) *Leidraad Psychogeriatrie B1*, Houten: Bohn Stafleu Van Loghum.

Droës, R.M. (1991) 'In beweging: over psychosociale hulpverlening aan demente ouderen', dissertation, Nijkerk: Intro.

Droës, R.M. (1997) 'Psychosocial treatment for demented persons with dementia; methods and effects', in B. Miesen and G. Jones (eds) *Care-giving in Dementia: Research and Applications*, vol. 2, London: Routledge.

Droës, R.M. (1998) 'Omgaan met de gevolgen van dementie. Psychosociale begeleiding en behandeling', *Neuropraxis* 2: 146–53.

Droës, R.M., van Tilburg, W., Jonker, C., Scheltens, Ph. and Slaets, J.P.J. (1999) 'Klinisch beleid bij dementie', in R.C. van der Mast and J.P.J. Slaets (eds) *Behandelingsstrategieën bij organisch psychiatrische stoornissen*, Houten: Bohn Stafleu van Loghum.

Duijnstee, M. (1992) 'De Belasting van familieleden van dementerenden', thesis, Nijkerk: Intro.

Ekkerink, J. (1997) 'Benaderingswijzen bij dementie', in M. Allewijn, F. de Groot, C. Hertogh, B. Miesen and H.J. Warners (eds) *Leidraad Psychogeriatrie B4*, Houten: Bohn Stafleu Van Loghum.

Engel, M. (1998) 'Systeemtherapie. Ontmoetingen vroeger en nu', in M. Allewijn, F. de Groot, C. Hertogh, B. Miesen and I. Warners (eds) *Leidraad Psychogeriatrie B5*, Houten: Bohn Stafleu Van Loghum.

Engelen, G.J.J.A. and Peeters, M.S.H. (1984) 'Dementie', in H.P.J. Buijssen and J.J.L. Derksen *Psychologische hulpverlening aan ouderen. Diagnostiek- Therapie- Preventie*, Nijkerk: Intro.

Erf, T. van der and Jong, E. de (1993) 'Overlijden. De impact van dementie op de familieleden', doctoral thesis, RU Leiden.

Erp, A. van, Miesen, B. and Spermon, M. (1999) *Leven met dementie*, Hilversum: Teleac/NOT.

Flapper, B. (1997) 'Wankelend onder een niet begrepen last', doctoral thesis, VU Amsterdam.

—— (1998) 'Dementie, Gehechtheid en Pesso's Psychomotore Psychotherapie', doctoral thesis, VU Amsterdam.

Gabbard, G.O. (1994) 'Dementia and other cognitive disorders', in G.O. Gabbard *Psychodynamic Psychiatry in Clinical Practice*, Washington, DC: American Psychiatric Press.

Glaser, B.G. and Strauss, A.L. (1965) *Awareness of Dying*, New York: Aldine.

Goldstein, K. (1952) 'The effect of brain damage on the personality', *Psychiatry* 15: 245–60.

Gorman, M. (1993) 'The phenomenology of early stage Alzheimer's and related disorders' paper presented at the Fifteenth International Congress of Gerontology, Budapest.

Grattan, L.M., Eslinger, P.J., Mattson, K.E., Rigamonti, D. and Price, T. (1994) 'Altered social self-awareness: empirical evidence for frontal lobe specialization for social self-knowledge' *Neurology* 44, suppl. 2: A292.

Grinsven, J. van (1996) 'Gedragstherapie. Oefening baart kunst', in M. Allewijn, C. Hertogh, B. Miesen and I. Warners (eds) *Leidraad Psychogeriatrie B3*, Houten: Bohn Stafleu Van Loghum.

Groot, F. de (1996) 'Dementie en Gehechtheid. Separatiereacties bij partners van dementerenden', doctoral thesis, RU Leiden.

Groot, F. de, Miesen, B. and Kerkhof, A. (1999) *'De Pijnlijke Situatie'. Beschrijving van een explorerend onderzoek naar emoties en interacties bij echtparen van wie een van de partners aan dementie lijdt*, doctoral thesis, RU Leiden.

Hagberg, B. (1997) 'The dementias in a psychodynamic perspective', in B.M.L. Miesen and G.G.M. Jones (eds) *Care-giving in Dementia: Research and Applications*, vol. 2, London/New York: Routledge.

Hamer, T. (1997) 'Mediatietherapie. De beste stuurlui staan aan wal', in M. Allewijn, F. de Groot, C. Hertogh, B. Miesen and H.J. Warners (eds) *Leidraad Psychogeriatrie B4*, Houten: Bohn Stafleu Van Loghum.

Haussman, C. (1992) 'Dynamic psychotherapy with elderly demented person with dementia', in G.M.M. Jones and B.M.L. Miesen (eds) *Care-giving in Dementia: Research and Applications*, vol. 1, London/New York: Tavistock/Routledge.

Hoen, M. (1998) 'Genormaliseerd wonen. Het alledaagse als therapie', in M. Allewijn, F. de Groot, C. Hertogh, B. Miesen and I. Warners (eds) *Leidraad Psychogeriatrie B5*, Houten: Bohn Stafleu Van Loghum.

Horn, M. de (1999) 'Besefscontext bij dementie. Ontwikkeling van een methode/procedure om besef te meten in het beloop van de ziekte', doctoral thesis, RU Leiden.

Houweling, H. (1987) 'Warme Zorg', *Ts. BKZ* 2: p. 39–42.

Huybrechtse, P. and Kouwenhoven, C. (2000) 'Coping met dementie. Onderzoek naar het effect van echtpaarcounseling bij patiënt en partner', doctoral thesis, RU Leiden.

Ingebretsen, R. and Solem, P.E. (1997) 'Caring for a dementing spouse. Attachment, loss and relationship-focused coping', in B.M.L. Miesen and G.G.M. Jones (eds) *Care-giving in Dementia: Research and Applications*, vol. 2, London New York: Routledge.

—— (1998) 'Spouses of persons with dementia: attachment, loss and coping', *Norwegian J. of Epidemiology* 2: 149–56.

Jacobs, M. (1995) 'Psychodynamische psychotherapie', in M. Allewijn, F. Gilson, H. Houweling, B. Miesen and I. Warners (eds) *Leidraad Psychogeriatrie B2*. Houten: Bohn Stafleu Van Loghum.

Jones, G. (1988) 'Validation therapy. Een andere benadering voor de psychogeriatrische bewoner', *Tijdschrift voor verzorgenden*, 94–9.

Jones, G.M.M. and Miesen, B.M.L. (eds) (1992) *Care-giving in Dementia: Research and Applications*, vol. 1, London/New York: Tavistock/Routledge.

Kapust, L.R. (1982) 'Living with dementia: the ongoing funeral', *Social Work in Health Care* 7: 79–91.

Kok, R. (1995) 'Diagnostiek van stemmingsstoornissen. Meetinstrumenten voor depressieve verschijnselen', in M. Allewijn, F. Gilson, H. Houweling, B. Miesen and I. Warners (eds) *Leidraad Psychogeriatrie B2*, Houten: Bohn Stafleu Van Loghum.

Kragt, K. and Holtkamp, C. (1996) 'Het effect van snoezelen op het welbevinden van demente ouderen', doctoral thesis, RU Limburg.

Lewis, L. (1986) 'Individual psychotherapy with person with dementia having combined psychological and neurological disorders', *Bull Menninger Clin.* 50: 75–87.

—— (1991) 'The role of psychological factors in disordered awareness', in G.P. Prigatano and D.L. Schachter (eds) *Awareness of Deficit After Brain Injury: Clinical and Theoretical Issues*, New York: Oxford University Press.

Lezak, M.D. (1978) 'Living with characterologically altered brain injured person with dementia', *Journal of Clinical Psychiatry* 39: 592–7.

Loo, E. van (1988) 'Over de beleving van dementie', doctoral thesis, RU Utrecht.

Mahy, M. (1987) *Memory*, London: J.M. Dent.

McGowin, D.F. (1993) *Living in the Labyrinth*, New York: Dell.

Miesen, B. (1985a) 'Meaning and function of the remembered parents in normal and abnormal old age', paper presented at the Thirteenth International Congress of Gerontology, New York.

—— (ed.) (1985b) *Als ik dat geweten had. Thema's in de omgang met dementerende ouderen. Een werkboek*, Deventer: Van Loghum Slaterus.

—— (1990) 'Gehechtheid en Dementie. Ouders in de beleving van dementerende ouderen', dissertation, Almere/Nijkerk: Versluijs/Intro.

—— (1992a) 'Attachment theory and dementia', in G.M.M. Jones and B.M.L. Miesen (eds) *Care-giving in Dementia: Research and Applications*, vol. 1. London/New York: Tavistock/Routledge.

—— (1992b) 'Care-giving in dementia: review and perspectives', in G.M.M. Jones and B.M.L. Miesen (eds) *Care-giving in Dementia: Research and Applications*, vol. 1, London/New York: Tavistock/Routledge.

—— (1993a) 'Alzheimer's disease, the phenomenon of parent-fixation and Bowlby's attachment theory', *Int. J. of Geriatric Psychiatry* 8, 2: 147–53.

—— (1993b) *Dementie dichterbij. Een handreiking aan verzorgenden*, Houten: Bohn Stafleu van Loghum.

—— (1997a) 'Awareness in dementia person with dementia and family grieving. A practical perspective', in B.M.L. Miesen and G.G.M. Jones (eds) *Care-giving in Dementia: Research and Applications*, vol. 2, London/New York: Routledge.

—— (1997b) 'Care-giving in dementia: the challenge of attachment', in B.M.L. Miesen and G.M.M. Jones (eds) *Care-giving in Dementia: Research and Applications*, vol. 2, London: Routledge.

—— (1998a) *Dement: zo gek nog niet. Kleine psychologie van dementie*, Utrecht/Houten: Kosmos-Z&K Uitgevers/Bohn Stafleu Van Loghum.

—— (1998b) 'Attachment behaviour in dementia: parent-orientation and parent-fixation (POPFiD) theory', in G.H. Pollock and S.I. Greenspan (eds) *The Course of Life*, vol. VII, New York: International Universities Press.

—— (1999) *Dementia in Close-up. Understanding and Caring for Persons with Dementia*. London/New York: Routledge.

—— (2000) 'Gehechtheid by dementie: van meet of aan geboader?', in M. Allewijn, F. de Groot, C. Hertogh, B. Miesen and H.J. Warners (eds) *Leidraad Psychogeriatrie C2*, Houten: Bohn Stafleu Van Loghum.

Miesen, B.M.L. and Jones, G.M.M. (eds) (1997) *Care-giving in Dementia: Research and Applications*, vol. 2, London: Routledge.

—— (1999) 'Psychisch leed dat bij dementie weer boven komt. Van een nieuw naar een oud trauma?', in L. Hunt, M. Marshall and C. Rowlings (eds) *Trauma's uit het verleden. Therapeutisch werk met ouderen in Europees perspectief*, Houten: Bohn Stafleu van Loghum.

Miesen, B. and Kuypers, N. (1998) 'Alzheimer Café: educatie en therapie', in P.W. Huijbers and M.M. van Santvoort (eds) *Nationaal Gerontologie Congres Ouder Worden '98*, Utrecht: NIG, 37.141.

Munnichs, J.M.A. (1998) *Sterven. Beleving, verwerking, begeleiding*, Houten: Bohn Stafleu Van Loghum.

Nies, H.L.G.R. (1989) 'De veelzijdigheid van het ouder worden', in Nies *et al. Handboek ouder worden*, Houten: Bohn Stafleu van Loghum.

Nieuwenhuyzen, N. van and Broersen, M. (1997) 'Muziektherapie. Als woorden tekort schieten', in M. Allewijn, F. de Groot, C. Hertogh, B. Miesen and I. Warners (eds) *Leidraad Psychogeriatrie B4*, Houten: Bohn Stafleu Van Loghum.

Phinney, A. (1998) 'Living with dementia', *Journal of Gerontological Nursing* 24, 6: 8–15.

Plaats, J.J. van der (1994) 'Geriatrie: een spel van evenwicht', dissertation, Assen: van Gorcum.

Pot, A.M. (1996) *Care-givers Perspectives. A Longitudinal Study on the Psychological Distress of Informal Caregivers of Demented Elderly*, Enschede: Copyprint.

Prins, S. (1997) *Dubbel verlies*, Utrecht: Kosmos Z&K.

Reed, B.R., Jagust, W.J. and Coulter, L. (1993) 'Anosognosia in Alzheimer's disease: relationship to depression, cognitive function and cerebral perfusion', *J. of Clin. and Exp. Neuropsychology* 15: 231–44.

Seltzer, B., Vasterling, J.J., Hale, M.A. and Khurana, R. (1995) 'Unawareness of memory deficit in Alzheimer's disease: relation to mood and other disease variables', *Neuropsychiatry, Neuropsychology and Behavioral Neurology* 8: 176–81.

Sevush, S. and Leve, N. (1993) 'Denial of memory deficit in Alzheimer's disease', *American Journal of Psychiatry* 150: 748–51.

Sipsma, D. (1995) 'Psychogeriatrische diagnostiek. Een eigen doorschouwing', in M. Allewijn, F. Gilson, H. Houweling, B. Miesen and I. Warners (eds) *Leidraad Psychogeriatrie B1*, Houten: Bohn Stafleu Van Loghum.

Smith, J. and Birchwood, M. (1987) 'Specific and non specific educational intervention with families living with a schizophrenic relative', *Brit. J. of Psychiatry* 150: 645–52.

Smits, C. (1996) 'Life review. Verhalen van duizend dagen en nachten als therapie', in M. Allewijn, C. Hertogh, B. Miesen and I. Warners (eds) *Leidraad Psychogeriatrie B3*, Houten: Bohn Stafleu Van Loghum.

Solomon, K. (1992) 'Behavioral and psychotherapeutic interventions with persons with dementia in the long-term care institutions', in G.T. Grossberg and P. Szwabo (eds) *Problem Behavior in Long-term Care: Recognition, Diagnosis and Treatment*, New York: Springer.

Solomon, K. and Szwabo, P. (1992) 'Psychotherapy for persons with dementia', in J.E. Morley, R.M. Coe, R. Strong and G.T. Grossberg (eds) *Memory Function and Aging-related Disorders*, New York: Springer.

Solomon, P. and Draine, J. (1995) 'Subjective burden among family members of mentally ill adults: relation to stress, coping and adaptation', *American J. of Orthopsychiatry* 65: 419–27.

Soudijn, K. (1995) 'Diagnostiek. Wikken en wegen', in M. Allewijn, F. Gilson, H. Houweling, B. Miesen and I. Warners (eds) *Leidraad Psychogeriatrie B1*, Houten: Bohn Stafleu Van Loghum.

Sparks, N. (1996) *The Notebook*. New York: Warner.

Starkstein, S.E., Vasquez, S., Migliorelli, R., Teson, A., Sabe, L. and Leiguarda, R. (1995) 'A single-photon emission computed tomographic study of anosognosia in Alzheimer's disease', *Archives of Neurology* 62: 415–20.

Sutton, L. and Cheston, R. (1997) 'Rewriting the story of dementia: a narrative approach to psychotherapy with persons with dementia', in M. Marshall (ed.) *The Cutting Edge of Dementia*, London: Centre for Policy on Ageing.

Tainsh, S. and Hinshelwood, D. (1997) 'Practical management of frontal lobe dementia: institutional perspectives', in B.M.L. Miesen and G.M.M. Jones (eds) *Care-giving in Dementia: Research and Applications*, vol. 2, London: Routledge.

Teunisse, S. (1997) 'Clinimetrics in dementia', dissertation, Enschede: PrintPartners Ipskamp.

Teunisse, S., Walstra, G.J.M. and van Crevel, H. (1994) 'De ernst van dementie', in M.M.A. Derix, A. Hijdra and W.A. van Gool (eds) *Dementie: de stand van zaken*, Lisse: Swets and Zeitlinger.

Threels, R. (2003) 'Het Alzheimer Café. Onderzoek naar het effect van psycho-educatie bij patiënt en partner', doctoral thesis, RU Leiden.

Ven, L. van der and Hectors, R. (1983) 'Reflecties over de begeleiding van familieleden van dementerende bejaarden', *Ts. Voor Gerontologie and Geriatrie* 14, 4: 149–56.

Verdult, R. (1993) *Dement worden: een kindertijd in beeld. Belevingsgerichte begeleiding van dementerende ouderen*, Nijkerk: Intro.

—— (1995) 'Empathisch communiceren met ouderen. Gevoelens zijn altijd waar', in M. Allewijn, F. Gilson, H. Houweling, B. Miesen and I. Warners (eds) *Leidraad Psychogeriatrie B2*, Houten: Bohn Stafleu Van Loghum.

Vernooij-Dassen, M.J.F.J. (1993) 'Dementie en Thuiszorg. Een onderzoek naar determinanten van het competentiegevoel van centrale verzorgers en het effect van professionele interventie', dissertation, Lisse: Swets and Zeitlinger.

Verwoerdt, A. (1981) 'Individual psychotherapy in senile dementia', in N.E. Miller and G.D. Cohen (eds) *Clinical Aspects of Alzheimer's Disease and Senile Dementia*, New York: Raven Press.

Warners, I. (1998) *Terug naar de oorsprong*, Houten: Bohn Stafleu Van Loghum.

Weiner, M.F. (1991) 'Dementia as a psychodynamic process', in M.F. Weiner (ed.) *The Dementias: Diagnosis and Management*, Washington, DC: American Psychiatric Press.

Weinstein, E.A., Freidland, R.P. and Wagner, E.E. (1994) 'Denial/unawareness of impairment and symbolic behavior in Alzheimer's disease', *Neuropsychiatry, Neuropsychology and Behavioral Neurology*, 7, 3: 176–84.

Wragg, R.E. and Jeste, D.V. (1989) 'Overview of depression and psychosis in Alzheimer's disease', *Am J Psychiatry* 146: 577–87.

Zorgkompas (1995) Utrecht: NIZW.

Chapter 10

Support programmes for caregivers of persons with dementia

A review of methods and effects

R.M. Dröes, J.J.M. Goffin, E. Breebaart, E. de Rooij, H. Vissers, J.A.C. Bleeker, W. van Tilburg

Introduction

Over the next decades the number of persons with dementia will increase substantially. A growing percentage of these elderly persons will stay at home longer. On the one hand this is due to the limited capacity of nursing homes and in-patient care facilities, on the other to the government policy to offer people in need of assistance/care the opportunity to remain in their own homes as long as possible. As a result, the care for these elderly persons will have to be offered in the home situation much more frequently. This extramuralization of elderly mentally frail care raises new issues, such as: how do we organize this care and who cares for the persons with dementia in the absence of the professional caregiver (Bleeker 1994, 1997)? Until now much of this care was provided by spouses and family members, and to a lesser degree neighbours and friends also played a role. Caring for an elderly person with dementia is no easy task and it implies an emotional, physical, social and in the long run also financial burden (Morris 1988; Huckle 1994). Since the early 1980s there has been a growing awareness in the health care sector of the burden that family members experience and of the capricious adaptation process they go through. This awareness was generated in part by research that showed that family members develop more physical and emotional health problems, as well as decreased feelings of well-being, than the general population (Clark and Rakowski 1983; Nuy *et al.* 1984; Eagles *et al.* 1987; Cohen and Eisdorfer 1988; Brodaty and Hadzi-Pavlovic 1990; Coope *et al.* 1995; Fuller-Jonap and Haley 1995; Pot 1996). Unless effective measures are taken, the severity of problems of informal caregivers is expected to increase in the future.

To assist the caregivers of persons with dementia and to prevent (premature) institutionalization of the dementing person in a nursing home, several support programmes were developed internationally over the past few decades, such as: support groups (Cuijpers 1992), respite care (for instance, day care, temporary admission into a nursing home and sitter services; Nies

1989; Diesfeldt 1992; Wächtler *et al.* 1994; Feinberg and Kelly 1995), information meetings, stress management training, more specific psychoeducational and therapy groups, and telephone support groups (Vissers 1994). In general, these interventions aim at one of the following effects (Cuijpers 1992):

- to reduce, or prevent an increase of the burden on the primary caregiver and to improve his/her health and well-being
- to improve the quality of care for the person with dementia
- to prevent, or delay, institutionalization of the person with dementia into a nursing home.

Until 2000, when we concluded our literature study, several literature reviews had been published on the effects of support activities on caregivers of persons with dementia (Toseland *et al.* 1989; Cuijpers 1992; Knight *et al.* 1993; Collins *et al.* 1994; Huckle 1994; Flint 1995; Bourgeois *et al.* 1996). Toseland *et al.* as well as Cuijpers focused on the so-called support groups. Flint wrote a review on respite care. Collins *et al.* (1994) and Bourgeois *et al.* (1996) confined themselves exclusively to interventions for family members of persons with Alzheimer's disease. Knight *et al.* (1993) put no restriction on the type of dementia and focused on interventions for caring relatives in general. Finally, Huckle's review offers a general outline of support programmes for carers of persons with dementia but fails to provide an overview of the intervention studies conducted up to that point. In view of the increased variety of support programmes and the growing number of people who will have to deal with the care of a person with dementia in their own environment, there is a need for such a review. In our opinion, a better insight into the offer and effectiveness of support programmes is a precondition to optimize the support for family caregivers.

In this chapter we therefore present the results of an extensive study of the literature on intervention studies that were conducted in the period from 1980 to 1999. We will focus both on the different support methods that were developed and the reasons for changes in the offer over the last two decades, as well as on the efficacy of the various types of support.

Search procedure, selection criteria and data analyses

The studies were collected on the basis of several strategies. First of all we carried out a computerized literature search covering the period 1980 to 1999 on several databases (MEDLINE, Index Medicus, PSYCHLIT, PsychINFO). Key words used were (combinations of): dementia, Alzheimer's disease, family, caregivers, caregiver burden, (social) support (networks), education, day care, institutionalization, effect size-statistical, experiment-controls. We screened the collected publications for relevant references and we contacted several experts on support for family caregivers of relatives with dementia in the UK, France and Italy, and asked them to add relevant publications to our list if possible. For our review we selected intervention studies:

- in which at least 80 per cent of the study sample consisted of family caregivers of a person with a dementia syndrome
- that focused on support activities for caregivers of persons with dementia who live at home
- in which the goal of the support was, among other things, to decrease the burden on the family caregiver, to improve the quality of care for the person with dementia, and/or to delay or prevent institutionalization of the person with dementia in a nursing home.

The studies we traced were arranged in chronological order and analysed on the following aspects: population sample, goals and contents of the support programme and the effects on the family caregivers and/or the person with dementia. We examined which changes took place in the offer of support programmes over the last two decades, and for what reasons. Finally, we tried to draw conclusions with regard to the effectiveness of the different types of support on specific variables.

Results

A total of 46 studies were traced that met the inclusion criteria. Two studies were conducted between 1980 and 1985, 13 between 1985 and 1990, 14 between 1990 and 1995, and 17 between 1995 and 2000 (see Chapter 11, Table 11.1, pp. 242–3).

Support programmes in the period 1980–84

For the period 1980–84 we found only two studies that met our criteria. Lazarus *et al.* (1981) used a pre-test–post-test control group design to examine whether a *support group* had a positive effect on the degree to which the central carers felt in control of their own lives, and on symptoms of being overburdened (anxiety and feelings of depression). The group, in which four carers of persons with dementia participated, met once a week for one hour, over a period of ten weeks. Important themes that were discussed were: acceptance of the illness, developing more realistic expectations about the future, the emotional confusion that dealing with a person with dementia can generate, the feelings of exhaustion due to the enormous responsibility, the attitude towards professional caregivers and coping strategies. The researchers found that the carers who had participated in the group experienced significantly more control over their own lives, and attributed less importance to what they refer to as 'family ambition' (the importance attached within the family to success, prestige and the opinions of others) than caregivers who had not participated in the support group (n = 3). No differences were demonstrated between these groups regarding affective symptoms.

The second study of this period examined the effect of *respite care* (Gilleard *et al.* 1984). George and Gwyther (1986) define respite care as temporary, substitute care for family members in need of assistance/care to relieve the central caregiver, when he/she is temporarily absent. Gilleard *et al.* conducted their study among 129 family members of persons with dementia who made use of elderly mentally frail day-care programmes in several psychiatric hospitals. They used a pre-test–post-test design without a control group. The expected outcome was that the burden on the caregivers would decrease because of the respite care. However, the researchers found no decrease of the burden experienced by the caregivers. Based on interviews with the caregivers three and six months after the start of the respite care, it became clear that they did feel they had derived benefit from the offered respite care. Satisfaction on this point even increased over time.

Support programmes in the period 1985–9

The period between 1985 and 1990 shows a considerable increase in the number of intervention studies on support programmes. In addition to the existing offer of support groups and respite care that were also the subject of intervention studies during this period, we also see more variety. Previously developed support activities are now offered, sometimes in combination with new elements, in the shape of programmes, and entirely new types of support activities and programmes are being developed.

Various researchers investigated the effect of *support groups* (Zarit *et al.* 1987; Meier Robinson 1988; Chiverton and Caine 1989; Russell *et al.* 1989). A controlled study by Zarit *et al.* (1987) compares three groups: a support group, a group that had individual and family talks (eight times), and a waiting list group (control group) that received no support. The support group was therapeutic in nature and focused on sharing feelings and emotions. The objective of the individual and family talks was to mobilize the social support system surrounding the person with dementia and his caregiver to a maximum degree. Both interventions aimed to reduce the stress experienced by the caregiver. Although the caregivers in both intervention groups felt less burdened and showed fewer psychiatric symptoms after the intervention, the improvement was not significantly larger than in the waiting list control group. The follow-up measurement one year later also demonstrated no effect. The caregivers that had had talks did feel significantly more supported than the caregivers in the support group.

Renewed analysis of the data (Whitlach *et al.* 1991) showed that the group which had had talks also experienced less stress related to their caregiver role after the intervention. On this aspect they differed significantly from the support group and the control group.

The support group studied by Meier Robinson (1988) was based on a social skills model. The assumption was that socially skilled caregivers of persons with dementia are better able to mobilize their social network, which reduces their feeling of burden and increases their sense of self-worth. In four two-hour meetings, the participants were trained to be assertive, initiate a conversation about caring for a demented person, and ask others for help. Based on a controlled intervention outcome study, Meier Robinson concluded that participation in this support group did not result in an increased sense of self-worth, but it did lead to a significant reduction of feelings of burden in the caregivers.

Chiverton and Caine (1989) carried out a controlled trial on a short-term support group that focused on providing information about dementia and learning communication skills and social skills. The coping behaviour of the participants (n = 20) proved to increase significantly, as did the knowledge of dementia and treatment methods, and the emotional competence.

Russell *et al.* (1989) also carried out an intervention study on an educational support group (n = 5), but they did not use a control group. Although they observed a significant increase in emotional well-being of the caregivers, they also concluded that these caregivers assess their problems as more serious. They explain this as a consequence of the increased knowledge about dementia: by participating in the educational support group, the participants realized more fully the consequences of caring for a person with dementia, in particular the fact that the care would become increasingly demanding.

Researchers also investigated *support groups* that gave extra attention to *stress management techniques* (Kahan *et al.* 1985; Gendron *et al.* 1986; Haley *et al.* 1987). Both Kahan *et al.* and Gendron *et al.* found a significant reduction in feelings of burden in participants in these groups. The support programme of Kahan *et al.* consisted of eight weekly meetings. The first hour of these meetings was educational in nature, with lectures on medical, neurological and legal aspects of dementia, common reaction patterns of people who are confronted with a family member with dementia, coping with behaviour problems, stress management, and how to organize a social network to relieve the central caregiver. The second hour was reserved for discussion, sharing experiences, role play to practise skills and instruction in stress management techniques. The effectiveness of this support programme was measured with a pre-test–post-test control group design. After the eight meetings the sense of burden proved significantly reduced in the participants from the support group (n = 22), whereas it had increased significantly in the caregivers from the waiting list control group (n = 18). Furthermore, the caregivers in the support group indicated they were less depressed, and their knowledge of dementia had increased significantly more than in the caregivers in the control group. Ninety per cent of the caregivers from the support group felt the programme to be very to extremely supportive, and satisfaction was highest about the lectures on dementia.

Gendron *et al.* (1986) used meditative relaxation and assertiveness training to expand the coping repertoire of central caregivers. To determine the coping skills at baseline, before the intervention started, the caregivers were shown 12 dramatized video fragments. Each fragment depicted a situation that is generally characterized by caregivers of dementing elderly people as difficult. Examples are: night-time unrest, incontinence (for urine or faeces), aggression, fire risks, illness of central caregiver and embarrassment in social situations by the person with dementia's behaviour. The caregivers were asked for each video fragment: 'If you were in this situation, how long could you cope?' Answers could be circled on a Likert-scale of 1 ('not at all') to 10 ('more than 5 years'). Eight caregivers received eight weekly training sessions. Four caregivers received no training at all and constituted the control group. In the post-test measurement and also in a follow-up after six months, the caregivers of the experimental group proved to be more assertive, better at solving problems and less stressed than the caregivers from the control group. Also, a difference in response to the video fragments was demonstrated. The trained caregivers estimated their stamina in the various problem situations measurably longer than during the pretest measurement. The researchers do not mention whether this change was statistically significant.

Haley *et al.* (1987) also investigated whether the addition of stress management techniques increased the effect of a support group. In addition to 10 support group meetings, 17 caregivers were offered progressive relaxation and lessons in cognitive techniques for coping with negative thoughts/ideas. A second group of caregivers (n = 14) participated only in the support group. The control group (n = 9) consisted of caregivers on a waiting list for support. Although the caregivers were very satisfied with the groups, no improvement could be demonstrated on aspects like depression, life satisfaction, and satisfaction with social support. There were significant differences on two aspects of coping with stress only: the caregivers from the waiting list control group expressed more emotion regarding the care than the family members from the two experimental groups. The caregivers that were offered both stress management and the support group used mood-regulating coping strategies more frequently (for example, turning to a new activity in order not to have to think about the problem anymore).

Burdz *et al.* (1988), as well as Seltzer *et al.* (1988) investigated the effect of *respite care*. This care consisted of temporary institutionalization (in both cases for a period of two weeks) of the person with dementia in a nursing home and in a hospital. In the Burdz *et al.* study, respite care proved to have a positive effect on the burden experienced by the caregivers, and it also had a positive effect, against all expectation, on the cognitive and physical functioning of the persons with dementia.

Seltzer's study, however, found no overall effect. In the case of those who functioned at a severely demented level at the start of the respite care, significant improvements were observed on mood, cooperation, communication and social contact; those who functioned at a less severe level deteriorated on the aspects mentioned during their institutionalization.

A newly developed support activity that was investigated during this period is a *cognitive stimulation programme* (Quayhagen and Quayhagen 1989). In this programme the central caregiver is shown how he can stimulate the person with dementia at home by means of structured activities (memory exercises, language/communication exercises and problem solving). The study revealed that the feelings of burden and well-being of the caregivers who had participated in the programme (n = 10) remained stable, whereas they increased and decreased respectively in those caregivers who had not participated in the programme (n = 6). Differences were also found between the persons with dementia in the stimulation group and those in the control group; whereas the level of cognitive functioning and behaviour problems remained the same over a period of eight months in the stimulation group, the cognitive functioning in the control group deteriorated, and behaviour problems in this group also increased. The difference between both groups was significant.

Sutcliffe and Larner (1988) studied the effect of two types of *individual support for the carers at home* (information and emotional support combined with relaxation exercises) by means of a pre-test–post-test control group design. A total of six weekly 45-minute housecalls were made. The group receiving emotional support improved significantly on mood, whereas the control group deteriorated significantly. This effect was still present 12 weeks after the housecalls.

Finally, in this period two studies (Brodaty and Gresham 1989; Lawton *et al.* 1989) were conducted into the effect of more *comprehensive support programmes*. Brodaty and Gresham (1989) studied the effect of a support programme that consisted of a discussion group and a phone circle for the caregivers and a memory training group for the dementing persons. The discussion group for the caregivers consisted of six meetings and was followed by setting up a phone circle. After one year the caregivers that had participated in the programme felt healthier than the waiting list control group. Furthermore, the persons with dementia who participated in the support programme lived at home considerably longer (postponement of institutionalization).

Lawton *et al.* (1989) investigated the effect of a programme that offered respite care (at home or in an institutional setting), a support group and case management. Except for the respite care, the control group received the same support. Measurements were carried out after 3, 6 and 12 months. Although the offer of respite care had no effect on feelings of burden of the caregiver (despite the caregivers' satisfaction with the programme), the results did allow the conclusion that the persons with dementia who utilized the respite care could remain at home for a considerably longer period.

Support programmes in the period 1990–94

In the period following 1990 up to 1995 we see that the development in support programmes continues. The offer keeps growing. Yet new intervention studies on previously developed and studied support activities are also carried out. For instance, the effects of the increasingly applied *support groups* are studied again during this period (Morris *et al.* 1992; Cuijpers 1993; Brodaty *et al.* 1994; Hébert *et al.* 1994). The support group studied by Morris *et al.* focused on the caregivers' coping strategies. In addition to coping with the emotional problems that caring for an elderly person with dementia brings, much attention was given to coping with practical problems, such as handling behaviour problems, the changing relationships with the rest of the family and dealing with all the organizations involved in the care. A control group attended five lectures on dementia. Both the caregivers that participated in the coping-support group (n = 13) and the caregivers that participated in the lecture series (n = 18) showed a significant increase in the ability to solve problems, knowledge of dementia and the emotional involvement in the care. The feelings of burden and depression, however, remained the same.

Cuijpers (1993) interviewed 110 participants in 21 already existing support groups, presenting them with questionnaires on feelings of burden, health and experienced social support on three occasions. He found no significant improvement on any of the mentioned variables. One of the explanations provided by the author was that effects possibly occur only in particular types of caregivers. Renewed statistical analyses did show that improvement had occurred on the aspects of general health and satisfaction about the caregiver role among people who worked, participants in groups that required a financial contribution, in caregivers of more apathetic persons with dementia and in carers who were less satisfied with their own role of caregiver.

The support group that was investigated by Brodaty *et al.* (1994) consisted of a combination of providing information about dementia and learning to cope with the behaviour problems of the person with dementia and with the stress this can cause in the caregiver. In this quasi-experimental study three groups of carers were compared: people who had attended at least one half-day of the workshop and at least four of the five other meetings (n = 33), caregivers who had attended fewer meetings (n = 22) and a waiting list control group (n = 26). Participation in the support group was expected to lead to a reduction of stress and feelings of burden, and an increase in life satisfaction, well-being and knowledge about dementia. However, no differences were found between the three groups in terms of effects.

Hébert *et al.* (1994) also studied the effectiveness of support groups. The 41 caregivers were randomly assigned to an experimental group (n = 23) and a control group (n = 18). The experimental group was offered a support programme consisting of eight weekly two-hour meetings. During these meetings the participants received information about the disease and they engaged in role play to learn to cope with behaviour problems. There was also discussion about the emotional consequences of caring for a person with dementia, and the participants were taught stress management techniques. Participants in the control group were offered information meetings by the local Alzheimer's association. Except on the aspect of 'knowledge about the disease', no significant differences were found between the two groups, either on feelings of burden, or on psychological reactions. The authors therefore concluded that the effect of this type of support group on the morbidity and burden of the caregivers is minimal. Nevertheless, 96 per cent of the participants were satisfied or very satisfied with the offered programme, and they found the offered knowledge and skills very useful in their daily lives. In other words, despite the fact that the support programme did not relieve their feeling of burden, they had still gained a new and better attitude towards the person with dementia.

In this period we also again find several studies on the effect of *respite care* (Wells *et al.* 1990; Conlin *et al.* 1992; Adler *et al.* 1993; Larkin and Most Hopcroft 1993). Wells *et al.* (1990) studied the effect of day-care programmes for the dementing person on a number of psychological symptoms of caregivers (n = 52), such as the practical and psychologcial problems they experience with the person with dementia, feelings of guilt, anxiety, depression and quality of life. The study was carried out in 16 elderly mentally frail day-care programmes in Australia. None of the psychological symptoms changed significantly as a result of using the day care. The researchers conclude that the day-care programme probably does not offer enough hours of care relief to effect any real changes in the mentioned psychological symptoms.

As in the study of Lawton *et al.* (1989), Conlin *et al.* (1992) gave the caregivers in their pilot study (n = 7) the choice whether they wanted to receive the offered respite care: at home or in an institution. The waiting list control group (n = 8) received the same offer, but only after the study was concluded. The respite care proved to have a positive effect on the stress experienced by the caregivers. No improvement was found with regard to mood.

Adler *et al.* (1993) offered central carers of American war veterans with dementia the opportunity to admit these veterans to a military hospital for two weeks. The aim was to provide relief to the caregivers (n = 37) and reduce their feelings of depression. On the day the person with dementia was sent home these feelings of burden and depression in the caregivers did prove to be significantly reduced. However, during the follow-up measurement two weeks later this effect had already disappeared. In the demented war veterans the researchers looked at the activities of daily living (ADL) and the degree of behaviour problems. No significant changes were observed here.

Larkin and Most Hopcroft (1993) studied the effect of a temporary admission (two weeks) of persons with dementia to a dementia unit in a hospital on the feelings of burden of their caregivers (n = 23) over a period of six months. The caregivers were interviewed at three points in time: before admission of the person with dementia to the hospital, just before his release, and two weeks after his release. The results showed that the caregivers experienced significantly less psychological stress just before the release of the dementing person than before admission (lower score on hostility, anxiety, depression and obsessive-compulsive behaviour). Two weeks after the person with dementia returned home, these effects had already diminished to such an extent that there was no longer any significant difference with the period before the admission. In other words, the effect of the respite care lasted only briefly. The experiences of the caregivers also revealed that they slept better and had the opportunity to go out or visit friends again during the institutionalization.

Interventions whose effectiveness was studied for the first time during this period are: a behaviour and medication intervention among persons with dementia and the effect of this intervention on their carers (Hinchliffe *et al.* 1992); emotional and social support through a telephone network (Goodman 1990); and a support activity consisting of offering individual advice and information to caregivers by a trained social worker (Weinberger *et al.* 1993).

In the study of *behaviour and medicine intervention* (Hinchliffe *et al.* 1992) a number of participants in a day-care programme (n = 16) and his or her caregiver were offered a made-to-measure intervention. For the central caregivers the key question was which behaviour of the person with dementia irritated them most, or which aspect of the behaviour they had a problem with. The interventions varied from, for example, sleep medication in the case of night-time unrest and diversion techniques to prevent sleeping during the day, to behaviour techniques and medication in the case of physical and verbal aggression. The intervention showed a significant increase in mental well-being of the caregivers.

Central caregivers who participated in a *telephone network* (Goodman 1990) were randomly assigned to a group in which the caregivers had weekly contact with each other by phone (n = 22), and a group that listened to a lecture on dementia by phone every week (n = 18). After three months the group switched, so that both groups eventually received the same programme. After the first three months both groups were more satisfied about the support they received from their social network. They initiated contact with family and friends more frequently. They also knew more about dementia than they did before participating in the network. However, during the second three-month period a reduction of the effect occurred in both groups, and the feeling of burden and the number of social conflicts increased. The total number of social contacts in both groups did remain higher than before participation in the telephone network.

Weinberger *et al.* (1993) investigated the effect of a support activity that was carried out by social workers, in which caregivers could get *individual advice and information* about the use of health care facilities and public funds and on how to cope with the person with dementia's behaviour problems. The offered advice and information had no significant effect on either the use of support services, or the spending patterns of these carers.

Finally, *integrated support programmes* were studied during this period. These programmes combined existing support activities for the person with dementia and the caregiver in one, usually long-term, comprehensive programme. These are the intervention studies by Mohide *et al.* (1990), Vernooij-Dassen and Persoon (1990), and Dröes and Breebaart (1994).

Mohide *et al.* (1990) studied the effect of a support programme in which 30 central caregivers of persons with dementia living at home were offered four hours of respite care at home, and furthermore received support from an especially trained nurse once a week. This nurse provided the carer with practical information about dementia and helped him or her cope with problem situations. In addition they could participate in a support group every month during a six-month period. The control group (n = 30) received regular home care and district nursing services. After its conclusion, the support programme proved to have had no effect on the feelings of depression and stress of the carers. However, a few trends could be observed. For example, the quality of life of the caregivers in the experimental group proved higher after the support than that of the carers in the control group. They were also more satisfied with the nursing assistance they received and saw their role as carer less problematically than the carers in the control group. Furthermore, a significantly higher percentage of the persons with dementia in the control group were admitted into a nursing home more quickly. The conclusion was that the experimental programme resulted in delay of institutionalization in a nursing home.

The support programme studied by Vernooij-Dassen and Persoon (1990) is comparable with the programme that was investigated by Mohide *et al.* It also consisted of four hours of home care by a specialized nurse, but the discussion group was more intensive (twelve times, two hours). The result of the support was that the female caregivers who lived with the dementing persons experienced increased feelings of competence. In the group of female caregivers who did not live with the persons with dementia, the support resulted in fewer nursing home admissions.

The Amsterdam Meeting Centres support programme that Dröes and Breebaart (1994) investigated in a pilot study (and subsequently in a controlled intervention study in 1996), consisted of case management, a bi-weekly, long-term discussion group and ten bi-weekly informative meetings to support the caregivers, as well as a day club for the persons with dementia (three days a week). Caregivers and persons with dementia could furthermore attend a consultation hour once a week and participate in a centre meeting once a month. In addition, recreational activities were organized regularly for persons with dementia and caregivers together (outings, drinks, etc.). The entire programme was offered in community centres. The goal was to offer practical, emotional and social support to the dementing persons and their caregivers: so that (a) the caregivers learned to cope with the problems in a different way and would be able to maintain the care for a longer period of time; (b) the persons with dementia would exhibit fewer behaviour problems; (c) admission into a nursing home would be postponed. In the first pilot study (with no control group) that was carried out with regard to this programme, a positive trend was observed in the carers on the burden they experienced. For the participants with dementia a positive trend was observed regarding non-social behaviour. At a group level, however, the changes were not significant.

Support programmes in the period 1995–9

For this period we traced 17 intervention studies, varying from support groups with or without family counselling, respite care and behavioural treatment group interventions to a new method of support by a computer network, tailored individual support and the more comprehensive multi-component service programmes.

Three studies investigated the effect of *support groups* with or without individual and family counselling (Mittelman *et al.* 1995; Cummings *et al.* 1998; Wilkins *et al.* 1999). Mittelman *et al.* investigated the effect of individual and family counselling during four months (six sessions), followed by a support group and follow-up counseling, if so desired, in 206 spouse caregivers of Alzheimer type patients. After eight months they found that caregivers who received this intervention were significantly less depressed and obtained more social support and satisfaction from their social network than caregivers who did not receive the intervention (control group). Survival analysis showed that the median time from baseline to nursing home placement was 329 days longer in the intervention group than in the control group (Mittelman *et al.* 1996). The risk of placement for patients in a nursing home also decreased significantly, with the greatest effect in persons who were mildly or moderately demented.

In a pilot study Cummings *et al.* (1998) investigated the effect of an 8-week psycho-educational support group of 90 minutes a week in caregivers (n = 13) of persons in early stage Alzheimer's. They found positive effects on perceived stress, preparedness for care-giving, caregiver competence and positive coping strategies.

In a pilot study Wilkins *et al.* (1999) also studied the effect of a psycho-educational support group (eight weeks, 90 min/week), in combination with weekly telephone calls. The group, which consisted of 11 women caregivers and was led by a clinical psychologist and a social worker, focused on building coping skills through stress reduction training, teaching cognitive-behavioural interventions to decrease depression and anxiety, providing information about resources for caregivers, and providing a supportive environment to address caregivers' current concerns. Though all caregivers rated the group as highly beneficial, after completion of the programme no effect on either burden, depression or anxiety was found. The immune status of the caregivers even deteriorated.

Two studies tested the effect of *a support group with an educational goal* on the caregiver (Zanetti *et al.* 1998; Belmin *et al.* 1999). Zanetti *et al.* (1998) found an increase of knowledge regarding dementia in caregivers (n = 12) who participated in a six-week educational programme of one hour a week, compared to caregivers who did not participate (matched controls). Three months after the end of the programme, the participants showed a significant reduction of their levels of stress associated with person's behavioural disturbances.

Belmin *et al.* (1999) report a positive effect of a health education programme of three three-hour sessions in three weeks on the burden of family caregivers (n = 19).

In this period we only traced one study on the effect of *respite care.* Zarit *et al.* (1998) report the findings of an evaluation of the psychological benefits of the use of adult day care by family caregivers assisting a relative with dementia. The study used a quasi-experimental design in which caregivers who used adult day care were compared with caregivers who did not use day care at any point during the three-month evaluation period and only small amounts of other respite services. Results after three months showed that the caregivers who used day care had significantly lower scores than the control group on two of the three measures of appraisal of primary stress (overload and strain). After one year the day-care group scored significantly lower on overload and depression than the control group. It was concluded that use of day care results in lower levels of caregiver-related stress and better psychological well-being.

Several researchers investigated the effect of *behavioural interventions* (Gendron *et al.* 1996; Burgener *et al.* 1998; McCurry *et al.* 1998; Ostwald *et al.* 1999) compared to, or in combination with, education or an informative support group. Gendron *et al.* (1996) compared the effect of a cognitive-behavioural group intervention plus telephone contact with an information support group for spouses of persons with dementia (n = 35). The cognitive-behavioural group intervention was delivered by a cognitive therapist in 8 weekly sessions of 90 minutes. The cognitive-behavioural group improved on assertiveness but demonstrated a decrease on two subscales of marital adjustment (global adjustment and satisfaction). The information support group showed increased scores for marital adjustment.

McCurry *et al.* (1998) studied the effect of behavioural treatment on sleep problems in caregivers of persons with dementia (n = 36) in a randomized controlled trial. Caregivers who participated in the behaviour therapy group showed improvement in sleep quality compared to their waiting list controls. No differences were found in depression, burden or problem behaviours of the person with dementia.

Burgener *et al.* (1998) investigated the differences in effect on patients (n = 54) and caregivers (n = 54) of four interventions: a combined education and behaviour intervention, an isolated education or behaviour intervention and no intervention (controls). The interventions were presented by a nurse in two 90-minute sessions. After six months an increase in knowledge was found for those caregivers who participated in the combined education and behaviour intervention programme.

Ostwald *et al.* (1999) in a three-year randomized clinical trial tested the effectiveness of a psycho-educational family group intervention in decreasing the caregivers' perceptions of the frequency and severity of behavioural problems in persons with dementia and their reactions to those problems, and in decreasing caregiver burden and depression. The intervention consisted of seven weekly, two-hour training sessions that included education, family support and skills training for 94 caregivers and their families. After five months the intervention group showed reduced negative reactions to disruptive behaviours and reduced caregiver burden compared to a waiting list control group. No effect on depression was found.

A totally new type of support was investigated in this period by Brennan *et al.* (1995): support via a special *computer network*. The assumption was that support via a computer network would lead to more (self-) confidence, better decision-making skills and a decrease of social isolation. All caregivers from the experimental group (n = 47) received a computer and modem, funded by donations, which was connected to their telephone line. The computer network gave the carer the opportunity to obtain information about dementia and the care of dementing persons from an electronic encyclopaedia. They could also get help via the computer for making care decisions (should I take away his/her keys?), and get in touch with other participating caregivers and a nurse specialized in dementia care through e-mail. The control group (n = 49) was trained to find organizations and institutions in the area they could turn to for help. After the experimental period the authors concluded that there was no difference in effect between the two interventions as regards the caregivers' change in decision-making skills and the degree of social isolation. Compared to the control group, the participants in the computer network did, however, demonstrate a significant improvement in self-confidence when making decisions.

Four studies focused on *tailored individual interventions* (Moniz-Cook *et al.* 1998; Riordan and Bennett 1998; Strawn *et al.* 1998; Newcomer *et al.* 1999). In a controlled trial Moniz-Cook *et al.* studied the effect of an individual intervention (6 to 12 hours) offered by a psychologist for four to fourteen weeks after assessment at a memory clinic. The intervention consisted of education and reinforcement of coping strategies. While the caregivers who received early intervention (n = 15) remained stable on well-being after 12 months, the control group (n = 15) deteriorated in this respect.

Riordan and Bennett (1998) found no effect on the psychological well-being of carers (n = 38) as a result of a support service that provided individually tailored practical and emotional help over one year. The service was provided by care assistants.

Strawn *et al.* (1998) examined the utility of a telephone intervention to provide support and assistance to caregivers (n = 14) of persons with dementia. The purpose of Telecare, which consisted of weekly telephone contacts from a so-called Caring Caller were: (a) to discuss the caregiver's current experiences of stress, anxiety, mood, and general health; (b) to serve as social support and caring human interaction; (c) to provide information regarding social service agencies. After 12 weeks of participation the caregivers experienced less general distress, hostility, and obsessive thoughts, and found caregiving somewhat less burdensome.

Newcomer *et al.* (1999) investigated the effects of the Medicare Alzheimer's Disease Demonstration programme on caregiver burden and depression in 5307 individuals. Applicants to the demonstration (all voluntary) were randomly assigned into treatment and control groups. Caregivers in the treatment group were eligible for case management and for up to $699 per month in community benefits. Principal findings were that persons in the treatment group had a high exposure to case management and a greater likelihood of community service use but showed a very small reduction in caregiver burden and depression over a 36-month period relative to those in the control group. The authors conclude that to substantially increase the effect on caregiver burden, the intervention possibly should be broadened into areas such as 24-hour care, crisis intervention, coordination with primary care or chronic disease management.

Finally, two authors studied the efficacy of comprehensive *integrated support programmes* both for persons with dementia and their caregivers (Brodaty *et al.*, 1997; Dröes, 1996; Dröes *et al.* 2000). Brodaty *et al.* (1997) report on eight-year experiences and the outcome of a ten-day residential intensive programme for caregivers followed by follow-up meetings and telephone contacts over twelve months in combination with a ten-day structured memory retraining and activity programme for the persons with dementia. The total programme was offered in a psychiatric ward of a general hospital. For the caregivers (n = 33) the programme was delivered by a social worker/

occupational therapist, a psychiatrist, a psychologist, a welfare officer and a physiotherapist. It consisted of a wide range of activities aimed at reducing caregiver distress, combating isolation, discussing themes such as guilt and seperation, increasing assertiveness, re-roling, stress management, improving coping skills (communication, therapeutic use of activities, reminiscence, coping with physical frailty), encouraging fitness and diet, informing on medical aspects of dementia, using community services, planning for the future and coping with problem behaviours. The patients had their own programme which consisted of occupational therapy, outings and relaxation classes as well as specific programmes such as group discussion, reminiscence therapy and a memory retraining programme. The intervention group was compared with a waiting list control group who received the intervention after waiting six months, and a third group of caregivers who received ten days respite care (while patients underwent their memory retraining programme) and 12 months booster sessions. Eight-year survival analysis indicated that patients whose caregivers received training stayed at home significantly longer and tended to live longer.

Dröes (1996) and Dröes *et al.* (2000) report on the effects of the integrated support programme, Amsterdam Meeting Centres, which was investigated in a larger sample of caregivers (n = 36) and persons with dementia (n = 33) in a pre-test–post-test control group design with matched groups. The control group consisted of caregivers of persons with dementia who used regular elderly mentally frail day care only. The results showed that caregivers who participated for seven months in the meeting centres programme felt more competent to care for the person with dementia than did their matched controls whose relative with dementia frequented day care. The persons with dementia who visited the meeting centres for seven months showed less behaviour problems (non-social and inactive behaviour) than those who participated in the regular day care.

Conclusions and discussion

The type of support for family caregivers of elderly persons with dementia who live at home that was investigated most frequently is the *support group*. The central feature of the support group is that the caregivers share similar experiences with fellow caregivers and therefore experience support and gain information (Glosser and Wexler 1985). However, a wide variety of interventions is placed under the umbrella of the support group concept. Wright *et al.* (1987) distinguish three types of support groups: groups aimed at education of the caregiver, groups aimed at mutual support of companions in distress, groups aimed at the expression of emotion, and of course, combinations of the three. Support groups that also include other activities, such as relaxation exercises or stress management are not uncommon (e.g. Kahan *et al.* 1985; Hébert *et al.* 1994). As a consequence the comparability of support groups is limited, and a general statement about the effectiveness of the support group is therefore not feasible.

Our literature study traced 18 outcome studies with regard to support groups, of which 12 reported positive effects, which, depending on the kind of support offered (social, emotional, educational), varied from an improved emotional well-being (Russell *et al.* 1989; Mittelman *et al.* 1995), more social support (Mittelman *et al.* 1995) and an increased subjective feeling of caregivers that they were again in control of their own situation (Lazarus *et al.* 1981; Cummings *et al.* 1998), to increased knowledge about dementia and dementia-related issues (Chiverton and Caine 1989; Hébert *et al.* 1994; Zanetti *et al.* 1998), increased experienced health and decreased feelings of burden in subgroups of caregivers (Cuijpers 1993; Cummings *et al.* 1998). In the more comprehensive support groups that also paid explicit attention to stress management (coping), positive effects were found on the feelings of burden of the caregivers (Kahan *et al.* 1985), and their problem-solving skills (Gendron *et al.* 1986; Morris *et al.* 1992; Cummings *et al.* 1998). Finally, in some studies significantly lower stress (Brodaty and Gresham 1989; Zanetti *et al.* 1998) and delay of institutionalization were found in caregivers who participated in a support group (Brodaty and Gresham 1989; Mittelman *et al.* 1995).

Respite care for the persons with dementia can offer temporary relief to the caregiver, regardless of the form in which it is offered (day care, temporary institutionalization, home care), and can also improve the behaviour of the person with dementia. Knight *et al.* (1993) concluded earlier on the basis of their meta-analysis that respite care has a significant influence on the feelings of burden of the caregiver. This is confirmed in five of the eight studies on respite care included in this review (Burdz *et al.* 1988; Larkin and Most Hopcroft 1993, Conlin *et al.* 1992; Kosloski and Montgomery 1993; Zarit *et al.* 1998), which demonstrates that not all of the caregivers experience a decrease of their feelings of burden.

The effect of the respite care on the persons with dementia is equally ambiguous. On the basis of descriptive research of day care in 21 nursing homes, Nuy *et al.* (1984, 1985) found that day care results in improved functioning of the person with dementia, especially in terms of communication and mobility. Furthermore, they observed a slight delay in institutionalization. Seltzer *et al.* (1988), however, report that only persons with severe dementia improved in terms of psychosocial functioning during a two-week hospitalization, whereas persons with a mild dementia deteriorated in this respect. No significant effects were achieved at a group level. Based on the variety of research results, Brodaty and Gresham (1992) note that respite care might be more effective if more attention were paid to individual characteristics and needs of the person with dementia and his caregiver. The question to ask, in other words, is 'What is the correct dose for the right person at the appropriate stage of the dementia?' (Brodaty and Gresham 1992).

We found six *individually tailored interventions* varying from housecalls in which information and practical and/or emotional support and/or relaxation exercises were given by a social worker, care assistants or a psychologist (after assessment in a memory clinic), to a telephone care intervention in which emotional and social support and information was offered, and a case management and financial support programme. The intervention by the social worker and the care assistants did not result in an increased psychological well-being of the caregivers. The four other interventions, however, seemed to stabilize the well-being (Moniz-Cook *et al.* 1998), or had small effects on stress/burden (Strawn *et al.* 1998; Newcomer *et al.* 1999), mood (Sutcliff and Larner, 1988; Newcomer *et al.* 1999) or use of community services (Newcomer *et al.* 1999). The limited number of studies, and the variations in interventions offered, do not allow us to draw definite conclusions on this type of support at this moment. Individual tailored interventions seem to be very important. However, the small size of outcome suggests that these interventions possibly should be offered continuously instead of temporarily (a few weeks) and should be combined with practical support and respite care to substantially increase the effect on caregiver burden (see also Newcomer *et al.* 1999).

Over the past decade several *comprehensive integrated support programmes* for persons with dementia and caregivers have been developed. The support activities varied from, for instance, respite care at home, in a community centre or in the nursing home combined with support activities for the care-giver such as: (a) individual assistance and a support group aimed at education and emotional support; (b) education and case management; (c) a discussion group, informative meetings, case management, individual consultation hour, and recreational activities.

Of the three studies that were conducted with regard to the type (a) programme, one study showed an increase in feelings of competence of the female caregivers who were living with the person with dementia. In female caregivers who did not live with the person with dementia, this support resulted in the postponement of admission into a nursing home of the person with dementia (Vernooij-Dassen and Persoon 1990). Postponement of institutionalization was also found in the two Brodaty *et al.* studies (1989, 1997) and in the (only) intervention study done on the type (b) programme (Lawton *et al.* 1989). In the controlled intervention study (Dröes 1996; Dröes *et al.* 2000) that was conducted with regard to the only type (c) programme that we traced, significant positive effects were found on the feeling of competence of the care-givers and behaviour problems (non-social and inactive behaviour) in the persons with dementia, as well as a tendency for postponement of institutionalization.

In view of the small number of studies conducted on comprehensive integrated support programmes for persons with dementia and caregivers so far, barely any general conclusions can be drawn about their effectiveness.

However, the results achieved so far are very promising. More research is therefore recommended.

We traced a number of single studies on *other types of support* that could not be placed in any of the categories presented here. The following initiatives are referred to: a telephone support programme, a combined behavioural and medication intervention, a cognitive-behavioural group intervention, a behaviour therapy group for sleep problems, a psycho-educational group intervention that focused on the perception of and coping with behavioural problems in persons with dementia, social skills training, a cognitive stimulation programme and support through a computer network. All in all, we may conclude that the majority of the support activities described here do appear to have some effect on the support experienced by caregivers, their knowledge about dementia, and/or their feelings of burden. However, all interventions were evaluated only once, so general conclusions about their effect are premature at this moment.

This overview of studies on support programmes for persons with dementia and their caregivers clearly shows that since the beginning of the 1980s interest in the emotional, physical and social support of caregivers of persons with dementia who live at home has increased. This has resulted in a variety of support activities and programmes. In the beginning only support groups and respite care were offered, but nowadays there are all kinds of activities, including telephone support programmes, support via the computer or trained nurses as case managers. Apart from single support activities there are also more comprehensive programmes.

The literature reveals several reasons for these *broader* programmes.The main reason lies in the complex nature of the problems that caregivers of persons with dementia encounter. The problems are so diverse, complex and burdensome that a single intervention is no longer expected to result in a substantial decrease in the burden experienced by the caregivers. The effect of respite care alone, for example, proved insufficient. Family caregivers indicated that in addition to practical support they also needed help in learning to deal with the stress (Gendron *et al.* 1986; Hébert *et al.* 1994; Dröes and Breebaart, 1994; Dröes, 1996). Support groups also proved too limited: in those cases the caregivers lacked practical assistance such as domestic help, sitter services and help with the home care (Haley 1987; Zarit *et al.* 1987). Other reasons mentioned in the literature for the changes in the support offer are: the importance of emotional support to reduce the vulnerability of the family caregiver (Vernooij-Dassen and Persoon 1990) and the importance of customized interventions, modified to the needs of the individual caregiver (Mohide *et al.* 1990; Duijnstee 1992; Hébert *et al.* 1994). In general, family caregivers have diverse needs and problems simultaneously, and they simply cannot be met and solved by one single support activity (Mohide *et al.* 1990; Vernooij-Dassen and Persoon 1990; Dröes 1994, 1996, 2000). Based in part on these reasons, the expectation that integrated, flexible and comprehensive programmes are more effective than separate support activities has increased.

With regard to the effectiveness of the intervention studies reviewed in this analysis, conclusions can only be drawn with some reserve. The theoretical models used to organize support programmes were varied. As a consequence there is considerable heterogeneity in the examined interventions, in the group of caregivers (the target group), the target variables the studies focus on, and the measuring instruments used to register the desired changes (see Kuhlman *et al.* 1991; Knight *et al.* 1993). Concepts such as support group and respite care may give the impression that there are some standard types of support, but in reality there are many substantial differences between the offered interventions, which makes comparison difficult. This complicates drawing any conclusions about the different types of support. We nevertheless made an attempt to do so.

Recently two systematic reviews of the effectiveness of psychosocial interventions for caregivers of people with dementia were published. The first focused on controlled trials in English-language journals (Pusey and Richards 2001) and the methodological quality of the study designs to draw final conclusions. The second focused on the question of what components or combination of components produce positive outcomes for caregivers of persons with dementia (Cooke *et al.* 2001). Pusey and Richards conclude that the overall methodological quality of the studies was poor, particularly with regard to sample size, and methods of random allocation. They found that individualized interventions that utilized problem solving and behaviour management demonstrated the best evidence of effectiveness. Cooke *et al.*, however, conclude that social components (e.g. social support) or a combination of social and cognitive (e.g. problem solving) components seem to be the most effective. To advance our understanding of the efficacy of psychosocial interventions for caregivers, Cooke *et al.* (2001) recommend a more systematic approach in future research. Intervention components need to be carefully contrasted in appropriately designed studies of sufficient size.

A rather striking feature of the intervention studies we examined is that they generally focus on mixed populations of persons with dementia and caregivers, without acknowledging the possibly different needs of spouses, adult children, other caregivers, or people with a different type of dementia, for example, Alzheimer's disease or Pick's disease. In their reviews, Toseland *et al.* (1989), Knight *et al.* (1993), Huckle (1994) and Cuijpers (1992) therefore advocate that future research focus on specific groups of caregivers and persons with dementia with similar problems. We agree with Knight *et al.* who state that the principle question is *which* interventions are effective for *what* kind of caregivers and persons with dementia, and how the effectiveness of interventions for caregivers of persons with dementia can be maximized.

References

Adler, G., Ott, L., Jelinski, M., Mortimer, J. and Christensen, R. (1993) 'Institutional respite care: benefits and risks for dementia patients and caregivers', *International Psychogeriatrics* 5, 1: 67–77.

Belmin, J., Hee, C. and Ollivet, C. (1999) 'A health education programme lessens the burden of family caregivers of demented patients', *Journal of the American Geriatrics Society* 47: 1388–9.

Bleeker, J.A.C. (1994) 'Dementia services: a continental European view', in A. Burns and R. Levy (eds) *Dementia*, London: Chapman and Hall.

—— (1997) 'The status of daytreatment for psychogeriatric patients in Europe', in C. Waechtler (ed.) *Die Gerontopsychiatrische Tagesklinik – 20 Jahre Erfahrungen*, Regensburg: Roderer.

Bourgeois, M.S., Schulz, R. and Burgio, L. (1996) 'Interventions for caregivers of patients with Alzheimer's Disease: a review and analysis of content, process, and outcomes', *Int. J. Aging and Human Development* 43, 1: 35–92.

Bouter, L.M. (1994) *Meta-analyse: Controleerbaar en reproduceerbaar literatuuronderzoek als basis voor rationele beslissingen in de gezondheidszorg*, Amsterdam: Amsterdam University Press.

Brennan, P.F., Moore, S.M. and Smyth, K.A. (1995) 'The effects of a special computer network on caregivers of persons with Alzheimer's disease', *Nursing Research* 44, 3: 166–72.

Brodaty, H. and Gresham, M. (1989) 'Effect of a training programme to reduce stress in carers of patients with dementia', *British Medical Journal* 299: 1375–9.

—— (1992) 'Prescribing residential respite care for dementia; effects, side-effects, indications and dosage', *International Journal of Geriatric Psychiatry* 7: 357–62.

Brodaty, H. and Hadzi-Pavlovic, D. (1990) 'Psychosocial effects on carers of living with persons with dementia', *Australian and New Zealand Journal of Psychiatry* 24: 351–61.

Brodaty, H., Roberts, K. and Peters, K. (1994) 'Quasi-experimental evaluation of an educational model for dementia caregivers', *International Journal of Geriatric Psychiatry* 9: 195–204.

Brodaty, H., Gresham, M. and Luscombe, G. (1997) 'The Prince Henry Hospital Dementia Caregivers' Training Programme', *International Journal of Geriatric Psychiatry* 12: 192–3.

Burdz, M.P., Eaton, W.O. and Bond, J.B. (1988) 'Effect of respite care on dementia and nondementia patients and their caregivers', *Psychology and Aging* 3, 1: 38–42.

Burgener, S.C., Bakas, T., Murray, C., Dunahee, J. and Tossey, S. (1998) 'Effective caregiving approaches for patients with Alzheimer's Disease', *Geriatric Nursing* 19: 121–6.

Chalmers, T.C., Smith, H., Blackburn, B., Silverman, B., Schroeder, B. *et al.* (1981) 'A method for assessing the quality of a randomized controlled trial', *Controlled Clinical Trials* 2: 31–49.

Chiverton, P. and Caine, E.D. (1989) 'Education to assist spouses in coping with Alzheimer's disease. A controlled trial', *Journal of the American Geriatrics Society* 37, 7: 593–8.

Clark, N.M. and Rakowski, W. (1983) 'Family caregivers of older adults: improving helping skills', *The Gerontologist* 23, 6: 637–42.

Cohen, D. and Eisdorfer, C. (1988) 'Depression in family members caring for a relative with Alzheimer's disease', *Journal of the American Geriatric Society* 36: 885–9.

Collins, C.E., Given, B.A. and Given, C.W. (1994) 'Interventions with family caregivers of persons with Alzheimer's disease', *Nursing Clinics of North America* 29, 1: 195–207.

Conlin, M.M., Caranasos, G.J. and Davidson, R.A. (1992) 'Reduction of caregiver stress by respite care: A pilot study', *Southern Medical Journal* 85, 11: 1096–1100.

Cooke, D.D., McNally, L., Mulligan, K.T., Harrison, M.J.G. and Newman, S.P. (2001) 'Psychosocial interventions for caregivers of people with dementia: a systematic review', *Aging and Mental Health* 5, 2: 120–35.

Coope, B., Ballard, C., Saad, K., Patel, A., Bentham, P. *et al.* (1995) 'The prevalence of depression in the carers of dementia sufferers', *International Journal of Geriatric Psychiatry* 10: 237–42.

Cuijpers, P. (1992) 'De effecten van ondersteuningsgroepen voor verzorg(st)ers van dementerende ouderen thuis: een literatuuroverzicht', *Tijdschrift voor Gerontologie en Geriatrie* 23: 12–17.

Cuijpers, W.J.M.J. (1993) 'De werking van ondersteuningsgroepen voor centrale verzorgers van dementerende ouderen', thesis, Katholieke Universiteit Nijmegen.

Cummings, S.M., Long, J.K., Peterson-Hazan, S. and Harrison, J. (1998) 'The efficacy of a group treatment model in helping spouses meet the emotional and practical challenges of early stage caregiving', *Clinical Gerontologist* 20, 1: 29–45.

Diesfeldt, H.F.A. (1992) 'Psychogeriatric day care outcome: a five year follow-up', *International Journal. of Geriatric Psychiatry* 7: 673–9.

Dröes, R.M. (ed.) (1996) *Amsterdamse Ontmoetingscentra; een nieuwe vorm van ondersteuning voor dementerende mensen en hun verzorgers*, Amsterdam: Thesis Publishers.

Dröes, R.M. and Breebaart, E. (1994) *Amsterdamse Ontmoetingscentra; een nieuwe vorm van ondersteuning voor dementerende ouderen en hun verzorgers*', Amsterdam: Thesis Publishers.

Dröes, R.M., Breebaart, E., Tilburg, W. van and Mellenbergh, G.J. (2000) 'The effect of integrated family support versus day care only on behavior and mood of patients with dementia', *International Psychogeriatrics* 12, 1: 99–116.

Duijnstee, M. (1992) *De belasting van familieleden van dementerenden*, Nijkerk: Intro.

Eagles, J.M., Craig, A., Rawlinson, F., Restall, D.B., Beattie, J.A.G. *et al.* (1987) 'The psychological well-being of supporters of the demented elderly', *British Journal of Psychiatry* 50: 293–8.

Feinberg, L.F. and Kelly, K. (1995) 'A well-deserved break: respite programs offered by California's statewide system of caregiver resource centers', *The Gerontologist* 35, 5: 701–6.

Flint, A.J. (1995) 'Effects of respite care on patients with dementia and their caregivers', *International Psychogeriatrics* 7, 4: 505–17.

Fuller-Jonap, F. and Haley, W.E. (1995) 'Mental and physical health of male caregivers of a spouse with Alzheimer's disease', *Journal of Aging and Health* 7: 99–118.

Gendron, C.E., Poitras, L.R., Engels, M.L., Dastoor, D.P., Sirota, S.E. *et al.* (1986) 'Skills training with supporters of the demented', *Journal of the American Geriatrics Society* 34, 12: 875–80.

Gendron, C., Poitras, L., Dastoor, D.P. and Perodeau, G. (1996) 'Cognitive-behavioural group intervention for spousal caregivers: findings and clinical considerations', *Clinical Gerontologist* 17: 3–19.

George, L. and Gwyther, L. (1986) 'Caregiver well-being: a multidimensional examination of family caregivers of demented adults', *The Gerontologist* 26: 253–9.

Gilleard, C.J., Gilleard, E. and Whittick, J.E. (1984) 'Impact of psychogeriatric day hospital care on the patient's family', *British Journal of Psychiatry* 145: 487–92.

Glosser, G. and Wexler, D. (1985) 'Participants' evaluation of educational/support groups for families of patients with Alzheimer's Disease and other dementias', *The Gerontologist* 25, 3: 232–6.

Goodman, C. (1990) 'Evaluation of a model self-help telephone program: impact on natural networks', *Social Work* 35, 6: 556–62.

Goodman, C.C. and Pynoos, J. (1990) 'A model telephone information and support program for caregivers of Alzheimer's patients', *The Gerontologist* 30, 3: 399–404.

Haley, W.E. (1987) 'Experimental evaluation of the effectiveness of group intervention for dementia caregivers', *The Gerontologist* 27, 3: 376–82.

—— (1989) 'Group interventions for dementia family caregivers: a longitudinal perspective', *The Gerontologist* 29, 4: 478–80.

Haley, W.E., Brown, S.L. and Levine, E.G. (1987) 'Experimental evaluation of the effectiveness of a group intervention for dementia caregivers', *The Gerontologist* 27, 3: 376–81.

Hébert, R., Leclerc, G., Bravo, G., Girouard, D. and Lefrançois, R. (1994) 'Efficacy of a support group programme for caregivers of demented patients in the community: a randomized controlled trial', *Archives of Gerontology and Geriatrics* 18: 1–14.

Hinchliffe, A.C., Hyman, I. and Blizard, B. (1992) 'The impact on carers of behavioral difficulties in dementia: a pilot study on management', *International Journal of Geriatric Psychiatry* 7: 579–83.

Huckle, P.L. (1994) 'Families and dementia; review', *International Journal of Geriatric Psychiatry* 9: 735–41.

Kahan, J.S. (1984) 'The effect of a group support program on decreasing feelings of burden and depression in relatives of patients with Alzheimer's disease and other dementing illnesses', *Dissertation Abstracts International* 45, 3: 963a–4a.

Kahan, J., Kemp, B., Staples, F.R. and Brummel-Smith, K. (1985) 'Decreasing the burden in families caring for a relative with a dementing illness: a controlled study', *Journal of the American Geriatrics Society* 33, 10: 664–70.

Knight, B.G., Lutzky, S.M. and Macofsky-Urban, F. (1993) 'A meta-analytic review of interventions for caregiver distress: recommendations for future research', *The Gerontologist* 33, 2: 240–8.

Kosloski, K. and Montgomery, R.J.V. (1993) 'The effects of respite on caregivers of Alzheimer's patients: one-year evaluation of the Michigan model respite programs', *Journal of Applied Gerontology* 12, 1: 4–17.

Kuhlman, G.J., Wilson, H.S., Hutchinson, S.A. and Wallhagen, M. (1991) 'Alzheimer's Disease and family caregiving: critical synthesis of the literature and research agenda', *Nursing Research* 40, 6: 331–6.

Larkin, J.P. and Most Hopcroft, B. (1993) 'In-hospital respite as a moderator of caregiver stress', *Health and Social Work* 18, 2: 132–8.

Lawton, M.P., Brody, E.M. and Saperstein, A.R. (1989) 'A controlled study of respite service for caregivers of Alzheimer's patients', *The Gerontologist* 29, 1: 8–15.

Lazarus, L.W., Stafford, B., Cooper, K., Cohler, B. and Dysken, M. (1981) 'A pilot study of an Alzheimer patients' relatives discussion group', *The Gerontologist* 21, 4: 353–8.

McCurry, S.M., Logsdon, R.G., Vitiello, M.V. and Teri, L. (1998) 'Successful behavioural treatment for reported sleep problems in elderly caregivers of dementia patients: a controlled study', *Journals of Gerontology Series B. Psychological Sciences and Social Sciences* 53: 122–9.

Meier Robinson, K. (1988) 'A social skills training program for adult caregivers', *Advanced Nursing Sciences* 10, 2: 59–72.

Mittelman, M.S., Ferris, S.H., Shulman, E., Steinberg, G., Ambinder, A., Mackell, J.A. and Cohen, J. (1995) 'A comprehensive support program: effect on depression in spouse-caregivers of AD patients', *The Gerontologist* 35, 6: 792–802.

Mittelman, M.S., Ferris, S.H., Shulman, E., Steinberg, G. and Levin, B. (1996) 'A family intervention to delay nursing home placement of patients with Alzheimer Disease', *JAMA* 276, 21: 1725–31.

Mohide, E.A., Pringle, D.M., Streiner, D.L., Gilbert, J.R., Muir, G. *et al.* (1990) 'A randomized trial of family caregiver support in the home management of dementia', *Journal of the American Geriatrics Society* 38: 446–54.

Moniz-Cook, E., Agar, S., Gibson, G., Win, T. and Wang, M. (1998) 'A preliminary study of the effects of early intervention with people with dementia and their families in a memory clinic', *Aging and Mental Health* 2: 199–211.

Morris, R.G., Morris, L.W. and Britton, P.G. (1988) *Developing Respite Services for the Elderly*, Seattle, WA: University of Washington Press.

Morris, R.G., Woods, R.T., Davies, K.S., Berry, J. and Morris, L.W. (1992) 'The use of a coping strategy focused support group for carers of dementia sufferers', *Counselling Psychology Quarterly* 5, 4: 337–48.

Newcomer, R., Yordi, C., DuNah, R., Fox, P. and Wilkinson, A. (1999) 'Effects of the Medicare Alzheimer's Disease Demonstration on caregiver burden and depression', *Health Services Research* 34, 3: 669–89.

Nies, H.L.G.R. (1989) 'Dagopvang en dagverzorging voor ouderen', *Tijdschrift Gerontologie en Geriatrie* 20: 67–72.

Nuy, H.R., Plaats, J. van der and Vernooij, M. (1984) *Dagbehandeling in verpleeghuizen*, Nijmegen: Instituut Sociale Geneeskunde, Katholieke Universiteit.

Nuy, H.R., Plaats, J. van der, Vernooij, M. and Heyendael, P. (1985) 'Geriatrische patiënt, thuismilieu en voorziening', *Medisch Contact* 40, 17: 521–6.

Ostwald, S.K., Hepburn, K.W., Caron, W., Burns, T. and Mantell, R. (1999) 'Reducing caregiver burden: a randomized psychoeducational intervention for caregivers of persons with dementia'. *The Gerontologist* 39: 299–309.

Pot, A.M. (1996) 'Caregivers' perspectives. A longitudinal study on the psychological distress of informal caregivers of demented elderly', thesis, Vrije Universiteit, Amsterdam.

Prins, J.M. and Büller, H.R. (1996) 'Meta-analysis: the final answer, or even more confusion?', *The Lancet* 348: 199.

Pusey, H. and Richards, D. (2001) 'A systematic review of the effectiveness of psychosocial interventions for carers of people with dementia', *Aging and Mental Health* 5, 2: 107–19.

Quayhagen, M.P. and Quayhagen, M. (1989) 'Differential effects of family-based strategies on Alzheimer's disease', *The Gerontologist* 29, 2: 150–55.

Rey, J.C. and Tilquin, C. (1994) 'SYSTED '94: dependency, the challenge for the year 2000', *Proceedings of the 5th International Conference on Systems Sciences in Health–Social Services for the Elderly and the Disabled*, Geneva.

Riordan, J. and Bennett, A. (1998) 'An evaluation of an augmented domiciliary service to older people with dementia and their carers', *Aging and Mental Health* 2: 137–43.

Russell, V., Proctor, L. and Moniz, E. (1989) 'The influence of a relative support group on carers' emotional distress', *Journal of Advanced Nursing* 14: 863–7.

Seltzer, B., Rheaume, Y., Volicer, L., Fabiszewski, K.J., Lyon, P.C. *et al.* (1988) 'The short term effects of in-hospital respite on the patient with Alzheimer's Disease', *The Gerontologist* 28, 1: 121–4.

Strawn, B.B., Hester, S. and Brown, W.S. (1998) 'Telecare: a social support intervention for family caregivers of dementia victims', *Clinical Gerontologist* 18: 66–9.

Sutcliffe, C. and Larner, S. (1988) 'Counseling carers of the elderly at home: a preliminary study', *British Journal of Clinical Psychology* 27: 177–8.

Toseland, R.W., Rossiter, C.M. and Labrecque, M.S. (1989) 'The effectiveness of peer-led and professionally led groups to support family caregivers', *The Gerontologist* 29, 4: 465–70.

Veldhuyzen-Van Zanten, S.J.O. and Boers, M. (1993) 'Meta-analyse: de kunst van het systema-tisch overzicht', *Nederlands Tijdschrift voor Geneeskunde* 137: 1594–9.

Vernooij-Dassen, M. (1993) *Dementie en thuiszorg*, Amsterdam/Lisse: Swets and Zeitlinger.

Vernooij-Dassen, M.J.F.J. and Persoon, J.M.G. (1990) *Het thuismilieu van dementerende ouderen. Een interventie-onderzoek naar effecten van professionele ondersteuning van gezins- en familieleden van dementerende ouderen*, Nijmegen: Instituut voor Sociale Geneeskunde, Katholieke Universiteit Nijmegen.

Visser, E.J. and Cornel, A. (1993) *Respite care voor mantelzorgers van mensen met dementie*, Utrecht: NIZW.

Vissers, H. (1994) 'Ondersteuningsprogramma's voor mantelzorgers van dementerende ouderen in Europa en de Verenigde Staten', doctoral thesis, Vrije Universiteit, Amsterdam.

Wächtler, C., Fuchs, G. and Herber, U. (1994) '15 Jahre gerontopsychiatrische Tagesklinken in der Bundesrepublik Deutschland', *Psychiatr. Praxis* 21: 139–42.

Weinberger, M., Gold, D.T., Divine, G.W., Cowper, P.A. *et al.* (1993) 'Social service interventions for caregivers of patients with dementia: impact on health care utilization and expenditures', *Journal of the American Geriatrics Society* 41, 2: 153–6.

Wells, Y.D., Jorm, A.F., Jordan, F. and Lefroy, R. (1990) 'Effects on caregivers of special day care programmes for dementia sufferers', *Australian and New Zealand Journal of Psychiatry* 24: 82–90.

Whitlatch, C.J., Zarit, S.H. and Von Eye, A. (1991) 'Efficacy of interventions with caregivers: a reanalysis', *The Gerontologist* 31, 1: 9–14.

Wilkins, S.S., Castle, S., Heck, E., Tanzy, K. and Fahey, J. (1999) 'Immune function, mood, and perceived burden among caregivers participating in a psychoeducational intervention', *Psychiatric Services* 50, 6: 747–9.

Wright, S.D., Lund, D.A., Pett, M.A. and Caserta, M.S. (1987) 'The assessment of support group experiences by caregivers of dementia patients', *Clinical Gerontologist* 6, 4: 35–9.

Yordi, C.L., Chu, A.S., Ross, K.M. and Wong, S.J. (1982) 'Research and the frail elderly: Ethical and methodological issues in controlled social experiments', *The Gerontologist* 22, 1: 72–7.

Zanetti, O., Metitieri, T., Biachetti, A. and Trabucchi, M. (1998) 'Effectiveness of an educational program for demented person's relatives', *Archives of Gerontology and Geriatrics* suppl. 6: 531–8.

Zarit, S.H., Anthony, C.R. and Boutselis, M. (1987) 'Interventions with caregivers of dementia patients: comparisons of two approaches', *Psychology and Aging* 2, 3: 225–32.

Zarit, S.H., Stephens, M.A., Townsend, A. and Greene, R. (1998) 'Stress reduction for family caregivers: effects of adult day care use', *J. Gerontol. B. Psychol. Sci. Soc. Sci.* 53, 5: S267–77.

Chapter 11

Coping in early dementia

Findings of a new type of support group

Ann Marshall

Introduction

The recent growth of memory clinics, improved assessment techniques and research into drugs to reduce cognitive impairment has led to earlier diagnosis of Alzheimer's disease and other types of dementia. However, at present very little is known about how people with early dementia cope with such a devastating illness, what they wish to know about their diagnosis and what kind of information and support is helpful to them (Pinner 2000).

In other illnesses, one way to provide support and information is through mutual support groups: these can be a way of dealing with the feelings of isolation which may result from the illness, as well as a source of information and ways of coping. 'Universality' (the feeling that one is not alone) is a very important part of any therapy group, as well as the opportunity for vicarious learning, catharsis, improving knowledge and altruism – helping others can boost self-esteem (Yalom 1985). Support groups have already been used extensively in the field of dementia with caregivers and have provided social support, coping skills and reduced stress and depression levels (Cuijpers *et al.* 1997). There is now growing evidence of the need for such groups, not just for the caregivers, but for the people with dementia themselves (Keady and Gilliard 1999).

This chapter will look at the development of support groups for people with early dementia. It will then examine some models and studies which contribute to our understanding of the emotional reactions and coping responses of a person faced with a dementing illness and the implications of these models for running a support group. Following this, issues of process and content will be considered and some case examples will be given. Finally, the problems of evaluating support groups in this area will be considered.

Background

Reports of groups which aim to provide emotional support for people with dementia have appeared in the literature since the 1950s (Finkel 1990).

However, these were usually based in inpatient settings with patients with moderate to severe dementia (Feil 1967; Akerlund and Norberg 1986; Austad 1992) or mixed groups of patients with functional and organic illnesses (Greene *et al.* 1993). Since the 1990s, with earlier diagnosis, reports have been published of groups specifically for people in the early stages of dementia. These groups have described themselves in various ways: 'early-stage Alzheimer's reassurance group' (Haggerty 1990); 'mutual support group' (Peach and Duff 1991); 'supportive seminar group' (Snyder *et al.* 1995), 'support group' (McAfee *et al.* 1989; Labarge and Trtanj 1995; Yale 1995; Hawkins and Eagger 1999; Marshall 2001; Cheston *et al.* 2001), 'memory group' (Thrower 1998), 'memory support group' (Scarboro 2000) and 'coping with forgetfulness group' (Barton *et al.* 2001).

Most of these groups have had sessions of about one and a half hours including time for refreshments. The aims of these groups have been to provide education and support, but they have used a wide range of models and techniques including psychotherapy, cognitive therapy, behaviour therapy, relaxation exercises, reminiscence and memory training exercises (Haggerty 1990; Labarge and Trtanj 1995; Scarboro 2000; Marshall 2001). An outline of each of these groups is given in Table 11.1.

Emotion and coping in early dementia

There are a few studies that focus on the emotional reactions and coping responses specifically in the early stages of dementia, but some useful ideas also come from stage models, those looking at later dementia and approaches applied to functional illnesses.

The subjective experiences of the very early stages of dementia have been described as 'slips and lapses' (Keady and Gilliard 1999) and 'a growing realisation that something is wrong' (Clare 2001). There may be recognition and concern (Cohen *et al.* 1984) and a struggle to find an explanation for what is happening (Miesen 1999), but also discounting and normalizing events such as trying to ignore the memory loss or seeing it as a normal part of getting older (Keady and Gilliard 1999). As the illness progresses, denial may take many forms such as not naming the illness, dissociation of affect, vagueness in discussing the condition, minimizing the severity of the impairment and refusing to seek information about the illness (Bahro *et al.* 1995; Keady and Gilliard 1999). The degree of denial may vary from complete denial of all problems, acknowledging the problem but not the cause or implications, for example, seeing the memory problem as part of normal ageing or not accepting help, and finally accepting the problem intellectually but not emotionally (Cheston and Bender 1999). Clare (2001) suggested that there are two tendencies with dementia: 'self-protective – denying or minimising the changes' and 'integrative – acknowledging the full extent of the changes and trying to integrate them into the self-concept'. She observed

Table 11.1 Summary of reports of support groups for people with early dementia

Authors	Type of group	Participants	Content
McAfee et al. (1989)	Six weekly sessions with speakers followed by seven support sessions and one 'social occasion' to end.	Early stage of dementia. Six participants with probable Alzheimer's disease and one with multi-infarct dementia.	Legal and financial matters, history of Alzheimer's disease and research, relationship, emotional aspects and coping skills.
Haggerty (1990)	Open-ended 'early-stage Alzheimer's reassurance group'.	'Beginning or middle stage of dementia with minimal cognitive impairment'. Six to eight participants present at one session.	Information about Alzheimer's disease, relaxation, cognitive therapy, reminiscence, reassurance, peer support.
Peach and Duff (1991)	Mutual support group. Initially four weeks, then became ongoing.	Alzheimer's or related dementia. Mental Status Questionnaire score '4–7.5. Thirteen participants had attended after one year.	Social, emotional, health, practical and spiritual issues.
Snyder et al. (1995)	Supportive seminar group. Eight-week closed group.	Diagnosis of Alzheimer's or related disorder. Four to five participants.	Daily living skills, self-esteem, relationships, health and legal matters and discussion.
Labarge and Trtanj (1995)	Support group 'Project Esteem'. Eight bi-monthly sessions.	Recent diagnosis of dementia. Ten participants.	Information and demonstrations about lost and intact memory functions, Alzheimer's disease, self-esteem, loss of roles, interpersonal loss, coping strategies, death.
Yale (1995)	Support group for patients newly diagnosed with Alzheimer's disease. Eight-week closed group.	Diagnosis of probable or possible Alzheimer's disease. Seven participants in the support group, six in the control group. Mini Mental Scale score 18–24.	Diagnosis, living skills, relationships, research and preparing for the future.

Thrower (1998)	Eight-week memory group which evolved into a six-hour peer support programme with a formal group in the morning, lunch and then social activities in the afternoon.	Eleven participants in the early stages of dementia.	Model of memory, memory exercises, strategies and aids, effects of emotion on memory, relaxation.
Hawkins and Eagger (1999)	Open-ended support group.	Six participants in early stages of dementia.	Diagnosis, research, driving, relationships, emotions, sex, treatment, services and legal issues.
Scarboro (2000)	Memory support group. Six weekly sessions.	Six participants in early stages of dementia.	Model of memory, coping skills, diagnosis, emotional reactions, old age, reminiscence and medication.
Marshall (2001)	Support group. Eight weekly sessions. Four-week baseline and follow-up phases.	Report of eight participants from two separate groups. MMSE scores 20–28.	Model of memory, memory aids, emotional reactions, anxiety management, relationships, assertiveness training and reminiscence.
Barton et al. (2001)	Coping with forgetfulness group. Seven weekly sessions.	Seven participants attending a day hospital for assessment of memory difficulties.	Causes of memory problems, memory aids and coping strategies, loss of independence, changes in social life and activities and worries about the future.
Cheston et al. (2001)	'Dementia Voice project'. Ten weekly sessions. Six-week baseline and ten-week follow-up phases.	Report of six groups with 42 participants with early dementia. Mean MMSE score 23. Nineteen participants completed all three phases and eight completed group and follow-up.	The main issues concerned the participants' lives and their memory problems; the many subtle aspects of forgetting.

that most people showed a mixture of both tendencies but usually adopted one more than the other.

In order to adjust to the cognitive impairments, the person with dementia may try and overcome the problems by using mnemonic aids (Labarge *et al.* 1988), sticking to a routine (Keady and Nolan 1995; Clare 2001), trying to cover up their memory loss as much as possible (Keady and Gilliard 1999), blaming others, or becoming aggressive as a way of externalizing the threat – explaining errors in terms of other people's actions or venting their frustration arising from the cognitive losses (Feil 1989; Cheston and Bender 1999). They may also withdraw from difficult or unfamiliar situations to cover up their memory loss (Keady and Gilliard 1999).

If they have family around them, the person with dementia has to 'negotiate a shared view' of the illness with a family member (Clare 2001). This may be prompted by the family member confronting the person with dementia about their unusual behaviour or seeking professional help on their behalf. They may then share some of their fears with this family member, but still hide the extent of the problem from them and continue to conceal it altogether from other people (Keady and Gilliard 1999). If, as is usually the case, the person with dementia is unable to communicate their feelings openly with their spouse, they will suffer from increasing emotional separation and isolation (Miesen 1997).

As the illness progresses, maintaining a sense of mastery and concealing the memory loss become increasingly difficult and so the person starts to rely more and more on the support of the people close to them and may become very dependent on their caregiver for a sense of security (Miesen 1992; Keady and Gilliard 1999; Cheston and Bender 1999). As they find it increasingly difficult to recall recent information, they may draw increasingly on their past (Miesen 1999). Living in the past may be a way of establishing a different, cognitively intact identity, a way of exploring and making sense of the current situation by drawing on past experience (Bender and Cheston 1997), or a way of coping by acknowledging the mastery of previous crises (Labarge *et al.* 1988). Retreating to images of the past may also be a way of seeking security in a strange and frightening situation (Feil 1989; Miesen 1992; Cheston and Bender 1999) or improving mood by recalling 'good times' (Keady and Nolan 1995). Other positive ways of coping which have been identified in studies of early dementia include the use of humour (Peach and Duff 1991; Keady and Nolan 1995), emotional management ('I talk to myself about calming down'), acceptance ('I can't change what is happening, so there's no use worrying'), 'modelling' – recognizing how other people have coped, focusing on the good things (Labarge *et al.* 1988) and comparing oneself to people worse off (Keady and Nolan 1995; Clare 2001).

The way in which a person with dementia reacts to their environment will depend very much on their social environment: Kitwood (1990) has emphasized the important role of interpersonal interaction in ameliorating or exacerbating the organic changes in dementia. He used the term 'Malignant Social Psychology' to describe the negative types of social interaction such as stigmatizing or invalidating which often occur towards people with dementia and take away the social roles which they could maintain. Apathy and withdrawal may occur because of the loss of these social roles – a person may defend himself against further attack by exaggerating their difficulties or fulfilling the role in which others have placed them (Bender and Cheston 1997). Feil (1989) proposed that it is the loss of social roles, together with sensory losses that lead to a retreat from reality and late-onset dementia (over the age of 75). Bender and Cheston (1997) suggested that denial and lack of awareness in people with dementia are not fixed entities, but more responses to the situation in which they find themselves. If the people around them behave empathically, they may feel safe and able to acknowledge their losses.

In addition to the social environment, many authors have also emphasized the importance of pre-morbid personality, developmental history including previous losses and defence mechanisms in explaining how an individual will cope with a dementing illness (Hausman 1992; Miesen 1997; Cheston and Bender 1999). Kitwood (1997) proposed that people who have lowered defences will be able to accept comfort and support, while those with an independent and obsessional personality may have strong defences against recognition and acceptance. Those with a passive and anxious disposition may be prone to apathy and despair. People with a low level of insight will tend to blame others when things go wrong or experience delusions. Those with a high level of awareness will remain open to what is happening to them without evasion or blame. Miesen (1997) used the term 'awareness concept' to describe a person's subjective experience and understanding of their dementia. He suggested that a person's attachment history is of particular importance in explaining their 'awareness concept' and thus determining how they cope with their illness and is linked to the 'self-protective' and 'integrative' tendencies identified by Clare (2001).

The main emotional reactions to the dementia have been described as anger, anxiety, suspicion, sadness, hopelessness and worthlessness (Soloman and Szwabo 1992); grief, anxiety, depression and despair (Bender and Cheston 1997; Cheston and Bender 1999), anger, guilt and sadness (Cohen et al. 1984); 'slow dismay' (Clare 2001) and mourning – 'saying good-bye to their previous self and accepting that things are not going to return to normal' (Keady and Gilliard 1999). Miesen (1997) has also drawn attention to the grieving process in dementia and suggested that the person with dementia has to cope with 'the same feelings that arise in situations which resemble separation, homelessness or displacement'.

Empirical studies have found a high prevalence of anxiety and depressive symptoms in dementia (Burns et al. 1990; Cummings and Victoroff 1990; Ballard et al. 1996). A study by Wands et al. (1990) looking specifically at early dementia and using the Hospital Anxiety and Depression Scale found that 38 per cent of 50 patients were in the borderline or clinical range for anxiety and 28 per cent were in this range for depression.

Psychodynamic models explain the development of anxiety, depression and paranoia in people with dementia by suggesting that the illness prevents them from adapting to the demands of old age. The weakening of ego resources and defences makes it difficult to cope with unresolved conflicts which may re-emerge in old age, there is a loss of mastery over one's self and environment, loss of ability to adapt to change and to direct energies into new areas and loss of ability to invest in others (Hausman 1992). Behavioural models applied to dementia emphasize the loss of pleasant activities as well as the loss of skills in dementia (Teri and Uomoto 1991; Teri 1994; Teri *et al.* 1997) and cognitive models suggest that some of the dysfunctional behaviours seen in dementia are attempts made by the person to cope with the anxiety caused by their confusion (James 1999).

Implications for support groups

The models described above emphasize the importance of understanding the subjective experience of early dementia, individual differences in reaction to the illness and ways to create a safe environment for people with dementia to express their feelings and acknowledge their losses.

Feil (1992), in her Validation approach, advocated encouraging people with dementia to express their feelings, listening to them with empathy, asking non-threatening questions to build up trust, being non-judgemental and not confronting people who deny their loss of ability. Miesen (1997) emphasized the need for people with dementia to grieve for their losses. Kitwood's model focused on ways to create an interpersonal environment which makes the individual feel valued and encourages the expression of a wide range of emotions, as well as facilitating choices, creativity and ways in which people can help others (Kitwood 1997). In a support group for early dementia, the participants can be encouraged to make choices about the way in which the group is run and helped to support others in the group.

Feil proposed using reminiscence techniques to help people with dementia to look at how they have coped in the past and Solomon and Szwabo (1992) suggested the use of reminiscence and life review to resolve present and past conflicts. Bender and Cheston's work suggests 'story-telling' – sharing stories about the past can be useful for creating an identity for an individual, can help them to make sense of current experiences by relating them to the past, enhance their self-esteem and also create a shared identity within the group. However, this approach has to be handled sensitively as for some people past memories are a source of pleasure and self-esteem and a way of making sense of the present, but for others they can be a painful reminder of their many losses. Individual difference in attitudes to reminiscence was documented by Coleman (1986).

Psychodynamic models for group therapy describe the importance of building up relationships with the group leaders and the other group members, emotional catharsis, the validation of emotions, the enhancement of self-esteem, roles and coping skills, reminiscence of past accomplishments and resolution of past issues and the development of insight (Shoham and Neuschatz 1985; Feil 1989; Haggerty 1990; Hausman 1992; Yalom 1985; Cheston 1997). They also draw attention to countertransference and emphasize some of the emotional reactions that may arise from working with dementia and the need to lower one's own defences to provide good care and treatment (Feil 1989; Kitwood 1997; Hausman 1992; Cheston 1997). The behaviour therapy model has generated effective therapies for reducing anxiety and depression and improving social skills in a wide range of settings and there have been some recent studies applying some of these techniques to people with dementia. Relaxation therapy has been found to have some beneficial effects with people with dementia (Welden and Yesavage 1982; Lantz *et al.* 1997). Other behavioural strategies such as increasing pleasant events and maximizing cognitive abilities have been found to be effective in reducing depression in patients with dementia and minor or major depressive disorder, although these have been applied by a caregiver (Teri and Uomoto 1991; Teri 1994; Teri *et al.* 1997). Attempts have also been made to use cognitive therapy techniques – helping patients to identify and challenge negative patterns of thinking with people with dementia (Teri and Gallagher-Thompson 1991).

Group process and content

In setting up a support group, there are many issues to consider; how to select participants for the group; whether to have an open or closed group; the best way to involve caregivers; how to plan the structure and content.

Selection for the group

The main selection criteria for the support groups in the literature has been the ability to participate constructively in the group (Haggerty 1990) – being able to express feelings and commitment to attending a group – and a diagnosis of dementia. (In Yale's 1995 study this was Alzheimer's disease; in the other studies, it was Alzheimer's and other dementias.) Some degree of insight into the illness is also an essential criterion for participation in the group and authors have defined this insight in varying ways: 'acknowledgement of memory loss and understanding of the implications of diagnosis' (Peach and Duff 1991); 'acknowledgement of memory loss and some recognition that this may be due to Alzheimer's disease or a related disorder' (Snyder *et al.* 1995); 'a recent diagnosis of dementia and awareness of the illness by the participant' (Labarge and Trtanj 1995); the participant has 'at least occasionally acknowledged their memory loss' (Yale 1995). Participants appear to gain some benefit from the group as long as they acknowledge some memory loss, without necessarily being open about all the implications (Marshall 2001).

The second important criterion is the degree of cognitive impairment. The participants are described as being in the early or early to middle stages of dementia and some studies emphasized specific cognitive test scores. These were 18 to 24 on the Mini Mental State Examination in Yale's study and 4 to 7.5 on the Abbreviated Mental Status Questionnaire in Peach and Duff's study. Other studies relied more on social and conversational skills (Snyder *et al.* 1995; Labarge and Trtanj 1995), although Snyder *et al.* suggested a score of 20 or above on the Mini Mental State Examination as a rough guide.

Other criteria used were no major psychiatric disorder such as hallucinations or delusions (Snyder *et al.* 1995) and no significant medical or psychiatric condition other than dementia (Yale 1995). Snyder *et al.* also mentioned the ability to read and to sit still throughout the duration of the group.

Thus cognitive status is important in grouping people of a similar level and tailoring activities to meet their abilities, but it is also important to take into account the person's ability to participate in the group, which will depend on personality, insight and social skills (Snyder *et al.* 1995). A pre-group interview is crucial to look at these issues, as well as to give a full explanation to the potential group member about what will happen in the group. Bender (2001) has described this as the 'informed consent interview'.

Open versus closed groups

In the literature about dementia support groups, there are examples of both open and closed groups. The advantages of an open group are that people can join at any time without waiting for the next group to start and can stay as many weeks as they wish (or until their condition deteriorates too far for them to participate). Discussions about issues can be developed over a long period of time and participants have the security of knowing that the group will always be there for them. The disadvantage is that new people have to integrate themselves into a group in which people already know each other and depending on how long people stay in the group, there may be people at different stages of dementia and at different therapeutic stages. Haggerty (1990) stated that in his group the less cognitively impaired members were encouraged to provide support both for new members and those with more cognitive impairment. However, he did not say how large these cognitive differences were and whether these caused any difficulties. People in the early stages of dementia may feel threatened by the presence of people at a more advanced stage (Feil 1992).

Involvement of caregivers

Previous studies of support groups have varied in the way in which they have involved caregivers: In McAfee *et al.*'s study the participants and caregivers met together for the information-giving phase of the study and then separately for the support phase. McAfee *et al.* reported that the caregivers 'felt a sense of empowerment' from their relative with dementia being included in the meetings. In Snyder *et al.*'s study, the participants and caregivers met separately for an hour and together for half an hour. Snyder *et al.* concluded that people talked more freely in the separate sessions, while the joint sessions were more about 'learning and reflection'. In Yale's study, the caregivers attended the last session. In other studies simultaneous sessions have been organized separately for caregivers (Labarge and Tranj 1995; Scarboro 2000). Separate sessions may be useful for the participants as they may not feel able to discuss some of their fears and feelings with their caregivers (Keady and Gilliard 1999; Marshall 2001). However, Clare (2001) suggested that effective strategies need to be identified to help couples who are struggling to negotiate a joint way of dealing with what is happening. Emmerson and Spaull (2001) have advocated joint sessions to minimize the patient–carer division and encourage couples to work as a team in managing everyday difficulties. Some shared time together may break down barriers and enhance communication (McAfee *et al.* 1989; Snyder *et al.* 1995), providing not just the opportunity to talk, but to find ways to reach a joint understanding so that the person with dementia may become an 'emotional equal' to their partner (Miesen 1997). This could reduce the isolation of the person with dementia and promote healthy rather than pathological grieving in both parties (Miesen 1997). A crucial area for research is to compare the effectiveness of joint and separate groups.

Structure

Holding sessions in the same place at the same time with the same therapist can create a secure environment, as well as having a small group of only six to eight participants (Haggerty 1990). Clear rules about confidentiality and making people feel comfortable to express themselves, or to listen as they wish, help to create a secure environment in which people feel safe to express their emotions. The group may be structured primarily as educational or non-directive, but clear educational tasks initially may make the participants feel secure, and then as the group progresses it can become less directive (Cheston and Jones 2000).

Certain techniques may be useful in the group to accommodate the cognitive impairments of the group members such as introducing one question at a time, restating themes and providing explanations, as well as reassurance if anxiety or confusion occur (Kasl-Godley and Gatz 2000). Summaries of main points from the sessions using flip-charts or handouts are useful as memory aids and can be shared with relatives (Snyder *et al.* 1995; Marshall 2001). If a group member has difficulty communicating, the group leaders should check whether they would like help to express themselves and then intervene when appropriate (Yale 1995; Cheston 1997). A hearing loop may also be useful as hearing loss can be a major issue for some individuals, adding to their confusion and social exclusion (Peach and Duff 1991; Marshall 2001). The provision of refreshments in the group may help to reduce stress and careful attention needs to be given to transport arrangements (Peach and Duff 1991).

Content

Almost all the support groups in the literature emphasize support in their aims and some also mention education: for example, 'to provide opportunities to share thoughts and feelings with peers and professionals' (Labarge and Trtanj 1995); 'to give individuals a sense of control when coping with everyday living' and 'to offer a supportive space where emotions can be talked about and acknowledged' (Scarboro 2000); 'to link up individuals with memory loss, provide a safe environment for sharing feelings and provide information' (Peach and Duff 1991); and to help the group members to deal with their memory loss by 'achieving a gradual balance between being overwhelmed and shutting it all out' (Cheston *et al.* 2001).

In many of the groups, the group leaders presented topics, at least initially, and the main issues discussed included daily living skills, legal and financial issues, driving, disempowerment, loss of self-esteem, relationships and dependency, ageing, other health issues which add to the memory loss such as poor hearing and the benefits of the group (Haggerty 1990; Snyder *et al.* 1995; Yale 1995; Scarboro 2000; Marshall 2001). The causes of Alzheimer's disease, current research and preparing for the future were also discussed in some groups (Peach and Duff 1991; Labarge and Trtanj 1995; Yale 1995; Hawkins and Eaggar 1999; Cheston and Jones 2000), although people did not want information about the later stages of the disease (Labarge and Tranj 1995). Some groups have also included specific techniques such as relaxation exercises, assertiveness techniques, cognitive therapy and reminiscence (Haggerty 1990; Marshall 2001). Labarge and Trtanj (1995) included information and demonstrations about memory in the first two sessions of the group, then started subsequent sessions with the request 'Tell us one good thing and/or one bad thing that has happened to you since we last met'. Cheston *et al.* (2001) used the phrase 'the purpose of

these groups is to think about what it's like when your memory isn't working as well as it used to'.

An example of a plan for an eight-week support group

- *Session 1*: introductions, aims of the group, discussion about confiden-
  tiality, memory problems, simple model of memory.
- *Session 2*: memory aids.
- *Session 3*: dealing with social situations, cognitive and assertiveness
  techniques.
- *Session 4*: emotions associated with having a memory problem, coping
  with emotions, relaxation.
- *Session 5*: further discussion about the effect of memory problems on
  relationships and about reducing anxiety.
- *Session 6*: participants' strengths – interests, hobbies, retained skills –
  past roles, reminiscence.
- *Session 7*: Preparing for ending of the group the following week, review
  of skills and techniques learnt in the group.
- *Session 8*: participants' views about the group, future groups, goodbyes.

The plan should be kept quite flexible, so that if material is covered quickly,
some of the next session's material can be covered or if participants want to
spend a long time or come back to a topic, then this topic might run into
later sessions. From the second session, the group starts with a summary
of the previous week's session and this is shown on a handout given to the
participant. A flip-chart is used to record the main points made by the
group leaders and participants in each session.

Case examples

Beatrice

Beatrice was a lively and outgoing person who had had a full social life, but
since the onset of her memory loss she felt that she had become depressed,
anxious and lacking in confidence in social situations. Beatrice described her
relationship with her husband as close, but he was undergoing treatment for
cancer and she tried to hide her memory problems from him. Beatrice went
out a lot with her family and joined social events with neighbours. Beatrice
was keen to attend the group and felt it might help with her confidence.

Beatrice was anxious in the group initially, but became more relaxed in
later sessions. She talked about the frustration and embarrassment which
her memory problems caused her and her dependence on her husband, but
did not talk about the causes of her problems or about the future. She found
social situations very difficult due to both hearing and memory problems.

As the group progressed, she talked about being more open with friends and acquaintances about her memory problems and said that they had become more understanding. Beatrice had many happy memories and talked a lot in the group about her past life and her family.

Beatrice said that she found it helpful to be with other people with the same problems, 'to know that I am not on my own' and to 'have a laugh'. Her husband reported that she had enjoyed the group and appeared more relaxed after the sessions. He also said that she often practised the relaxation exercises from the group.

Henry

Henry was a sociable, cheerful person with a good sense of humour. He was open about the impact of his memory loss on his life, reporting that it had made him depressed and withdrawn. He worried about the future and the progression of his memory problems.

Henry had a close relationship with his wife. He confided in her about his memory problems and found her supportive, but still kept many of his fears to himself. His wife was younger than him and still working and he was anxious not to burden her when she was so busy. He had few regular social activities and was keen to join the group for the company.

Henry contributed a lot to the group and interacted well with others. His mood fluctuated from week to week so that at times he was relaxed and jovial and at other times low in mood. He expressed anxieties about the future and sometimes said that he found it painful to look back at his past life and compare it to his present situation. His sense of humour was very evident throughout the group and he often made jokes relating to his fears, particularly about ageing.

Henry reported that he found it very comforting to be with people with the same problems, to see how they coped and to express his feelings. His wife reported that he was reluctant to go to the first few sessions but then started to enjoy it and was upset when the group came to an end.

Dorothy

Dorothy described herself as having always been a sociable person with a tendency to worry a lot. She had been very dependent on her husband, but he had died about a year before the group. Dorothy was very depressed and also socially isolated as she and her husband had done everything together.

Dorothy had a close relationship with her son who visited her regularly. He reported that his mother often expressed fears about her illness and what would happen in the future. Dorothy's father had also had dementia. When asked about her expectations of the group, Dorothy said that she hoped that it would help in some way.

Dorothy was very open about her memory problems and her grief and received a lot of support from other group members. She talked frequently about how her illness might progress, her fears about the future and her heavy reliance on her son. At times, she was able to laugh and joke with the others. She also shared some recollections from the past, but seemed to gain little comfort from these.

After the group, Dorothy reported that the sessions had been helpful to her because there were other people with similar problems and they had got on well together. Her son reported that he always read the handouts and found these useful in understanding more about his mother's illness and being able to help her, but felt that she remained very depressed.

Margaret

Margaret was independent, talkative and outwardly cheerful. She was open about her memory problems, but said that she did not feel that they had affected her life very much. However, her husband reported that she often became frustrated by her difficulties, becoming angry and blaming those around her. He did not feel that she confided in him very much about her problems.

Margaret had a very active social life and attended an exercise class regularly. She was happy to attend the group in the hope that she might be able to help others by offering advice.

Margaret acknowledged her memory loss in the group and talked about her heavy reliance on memory aids. She talked about her past career as a headmistress and gained a great deal of self-esteem from this and other roles she had played in the past. She often said in the group that she did not feel her memory problems had affected her life very much. She was very positive about the benefits of the group, but suggested that it was more useful for others, because their problems were worse or they did not go out as much as her, thus distancing herself from the others in the group. Her husband reported that she had not found the group very relevant to her.

Harold

Harold was an active, kind, placid, sociable and easy-going person. He acknowledged some problems with his memory but attributed them to old age and very much played them down. He described himself as a person who 'takes life as it comes' and rarely worried about anything. He continued to enjoy company, having some close friends and attended a local social club. He was unsure whether he needed to attend the group, but was willing to come along.

Harold appeared anxious in the group at times, but verbally denied any anxiety. He was generally one of the quieter members of the group, but interacted well, responding sympathetically to other group members. In the first weeks, he did not acknowledge his memory problems in the group, even saying that he did not need to use memory aids like everyone else. However, as the group progressed he became more open and at the seventh session he talked about having memory problems like everyone else and said it was helpful to be with other people 'in the same boat'.

After the group he said that it was easy to talk in the group and 'open up'. His daughter felt that he had enjoyed it and it had given him somewhere to go socially.

Evaluation

Current findings

There are many difficulties in evaluating therapies for people with dementia (Robb *et al.* 1986) and most studies of support groups have only used basic measures of evaluation such as analysing the content of group discussion (Snyder *et al.* 1995; Scarboro 2000) or giving group members an interview or questionnaire (Peach and Duff 1991; Labarge and Trtanj 1995). McAfee *et al.* (1989) assessed the participants' and caregivers' mood (using the Profile of Moods State) and knowledge about Alzheimer's disease before and after the group. The sample was small and there was no significant change in mood, but a trend to improvement for both participants and their caregivers and a significant increase on the knowledge test for the participants. Yale carried out a small controlled study with measures of mood taken before and after the group using the Hamilton Rating Scale for depression. She did not find any significant changes in the depression ratings, but interview data in her study suggested that the participants obtained many benefits from attending the group such as being more open about the memory problems with their caregivers. Marshall (2001) and Barton *et al.* (2001) also looked for changes in mood (using the Hospital and Anxiety Depression Scale) in a small number of participants and did not find significant changes from the beginning to the end of the group. However, there was a trend to a reduction in depression in Marshall's study and in Barton's study initial scores were very low, and in both studies caregivers reported improvements in mood in the participants immediately after the group. Cheston *et al.* (2001), in a much larger study with six ten-week groups, showed a significant reduction in anxiety and depression from the beginning to the end of the group compared to baseline and follow-up phases (ratings were made using the RAID – Rating Anxiety in Dementia scale and the Cornell Scale for Depression in Dementia). There was no significant change in mood ratings during baseline or follow-up phases. Further details of the groups in these studies are shown in Table 11.1.

Despite the limited research in this area so far, many different studies with varying types of evaluation have concluded that participants find the groups helpful (Peach and Duff 1991; Labarge and Tranj 1995) and that it is the social support aspect of the group which is most valued rather than the educational aspect (Hawkins and Eagger 1999; Thrower 1998; Scarboro 2000; Marshall 2001). As Yalom (1985) suggested, universality is a very important therapeutic aspect to any group. In addition, cognitive models of memory suggest that in dementia there may be deterioration in prospective memory, making it difficult to recall the specific content of the group, but implicational memory may be intact, so that the emotional atmosphere or 'message' of the group can be retained (Williams 1994).

Future research

As described earlier, anxiety and depression are often found in early dementia and studies of support groups for caregivers have found that those with initial high levels of depression or anxiety benefit from the groups in terms of mood improvement (Cuijpers *et al.* 1997). It would therefore be useful to carry out further research on the effect of support groups on mood, although finding appropriate ways to measure changes in mood in people with early dementia can be difficult.

There is some evidence that people with mild or moderate cognitive impairment can report their mood accurately (Gottlieb *et al.* 1988; Feher *et al.* 1992) although discordance has been found between patient, caregiver and clinician reports of the patient's mood (Teri and Wagner 1991). This discordance is usually due to patients with dementia who have a general tendency to denial, also denying low mood (Mackenzie *et al.* 1989; Teri and Wagner 1991; Feher *et al.* 1992), but in a few instances can be due to patients hiding their low mood from their relatives (Mackenzie *et al.* 1989; Marshall 2001). It is therefore advisable to use ratings of mood from the participants themselves and from their caregiver and information about the patients' tendency to denial may help in interpreting any discrepancies. Self-report measures which have been used in early dementia include the Hospital Anxiety and Depression Scale (Zigmond and Snaith 1983; Wands *et al.* 1990), which is sensitive to change but has not been tested for reliability and validity in the early dementia population, and the Geriatric Depression Scale (Yesavage and Brink 1983; Sheik and Yesavage 1986), which is also sensitive to change but has been found to have mixed results when looking at accuracy in the early dementia population (Boddington *et al.* 1998). The Worry Scale has been developed specifically for use in early dementia and measures eight emotions including anxiety and self-esteem (Labarge 1993).

Other measures which have been designed specifically for the dementia population, combine patient and caregiver reports and are completed by a clinician such as the RAID (Shankar *et al.* 1999) and the Cornell

(Alexopoulos *et al.* 1988). However, the Cornell was developed using nursing staff rather than a relative as the caregiver, and when using such measures it is important to be aware that a participant might still hide their feelings if interviewed with their caregiver.

Coping is another area which has been found to change in caregivers' groups (Cuijpers *et al.* 1997) and might be usefully studied in the groups for people with dementia themselves. Keady and Nolan (1995) have developed a checklist of 42 coping responses used in dementia (the IMMEL), which includes such items as 'using lists and other memory aids to help me remember', 'keeping my fears and feelings secret' and 'remembering all the good times I have had'. So far, significant changes in coping on individual items from the IMMEL have not been found with support groups (Barton *et al.* 2001; Cheston *et al.* 2001; Marshall 2001), but with further development such as grouping items using factor analysis, the IMMEL might become more sensitive to any changes in coping which do occur (Marshall 2001).

The ways in which individuals cope with their dementia and changes as a result of the support group may also be evident from the issues emerging in the group and these can be analysed qualitatively. For example, group sessions could be videotaped, transcribed and analysed to look at group issues and change. In everyday clinical practice where resources may be limited, a record could be kept of the issues raised in each session and how these are managed (Cheston and Jones 2000). Another approach is to ask group members to identify one way in which they wish to cope better as a result of attending the group and see whether they have achieved this at the end (Scarboro 2001). However, the participants in Scarboro's study found it difficult to identify one single area and it may be a task with which they require some support.

As people with dementia do not tend to communicate their feelings openly with their spouses (Miesen 1997; Keady and Gilliard 1999), a crucial area for future study is the issue of separate or joint groups. It would be very useful to compare these two types of groups, looking at their effects on mood and coping in both the person with dementia and their relative and the effects on the couple's relationship. Given the current research finding that participants value the mutual support aspects of the group the most, it would also be useful to compare psycho-educational with non-directive groups. In all such research, it is important to look at individual differences in personality and coping in the person with dementia and how these relate to outcome.

Due to the problems of measuring change in any psychosocial therapy in dementia, it is advisable to collect data from a number of different sources: from both participant and caregiver, and from different forms of data collection; quantitative measures, interviews and observations of the group. Collecting data from several different sources using one piece of evidence to corroborate another has been described as triangulation (Good and Watts 1989).

Conclusions

People with dementia should have the opportunity to share their feelings with other people going through the same experiences (Keady and Gilliard 1999). The group should aim to make each individual feel valued and facilitate choices, creativity, relaxation and the opportunity for group members to help each other (Kitwood 1997). There should also be an opportunity for participants to talk about their past life, to look at how they have coped in the past and build self-esteem, as well as create a shared identity for the group (Feil 1992; Cheston and Bender 1999). Research in this area has many methodological difficulties and is limited, but there is considerable evidence that these groups are useful because of the mutual support. A vital area for future research is to compare joint groups for people with dementia and their relatives with separate groups, looking at changes in mood and coping responses in both partners and whether feelings of separation and isolation can be reduced.

References

Akerlund, B.M. and Norberg, A. (1986) 'Group psychotherapy with demented patients', *Geriatric Nursing* March–April: 83–4.

Alexopoulos, G., Abrams, R., Young, R. and Shamoian, C. (1988) 'Cornell scale for depression in dementia', *Biological Psychiatry* 23: 271–84.

Austad, C.S. (1992) 'The wisdom group: a psychotherapeutic model for elderly persons', *Psychological Reports* 70: 356–8.

Bahro, M., Silber, E. and Sunderland, T. (1995) 'How do patients with Alzheimer's disease cope with their illness? A clinical experience report', *Journal of the American Geriatrics Society* 43, 1: 41–6.

Ballard, C.G., Boyle, A., Bowler, C. and Lindesay, J. (1996) 'Anxiety disorders in dementia sufferers', *International Journal of Geriatric Psychiatry* 11: 987–90.

Barton, J., Piney, C., Berg, M. and Parker, C. (2001) 'Coping with forgetfulness group', *Newsletter of the Psychologists' Special Interest Group Working with Older People* 77: 19–25.

Bender, M. (2001) 'The same, but different: psychotherapeutic group work with people with dementia', workshop presentation to the Psychologists' Special Interest Group in Elderly People Annual Conference, Oxford, 2 July.

Bender, M. and Cheston, R. (1997) 'Inhabitants of a lost kingdom: a model of the subjective experiences of dementia', *Ageing and Society* 17: 513–32.

Boddington, S., Krasucki, C. and Richards, M. (1998) 'To BDI or GDS? Which depression rating scale to use with older people', presentation to the Psychologists' Special Interest Group in Elderly People Annual Conference, Edinburgh, 2 July.

Burns, A., Jacoby, R. and Levy, R. (1990) 'Psychiatric phenomena in Alzheimer's disease III: disorders of mood', *British Journal of Psychiatry* 157: 81–6.

Cheston, R. (1997) 'Psychotherapeutic work with people with dementia: a review of the literature', *British Journal of Medical Psychology* 71: 211–31.

Cheston, R. and Bender, M. (1999) *Understanding Dementia: The Man with the Worried Eyes*, London: Jessica Kingsley.

Cheston, R. and Jones, K. (2000) 'A place to work it all out together', *Journal of Dementia Care* 8, 6: 22–4.

Cheston, R., Jones, K. and Gilliard, J. (2001) 'The impact of group psychotherapy with people with dementia', *International Journal of Geriatric Psychiatry* 16: 816–21.

Clare, L. (2001) 'Managing threats to self: the phenomenology of early-stage Alzheimer's disease', presentation to the British Psychological Society Centenary Annual Conference, Glasgow, 30 March.

Cohen, D., Kennedy, G. and Eisdorfer, C. (1984) 'Phases of change in the patient with Alzheimer's dementia: a conceptual dimension for defining health care management', *Journal of the American Geriatrics Society* 32, 1: 11–15.

Coleman, P. (1986) *Ageing and Reminiscence Processes: Social and Clinical Implications*, Chichester: Wiley.

Cuijpers, P., Hosman, C. and Munnichs, J. (1997) 'Carer support groups. Change mechanisms and preventive effects', in B. Miesen and G. Jones (eds) *Care-giving in Dementia: Research and Applications*, vol. 2, London: Routledge.

Cummings, J.L. and Victoroff, J.L. (1990) 'Noncognitive neuropsychiatric syndromes in Alzheimer's disease', *Neuropsychiatry, Neuropsychology and Behavioural Neurology* 3: 140–58.

Emmerson, C. and Spaull, D. (2001) 'British Psycho-educational Intervention (BPI) for people with cognitive impairment', unpublished document, Avon and Wiltshire Mental Health Partnership NHS Trust.

Feher, E., Larrabee, G. and Crook, T. (1992) 'Factors attenuating the validity of the geriatric depression scale in a dementia population', *Journal of the American Geriatrics Society* 40: 906–9.

Feil, N. (1967) 'Group therapy in a home for the aged', *The Gerontologist* 7: 192–5.

—— (1989) *Validation: The Feil Method*. Cleveland, OH: Feil Productions.

—— (1992) 'Validation therapy with late onset dementia populations', in G. Jones and B. Miesen (eds) *Care-giving in Dementia. Research and Applications*, vol. 1, London: Routledge.

Finkel, S. (1990) 'Group psychotherapy with older people', *Hospital and Community Psychiatry* 41, 11: 1189–91.

Good, D. and Watts, F. (1989) 'Qualitative research', in G. Parry and F. Watts (eds) *Behavioural and Mental Health Research: A Handbook of Skills and Methods*, London: Lawrence Erlbaum.

Gottlieb, G., Gur, R.E. and Gur, R.C. (1988) 'Reliability of psychiatric scales in patients with dementia of the Alzheimer type', *American Journal of Psychiatry* 145, 7: 857–60.

Greene, J., Tyjwana, A., Ingram, B. and Johnson, W. (1993) 'Group psychotherapy for patients with dementia', *Southern Medical Journal* 86, 9: 1033–5.

Haggerty, A. (1990) 'Psychotherapy for patients with Alzheimer's disease', *Advances* 7, 1: 55–60.

Hausman, C. (1992) 'Dynamic psychotherapy with elderly demented patients', in G. Jones and B. Miesen (eds) *Care-giving in Dementia: Research and Applications*, vol. 2, London: Routledge.

Hawkins, D. and Eagger, S. (1999) 'Group therapy: sharing the pain of diagnosis', *Journal of Dementia Care* 6, 5: 12–14.

James, I. (1999) 'Using a cognitive rationale to conceptualise anxiety in people with dementia', *Behavioural and Cognitive Psychotherapy* 27: 345–51.

Kasl-Godley, J. and Gatz, M. (2000) 'Psychosocial interventions for individuals with dementia: an integration of theory, therapy and a clinical understanding of dementia', *Clinical Psychology Review* 20, 6: 755–82.

Keady, J. and Gilliard, J. (1999) 'The early experience of Alzheimer's disease: implications for partnership and practice', in C. Adams and C. Clarke (eds) *Dementia Care: Developing Partnership in Practice*, London: Ballière Tindall.

Keady, J. and Nolan, M. (1995) 'IMMEL: assessing coping responses in the early stages of dementia', *British Journal of Nursing* 4: 309–14.

Kitwood, T. (1990) 'The dialectics of dementia: with particular reference to Alzheimer's disease', *Ageing in Society* 10: 177–96.

—— (1997) *Dementia Reconsidered*, Buckingham: Open University Press.

Labarge, E. (1993) 'A preliminary scale to measure the degree of worry among mildly demented Alzheimer Disease patients', *Physical and Occupational Therapy in Geriatrics* 11, 3: 43–57.

Labarge, E. and Trtanj, F. (1995) 'A support group for people in the early stages of dementia of the Alzheimer type', *Journal of Applied Gerontology* 14, 3: 289–301.

Labarge, E., Rosenman, L., Leavitt, K. and Cristiani, T. (1988) 'Counseling clients with mild senile dementia of the Alzheimer's type: a pilot study, *Journal of the Neurologic Rehabilitation* 2: 167–73.

Lantz, M., Buchalter, D. and McBee, L. (1997) 'The Wellness group: novel intervention for coping with disruptive behaviour in elderly nursing home residents', *The Gerontologist* 37, 4: 551–6.

McAfee, M., Ruh, P., Bell, P. and Martichuski, D. (1989) 'Including persons with early stage Alzheimer's disease in support groups and strategy planning', *American Journal of Alzheimer's Care and Related Disorders and Research*, Nov–Dec: 18–22.

Mackenzie, T., Robiner, W. and Knopman, D. (1989) 'Differences between patient and family assessments of depression in Alzheimer's disease', *American Journal of Psychiatry* 146, 9: 1174–8.

Marshall, A. (2001) 'Coping in early dementia: findings of a new type of support group', unpublished PsychD thesis, University of Surrey.

Miesen, B. (1992) 'Attachment theory and dementia', in G. Jones and B. Miesen (eds) *Care-giving in Dementia: Research and Applications*, vol. 1, London: Routledge.

—— (1997) 'Awareness in dementia patients and family grieving', in G. Jones and B. Miesen (eds) *Care-giving in Dementia: Research and Applications*, vol. 2, London: Routledge.

—— (1999) *Dementia in Close Up*, London and New York: Routledge.

Peach, E. and Duff, G. (1991) 'Mutual support groups: a response to the early and often forgotten stage of dementia', *Practice* 6, 2: 147–57.

Pinner, G. (2000) 'Truth-telling and the diagnosis of dementia', *British Journal of Psychiatry* 176: 514–15.

Robb, S., Stegman, C. and Wolanin, M. (1986) 'No research versus research with compromised results: a study of validation therapy', *Nursing Research* 35, 2: 113–18.

Scarboro, J. (2000) 'Developing and evaluating a memory support group for people with memory difficulties', *Newsletter of the Psychologists' Special Interest Group Working with Older People* 73: 33–5.

Shankar, K., Walker, M., Frost, D. and Worrell, M. (1999) 'The development of a valid and reliable scale for rating anxiety in dementia (RAID)', *Ageing and Mental Health* 3, 1: 39–49.

Sheik, J. and Yesavage, J. (1986) 'Geriatric Depression Scale (GDS): recent evidence and development of a shorter version', *Clinical Gerontologist* 5, 1/2: 165–72.

Shoham, H. and Neuschatz, S. (1995) 'Group therapy with senile patients', *Social Work* 30, 1: 69–72.

Snyder, L., Quayhagen, M., Shepherd, S. and Bower, D. (1995) 'Supportive seminar groups: an intervention for early stage dementia patients', *The Gerontologist* 35, 5: 691–5.

Solomon, K. and Szwabo, P. (1992) 'Psychotherapy for patients with dementia', in J. Morley, R. Coe, R. Strong and G. Grossberg (eds) *Memory Function and Ageing-Related Disorders*, New York: Springer.

Teri, L. (1994) 'Behavioural treatment of depression in patients with dementia', *Alzheimer's Disease and Associated Disorders* 8, suppl. 3: 66–74.

Teri, L. and Gallagher-Thompson, D. (1991) 'Cognitive-behavioural interventions for treatment of depression in Alzheimer's patients', *The Gerontologist* 31, 3: 413–16.

Teri, L. and Uomoto, J. (1991) 'Reducing excess disability in dementia patients: training caregivers to manage depression', *Clinical Gerontologist* 10, 4: 49–63.

Teri, L. and Wagner, A. (1991) 'Assessment of depression in patients with Alzheimer's disease: concordance among informants', *Psychology and Ageing* 6, 2: 280–5.

Teri, L., Logsdon, R., Uomoto, J. and McCurry, S. (1997) 'Behavioural treatment of depression in dementia patients: a controlled clinical trial', *Journal of Gerontology: Psychological Sciences* 52b, 4: 159–66.

Thrower, C. (1998) 'Support and a crucial sense of belonging', *Journal of Dementia Care* 6, 3: 18–20.

Wands, K., Merskey, H., Haschinski, V., Fisman, M., Fox, H. and Boniferro, M. (1990) 'A questionnaire investigation of anxiety and depression in early dementia', *Journal of the American Geriatrics Society* 38: 535–8.

Welden, S. and Yesavage, J. (1982) 'Behavioural improvement with relaxation training in senile dementia', *Clinical Gerontologist* 1, 1: 45–9.

Williams, J. (1994) 'Interacting cognitive subsystems and unvoiced murmurs. A review of *Affect, Cognition and Change* by John Teasdale and Philip Barnard (1993)', *Cognition and Emotion* 8, 6: 571–9.

Yale, R. (1995) *Developing Support Groups for Individuals with Early-stage Alzheimer's Disease: Planning, Implementation and Evaluation*, Baltimore: Health Professions Press.

Yalom, I. (1985) *The Theory and Practice of Group Psychotherapy*, New York: Basic Books.

Yesavage, J. and Brink, T. (1983) 'Development and validation of a geriatric depression screening scale: a preliminary report', *Journal of Psychiatric Research* 17: 37–49.

Zigmond, A. and Snaith, R. (1983) 'The hospital anxiety and depression scale', *Acta Psychiatrica Scandanavia* 67: 361–70.

Chapter 12

The loss of meaningful attachments in dementia and behavioural stage-specific implications

Gemma M.M. Jones

Introduction

There has been increasing interest in using Bowlby's attachment theory to understand behavioural changes in dementia and plan new care interventions. This chapter seeks to extend the concept of attachments to persons, to attachments to objects and environments. The focus is to try to understand how, as attachments are diminished, broken or detached from, they can perhaps be replaced by other things that may fulfil the same or a similar need.

First, some examples and overall concepts on attachment are considered. Thereafter, several examples illustrate how persons with dementia struggle to secure and hold on to important things, as well as the responses with which such efforts are met. Using Bowlby's thoughts on attachment in old age, Miesen's POPFID theory and Feil's behavioural staging and the validation method, the move is made to specific practical uses of the attachment concept, across the stages of the dementia process.

It is hoped that professional carers will increasingly plan interventions to meet the many needs of persons with dementia; those that are tangible as well as those that are more difficult to identify, perhaps qualitatively, which are most important of all. This chapter concludes by giving suggestions for some practical interventions.

Attachment and detachment

To start to think about this topic in a broader context means to acknowledge all the things that persons can be attached to. Even better, to know what we are really attached to, we need to identify those things we fear losing. On reflection, this list can be endless, however there are some overall categories that are listed in Box 12.1. It is the increasing impact of missing, searching for and trying to hang on to these things over the course of a dementing illness that is considered first in this chapter.

What emotions underlie attachment? Surely they have to do with the value, to an individual, of the things that they are attached to. What sorts of

---

Box 12.1   The range of things we can be attached to

We have attachments to:

- persons, family, friends, heroes, role models, mentors, associates
- objects, necessities, treasures, collectibles, symbols
- beliefs, ideas, concepts, values
- memories, thought patterns, fantasies
- routines, ways of organizing things
- activities, work, roles, duties
- physical environment, emotional atmosphere
- animals, plants, places, nature
- financial securities

---

value? There are many sorts of values: emotional, spiritual, social, physical, intellectual, aesthetic and monetary. The emotional value of things can be described by drawing from a pool of words such as utility, meaning, safety, purpose, familiarity, comfort, etc. It goes without saying that over time any given 'thing' can take on a different value in our lives.

In addition, it seems reasonable to assert that some things will be of core value to all persons, and other things will have value only to a given individual. We will continue to see an expression of 'the desire for' and 'need of' a range of things throughout the dementia process. An understanding of how persons try to gain proximity to, secure, and hold on to such needs is necessary for both carers and caregivers.

The underlying assumption behind all of this is that access to other persons and objects is desired because of a felt need and purpose. Without people and things, life becomes a prison of searching endlessly and aimlessly for them, and when they cannot be procured returning to and remaining with memories of them.

Your handbag or pocket contents

To make the following examples more personal, let's first briefly consider what some (typical?) adults find necessary to keep near them throughout the day. Table 12.1 gives such a representative listing, compiled from volunteer friends and family members. You will note that, as mentioned above, some things appear for all persons and some are very individual.

Example 1: The often lost handbag

Although this example is a very specific one, about what happens to a lady's handbag and the contents over time, the purpose of noting it here is to

Table 12.1 Typical female handbag and male trouser (shirt or coat) pocket contents over time

Young adult female	Middle-aged female	Mid-seventies female	Male in his mid-forties	Male in his mid-seventies
Change purse Credit cards	Change purse Credit cards Wallet	Change purse	Change purse Credit cards Wallet	Wallet
Keys	Keys	Keys	Keys	Keys
Make-up	Lip balm	Make-up	Business cards	Loose change
Tissues	Tissues	Tissues	Hanky	Hanky
Sweets	Mints	Sugar cubes	Phone number list	Glasses and case
Cell phone	Comb	Pen	Bandaids	
Leather gloves	Cologne wipe	Rain cap	Pen	
Comb	Photos	String bag	Penknife	
Perfume	Matches	Address book	Pocket diary	
Photos	Swiss army knife	Sweets	Cell phone	
Tampons	Pencil/pen/yellow highlighter/paper	Spare batteries	Glasses and case	
	Band aids	Pension book	Pencil	
	Tampons	Glasses case	Paracetemol	
	Sewing kit	Brush		
	Aspirin	Silky scarf		
	Phone list			
	Toothpaste			
	Toothbrush			
	Blank paper			
	Spoon			
	Toothpick			
	Pop-up children's book			

stimulate thought about all the things that persons with dementia 'cannot hold on to' or 'remain attached to' of their own volition and control. The example could just as easily be about the distress felt by gentlemen at losing their wallets or pension books, or indeed dentures, glasses (but interestingly enough, very rarely hearing aids).

Table 12.2 How handbag contents can be lost and replaced over time by someone with dementia who is starting to be disoriented in time and is struggling to hang on to the safety of normal behaviour patterns (handbag contents were recorded from memory, after seeing owner emptying and/or checking the contents in the presence of staff)

Handbag contents noted upon refinding it over time as it was being emptied and checked	
Start	• Red change purse with some small coins, tissues
	• Jaffa Cake wrapper, keyring without keys, a button
Week 7	• Empty red change purse, paper tissues
Week 8	• Empty red change purse
Week 10	• Empty red purse, one pair of tights, one pair of panties
	• Jewelry case, three necklaces (one broken)
	• Two pairs 'borrowed' glasses, hairbrush
Week 15	• Empty red change purse, two pairs 'borrowed' glasses
	• One pair tights, one slip, one brooch, one blue change purse,
	• One powder compact
Week 18	• One pair tights, one powder compact
	• One paper tissue, one well-used lipstick
Week 25	• *Another handbag* and a plastic bag
	• Empty blue change purse, almost finished lipstick
	• One pen with cap
	• One powder compact, three paper tissues

Source: This listing is a composite one from unpublished data by R. Gladhill and G.M.M. Jones (1998).

Let's now consider a particular lady with dementia, who was residing in a care facility and trying very hard throughout the day not to lose her handbag. Despite her best efforts, which included taking it along to the dining room, the lounge, the toilet and keeping it under her pillow at night, she still lost the handbag (usually left behind), as well as the contents from time to time. Her distress at losing it was great on every occasion.

The point made by the information shown in Table 12.2 will be all too familiar to most readers. So familiar, that it becomes hard to imagine that it could be shocking to readers who do not have experience of dementia. From the perspective of the normal adult world, it would be inconceivable that staff would go through other persons' handbags to retrieve and find contents, and even to lock them away in closets to avoid the nuisance of forever being bothered by having to search for them. Yet such things do happen, and the handbag is just one little example of a much larger class of things to do with understanding what the value of personal property is, as well as what types of objects and decorations could be provided by a care facility to enhance day-to-day well-being for persons who at some point in their illness will often feel 'lost', 'stolen from' and 'not useful'.

What is striking about the listing in Table 12.2? Perhaps, it is the very contents, the basic original ones as well as the 'acquired' ones. Perhaps, it is the very acquisition of another (someone else's) handbag and change purse. Perhaps though it is the thought at how much searching and effort must have gone into finding the new acquisitions, as well as how often there must have been desperation at noticing that some of the contents were missing.

As expected, members of staff responded to this lady's recurring plight in a variety of ways. Some seemed to realize (likely from their own experience) that it feels terrible to lose one's handbag, and that those feelings do not subside until it is found. They tried to start searching with her immediately. Others responded more matter of factly (perhaps because they had already spent many hours searching for missing handbags), pointing out to her that it didn't really matter because she 'didn't keep anything in the handbag anyway'. Still other members agreed to help look for it when there was time to spare (perhaps because they had not spent as many hours looking as their colleagues, or perhaps because they were aware that the very feeling of a handbag, regardless of what was in it was important).

Have you ever seen staff take handbags away from ladies? Perhaps you have heard something like the following: 'Mrs X. You don't need that handbag. It causes nothing but trouble for you and for us. Last week you lost it three times. Mrs Z thought it was hers and when we took it away from her we had both of you upset for hours. We've spent hours again today trying to find this handbag. It's such a waste of everyone's time. There's nothing in it, look, just some tissues, some sugar packets, and, I don't believe it, Mrs A's dentures! Tell you what. I'm going to put it in the cupboard up here. If there's anything you want, just come to us and we'll get it for you. It's not even possible to get a good night's rest with that thing under your pillow. You really don't need it here.'

Although there is truth in this statement that there is almost 'nothing' in the handbag, the reality remains that most of us 'feel lost and anxious' without our handbags. Its value is as much symbolic as it is in its literal presence, one of the few possessions left – the thing that has functioned as a lifesaver throughout life still 'feels like' a lifesaver. How can we teach staff that a handbag (without much in it), or a watch (even though it may not work), or a necklace (with much wear), or a tweed cap (that is not needed for warmth), or a newspaper (even though it's a month old) can bring feelings of security and normalcy, which are valuable, beyond the literal value of these objects?

What is the most common item in the separate listings in Table 12.1? A change purse, and tissues. Are these not universal lifesavers of sorts?

Example 2: The restless night prowler

This next example illustrates some of the same things as in example one, but in single 'snapshot mode'. It gives a glimpse of what that lady must have felt when she noticed things missing from her handbag.

One night, about 2 am a gentleman in his eighties was pacing up and down a long corridor in a residential setting. He had had his own insurance agency and had been a meticulous businessman. At this point in his illness he was 'lost in time and space' almost all of the time. He was heard to be speaking to himself saying, 'Where am I to go now? Where can I find a safe place around here? Things disappear here. They just take things and never give them back to you. How is a body supposed to work like that?' His arms were fully laden with a roll of toilet paper, some washing-up liquid, a cardigan, a lady's housecoat, and the top tier of the cardex system from the nursing station. It was clear that he had been in the bathroom, past the nursing station and in someone's bedroom to collect these things.

The nurse who first found him said, 'My goodness, you're really loaded down. Can I help you carry some of those things?' He seemed relieved and handed some over. She continued, 'You look tired. Where were you heading for?'

'I have to find a safe place to put these so I can find them again and finish my work. I've been trying to get things all in order, and it's impossible when they keep disappearing. So now I've got them again, and that's been a big job. What am I going to do? Where can I put them? There aren't many safe places around here you know.'

She replied, 'You just wanted to keep things safe and all sorted out and it's almost impossible?'

'Yes, can you help me?' he asked.

No reply was possible because two other members of staff arrived, spotted the gentleman with his booty and loudly started laughing at him saying, 'That's Mrs C's housecoat. You've stolen it from her bedroom. Why would you steal a lady's housecoat? And our cardex! So that's where it is. You don't need to steal toilet paper here you know, there's plenty in the toilets. Now we'll just take these things and put them back where they belong and you get back to bed and stay out of trouble.'

The gentleman burst into tears, protesting that he was no thief but that there surely was a thief around. Then he became angry. The first nurse interjected to her colleagues, 'Mr A was just explaining that he's trying to keep things organized in his life. He has important filing to do and he really needs a safe place to store his things so that he can find them again. He's very frustrated and won't find any peace until he knows someone is listening to him and helping him. Let's show him where these things can be safely put in the nursing station and he can help us with some filing tomorrow. He's very tired from searching for somewhere safe to put these special things.'

The relief on the gentleman's face was enormous. He walked along, saw that everything was carefully placed on the counter of the nursing station, and was escorted back to bed. It is unlikely that this gentleman would remember this specific incident in the morning. However the need to 'try to find and sort his things and keep them in order' will still be there. If staff do not find something and some place for him to 'work' (perhaps a table, some paper, pencils and a filing box with index tabs and cards), he will start his search again the next day. If this doesn't happen, how many minutes of the day will care-giving staff have to spend checking up on him, assuaging irate or irritated residents who have found him in their bedrooms, and returning whatever new booty he has acquired throughout the day?

How important were the objects that this gentleman had carefully collected? What was their value to him, as well as how they were dealt with? What would have happened if the first nurse had not been there? What kind of education would it take for the latter two nurses to understand that he had been gathering a very specific set of objects with great purpose? If the first nurse had been junior to the latter two, would her lead have been followed?

Example 3: The Ukrainian lady who needed bread rolls and cutlery

In another long-term care facility, there was a lady who had immigrated from Ukraine 50 years earlier. Although she had learned to speak English, she lost that ability gradually. She only spoke in short Ukrainian phrases. She was currently disoriented in time, ceaselessly wandering everywhere in the residence and speaking to herself in low voice tones. The only history available to staff about this lady was that she had known 'very poor times in the old country' in her earlier life.

Each day, this lady somehow managed to procure and hide breadrolls under her armpits. They remained there throughout the day. She also collected various pieces of cutlery, rolled them in towelling and carried them with her. Helping her to bed in the evening was always a surprise. Yet staff did not take the further step of realizing that because they had disarmed her of the cutlery and removed her food stores, she would wake up each morning and start collecting again. Would she have continued to do that if her bedside surrounds, which were devoid of a single personal or familiar object or possession, had been filled with things? Perhaps on waking and seeing familiar, needed objects (a jar full of teaspoons, cards, a sealed pack of biscuits, and other things) her behaviour pattern would have changed. Perhaps also then she might have found a little rest to enjoy the music that was performed at times, or the crafts and daily activities. As it was, this lady's collecting and pacing continued.

Where did these urges come from? What would have become of such urges when she was no longer able to walk? Her relentless wandering will likely have been anxious rocking backwards and forwards and trying to grab whatever was visible nearby at mealtimes. Perhaps her quiet phrases in Ukrainian will have become swear words and expletives out of further frustration. (In the behavioural staging framework, this would be described as stage three behaviour. See the bookcase metaphor, Chapter 3.)

Miscellaneous examples

There are countless examples of such behaviour, where persons with dementia who are disoriented in time are still trying to be helpful and productive in the absence of many familiar objects with which to do their 'work'.

A former farmer, who had always repaired everything himself in life, had been itching to give the workmen who were fixing up the care home a hand. His requests to be of some use fell on deaf ears. One lunch break when the workmen were not attending to their tools, he saw his chance to do something useful. He borrowed their tools and sawed the couch in the lounge in half. Then he proudly announced to the staff that he'd made two chairs for them.

A former orthodontist attended a day centre for persons with dementia several times a week. He did not mix with other visitors there, but wandered around looking for pens, rulers, paper, small things. Staff noticed that he did not eat his meals, but only 'played and messed with his food'. Later, they noticed that it wasn't random 'messing', but rather that he rolled up tiny portions of mashed potato, squashed them into a more tubular shape and lined these up carefully all around the edge of his plate. This gentleman was making teeth with the only thing available to him that looked like mould material, mashed potatoes. Fortunately, his family still had some of his old work tools, sample teeth and moulds at home. Some of these were brought in and kept at the day centre. This gentleman was given his own table to sit at, with the things that were important to him, and he was happy while 'he felt' as if he was at work. The coffee and meal breaks were then a normal part of the working day for him.

There are also stories of mothers who tidy and polish and fold everything in sight, who think that they are the only ones 'doing all the work around this place' (the care facility). There are former teachers who feel as if all those around are former staff and pupils, who still need to be carefully observed and monitored. Most memorable perhaps are the nurses who never stop nursing.

It would seem that our need to be 'useful', to do familiar things and interact with familiar objects, does not leave us even if we get a dementing illness and become disoriented in time.

Fortunately, some of the new day-care facilities such as the one at Marienhaven, in Warmond, the Netherlands, are designed to allow many different needs to be accommodated in one large room. (It has been built with a kitchen area, a large table for cards and games, another area for crafts and plant potting, an area which feels like a living room, and even an area which feels like an office setting with desks and book shelving.) How much formal attention is given to these needs in other permanent care settings (or even sometimes in a person's own home where everything is tidied away, well out of view or easy access)?

Increasing, replacing and substituting attachments

When, spiritually and philosophically, the natural course of life leads us increasingly to consider the value of voluntary detachment, it may seem odd to be discussing the need for increasing, replacing and substituting attachments. The key difference between the care-giving framework for persons with dementia and the spiritual/philosophical stance has to do with the 'perceived need for' and 'voluntary nature of relinquishing' the things from which one detaches.

When weakened cognitive and memory functioning do not allow a person to access and transit through their memories with normal control (on command), it is the emotional, physical and spiritual needs which exist within the 'present reality' (of wherever a person perceives themselves to be), which are dominant. If a person feels safe, at home, at work, in the company of persons who 'feel familiar', contentment is experienced. If instead fear, estrangement, alienation, isolation are perceived and experienced, persons seek to alleviate this in whatever ways they can. This includes not only seeking out other persons and objects for comfort, returning to memories of happier times, but also self-stimulatory movements and changes of location (usually trying to 'go home').

Bowlby's thoughts on attachment

Although it was developed through work with children, attachment theory has shown itself to be a powerful concept in helping us to think about the behavioural changes in dementia in recent years, and also to point the way to some pertinent care-giving interventions (Bowlby 1969, 1973, 1980). Bowlby himself, only very cautiously, speculated about attachment in old age, as an old man a few years before his death.

Bowlby (1986) spoke of attachment as 'a pattern of behaviour which is care-seeking and care-eliciting from an individual who feels they are less capable of dealing with the world than the persons from whom they are seeking care'. Actual behaviours that could be considered 'attachment behaviours' are listed in Box 12.2. This listing is not exhaustive, but certainly includes the key behaviours discussed in the literature. Note that the latter ones are also considered to be grieving behaviours.

Bowlby's thought on attachments in old age

In a not well-known interview Bowlby was asked about 'the meaning of children for old people'. He answered: 'I believe that old people who have children and grandchildren who they see quite a bit of, are happier, and altogether more contented individuals than those who do not. I believe the difference is very marked in fact, unmistakable' (Bowlby 1986).

Box 12.2   Typical attachment behaviours used to try to secure the proximity of important others

- calling after a person when they try to leave
- searching for them
- leaving to find them
- following them, worrying about them, asking after them, holding on to them
- requesting their presence often
- shouting for help, eventually becoming frustrated, irritated, angry, aggressive, withdrawn

---

Furthermore, he was asked whether he thought 'bereavements or repeated losses had a cumulative effect'. He replied: 'One idea is that if a child has had experience of separation, then . . . he wouldn't be so upset next time. [But] the reverse is true. There is no doubt about that. We know that [with] repeated bereavements – each one comes harder than the last' (Bowlby 1986). His reply, although not the view of the author, is daunting. How serious and how important he took broken attachments or separations to be.

When pressed about 'the consequences of attachment for the total life-span' he answered thus: 'It was about 1968 that I realized that making a secure attachment is something which a lucky individual not only makes in childhood but is all part of being a healthy stable adult.'

In reply to being asked about the 'consequences different attachment patterns have for later life' he said: 'I think that a person who has had secure attachments is more capable of facing death than a person who hasn't.' Bowlby did not speak about the meaning of attachments to persons with a dementing illness, but Miesen has.

Miesen's extension of Bowlby's work and Popfid theory

The implications of Bowlby's thoughts, when extended to a person's needs and behaviour during a dementia process, lead us to reflect upon the meaning of past, current and future attachments. Miesen thinks that, depending on a person's previous attachment history, some persons with dementia experience more difficulties than others as a result of the types of attachments they formerly had with key persons in their life. Extending this thinking brings us to the realization that the experience of dementia is a long-term overwhelming process of yet more broken attachments of many sorts.

Miesen has looked at the attachment behaviours shown by persons with dementia when they become disoriented in time (Behavioural Stage 2 of dementia, Feil 1992; Jones 1997). At this stage of their illness they inevitably speak about parents (who are deceased) as being still alive. After examining how this phenomenon begins and develops over the course of the illness, he coined the terms 'Parent Orientation' and 'Parent Fixation' (see also Miesen 1992). POPFID is an acronym for Parent Orientation Parent Fixation in Dementia. Parent Orientation refers to when persons with dementia, openly or secretly, think increasingly frequently about their deceased parents. Parent Fixation refers to when persons with dementia refer to their long-since deceased parents as being alive or present. This may be a transient or permanent phenomenon.

The attachment behaviours listed in Box 12.2 (p. 270) are similar for persons in Behavioural Stage 2 of dementia, who are trying to hang on to someone they perceive as safe and connected to them, and to try to find key persons, who they do not remember are deceased, again.

Miesen emphasizes that caregivers often do not realize how much their presence with a person with dementia is a symbolic presence, also representing past experiences with key persons in their life, from whom they sought or received safety and nurture.

He holds that there are three patterns to such behaviour, which caregivers need to be aware of: parent fixation that does not stop; parent fixation that stops intermittently; parent fixation that stops entirely. The key implications of his work for carers and caregivers rest on three main concepts:

1   Attachment behaviours in dementia need to be recognized for what they are – 'attachment' behaviours as opposed to 'nuisance attention seeking' behaviour.
2   Such behaviour comes from feeling unsafe and alone in a world, which becomes increasingly unfamiliar.
3   Carers should realize the importance of 'their own presence' and 'the safe presence of others' in providing optimal care for persons with dementia.

Figure 12.1 shows how Miesen's theory corresponds with the Feil's behavioural stages of dementia. The latter will be discussed next.

Feil's Validation method and the implicit assumptions about attachment

Feil's Validation method (1982, 1992, 1993; Jones 1997) comprises a number of key concepts and assumptions which are closely linked to attachment theory, though Feil has not used this as an underpinning to her own work. The Validation method includes a description of the four 'stages of Resolution' which the author has adapted and described as four 'behavioural stages' of the dementia process (Jones 1997). These stages were intended to describe

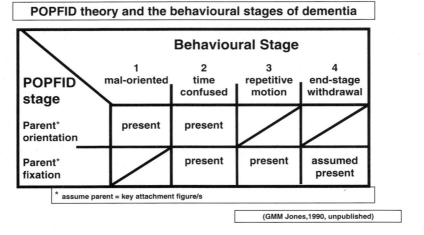

Figure 12.1 How Miesen's stages link with the behavioural staging of dementia. Parent fixation begins as time perception is lost in Behavioural Stage 2.

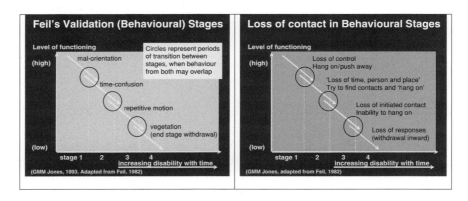

Figure 12.2a (left) The behavioural stages over time, including the transition interval between stages, when behaviour from two stages may occur simultaneously for a while.

Figure 12.2b (right) The increasing difficulty a person with dementia can have in trying to 'hold on' to important things in life.

primarily individuals with uncomplicated Alzheimer-type dementia and slow progressive multi-infarct type dementia. They are shown in Figure 12.2a. The increasing difficulties that are experienced by persons with dementia, to find and hold on to meaningful persons and objects in life are shown in Figure 12.2b.

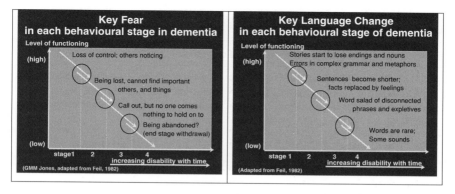

Figure 12.3a (left) The changing fears superimposed on a graph of the behavioural stages over time.

Figure 12.3b (right) The key language difficulties that are occurring simultaneously with the fears in each behavioural stage of dementia.

Feil's method emphasizes empathy to try to understand the world that is real to the person with dementia through a number of verbal and non-verbal techniques. It also seeks to identify and minimize whatever fear/s are (re)experienced in the different stages of the dementia process. (The key fears are shown in Figure 12.3a and Table 12.3.) Emotional and behavioural self-expression are encouraged at whatever stage of the illness a person is in. They are seen as important attempts to communicate in the face of greatly reduced language ability (shown in Figure 12.3b and Table 12.4).

Examples of the emotional tone arising from typical statements of persons in each stage are shown in Table 12.3. Among the one-to-one, stage-specific communication methods prescribed, 'validation' of the emotions experienced stands as the cornerstone. These emotions 'come out' even when speech is greatly diminished. The Validation method also incorporates a stage-specific group method for persons in Behavioural Stages 2 and 3 of dementia, in the belief that social continuity is critical to well-being throughout the dementia process.

The overall goals of this vision of care are to help make a person feel as happy (safe) as possible in the hope that their internal process of resolving life is facilitated so that the person can die in peace. All behaviour is assumed to be meaningful (Feil 1982). This goal links in closely with Bowlby's earlier quote. The goals of Validation group work are to enable a person to experience social contact in a safe, supportive environment, with persons of a similar cognitive ability.

Feil believes that as persons with dementia lose attachments, remaining people and possessions become increasingly important because they may

Table 12.3 Emotional tone arising from typical statements of persons in each behavioural stage

Emotional tone of the stages	Emotion-laden comments Stage 1
1 Frightened of losing control, independence, and not appearing normal. Request help, but often fight it.	• Sometimes I wonder if I'm going crazy • All this forgetting, it's very scary • It doesn't matter how hard I try, it gets worse
2 Frightened of being lost in time and place. Request help and hang on to carers, try to keep them always in view.	• Someone stole my. . . . He's poisoning me • That lady over there is crazy; shouldn't be here
3 Frightened of being isolated, request help often, limited ability to hold on to carers and objects.	• They don't like me, there's a conspiracy here
4 Withdrawn, will sometimes hold your hand desperately, resigned to abandonment?	• One mother can look after ten children, but. . . .

Emotion-laden comments Stage 2	Emotion-laden comments Stages 3 and 4
• It's like my bedroom, almost the same, but it's not mine • I'm not old – I still go in to work every day you know • I don't know where I am. What am I supposed to do? • No one will tell me what's going on, and I have to know • You have to leave now, I have to cook for the children • It's getting dark, mother and father will be coming for me • Mother would like you, we could have tea together soon	• Not much left, losing me, hang on • The photo, don't know how, spatter than good • Help, help, nurse, nurse! . . . • Dirty slapper, slut, shut up, shut up, shut up • Furtle durtle, murtle durtle, durtle durtle • Singing, humming, whistling, swearing • Monosyllables and noises • Words are rare

function as reminders of things lost, symbols of things lost, and as symbols of 'the only things remaining'. In this way they may become increasingly important as 'things which must not be lost at any cost'. The case histories given attest to this latter view.

Feil would say that the key fears change at each behavioural stage of dementia, as does a person's ability to explain what they are experiencing (Table 12.4). (Note that nouns are lost from speech first, typically. This causes great problems for the listener.) Feil's view, like Miesen's, assumes that persons, objects, environments and activities in present time can represent these things from the past in two senses. They can be mistaken for actual persons and things in past time, or, they can function as symbols of these

Table 12.4 Key fears and language changes occurring in the four behavioural stages of dementia

Key fears in Alzheimer-type dementia	Key language changes in Alzheimer-type dementia
Stage 1 Frightened of losing control, independence, and not appearing normal. Request help, but often fight it.	**Stage 1** • trouble finding nouns • difficulty using complex tenses, metaphors
Stage 2 Frightened of being lost in time and place. Request help and hang on to carers, try to keep them always in view.	**Stage 2** • shorter sentences, vague nouns • invent new words to replace 'lost' ones
Stage 3 Frightened of being isolated, request help often, limited ability to hold on to carers and objects.	**Stage 3** • word 'salad'/doodle, few whole sentences • repeated phrases for self-stimulation/ attention • may be left only with swear words, singing or whistling
Stage 4 Withdrawn, will sometimes hold your hand desperately; frightened of abandonment?	**Stage 4** • few words, vocalizations

things because in some way they feel like them. (See Chapter 3 on the bookcase metaphor for a further explanation of the link to this type of emotional memory storage.)

Behavioural staging, practical care issues and stage-specific care

How does knowing the behavioural staging link in with more practical daily observations of persons with dementia who reside in temporary and long-term care settings? Table 12.5 shows how the answers to everyday questions – such as 'Where are persons with dementia mostly found? Who do they feel safe with? Who do they feel least safe with?' – can be linked to the behavioural stage of dementia.

What are the implications of attachment for home and residential care settings?

If you cannot imagine what someone is missing, you will be caught off guard by their behaviours to restore or retrieve what they need. If you already

Table 12.5 Behavioural staging can shed light on many practical questions related to caring for persons in a variety of stages in care settings

Who is of prime importance to a person in a given behavioural stage?	Where can you expect to find persons in particular stages in residential settings?
Stage 1 • Some family members • Those seen as being important (doctor, pastor, the 'workers' in care settings) • Those who seem normal/in control of themselves, able to use social convention	**Stage 1** • Sitting in the best places, at the nursing station, with 'normal' elderly, in the admin office, near entrances, doorways near toilets
Stage 2 • Anyone who makes eye contact and approaches whom they can see, and who feels 'safe' or familiar	**Stage 2** • Wandering, sitting wherever there is an empty space, but rarely in their own place, in other people's rooms, trying to escape, thinking they're at home or at work, cleaning, refolding linen, in their own room repacking things endlessly
Stage 3 • Anyone who enters their visual field or whom they can grasp	**Stage 3** • Seated in a corner, if noisy and swearing, away from other residents down a corridor, in bedroom
Stage 4 • Anyone who can break into the withdrawn state with words or sensory stimulation	**Stage 4** • In room, in bed, seated for several hours in dining room or lounge, in the corner

When are persons most troubled?	When are persons least troubled?
Stage 1 • In the presence of those in later stages of dementia, • When offered help that they don't want (but may need) • When feeling excluded, unfairly treated, or patronized • When aware of errors, or others noticing them • When contradicted/or asked for an explanation of why they have done something or think something	**Stage 1** • When near 'normal' or 'important' persons • In the presence of meaningful possessions • Doing normal activities • In some select group settings • In respectful, non-judgemental, one-to-one dialogue
Stage 2 • When they feel lost, frightened, can't find familiar people or objects, and when not acknowledged	**Stage 2** • Near others who remain in their field of view • Doing familiar work/routines • Exploring/organizing familiar objects

Table 12.5 (cont'd)

When are persons most troubled?	When are persons least troubled?
	• When they feel 'as if they are at home' • When giving opinions or life experience wisdom
Stage 3 • When they can't obtain/retain the presence of those they perceive around them (isolated)	**Stage 3** • When they are exploring familiar objects • When they feel safe near others, during positive sensory stimulation: singing, movement, in groups
Stage 4 • When they feel abandoned (quiet moaning)?	**Stage 4** • When perceiving human touch, speech, music

have a feel for what is being missed by someone, you can try to intervene as the first nurse did in the second case history about the gentleman and his booty. If you can start to meet his needs during the morning, the anxiety and restless behaviour will be less likely to grow throughout the day and into the night.

Use of an apron or tabard to keep important objects close by

When handbags and pocket contents are lost forever, another option can be tried. (Feil first spoke of such 'Validation Aprons', after getting the idea from a Canadian lady in 1982.) An apron, tabard or tool pouch can be adapted in many ways, to keep important objects close by. The key is to have many pockets on them, and objects attached with Velcro, so that they can be removed for laundering. One side of the Velcro is attached to the object, so that it can be adhered to any of the several long strips of Velcro sewn along the width of the apron, between pockets. Tabards are preferable for some persons, because they distribute the weight of the apron over the shoulders rather than across the neck. It was surprising to see how many persons wanted to keep them on for many hours of the day.

Figure 12.4 shows photos of two different ladies (both in Behavioural Stage 2 and not very mobile) who had been withdrawn, tearful and difficult to get any contact or communication with. Both aprons were filled with objects such as pretty cards, pieces of lace, doilies, ribbons, a lace head-kerchief, keys, brightly coloured fabric samples, a change purse, measuring tape, a tiny cloth doll, a garter, real nylon stockings, some clothes pegs, a

Figure 12.4 Two ladies (in Behavioural Stage 2) with aprons for important objects

polishing cloth, pens and paper. Both ladies transformed within minutes of wearing the aprons. The lady on the left in Figure 12.4 found the lace headkerchief, put it on herself, began to sing hymns and explore the contents of the pockets. The lady on the right in Figure 12.4 found a cloth and small rag doll and began to speak and interact with those around her, by showing them all the items she was finding.

Over the years, many variations of apron and tabard have been experimented with. With some individuals it is easy to successfully predict which objects they will enjoy. With others, it is trial and error, hit and miss. Occasionally, some persons do not seem to respond to the objects in the apron, as if they were not even aware they were there.

Men's work tabards are made from denim and corduroy fabric, whereas women usually prefer patterns more akin to those they will have been used to in the past. Some men have reacted well to having small blocks of wood and sandpaper, rulers and pencils in their tabards. Small pieces of wood with holes drilled into it with large nuts and bolts through them, have also worked well for some men. Ladies usually enjoy brightly coloured fabrics, lots of lace, and even quilted fabric, or appliquéd pieces of crochet work or embroidery.

Such tabards are individually made up for each person, in collaboration with family and friends. It is best to make two at the same time, so that when one is in the laundry, the other can still be worn. Some are worn all day long, others are worn only during the afternoon, when energy is at a 'low ebb' and yet the person is not sleepy.

Special tabards have been sewn for persons who repeatedly undo all their buttons or zipper and often sit in a lounge area unaware of their state of being 'undressed' in front of others. These have had zippers, pop-studs, Velcro and pockets with extra flaps for buttons and buttonholes sewn on. It appears that sometimes undoing buttons is the only thing a person can still do. It is done for stimulation rather than literally to undress oneself.

The tabard concept, or seating someone at a table with activities and objects that are meaningful for them, has been tried successfully with some persons with dementia who masturbate in lounges, unaware of the presence of others. We do not yet know how much of this behaviour occurs out of sheer boredom and the need for some sort of stimulation whilst the person is unaware of the presence of others.

Stage specific activities and group work

Some care facilities for persons with dementia are still trying to provide one activity at a time for persons in all stages of dementia. Although very skilled, many activity therapists have not had specialist training in dementia and do not know exactly why this is an impossible task. For example, persons in Stage 1 are often ultra-critical of those in more advanced stages, who are disinhibited, may swear out loud, cannot remember rules for games and cannot not use adult etiquette. Persons in Stage 2 will start to wander if they cannot follow a task or are being harshly spoken to (by more cognitively intact residents). Persons in Stage 1 are often exasperated by persons in Stage 3 who repeat the same phrases and words or swear endlessly, and/or who make repetitive movements.

From this perspective, 'bingo for everyone' can hardly satisfy any person's real needs. With this in mind, the list shown in Table 12.6 is intended to be a rough guide for which activities and types of group work are most success-ful for persons in a given behavioural stage. As long as there are several tables in a room, individuals can be meaningfully occupied with an activity that suits their particular ability, whether it is a group activity or just inter-acting with objects that have special significance for them. (One lady was totally happy carding wool for many hours of the day and watching others. Another gentleman shredded newspapers, for pet litter, to give to the children who came to visit other residents.)

Box 12.3 gives a list of the types of objects which have been found useful in specialist dementia units, especially for persons in Stages 2 and 3.

Table 12.6 A sample list of stage-specific activities typical of what persons with dementia can still manage

Sample stage-specific activities and group work

Stage 1: propriety and normalcy of activities is important	• Reality orientation • Current events group • Factual reminiscence • Games with few rules • Dining group • Outings • Exercise groups • Serious cooking • Music appreciation
Stage 2: the enjoyment of the process and social interaction	• Validation group • Music therapy • Fun cooking • Dance and movement • Reminiscence • Make-up group • Bingo (with helper)
Stage 3: sensory stimulation and spontaneity	• Validation group • Sensory stimulation • Snoezelen • Music/movement • Feel-box type game • Wheelchair dancing
Stage 4: one to one	• Sensory stimulation • Music massage • Passive range of motion (ROM)

Box 12.3   Examples of useful objects for care facilities for persons with dementia

Some suggestions for objects that appeal to many persons in Stages 2 and 3

1 A taperecorder is preferable to a stereo for playing music. Collect a wide variety of tapes, different types of music, poems, stories. They can be played quietly during 'individual activity' time.
2 A good supply of trays for putting the following objects on:
   • stacks of newspapers for shredding (to give to children for their pets)
   • colourful picturebooks
   • postcard collection

- file cards with pictures of 'faces with different expressions' for sorting (you need to make these), pictures of famous people like the 'royals'
- magazines, old picture calendars, for looking at and cutting things out of
- selection of used birthday and Christmas cards for looking at, sorting, cutting
- bright large fabric squares for folding
- spare paper
- hole punch
- filing boxes with alphabetical indices and filing cards with pictures on them
- microwave playdough (for sculpting), and other types of modelling materials
- textiles, fabrics for cutting into squares, stuffing, polishing cloths
- box/basket of old linens (lace, doilies, embroidered napkins, headrest cloths, etc.)
- sewing box containing usual things, thread, thimbles, measuring tape, chalk, etc.
- button box (obviously to be kept out of reach of persons who compulsively eat non-edible things)
- misc. things, zippers, Velcro, curtain hooks, pom-poms
- wood polish/wax and polishing cloths
- containers of bolts, screws, nuts, etc. with an ice-cube tray into which they can be sorted
- simple woodworking tools, sand, sandpaper, torches
- small pieces of wood, blocks, edging, some with holes drilled in them
- bag of wool and carding combs
- brass objects, brasso, gloves and polishing cloths
- spare handbags and shopping bags, small suitcases or overnight bags
- make-up collection (nail polish, rouge, powder compacts, eye shadow, perfume, etc.)
- costume jewellery collection
- silk flowers, baskets, oasis, for making arrangements
- instruments that can be easily hand held, rainsticks, tambourines, bells
- safety darts, skittles, bagatelle
- soft toys, dolls
- simple (board) games like Sorry, Snakes and Ladders, Scrabble,
- dominos (which will be used for all sorts of amusement, but rarely for the actual game)
- spongy balls, beanbags, wooden or plastic shapes
- unusual objects, prisms, rubix cubes
- watches, old spare keys, wallets
- old clocks (that can be dismantled)
- aprons
- old dried tea leaves, crepe paper, sand, glue, paints (for making pictures)
- small boxes, brown paper, gift-wrapping paper

Conclusions about attachment and dementia interventions

It is important to acknowledge that 'attachment figures' for persons with dementia can be care-giving staff themselves, who know about the importance of and can freely provide close physical proximity and emotional contact. Their presence can function as a symbol for others with whom the person has been close to in life. Other persons/residents, who 'feel familiar' and do not question the behaviours of the person, can also be attachment figures (they will usually be in Behavioural Stage 2, disoriented in time).

Care-giving staff need to be aware that 'attachment objects' can be used for a variety of purposes. They can be used as landmarks (visual handles) when strategically placed around the environment, particularly to make a person's bedroom door easier to find. Attachment objects can also serve as a way of helping to provide activities to occupy time meaningfully. Their success will depend on their familiarity and the routines they were used in. (Those with a low complexity and memory load will be most successful after Behavioural Stage 1.) Attachment objects need to be readily visible and reachable as needed. Often open shelving is a better option than having such things behind closed doors and in other rooms. Table 12.7 summarizes these pointers.

There can never be anything more important than the presence of caring others. In such presence happiness is also possible for persons with dementia, as Figure 12.5 attests.

Table 12.7 Summary for caregivers of stage-specific 'attachment concept' implications

- Recognize 'attachment behaviour' (verbal and non-verbal requests for a carer's closeness)

- Provide access to a range of meaningful objects in the environment, and directly accessible within the visual field

- Provide opportunities for one-to-one communication, safe social interactions (with caregivers, and residents who feel safe to the person with dementia), and where speech prohibits social interaction, access to social events which allow a person to hear/observe/feel the atmosphere of social stimulation

- Try to replace losses with new attachments (a key or primary care-giver who understands the specific needs of the person, new contacts, including with those in a similar behavioural stage, meaningful objects and proximity to them when needed)

- Recognize both the literal and symbolic meanings of oneself, others, and objects to a person with dementia, and how this can change over the course of the illness

Figure 12.5 A lady who had been restless, asking after her father and mother, settles down with the close contact of a carer.

Notes

I am indebted to my many students and course participants over the years for their passionate response to this subject matter, and for their own various examples.

Feil's Validation V/F is a registered trademark.

All photos by Gemma M.M. Jones.

References

Bowlby, J. (1969) *Attachment and Loss, vol. 1: Attachment*, London: Hogarth Press.

Bowlby, J. (1973) *Attachment and Loss, vol. 2: Separation: Anxiety and Anger*, London: Hogarth Press.

Bowlby, J. (1980) *Attachment and Loss, vol. 3: Loss: Sadness and Depression*, London: Hogarth Press.

Bowlby, J. (1986) *Attachment, life-span and old age*, eds J. Munnichs and B. Miesen, Houten: Van Loghum Slaterus Press.

Feil, N. (1982) *Validation, The Feil Method*. Cleveland, OH: Edward Feil Productions, 4614 Prospect Ave., Cleveland, Ohio 44103, USA.

Feil, N. (1992) 'Validation therapy with late-onset dementia populations', in G. Jones and B. Miesen (eds) *Care-giving in Dementia: Research and Applications*, London: Routledge, pp. 199–218.

Feil, N. (1993) *The Validation Breakthrough*, London: Health Professions Press.

Jones, G.M.M. (1997) 'A review of Feil's Validation method', *Current Opinion in Psychiatry* 10: 326–32.

Jones, G.M.M. and Miesen, B.M.L. (1990) *Care-giving in Dementia: Research and Applications*, vol. 1, London: Routledge.

Miesen, B. (1992) 'Attachment theory and dementia', in G.M.M. Jones and B.M.L. Miesen (eds) *Care-giving in Dementia: Research and Applications*, London: Routledge, pp. 38–56.

Miesen, B.M.L. and Jones, G.M.M. (eds) (1997) *Care-giving in Dementia: Research and Applications*, vol. 2, London: Routledge.

Part IV

Family and professional caregivers

Chapter 13

The care-giving stress process

Anne Margriet Pot

Introduction

Until the 1980s, carers of relatives with dementia were so-called 'hidden victims' of Alzheimer's disease. The attention of clinicians and researchers was merely directed at persons with dementia, and not at their family carers. Zarit and colleagues were among the first researchers who illuminated what they called the *burden* of providing care to a relative with dementia (Zarit *et al.* 1980). They developed a scale, 'The Burden Interview', covering areas most frequently mentioned by carers as problems, including carers' health, psychological well-being, finances, social life and the relationship between the carer and relative with dementia. Results of their early study showed that persons with dementia receiving more visits from children (other than the primary carer), grandchildren and siblings had carers who reported less burden.

After this study was published, there has been an explosive growth of care-giving research, focusing on the negative effects of providing care on carers and on interventions to reduce or prevent these effects (Schulz *et al.* 1995, 2002). These studies were carried out in the USA, UK, Netherlands and other European countries, as well as in countries like Japan and Australia. The results of these studies reveal that providing care to a dementing family-member has no single cure. It affects not only the roles and activities of carers, but may also have serious consequences for their mental and physical health and may even increase their risk of dying.

The stress of carers is an important issue for public health care, because of their central role in the care of persons with dementia and the negative health consequences they may experience (see also Duijnstee 1992). It will become even more important in the near future, because of the expected increase in numbers of elderly persons with dementia and their family carers (RGO 2002). The pressure on these family carers will only further intensify, due to the expected shortage of professional care for persons with dementia.

In this chapter, the care-giving stress process will be discussed. A theoretical model will be presented for understanding the stress process of carers of persons with dementia, including patient and carer characteristics and situational aspects. Evidence on the relationships between components included in this model will be presented. Finally, some implications for preventing care-giving stress will pass in review.

Case

Mrs Brown has great difficulty with the apathy of her husband. Her always active husband has become lazy and forgetful. She asks him repeatedly 'Do you remember who visited us yesterday?' and 'What did we eat yesterday evening?' Her husband becomes angry and starts to shout in response to these enduring questions he cannot always answer. After a while, Mrs Brown calls in the aid of the GP because of her husband's aggressive behaviour. Several characteristics of Mrs Brown and her environment may contribute to the difficulties she goes through with her husband.

Family carer understanding of the illness

This case illuminates the importance of knowing the diagnosis of dementia. If Mrs Brown does not know that her husband has dementia, her continuous checking of his memory is not surprising. She may ask herself 'What's wrong with him?' She will persist in her questions, especially when he sometimes knows the answer and sometimes does not. However, knowing the diagnosis is not enough.

In addition, it is important that family carers understand what kind of behavioural consequences dementia may have to prevent misinterpretations. If Mrs Brown does not know that apathy may result from dementia, her interpretation of her husband's behaviour as laziness is sensible. In addition, she may misinterpret his aggressive behaviour as a way to hurt her purposefully.

A carer's misunderstanding of the illness will determine his/her reaction to the patient. This case of Mrs Brown shows that things can get completely out of control. Mrs Brown could not handle the interaction with her husband any more and went to the GP.

Appraisal of providing care

Imagine that Mrs Brown is still working and has a job. She may get conflicts at work because the care of her husband takes up too much of her time and attention, which is needed for her job. She is often late at the office and when she is present her attention is distracted by phone calls from (or regarding) her husband. She feels under pressure from her care-giving role, which will lead to her own health problems.

Emotional and physical health of the carer

The emotional health of the family carer determines his/her flexibility in providing care. For example, if Mrs Brown feels under pressure by caring for her husband, if she feels sad and helpless, if she has sleeping and eating problems, if she does not have any expectations of the future any more, no doubt she will react to her husband in a less flexible way. For example, she may react by shouting at her husband. In addition, her emotional functioning may also have consequences on her physical functioning.

The physical health of carers determines how much care they can safely provide. Carers who are physically ill, disabled or frail may put themselves and the person with dementia at risk when they take on too much care. If Mrs Brown is frail, she may need help with doing the shopping at an early stage, because she cannot do this with her husband any longer.

Resources for family carers

Some care resources may facilitate the care of a relative with dementia. Initially, a carer's personality may play a role. If Mrs Brown feels no control over the interaction with her husband, the situation will not improve. However, if she feels some control over the things that happen to her husband, that they are not mere pawns in the system, a sense of cooperation and control will facilitate providing care.

Mrs Fortune, whose husband also has memory problems, sat down with her husband and told him what a pleasure it was when they visited their daughter the day before and what a delicious meal she had cooked for them. Mr Fortune is glad his wife reminds him of this special event. We may assume that Mr Brown would react in a less aggressive way if his wife was able to change her way of coping with his memory problems.

Another aspect that may change the care-giving experience is social support. Support may be offered in different ways (emotional, practical, informational or financial) and by different members of the family carers' support network (family members, friends, neighbours) or by professional sources. Mrs Brown, though frail, feels supported by her son who is willing to do the shopping with her once a week. However, when her son does not want to help her because he does not want to see his father, this may be a tremendous stress for Mrs Brown. Thus, social support may facilitate the care-giving process, but family conflict may also be a serious stressor. The same holds for professional resources. A paid home help may be of great help to Mrs Brown, but if a different home help is supplied each time it may be very stressful for her.

Background factors

Background factors may also play a part in the care-giving process. For example, Mrs Brown may feel more distressed about providing care for her husband than she felt when she cared for her mother with dementia some years ago. Her commitment to providing care for her husband may be relatively stronger, as in a 'child–parent' care-giving relationship. The quality of the previous relationship may also play a role in the care-giving stress process. Imagine that Mrs Brown has been belittled by her husband throughout her life; providing care for him without 'taking revenge' may be a difficult job for her.

Theoretical model

Providing care for a person with dementia may lead to distress in carers. However, carers can differ greatly in the amount of distress they experience, even as a result of very similar conditions. As illustrated above, several characteristics of family carers and their environment may influence the care-giving stress process.

Figure 13.1 shows a general model of the stress process (adapted version of the model described by Aneshensel *et al.* 1995; Pearlin *et al.* 1990). It is a simplified diagrammatic representation showing all the components of the care-giving stress process: stressors, outcomes, resources, background

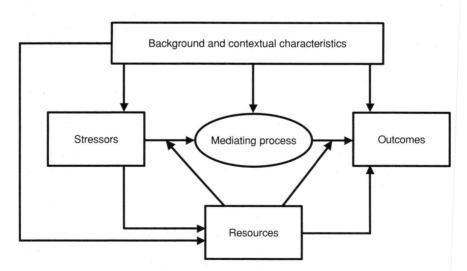

Figure 13.1 Stress process model
Source: Aneshensel *et al.* (1995, adapted version)

variables and a mediating process. *Stressors* refer to the difficult circumstances experienced by family carers that threaten their own health. The memory loss and apathy of her husband were stressors for Mrs Brown.

Outcomes refer to the short or long-term consequences of these stressors for the carer and may be thought of rather broadly. They may include the mental and physical health problems of the family carer, the unfolding of the 'post care-giving life course', such as the duration of grief and his/her mortality. As Schulz and Beach (1999) showed, carers of persons with dementia had a higher risk of dying, as compared to non-carers. Outcomes may also include transitions in the carer's caregiving career, for example, nursing home placement of the person with dementia. Outcomes for Mrs Brown were feeling sad and helpless, sleeping and eating problems, and having no expectation of the future anymore.

Resources may explain variations in the effects of stressors among carers in terms of outcomes. Resources may be social, personal or material in nature. The ways in which the carer feels a sense of mastery or self-efficacy and feels supported are important resources. They may alter the basic stressor–outcome relationship, by either increasing or diminishing the negative effects of stressors. This effect is also called the stress buffering or moderating effect. Knowledge of the stress buffering role played by resources is important because it may deliver the key for interventions to prevent or reduce care-giving stress. This is especially important because most stressors can hardly be changed. In addition, resources are also thought to act as intervening links between stressors and outcomes.

In the model shown in Figure 13.1, *background and contextual factors* are also included. The stress process unfolds within the context of social, economic, cultural, political and religious factors. As Aneshensel *et al.* (1995) stated: 'Individuals confront stressors not in isolation of other facets of their lives, but as the bearers of certain characteristics, the possessors of different statuses, and the occupants of positions within stratified social systems.' In other words, these factors will influence stressors, resources, outcomes and the mediating process.

An important background factor is the relationship between family carer and care recipient. Duijnstee (1992) has discussed this relationship in great detail in the first volume of *Care-giving in Dementia*. In summary, there is a hierarchical selection process in taking on the primary family carer role. When a partner is available, mostly he/she becomes the primary carer. If not, a child, friend or neighbour will place themselves in this role. In general, more daughters than sons act as primary carers.

In general, spouse carers are more able to be committed to this role than the children. This commitment may be based on three components. First, spouses may have a higher sense of moral commitment to care for their partner. Second, they have invested more in the care-giving relationship, both emotionally and with regard to time. Third, they may feel more social pressures to continue in their role. This perceived commitment to care has consequences for the carer stress process.

A mediation process between stressors and outcomes may be postulated. Aneshensel *et al.* (1995) view this process as 'stress proliferation', one stressor is a target for another. We view this mediation process as a cognitive process, explaining why certain stressors are related to a family carer's reaction in accordance with the concept of '*appraisal*' as formulated by Lazarus (1991). He stated that psychopathology may arise when the environmental demands dominate at the expense of personal interests. The primary function of appraisal is to achieve the best possible integration of the environmental demands with one's personal interests without slighting either. One constantly tries to balance these two forces. Translated to the care-giving situation, if the demands of the care-giving situation dominate at the expense of carer's personal interests, psychological distress can develop.

We gave an example of Mrs Brown to illuminate this theoretical concept of appraisal. Mrs Brown may have conflicts at work, due to often being late and the frequent phone calls from (or regarding) her husband, thus distracting her attention, or even because of the mistakes she makes as a result of thinking of her husband's needs instead of her job tasks. As a result she may develop psychological distress. In this example, the demands of the care-giving situation and her role as an employee are no longer in balance. The partner is preoccupied by the care-giving situation. We developed an instrument to measure the outcome of this mediating process, the 'Self-Perceived Pressure from Informal Care' scale (Pot *et al.* 1995).

Below, empirical evidence will be summarized on components and relationships between these components described in the theoretical model. The results described are primarily based on two studies (Schulz *et al.* 1995; Pot *et al.* 1997).

Carers' emotional and physical health problems

Initially, researchers used global instruments in which family carers were asked to relate health consequences directly to the care-giving situation. For example, a carer was asked if he/she became nervous or depressed by the contact with the person he/she cares for. To compare clinically significant emotional symptoms between carers, a control group of non-carers from the general population and standardized screening instruments or structured interviews were used. Researchers have increasingly focused on these kinds of instruments.

In several studies, screening instruments for psychiatric morbidity were used. For example, in our own study one of the instruments used to measure psychological distress was the 12-item version of the General Health Questionnaire (GHQ). The GHQ-12 consists of questions like: Have you recently felt constantly under strain? Have you recently been feeling unhappy and distressed? Have you recently been able to enjoy your day-to-day activities? These are scored on a four-point scale. A score of two or higher would indicate people who have a high risk of psychiatric morbidity. Of the family carers 66 per cent scored above the cut-off score of '2+'. This is about 2.5 times greater than in the general Dutch population (see Figure 13.2).

Another instrument to measure a broad spectrum of psychiatric symptoms used in studies on carers is the Hopkins Symptom Checklist-90 (SCL-90). It consists of 90 items to be answered using a five-point scale.

Family carers were also screened for depressive symptoms using among others the Center for Epidemiologic Studies Depression Scale (CES-D). This is a 20-item, self-report scale to be scored on a four-point scale. Examples of items are: 'I felt depressed', 'My sleep was restless' and 'I felt that people disliked me'. A cut-off 16+ was used, as an indication of being at risk for having a diagnosis of depression. Proportions of family carers at risk for depression range from 28 per cent to 55 per cent, compared to the figure of 15 per cent normally found in community surveys. Thus, these findings indicate that a substantial proportion of carers have depressive symptoms that are clinically relevant in the sense that they may need treatment. In other studies, using other instruments for measuring depressive symptoms, results concur with those mentioned using the CES-D.

Studies in which diagnostic interviews such as the Structured Clinical Interview for DSM-IIIR (SCID) or the Diagnostic Interview Schedule (DIS) were used also reported elevated levels of the diagnosis of depression and anxiety, as compared to population norms and control groups. Percentages of 20 per cent or higher were found for depressive disorders of spouse carers, and 18 per cent for adult children carers. The use of psychotropic drugs among family carers was found to be higher as well.

As Schulz et al. (1995) indicated, the precise amount of family carer 'psychiatric morbidity' is difficult to determine because of the ways in which carers are recruited for the studies in this field. In most studies, they are recruited from health care facilities. These carers probably have greater symptoms compared to family carers who have not yet asked for help. However, although the prevalence of psychiatric symptoms is somewhat lower in epidemiological studies, it is still higher in comparison to the general population.

Research showed that the negative consequences for family carers' 'physical health' are less distinctive than for their mental health (Schulz et al. 1995). Carers perceive their own health as being worse than that of non-carers. However, they do not show unambiguous differences on other aspects of physical health, like self-reported diseases, physical symptoms, and cardio-vascular functioning. The same trend holds for 'care consumption', such as number of doctor visits and periods of hospitalization. This may be due to a longer period of time being needed to show effects of caring on carers' physical health (Figure 13.2).

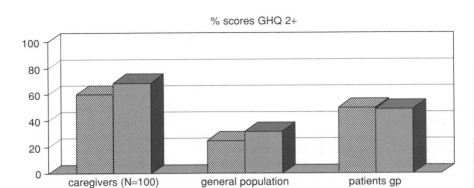

Figure 13.2 Prevalence of high psychological distress (GHQ-12 2+) in caregivers of demented patients in comparison with the general population and patients visiting the GP

Changes over time

The increased levels of psychological distress among family carers of persons with dementia living in the community raises the question of how carers' health changes over time. Different models have been postulated to describe this (Haley and Pardo 1989; Townsend *et al.* 1989). According to the *wear-and-tear model*, carer health deteriorates progressively as a person with dementia's functioning declines. Another possibility is that carer health either improves or stabilizes over time as the person with dementia deteriorates, as postulated by the *adaptation model*. A third model, the *trait model*, assumes that the mental health of carers remains stable due to carer 'stable resources' such as coping strategies, despite the worsening of dementia symptoms.

The course of a carer's health may be different from that of carers at a different stage of the 'care-giving career'. Caring for a person with dementia who is institutionalized may be less stressful for the family carer due to care-giving stressors ceasing to exist. On the other hand, nursing home placement may be experienced as an important life event; new stressors may be created related to the new environment. Therefore, health changes over time will be discussed separately for three groups: those who continue to provide care to a relative with dementia in the community; those with a relative who has been institutionalized; those whose relative has died.

When the relative stays in the community

Results of our own study in the Netherlands support the *wear-and-tear model* (Figure 13.3, Pot *et al.* 1997). During a two-year period, the mental

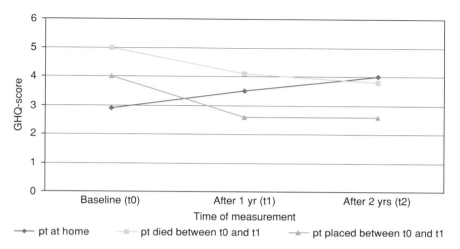

Figure 13.3 Changes in carer's psychological distress over two years

health of carers who continued providing care at home worsened when compared to that of carers of relatives who were institutionalized or had died in the meantime. The level of general psychiatric morbidity increased during the two years of providing care measured in this study. More support for the wear-and-tear model was given by a study among carers in the USA using the 28-item version of the GHQ (Gold *et al.* 1995).

An instrument that measures a 'wider range' of psychiatric morbidity, such as the GHQ-12 and the SCL-90, may be more appropriate for detecting changes over time among carers. In studies measuring the course of carers' depression, results showed no changes (Pruchno *et al.* 1990; Kiecolt-Glaser *et al.* 1991; Mullan, 1992; Collins *et al.* 1994). Furthermore, the effects of carer characteristics may influence changes over time in carers' psychopathology. Differences in health changes were found for male vs. female carers and spouses vs. others (Schulz and Williamson 1991; Zarit and Whitlatch 1992). It would be relevant to relate the change in carers' health to the change in functioning of the person with dementia in future studies.

After institutionalization

It is important to underline that the (care-giving) relationship does not come to an end after placement. (Chapter 18 attests to this.) Carers continue to provide care and remain committed to their relatives, although their tasks change. They often play an important role in representing their relatives when difficult decisions in treatment must be taken. Some carers visit their relatives every day and stay till they go to sleep. Thus, after placement some stressors (specifically related to the home care situation) come to an end, but new stressors related to the nursing home environment may arise. For example, the interaction with nursing staff may be stressful for family carers because nurses will care for their relatives in a different way, or because family carers sometimes get a sense of redundancy. Other interactions in care settings can be stressful too, such as the behaviours of other persons with dementia on the ward, the behaviour of other family members during visits, or even trying to visit with one's own relative who is adapting to the new environment. This is supported by the study of Whitlatch et al. (1991) showing that 'carers' own poor adjustment to the placement' and negative interactions with both their family member with dementia and families of other residents were related to depressive complaints.

In our own carer study, mental health tended to improve among those whose relative had been placed in a nursing home. This was demonstrated by a reduction of their psychological distress and depressive complaints (Pot et al. 1997). In another Dutch study, a reduction in carers' 'perceived pressure from informal care' was already found six weeks after institutionalization. An improvement in mental health was found three months later. Again, depressive complaints did not change (Meiland et al. 2001). These differences may be explained by the duration of follow-up: in the first study, carers' health was measured at least one year after institutionalization. In the second study, it was measured only 4.5 months after nursing home placement. Recovery from depressive complaints after institutionalization may take more time, although it would be unrealistic to expect that the mental health of these carers will become the same as for those without a relative with dementia.

It is worth while to study the course of carers' mental health and the effects of stressors after placement in European countries. Nursing homes and criteria for placement can be quite different from the USA, making it difficult to extrapolate US findings, which found no changes in carers' mental health after placement (Zarit and Whitlatch 1992; Lieberman and Fisher 2001).

After bereavement

In which ways do carers' health and ability to adjust change after the loss of the person with dementia? In the literature, positive as well as negative effects of bereavement have been assumed. Therefore, it is worth while to look in more detail at the theoretical models that lay behind these assumptions. This will illuminate the difficulties in predicting changes in carers' health and adjustment after bereavement.

According to the 'stress and coping model', the relief of care-giving may improve carers' health and adjustment because an important stressor is gone. However, it may equally be assumed that the care-giving experience, as a stressful life event, may reduce carers' health and adjustment after bereavement. A third possibility is that the care-giving experience may have both these (positive and negative) effects on carers' health and adjustment after the loss of the care recipient (Schulz *et al.* 1997).

According to the same model, there are more factors affecting carers' health and adjustment than the actual carer's experience, including things such as social support and carers' perceptions of control. In general, long-term exposure to a chronically stressful situation may deplete these resources. Carers' resources may be reduced at the time of loss of the person with dementia, due to the long time that carers have been involved in care-giving. This may have a negative effect on carers' health and adjustment (Schulz *et al.* 1997).

Whereas many studies were carried out on stress and coping models, surprisingly few studies discuss grief models to any significant extent (Meuser and Marwit 2001). Some findings suggest that carers adjust better after the death of the person receiving care, because they have been able to prepare slowly for the loss. However, other findings suggest that even after many years of care-giving, a lack of acceptance and resolution of grief may still exist.

Results of our own study showed no further significant deterioration in psychological well-being among Dutch carers after the person with dementia had died (Pot *et al.* 1997). This is in line with findings from other studies (Mullan 1992; Bodnar and Kiecolt-Glaser 1994). However, finding 'no changes' may also be due to temporal and individual variability in post-death adjustment. Temporal variability is supported by the finding that when subdividing the carers into recent and longer bereaved, those recently bereaved (less than six months) showed an increase in depression, whereas those who were bereaved for a longer period of time showed a decrease (Mullan 1992). When carers were asked whether anticipatory grieving has an ameliorating effect on post-death grief, the answer appears 'yes' initially and 'no' in the long run (Meuser and Marwit 2001). However, the accuracy of these accounts seems to be low and must be checked by longitudinal research. Finally, individual variability may play a role. A difficult pre-death period will probably lead to more difficulty following bereavement.

Stressors

In general, it is assumed that problems of persons with dementia, such as incontinence, aggressive behaviour and nocturnal restlessness, are especially troublesome for carers. Most studies indeed show that the occurrence and/ or severity of such behavioural problems as a whole are related to carers' psychological distress. These correlated more strongly than other disease-related stressors such as general severity of dementia, cognitive or functional decline of the person with dementia, or care-giving tasks of the carer (Pot and Van Dyck 1992). Although the total amount of behavioural problems affect the psychological well-being of the carer, it must be stressed that different carers may perceive behavioural problems in a different way, and that these problems will have different effects on them (see also Duijnstee 1992). Some carers perceive nocturnal restlessness as a great problem, get exhausted by it and develop depressive complaints, while others seem to be able to handle it without significant problems.

Mediating process

Knowledge of the mediating process (see Figure 13.1) is relevant for understanding why specific stressors, for example, behavioural problems of the person with dementia, increase carers' psychological distress. We developed an instrument to measure the outcome of carers' cognitive mediating process, the Self-Perceived Pressure from Informal Care scale (SPPIC, Pot *et al.* 1995). The scale consists of nine items to be scored on a five-point scale. We showed that these items are indicators of one dimension of 'self-perceived pressure from informal care' with a hierarchic order. Self-perceived pressure initially manifests itself in carers' thoughts of being too involved in the care-giving situation. Increasing pressure makes itself felt in perceptions of limits to performing other activities or roles and finally in conflicts at home and/or at work.

Using this instrument, we found (for spouse as well as child carers) that their perceived pressure explained why their care-giving tasks were related to their psychological distress. Child carers' 'perceived pressure from informal care' also explained why their parents' behavioural problems were related to the children's psychological distress. For spouse carers, the strong relationship found between behavioural problems and carer psychological distress was not explained by their perceived pressure. Maybe this can be explained by the fact that behavioural problems pose too great a demand on the quality of the spousal relationship. Another explanation may be that spouse carers are less capable of stepping back from the care-giving situation and maintaining a feeling of control with respect to their spouses' behaviour (Pot *et al.* 1998).

The relevance of this finding is that it may offer keys for interventions to prevent or diminish psychological distress of the carers. Carers' perceived pressure needs to be reduced if they are to continue providing care. For example, carers could be taught to prevent or to solve conflicts with family members or with colleagues at work, or to negotiate with them in order to get more practical or emotional support or more time for themselves. This finding also illustrates that interventions merely focused at stressors, i.e. taking over care-giving tasks by respite care may not be as effective as one would think. If carers' subjective experience of the care situation does not change, the psychological distress will not be diminished.

Resources

It is important to know which carers have an increased or a decreased risk for psychological distress under similar conditions or experiences. For example, do carers who receive more support experience less psychological distress when they provide the same amount of care for their family member with dementia than those who receive less social support? This information on so-called 'moderators' is helpful for planning interventions to prevent or reduce the psychological distress of carers.

However, the results are less clear than one may wish. Findings show that characteristics of the carer, such as personality characteristics and received social support, may have '*main* effects' on their psychological distress. However, results are mixed, especially for the role of factors such as coping strategies and social support. Schulz *et al.* (1995) concluded that of the many psychosocial and personality variables examined, those most often associated with depression included loss of self/boundary ambiguity, self-esteem/mastery, neuroticism and optimism.

Results about moderator or stress-buffering effects are scarce. We showed that 'the carers' appraisal' is an indication of their psychological distress regardless of their personality (degree of extraversion), coping strategies (emotion focused or problem focused), social support (instrumental or emotional) or physical functioning. In other words, if carers perceive much pressure they are in need of attention and support, regardless of their way of coping, personality, physical functioning, or the support they receive (Pot *et al.* 2000).

Background variables

Two demographic variables consistently found to be related to depression were socio-economic status and the carers' relationship to the person with dementia. Spouse carers are more distressed than non-spouse carers. This is not surprising due to the different commitment spouses versus others have to the person with dementia.

Benefits of care-giving

Empirical research has also been carried out about the benefits for carers. In some studies, carers were asked 'which positive aspects of providing care' they experienced. This question suggests a *psychological* perspective, it refers to the level of *experience*. In our own study we asked a similar question. Half of the carers answered that they could not think of anything positive. Regarding the burden of care-giving, this finding is not surprising. It might have been different if carers had been asked whether providing care 'had any positive *meaning*' for them.

This asks for research on a cultural anthropologic level. A positive meaning may be attributed to a negative experience. In terms of our Western culture, it may be assumed that 'bearing one's cross' may have a positive meaning. Regarding this essential terminological and methodological differentiation, it may be questioned what the value is of, for example, a recent study on Canadian carers in which 73 per cent could identify one specific positive aspect of care-giving, and an additional 7 per cent more than one (Cohen *et al.* 2002).

Consequences for the care-giving relationship

The negative health effects of providing care may have consequences for the care-giving relationship. Two consequences will be discussed in more detail: carer's behaviour towards the person with dementia, and the placement of the person in a long-term care facility.

Aggressive behaviour towards the person with dementia

Attention has increased recently towards studying the family carer's aggressive or other undesirable behaviour towards the person with dementia. This behaviour falls within a large scope of behaviour called 'elder abuse or mistreatment'. Great care is needed in using these terms. They stigmatize carers who are in most cases victims themselves.

Several studies show high prevalence rates of carers' aggressive behaviour towards the relative with dementia. In our study among Dutch carers, 11 per cent (18 out of 169 carers) reported that they had actually engaged in physical aggression by shaking, hitting or pushing the person with dementia. Half reported a frequency of once or more a month. These prevalences are in line with those found in other studies ranging from 5 per cent to 12 per cent for physical aggression (Paveza *et al.* 1992; Pillemer and Suitor 1992; Coyne *et al.* 1993). Most of the carers who reported physical aggression in our study also reported chronic verbal aggression (13 out of 18 carers). Of the Dutch carers 30 per cent (51 out of 169 carers) reported chronic verbal aggression only, by shouting, swearing, threatening or insulting the person with dementia (at least ten or more times in the preceding year) (Pot *et al.* 1996).

It would be of interest to discover whether particular characteristics of carers are related to their aggressive behaviour. In our Dutch study, both verbal and physical aggression were related to a greater degree of impairment of the person with dementia (in cognitive functioning and instrumental activities in daily living). Chronic verbal aggression was also related to the amount of care provided by carers. Physical aggression made to carers was related to a higher level of psychological complaints. This suggests that physical aggression is not just a mere extension of chronic verbal aggression.

It seems that carers who reported physical aggression were experiencing burnout (Pot *et al.* 1996). This topic is discussed in further detail in Chapter 17.

Institutionalization of the person with dementia

Another effect of providing care for the person with dementia may be upon the (negative) health status of the carer. We examined three sets of 'carer characteristics' with regard to their explanatory value of the effects of the institutionalization of person with dementia (Pot *et al.* 2001).

The first characteristic we studied was the *commitment* of informal carers to the care-giving relationship. This commitment may be based on their sense of moral commitment, their investments in the care-giving relationship (e.g. time or emotions) and social pressures (Johnson 1982). In addition, consequences of institutionalization for carers themselves may also determine their commitment to the care-giving relationship. For instance, when a carer and the person with dementia live together, institutionalization of the person has more far-reaching consequences than when they live in separate households. The type of relationship between carer and the person with dementia could be interpreted as a global measure of carers' commitment to the care-giving relationship. Spouses, in comparison to non-spouses, are more likely to be more strongly committed to the care-giving relationship. Therefore, it would be expected that the institutionalization rate of demented elderly people cared for by spouses would be lower than that of those persons cared for by non-spouses. This hypothesis was confirmed by our findings as well as those of others.

A second group of carer characteristics that may explain institutional placement is *psychological distress*. The general expectation was that the placement rate would be higher when carers experience greater psychological distress. However, empirical findings on the relationship between carers' mental health problems and a person with dementia's placement are ambiguous, mostly showing no clear relationship, like our own findings. The findings about carers' appraisal of the care-giving situation are also mixed. Interpretation of the seemingly conflicting findings is hampered because of the various instruments used, concerning burden, role overload, role captivity, family and job care-giving conflict, and carer competence. Our own findings, concerning Dutch carers, showed that spouse carers who perceived more pressure from caring, showed an increased amount of institutional placement. This suggests that spouse carers will only give in when the pressure is no longer bearable, regardless of their own health and personality. This is a matter of concern, especially in regard to the number of mental health problems and related aggressive behaviour against their relative with dementia, as described in the previous paragraph.

Third, that carers' *personality traits* could help shed more light on institutional placement was already suggested in 1990 by Pruchno *et al.* However, there was hardly any evidence of personality traits in relation to institutional placement. Therefore, research in this field is still explorative in character. We found that non-spouse carers, who were more extroverted, showed an increased likelihood of institutional placement of the person with dementia. An explanation may be that these carers discuss the difficulties of providing care and ask for professional help more easily.

Prevention of carer stress

As research has clearly shown, 'carer stress' is an important issue for public health care. Prevention of carer stress still receives too little attention. Too often support is merely offered in reaction to carers' problems. For example, in crisis situations when family members do not know what to do with certain behaviour problems of their relative with dementia, pharmacological treatment is offered or family care is taken over by professionals. Based on the findings about carer stress, a number of recommendations can be made for active prevention of such stress. Three points for attention are discussed below (Pot and Blom, 2001).

Including family support in the care plan for the person with dementia

With regard to the serious public health care consequences of providing care, professionals should not only systematically focus on the person with dementia, but also on their carers to prevent their stress from providing care. At the moment, professionals from different disciplines have several points of contact with family members. However, the aims of these contacts are often not well considered or remain implicit, and are not well coordinated in many cases. Even when professionals are used to working together in so-called multidisciplinary teams, several disciplines may have contact with relatives of persons with dementia without each other knowing about it, let alone in what way they are supporting these family carers.

Carers' problems, needs and potentialities should be included in care plans of the person with dementia to ensure adequate family support. The aims of this support are threefold: (a) to equip carers for their care-giving role as much as possible; (b) to prevent (an increase in) carers' health problems; (c) to postpone institutionalization of the person with dementia, so far as desirable. Professionals should also pre-arrange who is responsible for the content and management of this part of the care plan to prevent working at cross-purposes.

Enduring family support

The findings that during care-giving the carer's health problems do not resolve, but instead may become worse, imply that many carers need support from the beginning to the end of their relative's dementing process. Therefore, supporting carers of persons with dementia requires active care management during the entire course of the disease; also after a patient's institutionalization and sometimes even after his/her death.

This means that professionals should contact family members themselves at regular times – for example, once every three months – and at times when there are great changes in the person with dementia, carer functioning, or the care-giving situation. The usual *reason-for-encounter principle*, in which the client initiates contact with the professional and treatment is based on client's demand, will not be sufficient (Hertogh 1997).

By providing information and emotional support on a regular basis, carer problems may be prevented or treated in time. For example, when family carers are not well informed about the diagnosis and consequences of dementia, they may interpret behavioural changes in the wrong way, as was shown in the case of Mrs Brown (taking no initiative and losing things were attributed to laziness and nonchalance of the person with dementia). In addition, regular contacts may enable anticipation of crisis situations and carers may find it easier to ask for help at an earlier stage.

Combined family support

A third recommendation for preventing care-giving stress is to combine different intervention strategies, given that the findings show that carers' health problems are predicted by diverse factors concerning the person with dementia, the carer themselves, or the care-giving situation. Although the number of studies on diverse intervention programmes is not yet overwhelming, the ones that have been carried out suggest that these programmes have better results in comparison with simple interventions. Studies on the effects of simple intervention strategies in the 1980s and beginning of the 1990s – such as support groups and respite care – were somewhat disappointing.

The underlying hypothesis is that multiple intervention programmes are more intense and more flexible about focusing on the diverse problems of carers and the various needs they may have. An important principle of these intervention programmes is the systematic, long-term support for family carers on a regular basis. To give some idea of these intervention programmes, we will give some examples.

In the USA, Mittelman and colleagues (1995, 1996) studied an intervention programme consisting of three components. The first component consisted of individual and family counselling for the primary carer and family members over the entire course of the disease. Different strategies were included, such as strengthening communication between family members, teaching coping techniques and stimulating emotional and practical support for carers. Second, support group participation was offered with weekly meetings for an unlimited period of time. Third, ad hoc counselling from professionals in case of crisis situations was continuously available. Their research work suggests that enhancing long-term social support by such intervention programmes can have a significant impact on depression in carers and can substantially increase the time spouse-carers are able to care for the person with dementia at home, particularly during the early to middle stages of illness when nursing home placement is not generally appropriate.

Combined intervention programmes have also been studied in the Netherlands, such as the support provided by the Amsterdamse Ontmoetingscentra [Amsterdam meeting centre] (Dröes 1996). This programme consists of informational meetings, a support group for carers, a day-care programme for persons with dementia and consultations for carers and/or persons with dementia. This intervention delayed institutionalization and had positive effects on some carers' factors, e.g. coping with problems and feeling supported.

Recently, Mittelman and colleagues (2002) published a book that may be very helpful in creating a counselling programme to provide support and guidance to family members and friends who are caring for a person with dementia.

Concluding remarks

Research on family carer stress reveals that carers have health problems, that these health problems are not solved during the course of the caring for the person with dementia, but instead may increase. These findings are predicted by diverse factors relating to the person with dementia, the family carer and care-giving situation. These findings lead us to recommend systematic, ongoing and combined intervention programmes for carers of persons with dementia. The first studies of such programmes have shown positive results of such interventions. Whereas these programmes are not yet widespread, professionals should take care that the established care facilities and their own capacities in supporting carers are used to the maximum, especially with regard to informing the family carer about the disease and its consequences.

References

Aneshensel, C.S., Pearlin, L.I., Mullan, J.T., Zarit, S.H. and Whitlatch, C.J. (1995) *Profiles in Caregiving: The Unexpected Career*, New York: Academic Press.

Bodnar, J.C. and Kiecolt-Glaser, J.K. (1994) 'Caregiver depression after bereavement: stress isn't over when it's over', *Psychology and Aging* 9: 372–80.

Cohen, C.A., Colantonio, A. and Vernich, L. (2002) 'Positive aspects of caregiving: rounding out the caregiver experience', *International Journal of Geriatric Psychiatry* 17: 184–8.

Collins, C., Stommel, M., Wang, S. and Given, C.W. (1994) 'Caregiving transitions: changes in depression among family caregivers of relatives with dementia', *Nursing Research* 43: 220–5.

Coyne, A.C., Reichman, W.E. and Berbig, L.J. (1993) 'The relationship between dementia and elder abuse', *American Journal of Psychiatry* 150: 643–6.

Dröes, R.M. (ed.) (1996) *Amsterdamse Ontmoetingscentra: Een nieuwe vorm van onder-steuning voor dementerende mensen en hun verzorgers*, Amsterdam: Thesis Publishers.

Duijnstee, M. (1992) 'Caring for a demented family member at home: objective observation and subjective evaluation of the burden', in G. Jones and B. Miesen (eds) *Care-Giving in Dementia* 1: 359–79.

Gold, D.P., Feldman Reis, M.F., Markiewicz, D. and Andres, D. (1995) 'When home caregiving ends: a longitudinal study of outcomes for caregivers of relatives with dementia' *Journal of the American Geriatrics Society* 43: 10–16.

Haley, W.E. and Pardo, K.M. (1989) 'Relationship of severity of dementia to caregiving stressors', *Psychology and Aging* 4: 389–92.

Health Council of the Netherlands (2002) *Dementia*, Den Haag: Health Council of the Netherlands.

Hertogh, C.P.C.M. (1997) *Functionele geriatrie. Probleemgerichte zorg voor chronisch zieke ouderen*, Maarssen: Elsevier/De Tijdstroom.

Johnson, M.P. (1982) 'Social and cognitive features of the dissolution of commitment to relationships', in S. Duck (ed.) *Personal Relationships: Dissolving Personal Relationships*, London: Academic Press.

Kiecolt-Glaser, J.K., Dura, J.R., Speicher, C.E., Trask, O.J. and Glaser, R. (1991) 'Spousal caregivers of dementia victims: longitudinal changes in immunity and health', *Psychosomatic medicine* 53: 345–62.

Lazarus, R.S. (1991) *Emotion and Adaptation*, New York: Oxford University Press.

Lazarus, R.S. and Folkman, S. (1984) *Stress, Appraisal, and Coping*, New York: Springer.

Lieberman, M.A. and Fisher, L. (2001) 'The effects of nursing home placement on family caregivers of patients with Alzheimer's disease', *Gerontologist* 41: 819–27.

Meiland, F.J.M., Danse, J.A.C., Wendte, J.F., Gunning-Schepers, L.J., Klazinga, N.S. (2001) 'Burden of delayed psychogeriatric nursing home admission in patients and their informal caregivers', *Quality in Health Care* 10: 218–23.

Meuser, T.M. and Marwit, S.J. (2001) 'A comprehensive, stage sensitive model of grief in dementia caregiving', *Gerontologist* 41: 658–71.

Mittelman, M.S., Ferris, S.H., Shulman, E., Steinberg, G., Ambinder, A., Mackel, J. and Cohen, J. (1995) 'A comprehensive support program: effect on depression in spouse-caregivers of AD patients', *Gerontologist* 35: 792–802.

Mittelman, M.S., Ferris, S.H., Shulman, E. and Steinberg, G. (1996) 'A family intervention to delay nursing home placement of patients with Alzheimer disease: A randomized controlled trial', *Journal of the American Medical Association* 276: 1725–31.

Mittelman, M.S., Epstein, C. and Pierzchala, A. (2002) *Counseling the Alzheimer's caregiver. A resource for health care professionals*, USA: AMA Press.

Mullan, J.T. (1992) 'The bereaved caregiver: a prospective study of changes in well-being', *Gerontologist* 32: 673–83.

Paveza, G.J., Cohen, D., Eisdorfer, C., *et al.* (1992) 'Severe family violence and Alzheimer's disease: prevalence and risk factors', *Gerontologist* 32: 493–7.

Pearlin, L.I., Mullan, J.T., Semple, S.J. and Skaff, M.M. (1990) 'Caregiving and the stress process: an overview of concepts and their measures', *Gerontologist* 30: 583–94.

Pillemer, K. and Suitor, J.J. (1992) 'Violence and violent feelings: what cause them among family caregivers?' *Journal of Gerontology* 47: S165–72.

Pot, A.M. and Blom, M. (2001) 'Begeleiding van familieleden', in C. Jonker, F.R.J. Verhey and J.P.J. Slaets (eds) *Alzheimer en andere vormen van dementie*, Houten/Diegem: Bohn Stafleu Van Loghum.

Pot, A.M. and Dyck, R. van (1992) 'Belastende factoren in de zorg voor een dement familielid: een literatuuroverzicht' [The impact of care for a demented family member: a review of the literature], *Tijdschrift voor Psychiatrie* 34: 627–36.

Pot, A.M., Dyck, R. van and Deeg, D.J.H. (1995) 'Ervaren druk door informele zorg: constructie van een schaal' [self-perceived pressure of informal care: construction of a scale], *Tijdschrift voor Gerontologie en Geriatrie* 26: 214–19.

Pot, A.M., Dyck, R. van, Jonker, C. and Deeg, D.J.H. (1996) 'Verbal and physical aggression against demented elderly by informal caregivers in the Netherlands', *Social Psychiatry and Psychiatric Epidemiology* 31: 156–62.

Pot, A.M., Deeg, D.J.H., Dyck, R. van (1997) 'Psychological well-being of informal caregivers of elderly people with dementia: changes over time', *Aging and Mental Health* 1: 261–8.

Pot, A.M., Deeg, D.J.H., Dyck, R. van and Jonker, C. (1998) 'Psychological distress of caregivers: the mediator effect of caregiving appraisal', *Patient Education and Counseling* 34: 43–51.

Pot, A.M., Deeg, D.J.H. and Dyck, R. van (2000) 'Psychological distress of caregivers: moderator effects of caregiver resources?', *Patient Education and Counseling* 41: 235–40.

Pot, A.M., Deeg, D.J.H. and Knipscheer, C.P.M. (2001) 'Institutionalization of demented elderly: the role of caregiver characteristics', *International Journal of Geriatric Psychiatry* 16: 273–80.

Pruchno, R.A., Michaels, J.E. and Potashnik, S.L. (1990) 'Predictors of institutionalization among Alzheimer disease victims with caregiving spouses', *Journals of Gerontology* 45: S259–66.

RGO Health Council of the Netherlands (2002) *Dementia*, The Hague: Health Council of the Netherlands 2002/04.

Schulz, R. and Beach, S.R. (1999) 'Caregiving as a risk factor for mortality: the caregiver health effects study', *Journal of the American Medical Association* 282: 2215–9.

Schulz, R., Newson, T., Fleissner, K., Decamp, A.R. and Neiboer, A.P. (1997) 'The effects of bereavement after family caregiving', *Ageing and Mental Health* 1: 269–82.

Schulz, R. and Williamson, G.M. (1991) 'A 2-year longitudinal study of depression among Alzheimer's caregivers', *Psychology and Aging* 6: 569–78.

Schulz, R., O'Brien, A.T., Bookwala, J. and Fleissner, K. (1995) 'Psychiatric and physical morbidity effects of dementia caregiving: prevalence, correlates, and causes', *Gerontologist* 35: 771–85.

Schulz, R., O'Brien, A.T. and Czaja, S. (2002) 'Dementia caregiver intervention research: in search of clinical significance', *Gerontologist* 42: 589–603.

Townsend, A., Noelker, L., Deimling, G. and Bass, D. (1989) 'Longitudinal impact of interhousehold caregiving on adult children's mental health', *Psychology and Aging* 4: 393–401.

Whitlatch, C.J., Zarit, S.H. and von Eye, A. (1991) 'Efficacy of interventions with caregivers: a reanalysis', *Gerontologist* 31: 9–14.

Zarit, S.H., Reever, K.E. and Bach-Peterson, J. (1980) 'Relatives of the impaired elderly: correlates of feelings of burden', *Gerontologist* 20: 649–55.

Zarit, S.H. and Whitlatch, C.J. (1992) 'Institutional placement: phases of the transition', *Gerontologist* 32: 665–72.

Chapter 14

The Alzheimer Café concept

A response to the trauma, drama and tragedy of dementia

Bère Miesen and Gemma M.M. Jones

Anyone who has cared for someone over the course of a dementing illness will know that the title of this chapter rings true. That is not to say that there are not lighter and tender moments, but it is to acknowledge that something very heavy and serious occurs over the course of a prolonged terminal illness such as dementia. It is also true that it is difficult to speak openly about the feelings behind living through a trauma, drama and tragedy. The statement below contains a universal truth. It is this truth that has prompted many professionals to seek alternative ways of supporting those who undergo a dementing illness: both the families and the persons with a dementia themselves. This is the motivation underlying the development of the Alzheimer Café concept. The first part of this chapter will introduce the underlying concepts to the development of the Alzheimer Café. The second part is a brief manual providing details about the content, planning and running of an Alzheimer Café.

> Tragedy is not deep and sharp if it can be shared with friends.
>
> (Shalamov, quoted in Merridale 2000: 238)

> They were not doing enough to comfort the bereaved, their failings left the people with 'feelings of isolation and loneliness'.
>
> (Ibid: 287)

Introduction and background to the Alzheimer Café development

More than 60 Alzheimer Cafés (AC) exist in the Netherlands. The oldest has already been running for six years. The first Alzheimer Café in the UK, in Farnborough, is in its fourth year. There are Alzheimer Cafés in Belgium and the first ones have been opened in Greece, Italy, the USA and Australia. They are not, as the name would initially suggest, merely 'social get togethers' in a café style environment, but rather the careful combination and structuring of multiple levels of education and support offered within the context of a low threshold, understanding environment in the presence of health care professionals, persons with dementia and their family and friends.

A new type of support

The Alzheimer Café is different from other traditional types of support group such as those the Alzheimer Society has run for the partners of persons with dementia. Persons with dementia are included in, indeed are the focal point of the café talks and discussions in the presence of their family members, friends and others. The Alzheimer Café concept is about breaking through the pain of denial, acknowledging and providing space for the expression of the numerous emotions and practical difficulties that are involved in having and learning to continue living with this chronic, long-term illness.

The underlying assumption is that once the illness can be named and discussed in the presence of all affected, some of the denial, secrecy and pain surrounding it lessens. This in turn creates scope for new interactions and adaptations to live with the illness, not alone but 'in the same boat' with the many others also present at the Alzheimer Café.

Why is such support needed?

Dementing illnesses, the most common of which is Alzheimer's disease, cause chronic brain damage that can lead to psychological trauma, and for some, reopen 'old wounds'. The heart of such trauma stems from damage in the cognitive realm of functioning, resulting in 'losing control'. This can lead to all sorts of coping and compensation attempts, including controlling behaviour. In the affective realm of functioning, the essence of the trauma pertains to feeling unsafe and frightened. This leads to all sorts of attachment (i.e. proximity-seeking) behaviour.

Each person has to try to work through the reality that he/she is losing control over his/her life. For some, feelings that arose in a comparable situation of distress earlier in life can resurface again. The suffering is then 'doubled', as it were. The person with dementia is more aware of their illness and the situation than would appear on the surface, even if the person is denying the illness and not talking about it in first instance.

The emotional situation of the family is also extra difficult, because having a family member with dementia is like having an 'intangible loss'. Relatives face a complicated grieving process. The family starts to lose someone, while he/she remains 'visibly' with them for a long time.

This chapter will give a brief overview of how dementia can be seen as a trauma, drama and tragedy. It is this view of dementia that led to the development of Alzheimer Café concept, which is described as a new type of psychosocial intervention aimed at helping to reduce the emotional pain and isolation experienced by both persons with dementia and their families, within the context of a supportive, informative environment.

The second part of the chapter is a brief manual which was developed to help those interested in setting up an Alzheimer Café of their own. It is intended to provide introductory, general information and guidelines about the planning and structure required to host such gatherings according to the original philosophy of the Alzheimer Café.

At this juncture, it is important to note that there have been a number of groups who have set up gatherings and called them Alzheimer Cafés, without being aware that they are more than social gatherings. No doubt there are very great needs for social outlets for persons with dementia and their families and friends. The Alzheimer Café concept, however, is more than a social gathering because of the many levels of support and education built into it.

The psychological view of dementia today

Recent scientific and drug developments, however spectacular they may be, only offer persons with dementia and their families limited short-term comfort. In recent decades, psychology has brought new clarity to the subject of dementia, and Alzheimer's disease in particular. It has identified and clarified the effects of dementing illnesses for all those involved. From the perspective of psychology today dementia can be seen as a trauma, a drama and a tragedy. This point of view has far-reaching effects in terms of the treatment, support and care offered to persons with dementia and their families.

Alzheimer's disease: the trauma

In everyday language, the term 'trauma' not only refers to the existence of a wound or injury. It is also used to indicate a strong, shocking condition that can cause an enduring psychological disorder. The question underlying this theme is: How can dementia be understood to be a trauma? In the past decade research on care-giving in dementia (e.g. Jones and Miesen 1992; Miesen and Jones 1997) has radically and positively changed the general views about what treatment, support and ongoing care are required by persons with dementia and their families. It would be extreme to say that the views or perspective held previously were largely therapeutic nihilism and monodisciplinary/medical in nature, but from a certain point of view this generalization is not too far off the mark.

In short, psychological and psychosocial research has shown that persons with dementia remain involved in their illness, their living circumstances for far longer than had previously been assumed. In other words, we now speak of persons having an 'awareness context' of their illness, of something problematic happening to them, although this changes in nature during the course of the disease. This means that the phenomenon of 'coping' exists not only for persons experiencing chronic physical distress, but also for persons experiencing a dementing illness.

Research also shows that dementia entails an intense experience of loss, the core of which is both 'loss of control' and 'loss of security'. This can be seen, for instance, in the various ways in which the phenomena of 'constantly thinking about parents' or 'always wanting to go home' can be interpreted. These phenomena occur in nearly all persons with dementia, despite differences in level of cognitive functioning (Miesen 1990, 1993). This means that the behaviour of persons with dementia is not an exclusive consequence of their brain disease, but also a consequence of how they cope with it. In fact, persons with dementia react very normally to an abnormal situation, and not vice versa. This 'coping behaviour' is usually very individual in that it is affected by factors linked to personality and life history.

As far as the family (i.e. particularly the spouse) is concerned, their psychological situation vis-à-vis the person with dementia often remains nameless, without identity or status for a long period of time. It is not recognized as being both complex and continually complicated.

First, it has become clear that even though the person with dementia is still alive, the family are involved in a multilevel grieving process throughout the course of the illness. This is a process entailing working through many types of loss simultaneously. This means that the family has to learn how to cope with the gradual loss of the person with dementia, at the same time as thinking about and feeling 'bereaved' over a long period of time. This emotional process is just one of the many (often practical) problems that the family of people with dementia have to face.

Second, the nature of this process is a complicated one, in that the person one is losing is still present. This person is disappearing as it were from the spouse's life, but is not yet dying. The particular nature of this situation can be clearly compared to the situation of the family of someone who has been reported missing for a long time. With someone who has gone missing, the loved one is no longer physically there, but it is not clear whether he or she is dead. With dementia, the loved one remains physically present, but it is clear that they are slowly going away; it is not always clear how present they are. Paradoxically, the situation in the case of a person with dementia can therefore also be described as the opposite of that of a missing person. There can be a long delay in grieving for the actual loss of the person, and this can be extremely difficult to cope with.

In short, persons with dementia should no longer be described merely as victims of a catastrophe that they undergo only passively as the object of the catastrophe; quite the contrary. Persons with dementia should first be seen as a subject reacting with all their body and mind to their illness. This applies not only to the person with dementia but also to the family. The family is a witness to the catastrophe happening to the person with dementia. This means that the treatment, support and care for persons with dementia and their families cannot belong exclusively to the medical domain of the doctor (medical specialist, neurologist or psychiatrist). Treatment and support for persons with dementia also fall within the domain of the other health care professionals and a multidisciplinary approach is essential.

To conclude, Alzheimer's disease is a traumatic event, a disaster or catastrophe, for both the person with dementia and their family. The disruption this causes for their daily life comes with an array of feelings: insecurity and powerlessness, frequent emotional upheaval, ongoing distress and sometimes even collapse. Long-term grieving is an additional factor in this reality.

Alzheimer's disease: the drama

In everyday language, the term 'drama' not only refers to a play but also to a series of striking and moving events. The question underlying this section is: How can dementia be understood as a drama? One of the consequences of the above viewpoint is to consider that having dementia, or living with someone who has dementia, creates a cascade of unpredictable events and challenges all our learned ways of coping. It is this sequence of events which can be thought of as a drama. Many of these events are traumatic in themselves. Being affected by the catastrophe of the dementia is neither a 'one-off' event (known as Type I Trauma) nor a 'repeated event' (known as Type II Trauma) for either the persons with dementia or their family members. It is more aptly thought of as an unremitting series of unexpectedly traumatic events. The official diagnostic DSM-IV (this is the most recent version of the mental health diagnostic manual most frequently used by practitioners today) criteria for a post-traumatic stress disorder (APA 1994) are unsatisfactory to describe the full extent of what can happen by way of ongoing or sustained trauma over the course of a dementing illness. There is no respite from it. It remains, even though for periods of time one or both parties may find ways of coping with it. (It would seem obvious and necessary to develop new trauma criteria for dementia type chronic illnesses; to define a Type III Trauma which reflects the effects of the sustained trauma more adequately than the existing diagnostic criteria for trauma).

The trauma of dementia can thus become a drama because it entails a sequence of difficult events for both 'parties', which in principle only end when the person with dementia dies. (Grieving can be delayed, complex and pathological after such events, but this is beyond the scope of this chapter.) Both the person with dementia and their partner and family find themselves in a grieving process on account of the catastrophe of the dementia. Everyone knows, either from direct or indirect experience, how the relationship between a couple can be put under strain if a child in their family dies. (Of course it may be that both partners grow even closer to each other in the long term.) However, without intervention from others, many marriages cannot be saved because the couple have grown apart from each other. The underlying reason for this, more often than not, has nothing to do with a lack of love for each other. What has actually happened from a psychological perspective is that although the loss of the child is the same for both persons, two individual (and rarely synchronized) grieving processes come into play. Sometimes one partner is so greatly shocked by what is happening to him/herself, that they are unable to understand the situation of the other (even though they may be experiencing the same thing). This means that neither person is able to provide the support that is needed and longed for. This sometimes marks the beginning of the end of the relationship.

If this situation of loss is already hard, how difficult the situation of dementia must be to imagine. The fact that one of the partners has progressive cognitive decline puts this person at a disadvantage, compared to the other partner, in terms of dealing with, coping with and supporting the other through the catastrophe of dementia. That there is disparity between the cognitive and support abilities between partners often contributes to the drama of dementia.

Another potential consequence of the above viewpoint is that, in addition to the changing relationship between the person with dementia and the partner, each 'party' is doomed to emotional isolation if help does not come from others. Under normal circumstances, this would lead to an end of the relationship. In the case of dementia, this usually does not happen, even if one of the partners had perhaps been considering it previously. In the worst case scenario, the result is loneliness on both sides; i.e. two people gradually separating from each other emotionally, but who want to (or have to) remain living together under the same roof. This is a straight drama, pure and simple, and often an understandable source of hurt feelings, arguments or aggression.

Alzheimer's disease: the tragedy

In everyday language, the term 'tragedy' not only refers to a sorrowful incident, but also to a play ending in disaster after a string of difficult events, which taken together form a tragedy. The question underlying this viewpoint is: How can dementia also be understood as a tragedy, and what would prevent it from being such a bitter one?

Although the above text already provides an adequate prelude in terms of describing dementia as a tragedy, let's now consider our own professional role, which usually begins as that of an outsider. From a theatrical point of view, a tragedy or tragic play would not exist if there were no spectators. Over a period of time, the spectators themselves get caught up in what they are seeing. It practically goes without saying that those of us who are involved in the treatment, support and care for people with dementia and their family will sooner or later also be moved and genuinely affected by their trauma and drama. At some point, we change from being outsiders to becoming insiders. We automatically grow towards a more general involvement in the situation, which of course can vary greatly from one individual to another. But this is how we ourselves come to play a role in the tragedy of dementia. Why is this so, and what are the effects of such involvement?

There are many points of view in psychology that explain how this could be so, in particular the psychodynamic theories. Here, a brief outline will serve our purpose.

If you take a bird's eye view of persons with a dementia (or Alzheimer's disease in particular) and their families, you could easily describe the issues involved, from the point of view of a disaster area or a catastrophe. As already stated, one feature of this disaster area in many cases is that it goes unnoticed for too long a period of time. The result is that their plight has been given little or no status to date. People in dire need always look for something to hold on to or for security from anyone they can find. This makes them very vulnerable, and that is a dangerous situation. First and foremost, their vulnerability makes them uncritical of the treatment, support and care offered them. Whether our help is good or bad, skilled or unskilled, vulnerable persons accept any help they can get.

This gives us, the caregivers, a lot of power. High demands are therefore placed on our responsibility, expertise and self-knowledge. Every disaster area is an Eldorado for transference and countertransference processes (Miesen 2000). In this respect, it should be normal (and nothing short of professional) that we as caregivers, just as trauma teams, members of the fire brigade, policemen, first-aiders, etc., receive support and supervision. In our experience, volunteers are especially sensitive, making it all the more important that they also, like the professionals, receive close coaching and ample training.

The concept of the Alzheimer Café

As already stated, even the most spectacular medical developments in the field of Alzheimer's disease offer little comfort, even in the short term. It remains then to develop and invest more in psychosocial treatment, support and care. With this understanding, that dementia can be a trauma, drama, and tragedy, the Alzheimer Café is one new way of easing the distress of people with dementia and their families.

Guiding this concept are the research findings, which have shown that most families affected by dementia wish to continue living as normally as possible, despite the disease. In practice, the Alzheimer Café helps to emancipate patients/persons with dementia and their families by encouraging them to break out of their emotional isolation and to reduce or remove the taboo surrounding discussion of the illness.

In one sense, the Alzheimer Café can be thought of as a type of guided self-help group. From another viewpoint it can be thought of as a type of group therapy. There is also a sense in which it can be thought of as a stage on which the dramas of both the person with dementia and their family members are voiced or acted out collectively for the benefit of all who are trying to deal with their own trauma. A fellow psychologist, host of one of the Dutch Cafés, recently wrote that 'the programme of an Alzheimer Café is like a ritual that is repeated each month' (Peter Haex in *Denkbeeld*, October 2001, p. 7). Those who try to assist by providing treatment, support and care automatically become co-actors. However it is thought of, it meets the needs of some in a way that other types of support have not done yet. One participant in the Farnborough Café said that for him it was 'pure magic . . . it makes my month'.

'Tragedy is not deep and sharp if it can be shared with friends': this quotation from the beginning of the chapter was originally written in the context of the horror and terror of war and violence, but it can also apply to dementia. We can all bear witness to the distress that dementia causes (Miesen 2000: 9). The Alzheimer Café provides a way of recognizing the individual trauma, drama and tragedy of the persons with dementia and their family, as well as giving the disease a social status. The Alzheimer Café is intended to offer persons a safe place, where they express themselves and can be listened to, thus finding some comfort in their struggle of isolation and loneliness, at least for a while.

THE ALZHEIMER CAFÉ: A GUIDELINE MANUAL FOR SETTING ONE UP

Original document entitled, 'Handleiding Alzheimer Café', by Bère Miesen and Marco Blom.

Translated and adapted from the Dutch Alzheimer Society document by Gemma M.M. Jones (permission to be printed here), with special thanks to Ray and Elspeth Moran, April 2001.

I How it all started

On 15 September, 1997, the first Alzheimer Café opened its doors. The long-brewing idea of Dr Bère Miesen, clinical old age psychologist at the specialist research centre for old age psychiatry, 'Mariënhaven', in Warmond, the Netherlands, had become a reality. After several months of preparation, together with the Alzheimer Association in northern 'Zuid-Holland', he succeeded in launching something which is now being increasingly copied.

In his contacts with people with dementia and their families, Miesen had noticed that talking about the illness, even between partners or within a family, was often taboo. He was not alone in noticing this. Knowing that making dementia discussable and providing information about it and its consequences is very important for the acceptance of the illness, Miesen thought that it would be good if all those involved could meet each other in a 'relaxed forum' to exchange experiences and to talk about dementia. There would then be a place where people could share their experiences and sorrow.

Quotes from Bère Miesen

Dementia is a complete catastrophe. Both the person with dementia and their family deserve to be well supported. The recognition and admission of mental suffering can make life liveable again.

(*De Telegraaf*, September 1999)

In the outside world there is little recognition of the fact that both the person with dementia and those close to them are going through a grieving process.

(*VWS Bulletin*, June 1999)

What is understood by the word café?

How could such a 'relaxed atmosphere' be better described than with the word café? Miesen's idea of an Alzheimer Café first became reality in a lecture room at Leiden University. About 20 people attended the first meeting. A month later there were 35; a month later the number had risen to 54, and after three months the lecture room contained 80 people. It was clear that the initiative met a real need.

People from all over the country started coming. It appeared that there was a great need for a place where persons with dementia and those involved with them could talk calmly about the disease. People left the meetings feeling more resilient and also, importantly, with tips on how to deal with people with dementia. There was also interest from the national media. The fame of the Alzheimer Café also grew as a result of the seven half-hour television broadcasts in the series 'Living with Dementia', which were recorded by Teleac/NOT at the Alzheimer Café in Leiden.

Good examples will be followed

The enthusiasm grew. Soon on average more than 100 people were visiting the Alzheimer Café. A new meeting place had been found at a hotel in Leiden. Amongst the regular visitors were several representatives of other branches of the Alzheimer Association. They also decided to start Alzheimer Cafés in their regions.

Alzheimer Cafés were thereafter established in Delft and Utrecht. Zwijndrecht and Groningen now also have cafés. Other districts have since started and still others have begun planning and preparations. The wide interest resulted in a meeting on 'How to Establish an Alzheimer Café', organized by the Dutch Alzheimer Society. People from more than 15 districts took part. Several specialist nursing homes and care centres are also keen to use this concept. This led to similar initiatives in Dordrecht and Den Bosch. (For an up-to-date overview of the 60 places where Alzheimer Cafés are organized, you can consult the website of Alzheimer Nederland: http://www.alzheimer-ned.nl.)

Variations on a theme

To avoid reinventing the wheel, many initiators have made contact with the original founders or have made orientation visits to one or more Alzheimer Cafés. Nevertheless people are also looking for ways to make the idea more applicable to regional needs: different starting times, different locations or even another name, because the term café might be too restrictive. What remains important however is keeping to the original concept, which has turned out to be so successful. (The original idea behind naming the 'Alzheimer Café was to show that we are not afraid of the name, there is a life to live beyond any name or diagnosis, just as with cancer or M.S. 25 years ago.)

This is one of the reasons for putting the existing experiences down on paper. Initiators can make a considered choice before starting a café. They can benefit from the practical information in their preparations. Then they can devote their energies to running the meetings. If we think of all those having dementia and their carers, we realize that the quality of support can never be high enough. That is the single most important thing.

In a brief outline such as this, it is difficult to fully describe the fundamental principles, theoretical starting points and underlying vision of an Alzheimer Café. For this you really should attend one of the first meetings (of the thematic presentations) of the Alzheimer Café, and be closely involved for a longer time.

We have been helped by several articles by Bère Miesen which started off the development of an overview of the Alzheimer Café phenomenon. The core of his vision can be found in the following passage from the introduction to his book *Leven met Dementie* [Living with dementia]:

Underlying vision

The title *Living with Dementia* can be explained in two ways. On the one hand, it indicates the bewilderment, which starts when it becomes clear that a catastrophe is about to descend on the lives of the persons with dementia and their family. 'How do I handle an illness that threatens my life irreversibly?' The illness, either your own, or that of someone close to you, suddenly gets full attention. On the other hand, the title indicates that the moment that persons with dementia and their families have more or less accepted that a catastrophe has occurred, they can ask a new question, 'How do I lead as normal a life as possible, despite the illness?' Now, it is no longer the illness, but someone's life that is the focus of attention. The illness has, despite everything, been faced up to. This is the more positive approach to a process, which is often a long one, with a distinct beginning and an end.

The Alzheimer Café, a meeting place for persons with dementia, family, carers and other interested parties, helps with this process: to get from one point to the other, with as much support as possible. In short, the Alzheimer Café can be regarded as an intervention with aspects of both education and support. All the advantages of having a 'low threshold' (all inclusive), informal advice and consultation and 'self-help group type contact' with 'companions in distress' are offered/combined in a relaxed atmosphere. The term 'companions in distress' also applies to persons with dementia themselves. However, we don't hide from the facts; dementia represents a major catastrophe in the lives of all involved; it usually occurs unexpectedly. The mental pain, the powerlessness, the dislocation and the distress of the person with dementia and those close to them, therefore, form the starting points for discussions. How each person copes with the pain is very different and individual. If someone visits the Alzheimer Café he/she admits his/her sorrow and faces up to it. It is clear, that only then can someone go further.

Dementia is a chronic brain disorder that leads to psychological trauma, and for some reopens 'old wounds'. That is to say that each person has to work through the reality that he/she is losing the control over his/her life. And for some, earlier feelings, which arose in a comparable situation of distress, can resurface again. For example: emotional memories of powerlessness in situations of incest, POW camps, and violence in war, being deserted, or other traumatic experiences can be triggered again. The suffering is then doubled. The person with dementia is more aware of the illness and the situation than it would appear on the surface, even if he denies the illness and will not talk about it. The emotional situation of the family is also difficult, because it concerns an 'intangible loss'. Relatives face a complicated grieving process. The family starts to lose someone, while he or she remains 'visibly' with them for a long time.

It is important to gain certainty about the diagnosis as quickly as possible, and to lose as little time as possible in denying what is going on. This is the only way someone can take hold of their own life again, and take the steps or decisions which are necessary. This allows a person not only to take control of his own life again, but also to restore mutual contacts, albeit not necessarily in the same way as previously.

Some starting points

For the person with dementia

Some things may be going wrong, or difficult for you, but you are not crazy. Try to make the changes that you notice happening in yourself clear to those around you. Have your complaints investigated; nothing is worse than anxiety and uncertainty.

For the family

It is good to think of your own interests. Draw attention to the grieving process that you are going through. Seek emotional support from people you trust or your 'fellow companions in adversity'. Sometimes that can be a professional or caregiver who is more distanced from your situation. The attention you give yourself can also benefit the person with dementia. Seek help early for the practical problems; get enough sleep.

For others close to the person with dementia and their family

If you suspect or know that someone has dementia, don't be too quick to assume that the person 'doesn't want to speak about it'. Such a discussion might be easier than you think; often all you have to do is listen. Don't forget to ask the partner or children what the illness means to them; their problems are often greater than one realizes at first sight.

For professional caregivers

Try to make sure the diagnosis is established as soon as possible. Inform the person with dementia and the family about the meaning of the diagnosis. Inform them about how and where they can get help. Make sure the person with dementia and their spouse/partner get help as a couple. That way they can try to share their pain, reduce their feelings of loneliness, and be stimulated to work through their grieving and feelings of loss (Miesen 2000).

2 What is an Alzheimer Café?

By talking about the problems that having dementia brings, persons and families can better manage their own situations. Making the illness 'discussable' gives the person with dementia the feeling of being able to influence his situation. He/she also meets people in the same boat as him/herself. The family see that they are not the only ones with the feelings of powerlessness, dislocation and distress. With the coming of the Alzheimer Café, there is a place where they can go together and find out how others deal with the illness and its consequences. The visitors feel they belong and find recognition and acceptance. That in itself is unique. Furthermore, the Alzheimer Café brings together various aspects that the usual 'information evenings' lack. Although the meetings are partly therapeutic and have a strong educational side, a part of the evening is specifically for making informal contacts. In addition, its low threshold environment is unique. The range of people that visit a Café is great. Besides persons with dementia and relatives, friends, professional carers and students, other interested persons such as policy makers, journalists and representatives of the regional and national media sometimes attend.

Objectives

The Alzheimer Café has three main aims. First, information is provided about the medical and psychosocial aspects of dementia. Second, it emphasizes the importance about speaking openly about problems. Recognition and (social) acceptance are essential to this. Third, the Café promotes the emancipation of persons with dementia and their families, by preventing their becoming isolated. This all sounds rather therapeutic. However, as mentioned earlier, that is not to say that the course of an Alzheimer Café evening is as therapeutic as this sounds on paper. It is of prime importance that visitors can talk to each other informally and without interruption, exchanging experiences, for example, or informally consulting carers and specialists. It is precisely this relaxed atmosphere that breaks down the taboos and gives people the important feeling of belonging – the acceptance, acknowledgement and recognition mentioned earlier.

Changing themes

The Alzheimer Café has a different theme at each meeting, but the timing of the evening follows a fixed structure. After the welcome with coffee/tea comes half an hour of information. This could be via live interviews with persons with dementia and their family members, or videos of discussions with others who have visited the café. Often there is a lecture or a specialist who is interviewed before a video is shown. It will be evident that this is dependent on what the organizers and/or the guests prefer. After a break those present can discuss the evening's theme or bring up other topics. Hereafter, the meeting closes with more informal socializing and refreshments.

At the original café in Leiden, the order of the topics is not fixed but a certain 'thread' is followed. In each series, topics generally follow themes related to the chronological course of the illness. Naturally, all sorts of topics can be brought into this. The general 'thread' of the themes can be seen from the list of topics covered in the Teleac television series that was broadcast in 1999 (see box).

A   What's the matter?

A neurologist explains what dementia is, how it is diagnosed, and emphasizes the differences between normal forgetfulness, depression and dementia and provides relevant examples.

B   How does memory work and what happens in dementia?

A neuropsychologist explains about memory, how people remember and forget things, how 'memory testing' is done, and gives tips to help support memory functioning in the early stages.

C   It's getting a bit much for me!

A researcher explains that as dementia progresses, feelings of powerlessness increase and communication becomes more difficult. This is tied up with the realization that the person with dementia has a feeling that 'something is wrong', and their need to work through this emotionally. An overview of possible types of help is provided.

D   Who can I turn to for help?

A community health nurse and/or social worker are interviewed to answer the questions: 'May I turn to others for help?' 'When?' 'Where?' 'How do I start to do that?'

E   Admission to a day care/residential care facility?

A psychologist is interviewed to speak about: When the person with dementia can no longer be cared for at home full time, how is the decision to admit the person into a day care/residential care facility made, and what does this decision mean to all those involved?

F   How do I go on now?

A nursing home chaplain and former carer are interviewed. The person with dementia has gone through the last phase of their illness. After death, how do those emotionally attached to the person with dementia work through their grief? How does one look back when everything is finished? How does one pick up the threads of one's life again?

In the UK, other themes such as guilt, grieving, emotions, communication, 'Why is it so difficult to ask for help', and 'Hitting a brick wall', are also discussed, in an interactive way with the guests.

There are also Alzheimer Cafés, for example those in Delft and Utrecht, that change topics and consider regularly which topic is in the news. Of course it may be that the public asks for a specific topic which also could be followed up during the meetings. The following topics are amongst those that have been discussed:

- causes of dementia
- symptoms of dementia
- what dementia means: the first questions and uncertainty
- dementia at a young age
- living with dementia
- communication
- available help.

Very often, after a theme has been discussed, there are many comments made, questions asked and personal reactions given. The interviewer leads this discussion with the visitors. Those attending (including the professionals) are there as a sort of 'living example and resource' from which to draw further responses and concrete information.

Frequency and starting time

Meetings are held monthly, always on a fixed day, for example every first Monday in the month. The time and length of the meetings are also fixed. In general, gatherings are organized ten times a year, avoiding the holiday seasons. The opening times of the existing cafés vary somewhat. Some operate in the evenings, others during the day. Both have advantages.

Evening cafés attract more people, because family members and professionals are home from work then. However, it can be that some people don't come because they don't want to go out in the evenings. This is especially so in winter. If you plan to hold your café in the afternoon, the reverse is the case. Working people such as the children of the persons with dementia and the professionals often find it hard to get time off. Therefore, consider carefully who forms your target group and adapt your opening hours accordingly.

Type of location

The choice of location is important because the character of an Alzheimer Café is a low threshold one, appealing to as many persons as possible. Nevertheless, some districts have chosen to hold their meetings in a nursing home. The cost of accommodation and the desire of a nursing home to have a greater public profile can influence the choice of location. In Utrecht the large café room of a care centre is used; in The Hague the café is held in the city hall. Whatever organizations want to work in setting up a café, it is extremely important that they work towards the same objectives. It is essential that persons with dementia and their families (especially if persons have only been recently diagnosed) feel comfortable visiting an Alzheimer Café. Since the meetings are generally directed at persons in the earlier stages of dementia, it is usually better not to automatically choose a nursing home as a location.

Any results?

There surely are. Although the expected attendance at the first meeting of a new café must not be pitched too high, practice shows that the second meeting (generally through word of mouth publicity) attracts a bigger attendance. When someone has visited a café once, he or she often comes back. Such a person we call 'a regular' (core person). Families who come back together are called 'core families'. Their presence is essential to help other newcomers feel supported. At subsequent meetings the number of 'regulars' grows and new participants join.

Some quotes

- 'First I find it very informative and secondly it is good that you are not the only one with problems.'
- 'In short? Penetrating, emotionally gripping and very recognisable.'
- 'Initially I did not want to admit that I had it. But here it is accepted and that has helped me.'

In a survey by northern Zuid-Holland, findings showed that the Alzheimer Café formula was well liked. Exchanging information through informal conversations was much appreciated. Visitors thought that the aims of the café were being achieved. Communication was good, everyone was involved, and many people found the desired recognition and acceptance at such meetings.

Café lay-out and ambiance

There are various ways to lay out a café. The lay-out partly determines the Café's ambiance. For example, during the discussion time, you can let the leader of the discussion wander amongst the audience with a microphone. This ensures people's involvement and contributes to the low threshold feeling. Other cafés provide a podium on which the chairman and his guest speakers sit. Questions are posed and answered directly from the podium. With this form of presentation, the emphasis is more on the expertise of the speakers. Placing them on the podium does create a greater distance though. It is of course nice to give an Alzheimer Café a 'café-like' appearance to get the right atmosphere. Don't go to too much trouble though: tablecloths and candles on the tables dress the place up a bit.

Music

As you know, music is important for the atmosphere. To create the right ambiance in the café, light café-type music works well. It is perhaps a good idea to organize live music if that is possible. For example, some cafés have found that having a pianist goes down well. Naturally this depends on the venue. Of course, you can bring in other forms of live music. Be careful that the musical content of the meeting does not come to predominate so that the aim of the café is changed.

Information and aftercare

Providing an 'information stand' is a good addition to a café. Visitors can look at information material or even take it with them. If you have chosen the theme 'Dementia at a Young Age' it is a good idea to adapt the brochures and folders to this theme. It is guaranteed that some people will want to read through the material quietly at home. In order to offer a broader range of material, you can, for example, make contact with the local library. It may have some useful books to place on your stand for people to look at.

After an evening at the Alzheimer Café people sometimes still have questions that could not be answered during the evening. It is important therefore that help is available. It is preferable if this can be through your own staff or volunteers (core professionals). Any professionals present can also fulfil this function. It is important for the visitors that they can question the professionals informally.

We have seen that is useful to have a 'local contact address list' available. People can also be directed to the local and national Alzheimer helplines.

3   How is an Alzheimer Café meeting run?

Although we have already described how Alzheimer Cafés work in general, in this next section we explain this in greater detail. What elements are important for a successful Alzheimer Café evening? What are the most important things to consider? We will look at several practical issues in the course of a programme. We will also discuss the role of the interviewer or discussion leader, who is the equivalent of the spider in the web at every meeting.

Programme planning

The programme can be roughly divided into four fixed parts; the 'arrival and introduction', 'the presentation of a video or the talk in the form of an interview', 'the discussion' and 'the informal get-together' after the formal part of the meeting. Although you don't have to stick strictly to the times, practice shows that the discussion leader must ensure that the formal part of the meeting gets enough time. Arrival, the interval and the conclusion must not take up too much time. The official educational part of a café, on average, lasts up to one hour. Arrival and departure and socialization are in addition to this. Each of these can take up half an hour.

- 0.00   Arrivals with coffee and tea
- 0.30   Start, with introduction, video and/or interview/s
- 1.00   Interval with music and drinks
- 1.30   Discussion
- 2.00   End formal meeting
- 2.30   Informal session and departure

Arrival/reception

An ordinary café fills up slowly. This is also true of an Alzheimer Café. The visitors like to have the time to find a seat and get something to drink. About half an hour is often allowed for this, after which the evening can begin in a relaxed way. Experience shows that especially the regulars (core members) use this time to catch up with each other and make arrangements. Some people decide to travel to the meetings together. The organizers can be sure that some people will arrive as the talks start. If the Alzheimer Café has just started and perhaps the numbers attending are not very high, it is important to lay out the room so that people don't sit too far apart. It is better to keep some chairs aside, which can be put out in the case of a higher turnout. It is important for the organizers personally to welcome newcomers, to put them at their ease if necessary. They can be accompanied to a table in the room with regular/core family members and professionals to prevent them sitting right at the back or alone.

Introduction, video or interview

The formal part of the meeting begins with a welcome and introduction of the theme and speakers, the presentation/video and/or the interview/s. Half an hour is planned for this. The imparting of information on the theme is key. Usually, an expert is invited to give a lecture and be interviewed. This can be a monologue, a discussion between the lecturer and the interviewer/ discussion leader (with or without a person with dementia or a relative) or an interview with a family member and/or a person with dementia. A conversation or interview can, for example, take the form of a question and answer session. When choosing the expert, it helps to know if he or she is an experienced speaker. A good presentation encourages people to ask questions.

Another way of opening the evening is to show a video. This could also be part of the lecture. The TV series 'Living with Dementia' is suitable for use in a Dutch café, because they were recorded in a café setting. It is also possible to make a recording of an interview with someone with dementia and their carer in their home environment, and to show this during the meeting. This has been done at the café in Den Bosch. The person with dementia and her daughter were present at the café on the evening it was shown. Of course, permission for this has to be obtained.

Whether it is a lecture, video or interview, it is important that the audience can recognize itself in the material that is presented. In the lecture this can be achieved through taking statements from those involved. In using a video, guests can be asked to look out for what they recognize or have experienced themselves. Practice shows that a combination of businesslike communication of information and the recognition of individuals has the best chance of making discussion effective.

The interval

Contrary to what the name implies, 'the interval' is a very active part of the meeting for the organizers. They will be answering questions that persons do not want to ask in public, or they join in at a table where people are talking, whether it is about the evening's theme or not. They can use this time to collect questions and points for discussion to bring up after the interval. It is important that they know what the people's concerns are.

The information stand is often visited during the interval. The staff manning the stand can expect all sorts of questions. People with specific questions also often approach professionals who are regular visitors. It is important to have antennae for questions that go beyond the individual and that relate well to the theme of the meeting. Instead of answering the question immediately, the person asking it might also be encouraged to raise it in the general discussion.

Discussion

After the interval it is time for the discussion. The people in the room may react to what was presented before the break. This can range from questions for clarification, to a personal response lasting several minutes. For a good discussion it is important that the discussion leader keeps control. Ideally there are questions and answers, or discussion between the visitors. Moreover, the limited time must be properly divided between all the people who want to contribute, including those who don't push themselves forward.

To keep the discussion 'on the rails', it is sometimes necessary to agree some rules with the audience. In this way everyone knows what is allowed and what is not. This makes asking questions and the discussion simpler.

If someone repeatedly dominates with many questions, or always wants to ask their question first, or give their opinion on everything said, it will be appropriate to remind them politely that others also want to have a turn. Sometimes other visitors will point this out. In this way the Alzheimer Café can also be like a real café.

Informal socialization and departures

The rounding off of the discussion is also the end of the formal part of the meeting. Some of the visitors will leave almost at once. Experience shows that others will want to go on talking with each other while having a drink, just to recover from all the information and listening to other people's stories; the café atmosphere again takes over. In a number of Alzheimer Cafés there is dancing or singing afterwards. It is difficult to say exactly how long it takes for people to leave, but it is often about half an hour.

If they wish, the organizers of the Alzheimer Café can use the informal get-together to discuss subjects for future meetings with some of the visitors. In Delft, they have the custom of asking one of the visitors beforehand if they want to record their impressions of the café in a logbook. At the end of the meeting the visitor can fill in the logbook and, if necessary, discuss their impressions with an organizer. Other ways of evaluating the cafés have also been used. In Utrecht, people were asked their opinion via a questionnaire. In other places, candid responses to the organizers are recorded, dated and saved.

Discussion leaders

The same interviewer/discussion leader usually conducts the meetings of an Alzheimer Café. In the city of Den Bosch, however, there are two presenters. This has worked well. In Utrecht there are two discussion leaders who alternate with each other. Whichever form you choose, it is of the greatest importance that the way the discussion is led, and the division of roles between two presenters, is relatively similar. A great difference in style could impede the open atmosphere and can be a barrier to building a good relationship between the public and the discussion leader(s).

The discussion leaders play a crucial role in the planning of the café. They are responsible for the smooth running of the meeting and determine to a great extent what the participants get out of it. Ensure therefore that you appoint a discussion leader who can be relied upon to do all this. So far we have identified two variants of the discussion leader's role: the 'expert' and the 'presenter'.

The 'expert-type' interviewer can answer questions from the audience or otherwise give his opinion in the discussion. It is important that he or she is practising as a professional and knows the professional circuit. Sometimes he/she will know the visitors through his/her work. Normally this gives a trusting relationship and can increase the public's feeling of openness and security. A pitfall for the expert is that he or she answers all the questions and does not leave any space for the mutual exchange of experiences.

The 'presenter-type' interviewer ensures that everyone who wants to speak during the discussion gets the chance to do so. He leaves technical questions to be answered by the experts who are present. It is recommended in this case to operate with a fixed team of experts present at the café. It is helpful if the presenter can discourage the experts from using jargon and create a good relationship with the audience. A good presenter makes use of his ignorance and independence.

The perfect discussion leader does not exist. However, it is possible to list certain qualities that the 'ideal' leader would possess. The following qualities are important: knowledge of the different forms of dementia and of dealing with persons with dementia; experience with the problems of the partner and family; wide experience in leading group discussions; a relaxed manner of presentation, and a trustworthy personality.

Qualities of the discussion leader/interviewer

1   Complete respect for the questions and the persons asking the questions.
2   The ability to perceive and react well to signals from the audience.
3   The ability to pass on and paraphrase questions from the audience.
4   To be able to hold a 'companion' type of relationship with the visitors.
5   To be able to encourage open conversation, in a way that could also break through taboo subjects.

Perhaps you will feel from this description that an experienced psychologist would be the ideal discussion leader. This is indeed a good option, but of course not a strict necessity, especially if you choose to use two leaders or an experienced presenter in combination with a team of experts.

Whatever your choice, it a good idea to realize in advance that it is a difficult job and that you should regularly review whether the discussion leader is carrying out his/her role well and with enthusiasm. The leader must react well to signals from the audience. People with annoying questions, tears and laughter, moving stories, and insoluble problems can all be present at a café.

4   How to set up an Alzheimer Café

If you decide to organize an Alzheimer Café in your area, you would be wise to form a working party/group. A working party usually comprises three or four people from the organizing institution(s). It is easiest to divide the tasks amongst the members of the working party and to agree who will stand in for whom, in cases of absence.

Once the café is in existence, the working party need not be disbanded. Members can help with decorating the room, looking after refreshments, and manning the information stand. And of course they can take a role in setting the themes and the programme of the café.

There can be a considerable time between the decision to start an Alzheimer Café and the first meeting. The average preparation time is between three and six months. The opening of an Alzheimer Café often takes place on World Alzheimer Day, namely on or around 21 September.

Manual

To monitor the progress of the activities you should consider preparing a manual. A small job list can be drawn up for each area of work that comes up during the preparations. The list shows who will do what and when. At the meetings of the working party, the manual with the job lists can be regularly brought up to date.

Summary of manual

- Setting up consultation group
- Choice of location
- Choice of discussion leader
- Setting date and time
- Themes and introductions
- Publicity plan
- Regular evaluation
- Budget.

Working with a manual is, in general, more practical than just going ahead and relying on everyone's memory. In the latter case things are more easily forgotten. A manual is also convenient for new volunteers. You can begin drawing up a manual during preparations for the first meeting. There is no 'standard type' of manual because there are too many regional differences. However certain matters can be described.

Consultation group

Most of the cafés start up with the aid of a 'consultation group', sometimes known as a 'steering group'. The consultation group is a constructive, critical group of people who together act as a 'think tank' and 'advice group' for the working party. In practice the group meets every two to three months. In the beginning, this can be more often.

The members come mostly from the regional care sector, not just from one town or institution. This is the most practical arrangement because it provides broad support. The members can also play an important role in telling persons with dementia and families about the Alzheimer Café. They are the ideal group to tell others about the café. Ensure therefore that professional caregivers from all sectors are represented.

Choice of location

For an Alzheimer Café the location and ambiance are very important. Therefore, choose a good psychological and physical location. By a 'psychologically good location' we mean that the guests feel at home in the café. Take the example we referred to earlier: a nursing home might be a perfect place to hold a café, except that it can be threatening to persons who have just been diagnosed. Sometimes they don't want to be confronted in any way with persons in the later stages of the disease.

A physically good location has characteristics such as safety, ease of access, access for disabled, sufficient parking, and so on. Is the entrance in a dark alley, where people will feel unsafe? Is there a good transport connection from the station? Apart from the building, the room must meet certain requirements. The most important question is whether the room is right to create a convivial atmosphere.

Apart from the practical requirements that the room must meet (see below), certain facilities are essential. These can vary from meeting to meeting. For the discussion you can best use a mobile microphone, so that all participants are audible. A good sound installation will be required and perhaps a video screen. Think carefully what you will use and what equipment will be needed. For convenience make a checklist. And what are your rules on smoking?

Practical requirements

- Is the room too big? Can it be subdivided?
- Can tables and chairs be set out sensibly?
- Can people see properly? Can the lights be operated independently?
- Can everyone be heard? Is there noise from outside?

Refreshments

There is no question about this: refreshments must be available. It is best to arrange this with the manager of the location. Which drinks are always provided – only coffee and tea, or also soft and alcoholic drinks? Are you going to provide the drinks yourself or use the on-site catering? This affects the costs. Are you going to let the visitors pay for any/all of the refreshments, or only for alcoholic drinks? Is the first coffee free? Will there be nibbles provided for the tables?

Planning the meetings

In the preparation phase, it is wise to agree the topics for the first three or four meetings. Do this with the consultation group. The speakers can be invited as early as possible, and any videos can be organized. Usually the speakers are prepared to appear as a favour, or for expenses only. Confirm everything in writing, and provide practical information such as the route to the Alzheimer Café and where to park.

Sometimes the opening of an Alzheimer Café is enhanced by a regional symposium or an information campaign for the wider public. Ensure that the date, time and location are the same as the regular meetings. It is then more likely that your guests will be able to come at this time in the future and it will avoid unnecessary confusion.

Whether it is the first meeting or the hundredth, it is wise to evaluate every meeting. What went well? What went wrong? What could/must be improved? Show this evaluation regularly to the consultation group. Together you can ensure a good programme of meetings. Put the evaluation in writing. You or others may benefit from this in future.

Contacts with the press

You will, of course, want the café to become known, so that people come to it. Therefore it is wise to inform the local press about your plans at an early stage. Ask all the media for lists of copy deadlines. It can also be helpful to ring a newspaper and invite the editors to the first few meetings of your café.

Once you have made contact with the press, they'll be more receptive when you inform them about another meeting. This can be important for free publicity. You can announce the meetings in regional and local papers, free newspapers, on cable TV, or via regional television. You can also put up posters at the chemists, health centres, supermarkets and mobile shops.

Getting known in care organizations

Care organizations, especially the local Alzheimer society groups, are important for referring people to your Alzheimer Café. A number may be represented on the consultation group. Anyway, tell them about your existence. Apart from all mentioned above, also contact GPs, hospitals, social workers, church organizations, women's groups, etc. You can send them a press notice or brochures, offer to talk to them or send them an article for their house magazine. If you know people personally, invite them directly to visit the Alzheimer Café.

Acquiring visitors

Through the publicity in the press and the contacts with the institutions, you increase the potential number of visitors. People know of the existence of the Alzheimer Café, but of course that does not mean that they will also come. Some people come straight away, others need coaxing.

First-time visitors often have a watchful approach. Sometimes their partner or carer comes alone to have a first look to taste the atmosphere, see whether it is of any interest for them and whether the person with dementia will feel at ease. In this context every meeting of an Alzheimer Café must prove itself anew. Staff at the café give newcomers a special welcome and explain to them what happens. They can explain that visitors are free to come and go. Of course it is important to ask them afterwards what they thought of the meeting, and to invite them for the next time.

Word of mouth publicity

Don't expect 80 visitors for the first meeting. Assume that not everyone knows about the existence of the Alzheimer Café. Publicity needs time to take effect. Knowledge of the café will grow slowly. Keep contact with persons who have the potential to refer the café to others and try to get regular publicity. Once the Alzheimer Café is on the go, numbers will rise. Many persons with dementia and carers who come to a meeting for the first time do so on the recommendation of regulars or other frequent visitors of the Alzheimer Café. Professionals who are enthusiastic also encourage people to take part. The best advertisement therefore is happy customers. You can make use of this by including the experiences of visitors in the brochure, press release or flyer. If you can use your local radio station, don't hesitate to invite 'a regular attendee' to tell his story. This usually generates plenty of response from the listeners. The internet could be another medium to become known.

5 Alzheimer Café an open book?

In this guideline manual, a number of frequently raised topics have been covered that may be useful to those interested in starting an Alzheimer Café. Much more could be said, some of it anecdotal, some very practical. To have this on record, we regularly gather all sorts of ideas, cries from the heart and pitfalls. We make this information available to interested parties. Hopefully this generates more reactions. In this way we continue to discuss and develop the concept. The next section illustrates some of the comments received to date.

Having persons with dementia present in the café

It is not always easy to attract persons with dementia to the café initially. We found it difficult to reach them. We went to the neurologist at the memory clinic and to several staff at a day centre and asked for their cooperation. They are in close regular contact with persons in the earlier stages. We should have thought of going to these contacts earlier.

Consultation with visitors

If visitors like the café, they come back more often. In that way you automatically get a 'group of regulars'. It is nice if these visitors themselves suggest some themes. We think that through this consultation the visitors come to view the café as their 'own'.

Proposals for discussion

We have had good experiences with using proposals to get a discussion going. It does add an element of control to what is being discussed. You should prepare it well with the presenter. You have to know what he/she is going to say before the interval.

Keep the music volume down

You must have been somewhere where the music was so loud that you could not hear yourself speak. It is also very irritating in an Alzheimer Café if the music is so loud that people find it hard to hear each other. For people with a hearing aid it is a problem anyway. Music is fine, but keep it in the background so it does not obstruct conversation.

Attracting people from the whole region

People ask us regularly if we will set up an Alzheimer Café in other places in the region. This happens despite the fact that we have indicated that the one café has a regional role. How do we deal with this? The existing organization already requires lots of energy and resources.

Persons with dementia

Persons with dementia are at the centre of the Alzheimer Café. We have to try to remember this constantly and consistently. It is our aim to include persons with dementia in every way possible, in addition to them enjoying the time spent at the café. If they have special opinions, skills or talents, plan on using them; for example, exhibiting someone's artwork or letting them play the piano at a meeting. Try to be conscious of valuing them. The challenge lies in always remaining conscious of this.

References

American Psychiatric Association (1994) *Diagnostic and Statistical Manual of Mental Disorders* 4th edition, Washington D.C.: APA.

Jones, G.M.M. and Miesen, B.M.L. (eds) (1992) *Care-giving in Dementia: Research and Applications*, vol. 1, London: Routledge.

Miesen, B.M.L. (1990) *Gehechtheid en Dementie* [Attachment and Dementia], PhD dissertation, Imere/Nijkerk: Versluys.

—— (1993) 'Alzheimer's disease, the phenomenon of parent fixation and Bowlby's attachment theory', *International Journal of Geriatric Psychiatry* 8: 147–53.

—— (2000) *Dementia in Close Up*, trans. G.M.M. Jones, London: Routledge Tavistock.

Miesen, B.M.L. and Jones, G.M.M. (eds) (1997) *Care-giving in Dementia: Research and Applications*, vol. 2, London: Routledge.

Shalamov (2000) 'Kolyma Tales', in C. Merridale *Night of Stone: Death and Memory in Russia*, London: Granta, pp. 238, 287.

Chapter 15

Caring together for persons with dementia

The role of the district nurse in home care

Mia Duijnstee and Wynand Ros

A brief introduction to homecare in the Netherlands

Home care in the Netherlands is defined by the National Council for Public Health (NRV 1989) as nursing care, family care, treatment and support provided in the homes of clients by professionals and aided by self-care, informal care, and volunteers and specially geared to enabling clients to remain at home as long as possible. Home nursing organizations offer a package of services, comprising nursing, support, and counselling related to illness, recuperation, disability, old age and death. (This includes help, advice and other care during and after pregnancy and in the area of child health during the first year of a child's life, including regular check-ups. Nursing equipment is also available on loan for a maximum of six months.)

Home help supplies basic help to households when illness, handicap or old age makes it difficult for individuals to cope alone and when informal support by family, friends and neighbours have proved inadequate. Household assistance is the core product of home help. This encompasses activities in the area of domestic work, nursing care and counselling and is designed to safeguard the independent functioning of a household. Home care is largely provided by not-for-profit agencies. As described by the Steering Committee for Healthcare Scenarios for Public Health (STG 1993) these services can be grouped into the following categories:

- Care and support in activities of daily living (ADL): help with feeding, washing, toileting; transfers from bed and chair; dressing; mobility in the house; care for feet and nails and encouragement of self-care in ADL activities.
- Care and support in instrumental activities in daily living (IADL): domestic help of all kinds; cleaning; meal preparation; laundry; shopping.
- Support in medical care: supervision of medication, therapy, diet, teaching how to control pain, prevent complications and instruction in use of aids equipment.

- Social support (including education and counselling): information on sickness and changes in living circumstances; advice about therapy, lifestyle, nutrition and equipment; assistance in arranging sources of help and psychosocial support.
- Parent and child care, including maternity care and child health clinics.
- Prevention and health education.

This description is based on van der Linden and van Dam (1998: 73–4).

A request for help

Whenever a home care organization is confronted with a care need, it is very unlikely that it will be phrased as a request to support the family carer. As a rule, assistance is being applied for to take over certain caring and nursing tasks. Although the care need is often formulated in terms of the person with dementia, in actual practice the district nurse will soon meet the person with dementia's relatives. First of all, the district nurse meets the family members as fellow care workers. This requires a form of cooperation in which professionals and family members work side by side as 'partners in care'. From the very first introduction, but in later stages too, what is needed is not only consultations on what is to be done, i.e. about the care content, but also on the way in which care is being provided and on how district nurse and caregiving relative should deal with one another.

Once a partnership has been established and the district nurse has succeeded in gaining the family's trust, the foundation is laid to meet the family member in a later stage as someone also in need of care. For many of them do not give care without experiencing consequences. To a greater or lesser extent they all encounter the entailing problems. On the one hand these problems are related to the objective characteristics of the care situation, such as a person with dementia's illness, financial circumstances, the health of the family carer and the extent to which others assist with the care. On the other hand subjective characteristics of the family carers themselves play a part. This refers to the way in which the family carer is dealing with the situation, the extent to which he or she is able to accept the illness and the care and the motivation to provide care to the person with dementia. Effective support requires insight into the combination of objective and subjective characteristics and understanding of the shift in the burden over time (Duijnstee and Blom 1995).

Partnership

In home care, professional care and family care are dependent on each other. Professional home care cannot manage without the family carers and the family carers cannot cope without the district nurses. Both forms of care, however different, are equally important in home care for persons with dementia. Some district nurses will indeed think of family carers as 'colleagues' and approach them accordingly. Others, on the other hand, think of themselves in terms of 'administering angels'. They come to 'help' the family from the perspective that the family can no longer cope. From this perspective they will be inclined to take on a leading role more readily. In some situations, however, the district nurse is manoeuvred into this position as a matter of course. In some cases the family will take a dependent position from the very start and be perfectly ready, as it were, to hand over the care entirely. This can be observed in family carers for whom the care has become too much, and also with family carers who dislike giving care or feel condemned to it; for example, a daughter who promised her mother on her deathbed that she would take care of her father, a person with dementia, not realizing that this would go on for years, and that it would create great tension in her own family.

In situations such as these, the district nurse would be well advised to take charge. This will then enable the family carer to step back a little, calm down and bring the amount of care in proportion to what they are willing and able to do. However, in general, family carers would feel 'put out' if a district nurse takes charge too soon. In such cases they will feel they do not get recognition for being the primary carer. If the family carers are forced to defend their positions, this is a poor basis for cooperation. It is detrimental to the partnership concept from the very start.

If, upon introduction, a district nurse immediately starts to draw up a care plan that focuses on the 'division of care', such 'taking control' becomes almost too blatant. District nurses and family carers are then placed in a position of negotiation. This is the wrong approach. Not enough time was taken to explore at leisure which are the parties' possibilities and impossibilities. There is no mutual target setting and there is every risk of a situation developing in which family carers and care workers are diametrically opposed. Division of care should not be at issue in the first contact, but should be the outcome of a process. By presenting a care plan, the district nurse – with or without realizing it – takes on the role of director, while the play is already in full swing. First of all, insight must be gained into who takes on which part and why. There must be a reason why a daughter living next door to her parents does not help her mother at all with the care for the father who has dementia.

The way in which the roles are divided within a family hides an entire history. The division of roles and positions reflects mutual relations and ways of dealing with one another. Without insight into these matters there is a risk of presenting proposals that disrupt the balance within the family (Duijnstee and Blom 1995). Suggestions to divide the care across more 'shoulders' in the family will succeed more readily if the district nurse knows why the responsibility lies with this particular person. Did the family member in the care role choose this role for herself or was she manoeuvred into it by others? How were the roles of onlookers and participants created within the family?

This stage of 'information exchange' is the basis for a jointly carried decision about the most effective care and the best division of roles in care. Such an approach increases the chance of achieving a cooperation plan that is carried by all participants. As a rule, there is a triad: the person with dementia, the family carer, and the professional. However, sometimes this is a dyad. When a person is not able to define his/her own care need, as in the case of a child with a chronic disorder or a person with dementia, cooperation agreements are arrived at without consulting the person. In all other cases, however, the care and the entailing cooperation will be given in the triangle: self-care, family care, professional care.

The study

Questions on the cooperation between district nurses on the one hand and patients and family carers of persons with dementia on the other have been studied by the Department of Nursing Science at the University Medical Centre Utrecht. The results are of interest to everyone in home care who has sometimes wondered why in some cases contacts between person with dementia and family carer run smoothly and all parties involved feel they are working together, and why in other cases things are so very difficult.

The study discussed in this chapter investigated 23 practice situations in home care from all over the country. In-depth interviews were conducted with the patients involved, their family carers and the district nurses. Questions pertained to their mutual relations, their mutual expectations (wishes, needs and matters that influence the mutual relationship and that have more to do with the organizational side of home care). Analysis of the interview responses not only provided a surprising view of a number of dilemmas that district nurses often contend with, but also revealed the creative solutions that district nurses, ever inventive, come up with.

Cooperation is not the right term

Working on the intersection of daily life and illness is characteristic of home care work. For a district nurse it is essential to form a relationship with the person with dementia and family carer in order to do a good job, in the home situation. In this context district nurses often indicate that they cooperate with family carers, which implies that they are equals in the relationship. For many family carers, however, the term 'cooperation' is not a relevant one. Family carers in particular, but patients too, do not describe contacts with district nursing in terms of cooperation. And in fact they are right. If one studies the theories on cooperation, one soon finds that cooperation is more than striving for a similar goal (Hendrix *et al.* 1991; Henneman *et al.* 1995).

Other aspects of cooperation are equality, mutual dependence and taking part in the relationship on a voluntary basis. The care at home can become unbearable to the family carer if district nursing is not available. It is unlikely that district nurses will experience a similar sense of dependence. In the care for persons with dementia with a chronic disorder, family carers are often an important link to complete the care at home. If this cannot be achieved, this is not so great an issue for the home district nurse. An attempt will be made to call in other disciplines or to approach voluntary work. If it turns out to be impossible to effect care extramurally, intramural alternatives will be explored. There are also considerable differences as to what might be a voluntary basis. Of course, as a rule the person with dementia and family carers asked for home care themselves. In that sense one might call it 'voluntarily', but if you look into their hearts many will tell you that they applied for home care by force, necessity, under pressure of the circumstances. In addition to that, professionals have chosen care, whereas care simply happened to family carers. In order to do justice to these differences the phrase 'caring together' would be more appropriate. The study results show that with respect to this caring together three aspects are relevant. Summing up we present them under the denominators of: relational aspects, functioning aspects and organizational aspects (Duijnstee 2000, Ros *et al.* 2001, Duijnstee 2003).

Relational aspects

Family carers and district nurses agree that the care relationship runs smoothly if and when both parties take each other's possibilities into account and discuss many subjects together. As one family carer phrased it: 'The district nurse takes time to discuss things. If I want to talk and she does not have the time, we can discuss it the day after. She will come back to it of her own accord. I do not have to bring up the subject myself.'

A district nurse who feels the care relation is in good order says about the family carers: 'They try to think along with you and they understand things very well. Some people don't understand how home care works, but for these people just a few words suffice. They show understanding towards us, too.'

Effective communication is crucial to the development of a sound care relationship. People should be able to listen to each other's points of view and to put their own views into words. In this, district nurses are required to realize that family carers aren't professional district nurses. Therefore they aren't all as skilled in stating their own wishes and needs, setting targets and making agreements regarding care-giving.

It is not always easy for family carers to state their wishes and ideas

The extent to which family carers can openly state their wishes and needs correlates with the extent to which they feel dependent on the district nurse. Their response to this dependency varies.

Sometimes there is complete acceptance due to deeply felt gratitude. These family carers are so glad that there is care that they make no demands and take negative side-effects in their stride.

A different response is that of forced acceptance, but not without frustration. Although these family carers do not express any comments about the care, they would like to do so. Because of their dependence they feel obliged to accept the situation as it is. They are afraid that comments might put the provision of care at stake.

On the other hand, other family carers who also keep their comments to themselves do try to have control over the situation. They lessen their dependence by taking over care from district nursing. They usually don't do this openly. For example, they might put out the things (that are needed to wash the person with dementia), choose the clothes for that day, and so on. Thus they take back into their own hands part of the direction of the care. They do this in a 'safe' way and avoid conflicts.

There are also family carers who do express criticism openly. They depart from the concept of equality in the care situation. They want to have a degree of influence over the care situation which is similar or equal to that of district nurse. They make their influence felt in various ways. Some family carers look for a solution by exchanging personal information with the nurse. They feel they have to reveal too much about themselves, and they balance the scales as it were by asking the nurse a number of personal questions.

Finally, there are family carers who resist such dependence and make demands. This is the most active attitude that family members can adopt towards district nursing. They pay attention all the time. They don't want to become dependent on district nursing and refuse to give up control. They will address district nursing and home care organization regarding agreements made.

They will come up with solutions themselves to streamline the care provided by district nursing with their own ideas on the subject. An example of this was a list of instructions that a family carer drew up for the district nurse. It stated in detail all the things that were to be done for the person with dementia and how to do them.

Enhancing the input of family carers

Home care staff prefer people who are able to state their wishes and needs clearly and who are also able to discuss care issues openly if they are not satisfied with it. This preference is understandable. It is more difficult to detect what goes on inside people's minds and what is expected from home care through subtle non-verbal signs and painful evaluation talks than when it is directly stated. Family carers on the other hand often have good reasons for not being too demanding. The care relationship affects their personal and private lives deeply. Out of fear of conflicts and differences of opinion with district nurses who have sometimes been visiting their homes several times a week for years on end, many people keep criticism and comments to themselves. Their dependent position results in a striving for a harmonious relationship with the district nurses. That is why it is important that district nurses encourage family carers to give their opinion clearly. Asking for opinions more directly and consulting with them can do this. Questions such as 'How do you feel about it?' or 'What would be an ideal situation for you?' can help here. Equally important is paying attention to indirect signals.

Pay attention to non-verbal signals

We already indicated that family carers who feel very dependent on home care often adopt a compliant and wait-and-see position. This can prevent them from presenting their wishes and questions on the care, let alone that they will comment on or criticize the care. However, this does not mean they would not like to do so, or that they don't give off any other signs or indications. Evasive behaviour, irritability or tears in someone's eyes can be important clues. It is sometimes also necessary to spot the question behind the question. For example, if the family carer says 'You must be very busy', this does not necessarily mean that she is thinking of the district nurse's pressure of work exclusively.

Prevent one-sided agreements

For many district nurses, making agreements is a way to direct the care. In the cooperation with colleagues this is often a very adequate method. Once agreements have been made, it is reasonable to expect that they are carried out. This is not the case with family carers. They will sometimes consent to methods that they do not in fact agree with. They don't want to create the impression that they aren't willing to give up a great deal for a parent or spouse with dementia. It also happens that family carers are unable to realize the full extent of what they are promising. Their work is not so structured and planned as that of district nursing. They sometimes promise to take on care tasks that present themselves, but later on it appears that they were so busy that they were unable to meet the nurse's request.

Recognizing expertise: two types

The attitude that district nurses adopt towards family carers' expertise is also important. Family carers feel less dependent on district nurses if they pay attention to the expertise that family carers have developed regarding the illness and care of the relative. Family carers are 'experiential experts' and they expect that home care staff recognize this expertise. With regard to the attitude of professional district nurses towards this 'experiential expertise', two roles can be distinguished: 'the role of expert' and 'the role of partner'.

In the 'expert role', district nurses act on the basis of their professional knowledge. With regard to the specialized nursing-related acts and knowledge of provisions and aids, professionals will often know more than the family carer. With regard to knowledge of the illness and the treatment thereof, this is already less a matter of course. And with regard to the question of how the person with dementia responds and how best to deal with it, family carers are often more knowledgeable.

District nurses who operate on the basis of the expert role put themselves above family carers. They feel their own role in daily care is more important than that of the family carer, which gives family carers the feeling that their expertise is not being recognized. As a result, family carers do not feel supported, but rather they feel dominated. In such a situation it cannot be expected of family carers that they feel free to advance their opinions. There can be no open discussion at all. It may also happen that family carers will accept the expert role of care providers, but then there is a risk that their own expertise will not be called upon sufficiently and that they will then end up in a pattern of increasing dependence.

District nurses who operate on the basis of the 'partner role' act as fellow team players and do not place themselves above, but rather next to the family carer. These care professionals attempt to arrive at a division of tasks by means of an open discussion about care. By discussing the care and the situation with each other, care professionals try to map out the situation. Only then can they assess how they can function optimally in that context. In such a situation the district nurse recognizes and values unequivocally the expertise of the family carer, as a result of which mutual respect can develop. Thus a sound care relation can be built in which knowledge and information can be mutually exchanged and in which the family carer finds the encouragement to communicate with (more) openness with the care professional.

Showing appreciation

District nurses can also increase the input into the care relationship with family carers and persons with dementia by explicitly showing their appreciation for the specific contribution to the care, or for the way the family is functioning (see also McElheran and Harper Jacques 1994). This expression of appreciation must meet certain requirements. It must be worded in a way that will appeal to family carers. In addition the appreciation must refer to actions and attitudes that the informal carers themselves feel are important. Depending on the 'stage' in the care relationship, a professional can have several objectives for showing explicit appreciation. At the outset of the care relationship the main objective is to bring out the strong characteristics of people, to compensate for their sense of helplessness and dependence and to help them gain self-confidence. In a later stage, it is a sound means to combat feelings of impotence and to find new sources of energy. In addition, positive expressions enhance the relationship with the nurse or district nurse. In this context, expressions of appreciation should not be used as a way of smoothing out or denying problems in the care relation.

Functional aspects

So far, some points about the relational aspects of caring together have been considered. Next, the more functional sides of the care relationship will be dealt with. This concerns questions like 'Which way do the priorities lie with regard to the district nurse's tasks?' Roughly speaking, there are two lines of approach regarding the care: the perspective of the illness and the daily existence perspective. Here they are described separately in order to arrive at a clear message. In addition we will discuss the differences between 'professional' and 'personal' standards.

The perspective of the illness

Our study confirms that what is crucial to the care relationship's quality is the extent to which the district nurse is able to base her actions on the position that the meaning of the illness holds in the individual lives of the person with dementia and the family carer. Things go wrong if and when district nurses operate solely from an illness perspective. There are several reasons for this. District nurses who base their actions mostly on an illness perspective will often assume that the family carer has knowledge of the illness and accepts its consequences.

Family caregivers on the other hand are often quite willing to learn to accept the illness, but usually their acceptance does not extend to the fact that they will allow the illness to control their lives. Because of this, district nurses in turn sometimes feel that there is a certain opposition, and this makes the relationship somewhat difficult. This is the case when, for example, a family carer refuses to get rid of tablecloths or other stuff that, in her opinion, contribute to a homey atmosphere, whereas the district nurse feels that it is important to the safety of the person with dementia to remove them. Even if district nurses want the best for their clients, if they do not take the perspective of the family carer into account they will unintentionally put themselves in the position of expert and thus unintentionally undermine the relationship of trust.

No room for other roles

Some district nurses are unable to look upon a family caregiver other than as a person whose only role and activity is to take care of a family member with dementia. They overlook the fact that the family carer can also have the roles of parent, spouse or colleague. On that basis, they might make other choices than he or she would solely from a carer's perspective. If family carers continue to pursue activities away from the home, for them this is often just a way to go on giving care.

The existence perspective

Family carers who are trying to learn to live with the illness will sometimes set priorities that may amaze district nurses. Take the following example. The district nurse feels that the family carer should adapt herself to the restrictions of the illness of her husband and should therefore move to a flat. The wife prefers the discomfort of stairs to giving up a life to which she is used. She is afraid she will become socially isolated if she moves to a flat and that friends and acquaintances won't be able to drop by quite so easily. The fact that family carers refuse to adapt themselves completely to the illness is often a survival strategy that has little to do with acceptance – or lack of it – of the illness. They want to lead their own lives as much as possible and therefore they don't want to think of the illness and its consequences all the time.

Aspects of intimacy

Some district nurses pay little attention to the family carer's aspects of intimacy. They only think of the actions that are required and the best way of carrying them out and they will disregard their implications for the relationship between family carer and person with dementia. For a family carer, some parts of the care can be difficult to reconcile with his or her personal relationship to the person with dementia. If, for example, a family carer refuses to wash or feed her demented husband any longer, this need not imply that her relationship to the person with dementia is not a good one. Perhaps she refuses to do it because she wants the relationship to stay as good as possible. She is afraid her husband won't permit washing or feeding all that easily. She may be afraid that she won't be able to control herself if he pushes her away or starts calling her names.

Privacy

Many family carers regard the presence of district nurses in the house as an infringement upon their privacy. Not only does the district nurse know a lot about them, but they are barely managing to guard the boundaries of their own privacy. Family carers who dislike this will often try to protect their privacy in all sorts of ways. Sometimes they do this by undertaking the care themselves at certain times, for example, in the evening or during weekends. Others will go even further and state plainly the conditions upon which the district nurses can come into their house (for example, that they must not come from the same village). Some family carers will prepare in advance all the equipment the district nurses need to provide care, to prevent them from going through their cupboards.

Professional and personal standards

This brings us to the second area of tension: that between professional and personal standards. Family carers will be quick to look upon the well-meant comments of district nurses on their situation as a form of interference. If the district nurse's standards clash with those of the family carer and the demented person, all sorts of frictions and misunderstandings will arise. We came across one example where a district nurse found that a family carer stubbornly refused to give up certain tasks, in spite of her own poor health. After enquiring for the reasons behind this, the district nurse discovered that these particular aspects of the care were very important to this lady. She was set on tending to these matters for her husband, herself, even if it took up a lot of her strength. On the basis of her professional standards, the district nurse should take over as many tasks as possible from this family carer, but in this case she decided to respect the family carer's wishes. As a result of this they got on quite well from that moment. It is useless to try and enforce professional standards if this is counterproductive.

Of course there are limits to adapting to the standards of family carers and persons with dementia. If a district nurse finds that wounds are not treated correctly, he or she will have to take action. And of course you do not have to accept a violation of your personal standards if someone is verbally aggressive or pinches your bottom.

Personal standards

In particular, our study showed that a difference in personal standards between the district nurse and the family carer can have enormous consequences for their mutual relationship. For example, take standards with regard to what is clean and proper and what isn't: many family carers simply hate to see incontinence diapers left lying about on the bathroom floor, or a basin of washing water left standing, wet towels on the bed or a dirty lavatory bowl after the district nurse helped the person with dementia to go to the toilet. They wonder if the district nurse would do these things in her own home and feel they are not being taken seriously. They are very busy as it is, and then they also have to clear up after the district nurse or home care staff.

Frictions can also arise due to differences in opinion on how people should 'behave' towards each other. A family carer told us how hurt she was by a district nurse's negative comments on the way she teased her ill husband about the smell of his stools. The wife knew very well how her husband would feel about her remarks, and furthermore she felt that she could behave as she liked in her own home. Our study also shows that many family carers do not take kindly to comments on the way the household is run or the way the house is furnished. One family carer told us that it makes her really tired that whenever new district nurses come to the house they will always, time and again, make new plans for renovations – as if she herself had not thoroughly investigated every option.

Organizational aspects

Finally, we will pay attention to organizational aspects. This involves the questions: how do district nurses handle the rules and restrictions of their jobs and how does their attitude affect the relationship to the person with dementia and the family carer? Of at least equal importance is the question: how can the home care organization create room for the development of the best possible care relationship?

In carrying out their job district nurses have a relatively large degree of autonomy. They are personally responsible for the care relationships they enter into. In principle, they decide for themselves how they carry out their tasks. And yet it appears from our study that district nurses at times feel restricted in their possibilities by the rules of the home care organization. It is not for nothing that the term 'stopwatch care' became a well-known concept in home care. In the Netherlands, this means that sometimes 'product-based thinking' prevailed too much in home care. Under these circumstances district nurses often face dilemmas. If they abide strictly by the maximum amount of time that is to be spent on a specific care situation (or by the tasks that can be carried out within the care situation), they won't always be able to meet the needs of the person with dementia and his family carer. How does this affect the care relationship? District nurses, persons with dementia and family carers alike are averse to variable hours, different faces all the time, restrictions with regard to the task content and the pressure of work. What is the problem for the various parties involved and how do they handle it?

Variable hours

District nurses do not always succeed in providing care at the exact time agreed upon. This has various causes. Appointments may take longer than expected and, in the case of regular routes, those at 'the end of the shift/route' experience more delay. Furthermore, deputy and temporary staff are not always aware of agreements made. If a district nurse shows up at varying hours, this may seriously disrupt the daily life of family carers and persons with dementia. Because 'the nurse' can arrive any time, family carers can't go out to do a little shopping or take up something else. They spend their time waiting. Others feel tension when the district nurse is late: the family carer may not be in time for work, and the person with dementia won't be ready when the day-care bus comes round. Some district nurses feel that the varying hours are a fact of life they can do nothing about. They realize it is unpleasant for family carers, but they expect them to accept the situation anyway. Others try to meet the family carer halfway by ringing them up when they will be a little late, or by varying their shifts every now and then so that it isn't always the same people that receive help last.

A district nurse who takes the daily occupations of her clients into account as much as she possibly can says: 'It's a matter of give and take. Most people want to be helped early on and that is not possible. So you must switch from time to time. One day this client gets early help, then another. That's how you try to keep everybody happy.'

The fact that one district nurse handles her shift with more flexibility than another, gives some family carers the impression that this is a matter of 'desire to oblige' or 'willingness': 'The district nurse said that he could not come earlier and I have never been able to understand that. He said that he has to drive a longer way round and adapt his shift and he won't. But another nurse never had a problem with it and would come to me early in the day. So there are great differences with these hours, one person will oblige and the other will fold their arms and say it is impossible.'

Different faces all the time

Many persons with dementia and family carers find it difficult to accept the large number of 'different faces': strangers around the house again and again who do not know them and their situation. Usually they understand that this is not the individual district nurse's fault and that it is unavoidable in work with part-timers and temporary staff due to vacations and illness. In spite of this, they find it difficult to accept. It can upset the person with dementia and family carers indicate that it makes it practically impossible to form a relationship of trust with district nurses. In addition they are obliged to explain routine matters again and again each and every time. (How best to approach the person with dementia, how to operate the shower, where they keep the clean clothes, and so on.) This isn't just a bore, it is also very tiring. Continuity is important in a care relationship.

Many district nurses are also troubled by the lack of continuity in their contacts with clients. Some feel this is not their fault and they expect the clients to show some understanding. Others refuse to accept the situation for what it is and try to lessen the disadvantageous effects of the changes, for example, by ensuring a proper transfer of duties to other staff about what has to be done, and how best to care for the person with dementia. This is less of a problem in home care organizations in which district nurses work in regular teams or shifts. In such cases, persons with dementia and family carers see the same group of people all the time.

Clearly defined tasks

District nurses are not allowed to perform every activity. Their tasks have been clearly defined and laid down. For example, domestic chores are not a part of their job. Research shows that some district nurses are very strict about this, whereas others apply the rules with more flexibility and decide for each situation what they will or will not do:

> I know that officially household work is not one of our tasks, but I simply do it. It is no trouble at all. If you know that a domestic help will come in at any minute, you won't. And if, every day, dishes are piled up in the sink and the wastepaper basket is stuffed and the floors are stained, then I feel that this is not my job and that domestic help should be given. But sometimes there's a bit of a mess, for example, cups and saucers all about the room and a stained table. Well, then I just clear the cups away and wipe the table. It's no trouble and it looks nice at once. But I won't do all the dishes or some such thing.

This district nurse avails herself of the room she has, but her criteria remain subjective. Some district nurses are aware of this and will therefore try – in consultation with their colleagues – to arrive at clear objective agreements that they can explain to family carers. This was the case, for example, with one family carer who asked if the district nurse would give her husband his breakfast after his bath. She had to go to her choir rehearsal early in the morning. She had already asked the sitter and the domestic help and neither of them could get her husband to eat a morsel. She had noticed that the district nurse had more influence over her husband.

Pressure of work

It is a well-known fact that work pressure facing district nurses is considerable. Many of them feel that as a result of this they don't do right by their clients, that important aspects of the care (such as personal contacts with the person with dementia and the family carer and the transfer of information to colleagues) suffer:

> If the pressure of work becomes so great, several things just won't get done. It may happen that because of being so pressed for time you can't write things down properly for each other. Sometimes you can set this right as you go along, but after a week off and a different nurse in charge, you simply don't know all there is to know. Things to do with nursing, such as a decubitus ulcer, will be passed on to you, but informal things just don't get passed along any more.

Family carers have a great deal of understanding and admiration for their district nurses, but dislike it if they are in too much of a hurry or complain about the pressure of work all the time: 'They are all so very busy, but some are just too busy. They will rush in and buzzzz. They are pressed for time and dress my wife in a slipshod manner. I don't think right.'

Dealing with organizational restrictions

The way in which district nurses deal with the home care organizations' rules varies from rigidly to flexibly. These various attitudes all influence the care relationship in different ways.

Rules are rules

District nurses who consider the restrictions of the organization to be an 'established fact' usually feel the need for great clarity, predictability and structure. First of all they will be guided by the organizational rules and they feel they cannot change the ensuing restrictions. Rules are rules. That is why they expect understanding from family carers and do not like it if they express criticism. They feel that looking for other solutions isn't their responsibility. Such an attitude will offend most family carers, in particular if they find that other district nurses are able to apply those very same rules with more flexibility.

Explaining, but taking no action

Fortunately most district nurses do not adopt such a rigid attitude. They realize that such an attitude results in frustration in their clients and in friction in the care relationship. They explain and show understanding towards their clients, but they do not attempt to bend the rules accordingly. In this case family carers tend to accept the situation more readily than in case of the rigid attitude. And yet insight into the situation does not automatically result in understanding or acceptance. For some family carers the organizational restrictions are so much of an impediment that they will continue to resist them in spite of the explanation. District nurses who feel that explaining alone is the best strategy to deal with organizational restrictions are at risk of hiding behind the rules. Some go one step further and make out that the home care organization is 'a mutual enemy'. By acting as helpless victims of the organization, they make it their client's problem entirely. Thus, there is a risk that the care relationship will deteriorate into a complaint relationship that is not to the good or the well-being of any of the parties involved.

A flexible attitude within the possibilities

Not all district nurses feel so bound to the rules and regulations of the home care organization. Some manage to bend the rules as they see fit in order to meet the wishes and needs of their clients as much as possible. These district nurses do not derive their confidence from set tasks and rules. They do what they think is best for the client. They are not afraid of being called to account by colleagues regarding their choices. For each situation, they will consider what their options are. They know how far they can go in this and do not cross the lines of their professional responsibility.

Yet a flexible attitude does not solve all the problems. Often it is a case of personal and incidental choices. Today a district nurse will decide to stay a little to talk to the family carer, but what will happen tomorrow? This flexible attitude can be confusing to family carers. In addition, it can result in mutual tension between the district nurses. Some district nurses point out the risk presented by this 'accommodating attitude' in some colleagues in that it gives family carers an opportunity to play off district nurses against each other.

Solutions that cover the problem structurally

District nurses who take full advantage of the latitude present for action often appear to come up with creative solutions. They succeed in bending the rules to their clients' advantage and do not resign themselves in advance to the organizational instructions. They stand by their job and explore the possibilities and restrictions in the interest of the person with dementia and family carer. But this too has its limitations. However attractive it may seem at times, it is not a solution to bend the rules of the organization structurally in the interest of the clients. The organization will then never become aware of the problem.

Making the best possible use of the latitude present:
structural solutions

Finally, there are district nurses who look for more structural solutions. They have a clear insight into their own needs and the needs of their clients, the team and the organization. They consider matters from various perspectives and are not afraid of confrontations. They feel competent and secure about their role and the possibilities and restrictions of their profession. Realizing that they are part of an organization, they attempt to acquire structural freedom of action within the organization, in consultation with all parties involved.

An example of this is the aforementioned district nurse who was also asked to give a person with dementia his breakfast on Wednesday morning. In principle this was not a part of her job. However, she understood that this restriction is unpleasant for the family carer. In this case it was an impediment for the family carer to continue to participate in a small part of the life she used to lead. Instead of adopting a flexible attitude (i.e. if she is the one to visit the person with dementia on a Wednesday to give him a bath), she sets out to look for a more structural solution. She discussed the issue during team consultations and arrived at a solution – for all colleagues and temporary staff who take her place in case of sickness or vacation. The new solution takes into account the wishes of the family carer as well as the restrictions of the organization. Hence, other district nurses will also take over the task, except during vacations, for then there is a shortage of staff. The district nurse takes full advantage of the latitude present and arrives at a structural solution that is carried by the entire team and offers clarity to the family carer.

An optimal organizational structure

In order to arrive at sound care relationships, district nurses need job conditions that enable them to work in teams. In addition it is necessary that an organization's structure will offer latitude to professionals to act independently. A flat organization structure is better suited to this than a hierarchical one. In assessing the work, it is important that not merely individual achievements are taken into account. The results of cooperation are important too. Translated towards home care, this implies that when assessing district nurses employers should also take the quality of the care relationship (with the person with dementia and the family carer) and the cooperation with colleagues into account. A home care organization that recognizes the role of family carers within the care relationship, creates conditions that make it possible to care and to continue to care – together with the family carer – and to produce creative solutions within existing structures.

References

Duijnstee, M. (2000) 'Mantelzorg, ondersteuning en afstemming', *Handboek Verpleegkundig consult*, Houten: Bohn, Stafleu Van Loghum.
—— (2003) 'Vaste teams: continuiteer belangrijk via patient en matelzorg'. *Verpleeg Kunde Nieuws* January 17: 2.
Duijnstee, M. and Blom, M. (1995) 'Thuis in familiezorg. Niet alleen bij een patiënt, maar bij een heel systéém over de vloer', *MGZ* 23: 4–7.
Duijnstee, M. and Keesom, J. (2000) 'Relatie Wijkverpleging, patiënt en mantelzorg onderzocht. Normen en waarden aanpassen', *Verpleegkunde Nieuws* April: 30–32.
Hendrix, H., Konings, J. and Doesburg, J. (1991) *Functionele samenwerking: werkboek voor samenwerkingsverbanden in de zorgsector*. Baarn: Nelissen.
Henneman, E., Lee, J.L. and Cohen, J. (1995) 'Collaboration: A concept analysis', *Journal of Advanced Nursing* 21.
Linden, B.A. v.d. and Dam, Y. van (1998) 'Home care', in A.J.P. Schrijvers (ed.) *Heath and Healthcare in the Netherlands. A Critical Self-assessment by Dutch Experts in the Medical and Health Sciences*, Utrecht: De Tijdstroom, pp. 73–81.
McElheran, N. and Harper-Jacques, S.R. (1994) 'Commendations: a resource intervention for clinical practice', *Clinical Specialist* 8: 1.
Nieuwstraten, A., Mercken, C., Duijnstee, M. and Ros, W. (2000) *Samen zorgen: wijkverpleging in relatie tot person with dementia en mantelzorg*, Baarn: Intro.
NRV, National Council for Public Health (1989) *Discussienota Thuiszorg* [Discussion paper on home care], Zoetermeer: NRV.
Ros, W., Duijnstee, M., Nieuwstraten, A. and Mercken, C. (2001) 'Thuiszorg en mantelzorg', in *Handboek Thuiszorg*, vol. 1, Amsterdam: Elsevier, B2.3–12.
STG, Steering Committee on Future Health Scenarios (1993) *Primary Care and Home Care Scenarios 1990–2005*. Rijswijk: STG.

Chapter 16

The power of abuse

Gilda Newsham

Introduction

Forty years as a nurse and nursing home inspector have taught me that abuse can still shock and offend me. It is easier to dismiss altogether than to accept the solitary fact that it cuts across all social classes and encompasses all care settings. It is impossible to give more than a brief overview of adult abuse within a single chapter. The main focus will be specifically on persons with dementia, how best to support, care for, respect and above all protect them.

Eight types of abuse and the main indicators thereof are outlined. Eight case histories have been chosen, one to supplement each section. Sadly, each is a true story, though the details have been disguised. The purpose of the case histories is multiple: to highlight the courage of some carers in exposing the abuser/s; to encourage every person to stand up for what they believe in; to ensure that all persons requiring care are treated with respect and dignity; and to show how abuse may be present even in the most unexpected settings: 'There can be no secrets and no hiding place when it comes to exposing the abuse of vulnerable adults' (Dunn 2000).

Definitions of elder abuse

Elder abuse is a complex phenomenon and there is no 'uniform, comprehensive definition of the term' (Johnson 1986: 168). It is however important to define abuse for several reasons. First, as pointers towards the social problem in question, they guide the enquirer towards a clearer understanding of what the issue involves. Second, definitions help to focus on the social problem in question and differentiate that specific area of concern from other phenomena. Third, definitions are also necessary to guide professionals and permit intervention (Biggs *et al.* 2000).

The following definitions of abuse have been selected because they capture the meaning of the misuse of power over vulnerable person/s and the ensuing breakdown of trust. This is how the concept of abuse will be treated in this chapter.

Abuse is a violation of an individual's human and civil rights by any other person or persons.

(Dunn 2000)

Elder Abuse is a single or repeated act or lack of appropriate action occurring within any relationship where there is an expectation of trust, which causes harm or distress to an older person.

(Action on Elder Abuse mission statement)

The wilful infliction of injury, unreasonable confinement, intimidation, or cruel punishment with resulting physical harm, pain or mental anguish.

(Stevenson 1999)

Abuse within the practitioner–client relationship is the result of the misuse of power or a betrayal of trust, respect or intimacy between the practitioner and the client, which the practitioner should know would cause physical or emotional harm to the client.

(Nursing and Midwifery Council 2002)

Which adults are vulnerable? The age range for adult abuse is from 18 years onwards. The traditional definition that is commonly referred to as 'elder abuse' appertains in the main to persons over the age of 65 years:

Vulnerable adult, a person aged 18 years, or over, who is or may be in need of care services by reason of mental or other disability, age or illness and who are or may be unable to take care of him or herself, or is unable to protect him or herself against harm or exploitation.

(Law Commission 1995)

For the purposes of this chapter the term 'adult' abuse will prevail and be taken to include all care services provided in any care setting or context.

Prevalence of adult abuse

Most people conceive, naively perhaps, that most professionals and carers are basically kind. If this is so, why does abuse continue to emerge and why do repeated scenarios occur over and over again? In 1992 a UK national prevalence study was published. This showed that up to 5 per cent of older people in the community were suffering from verbal abuse and up to 2 per cent were victims of physical or financial abuse (Bennett and Ogg 1992).

Prevalence of adult abuse in nursing

On the 15 March 2001 the United Kingdom Central Council for Nurses, Midwives and Health Visitors (UKCC) stated a need for urgent action to deal with the rising number of allegations of misconduct. The number of allegations received in January and February 2001 was up more than 60 per cent on the previous year. Statistics also show that 113 nurses were struck off the register in the year 2000, 53 per cent more than 1999. A Senior RCN (Royal College of Nursing) member stated: 'The number of nurses removed from the register is a tiny proportion.' This may be the case, but how many reported cases received a 'caution', were dismissed through lack of evidence, or failed to be reported at all (Professional Conduct Committee UKCC 2001)?

Types of abuser

There are many types of abuser, but for the purposes of this chapter, four have been identified.

1   *The sadistic abuser.* These are people who systematically and intentionally abuse and are incapable of feeling remorse or guilt. They are quite prepared to blame others and will deny without a second thought any allegations made against them.
2   *The reactive abuser.* Care environments can be harsh and oppressive for staff with multiple demands being placed on their time. At the end of a hard day, carers may be stretched to their limits and responses may become unpredictable and unsafe. Carers should be able to tell their managers or nurse/doctor/social worker when they are near breaking point and when the care they are giving is getting too much to handle. A small break is often all that is needed, plus the fact that they have been able to share their concerns. Sadly, many will hold back, for to ask for help or support may be seen as a sign of weakness.
3   *The ignorant abuser.* Carers often follow instructions without question or thought. On occasions these actions may be outside the interests of their patient/client/relative. In simple words they choose to turn a blind eye or take the line of least resistance. For all carers who observe action or no action without due consideration and do nothing, have simply condoned the abuse and are guilty by association.
4   *The lazy abuser.* It is unacceptable for carers to rush duties in order to allow themselves longer break periods. This does occur and cannot be discounted as a form of abuse. No one likes to be rushed when receiving care. For persons with dementia they will become disoriented and each and every one will at the very least feel less valued.

The settings of abuse

Vulnerable adults may be abused by a wide range of people, including relatives and family members, professional staff, paid care workers, volunteers, other service users, neighbours, friends and strangers. There are also the people who deliberately set out to exploit vulnerable persons. Abuse may take place in any setting. It may occur when a vulnerable adult lives alone or with a relative/friend. It may also occur in a nursing or residential home, hospital, health clinic, day centre, custodial setting, from community service workers and in public places thought to be safe.

Causes of abuse

Persons with dementia are amongst the most vulnerable in society. Many have challenging behaviour that can put to the test the soundest ethical and philosophical beliefs of many carers. It is a sad fact that in Western cultures intellect is a major constituent of being valued. To lose one's intellect is so often the beginning of the loss of dignity and value as an individual – a frightening reality. There are multiple reasons that may trigger or even set the scene for abuse. They are presented in Box 16.1 and are only a sampling of the many possible reasons for abuse.

Although many professionals are direct caregivers to patients/residents, few have received training in dementia care. Abuse may therefore result from the actions or non-actions of individual members of staff because they

---

Box 16.1   Causes of abuse

- Inadequate training, especially in specialist areas like dementia care.
- Minimal supervision of staff from management. Staff may work in isolation.
- Poor communication between disciplines.
- Lack of knowledge regarding policies and procedures.
- Absence of appropriate risk management processes.
- Poor or limited resources.
- Unsuitable architectural design.
- Imbalance of high dependency needs and staffing levels.
- Poor attitudes and behaviour of staff and managers.
- Low status ascribed to the work. Lack of appreciation. Low pay.
- Failure to see the pattern of events.
- Social isolation. Those who are abused usually have minimal social contacts.
- History of a poor quality long-term relationship between the abused and the abuser.
- A pattern of family violence. The person who abuses may have been abused.
- The person who is abused may be dependent upon the person abusing them for accommodation, financial and emotional support.
- The person who abuses has a history of mental health problems, personality disorder or drug-related problem.

lack the knowledge and understanding of how best to cope with persons who require a high level of assistance.

Nurses who have attended dementia training programmes report that the knowledge they gained changed their way of providing care, which in turn influenced the residents' behaviour (findings substantiated from the evaluation returns submitted following courses hosted by the Alzheimer's Society, Lymington and District Branch, 'Care Giving in Dementia: A Positive Vision').

Types of abuse

Eight types of abuse have been selected. At the end of each section, an outline of some of the indicators to aid recognition is listed. These may help in raising a suspicion, but it is well to remember that many of the possible indicators may be no more than a sign of a medical or psychological condition. Having awareness and monitoring a suspicion is all-important. Keep a record of concerns, together with dates, names, places, etc. Check local policy and procedure. Do not be afraid to seek help from a senior member of staff. Box 16.2 lists the types of abuse that will be dealt with in this chapter. The primary focus must always be the protection of the vulnerable adult.

Physical abuse

This includes hitting, slapping, pushing, kicking, pinching, force feeding, restraint, misuse of medication, inappropriate sanctions or rough handling.

Indicators

- Injuries inconsistent with how they happened.
- Lack of explanation by carer as to how injuries occurred.

Box 16.2   Types of elderly abuse

1 Physical abuse
2 Verbal abuse
3 Psychological abuse
4 Financial abuse
5 Institutional abuse
6 Abuse by neglect and acts of omission
7 Sexual abuse
8 Discriminatory abuse

- In a care setting, no accident or incident records or minimal information recorded. No cross-reference made in care plan.
- Injuries inconsistent with the lifestyle of the individual.
- Multiple bruising, particularly on one part of the body or on the well-protected areas of the body.
- Clusters of injuries, for example, slap marks, finger marks, burns/friction marks on legs arms and torso.
- Injuries at different stages of healing, or not properly treated.
- Loss of weight, dehydration and/or malnourished without illness-related cause.

Verbal abuse

This includes swearing at residents, calling persons inappropriate names, shouting, talking over the head of a person, deliberately telling an untruth without justifiable reason.

Indicators

- The abused person may not be allowed to speak for themselves, or see others, without the caregiver (suspected abuser) being present.
- Seeking shelter or protection.
- Unexplained reactions towards particular individuals.
- Unexplained reactions towards particular settings.
- Withdrawal and/or marked change in normal pattern of behaviour.
- Change in sleep pattern.
- Verbal abuse, attitudes of indifference or anger towards a specific person or persons.

Psychological abuse

This includes threats of harm, abandonment, deprivation of contact, humiliation, intimidation, withdrawal from services and/or contact with others, isolation, coercion, controlling or blaming, denial of choices and opinions and denial of privacy.

Indicators

- Evidence of lack of consideration and understanding of persons with dementia.
- Privacy denied in relation to care, feelings or other aspects of life.
- Denial of freedom of movement. (If restraint is ever used it must be justified. Restraint can only be accepted when a full assessment has

been undertaken by a multidisciplinary team and the restraint must be regularly reviewed. All must be carefully documented.)

- Air of silence when alleged perpetrator is present.
- Increased confusion or disorientation.
- Withdrawal, signs of fear, tearfulness, agitation.
- Sudden change in behaviour patterns.
- Weight loss/gain, change in appetite.

Financial abuse

This includes theft, fraud, exploitation, pressures in connection with wills, property, inheritance and financial transactions. Use of money or property without the informed consent of the vulnerable person or the misuse or misappropriation of money, property, possessions or benefits by person/s responsible.

Indicators

- Unusual or sudden financial transactions.
- Sudden or unexpected change of will.
- Loss of valuable possessions.
- Unexplained change in material circumstances.
- Sudden inability to pay bills.
- Extraordinary interest by family or carer/s in person's assets.
- Disparity between assets and satisfactory living conditions.

Institutional abuse

This may be defined as abuse or mistreatment by a regime as well as by individuals within a residential or nursing home. It is often difficult to determine abuse in residential settings as many organizational practices may be seen as inadequate rather than abusive. Abuse may arise due to poor levels of care in regard to: nutrition; clothing; nursing and personal care; environment; staffing/leadership/management; training; health and safety standards.

Indicators

- High percentage of pressure damage.
- High number of accidents/incidents/deaths.
- Poor standards of hygiene.
- Minimal evidence of promotion of continence and management of incontinence.
- Poor care planning.

- Poor design layouts within the home.
- Poor understanding of core values and specialist needs, example: dementia.
- High level of sickness and turnover of staff.
- Poor staffing levels. Poor calibre of staff.
- Little or no regard for individual needs, cultures, religion or ethnicity.

Abuse by neglect and acts of omission

This includes lack of understanding or ignoring medical or nursing needs; failure to provide access to appropriate health, social care or educational services; the withholding of the necessities of life, such as medication, nutrition, specialist services and equipment.

Indicators

- Poor calibre staff, minimal evidence of appropriate training.
- Inappropriate and improper use of medications.
- Low staffing levels.
- Deterioration in health without any sound reason or obvious cause.
- Poor and occasionally sudden immobility.
- Malnutrition/dehydration.
- Inadequate clothing, heating, lighting, hygiene.
- Lack of social stimulus.
- High percentage of pressure damage.

Sexual abuse

This includes rape and sexual assault or sexual acts to which the adult has not consented, or could not consent to, or was pressured into consenting as well as inappropriate touching, sexual innuendoes, sexual harassment and/ or sexually suggestive language.

Indicators

- Genital/urinary infections.
- Bruising or bleeding in genital/anal areas, or higher thigh areas. Stained or bloody underclothing.
- Unusual mood swings. Restlessness and agitation.
- Unexpected difficulties in sitting or walking.
- Evidence of fear when being offered a bath or assistance with personal care.
- Disturbed sleep pattern.
- Reluctance of person to be alone with an individual known to them.

Discriminatory abuse

This includes all forms of harassment, slurs and/or denial of basic rights, including racist or sexist behaviour, and abuse based on a person's mental or physical disability.

Indicators

- Lack of understanding and training in the needs of individual cultures and beliefs.
- Lack of understanding and training in the needs of specialist groups, e.g. dementia.
- Denial of religious, spiritual or cultural needs.
- Lack of understanding of core values, for example, privacy, choice and fulfilment.

Case histories

The following are all examples of abuse that have occurred. They have been made anonymous to protect the persons involved. Every effort has been made, however, to keep the main features, so that we can learn from such examples and move forward. Many of the examples relate to the community or nursing homes and to nurses as the abusers. This in no way infers that the majority of abuse occurs in these settings, or that nurses are the main abusers. The following examples of abuse could have occurred in any setting and been perpetrated by any person or persons involved in care.

Case history one: Physical abuse

The health authority nursing home inspector received a call from the manager of a nursing agency. The inspector was advised that the matron of a nursing home had contacted the agency manager to complain about the professional conduct of the registered nurse whom they had placed at the nursing home for the night period. At the morning handover, the nurse had told the day staff that she had found a super way of keeping Mrs D (a resident) quiet. Mrs D suffered from Alzheimer's and was in Behavioural Stage 3 of the disease. It was common for her to make continuous repetitive motions with sounds and words. To keep her quiet the nurse had taped up Mrs D's mouth with sticky tape. This had apparently stayed in place throughout the night.

It is difficult even to begin to imagine the immense discomfort, disorientation and anxiety this resident must have suffered. Added to that, the dangers of Mrs D choking were considerable. The case was reported to the UKCC, but was lost some two years later through lack of evidence. The nurse continues to work. (See Box 16.3.)

Box 16.3 Physical abuse

- Professionals can also be guilty of abuse.
- Professionals do not all work to the same standards.
- The restraint used was also psychological abuse and neglect.
- Unqualified staff often feel unable to challenge the nurse/person in charge.
- The stress of caring for persons with dementia can push a person to unacceptable limits.
- Staff need to have ongoing training, development.
- Records must be kept from the first reported instance of alleged abuse. These must be factual (not opinion) and contemporaneous. Do not jump to conclusions.
- It is extremely important to follow local policies and procedures. Remember the primary focus is always on the vulnerable adult.
- Signed and dated statements should be obtained from witnesses at the first possible opportunity while facts are still clear in their minds.

Case history two: Verbal abuse

Anne Marie had worked as a care assistant at 'The Nursing Home' for four years and had left to undertake a position as receptionist at the local GP surgery. Her cousin was a practice nurse at the surgery and Anne Marie shared her concerns regarding 'The Nursing Home' with her. She expressed relief to be no longer working there. Her concerns were: poor staffing levels with little or no direct supervision of care staff; lack of equipment, particularly incontinence supplies, residents were left in wet pads and also wet beds for long periods of time; black dustbin liners were placed under draw sheets on the beds. They were wiped, folded and placed in a bedroom drawer for re-use later. The food served was minimal; there was no choice and second helpings were never offered.

The person in charge, who was also the proprietor, was verbally abusive to the residents. He would become exasperated and call them names such as 'stupid old bat', 'silly old cow', and many more. He would raise his voice and was often rough in handling the residents. He would occasionally apologise afterwards, stating that they would try the patience of a saint. Anne Marie stated that when relatives or visitors were present he was all 'sweetness and light' and came across as caring and totally committed to his work as a nurse. After further consideration and with the support of her cousin, Anne Marie took her concerns to the health authority inspectorate. They agreed to her request for confidentiality.

The inspectors made an unannounced visit to 'The Nursing Home'. The time of the visit coincided with the lunch period and they were able to observe the meal being given. Portions were on the small side and this was discussed at length. The proprietor insisted that a number of residents would still leave some of the food served and that large portions were offputting. He advised the inspectors that some residents had supplementary nutritional drinks prescribed by their GP to support their nutritional needs. This was supported by nutritional assessments outlined in the care plans.

The staffing roster identified the staffing levels to be in accordance with the minimum laid down by the registering authority. The inspectors took the opportunity to speak to some of the staff. They led the discussions round to management of incontinence and did discover that black bin liners were being used. The proprietor advised the inspectors that this was a temporary one-off situation due to the supplier letting them down on their last order. On checking the care plans, no pressure damage was noted, as might have been expected with poor management of incontinence.

Regarding the verbal abuse, there was nothing further they could do. They checked the policies and procedures and noted that there was one on core values and adult abuse. Training on this had been given to the staff. Ironically the document 'Action on Adult Abuse' drawn up jointly by the health authority and social services was pinned up on the notice-board. It was difficult to pick up any possible indicators from the residents. Due to the time of day there were no other persons present. The inspectors had no alternative but to draw their visit to a close with the proviso that they would be visiting again shortly to check incontinence supplies. (See Box 16.4.)

Box 16.4   Verbal abuse

- Besides alleged verbal abuse, the nurse was also guilty of alleged physical abuse (rough handling), psychological abuse (the verbal abuse was intimidating and frightening), and neglect (to use black bin liners was degrading and totally unprofessional even on a short-term basis).
- It is difficult to prove abuse when the victim has cognitive impairment. They are unable to confide in a relative/friend/prime carer. The only way forward is to seek out possible indicators.
- To witness any form of abuse and do nothing is to condone the abuse, and as a result be guilty by association.
- Monitoring may be more productive than active intervention or confrontation.
- Some forms of abuse may eventually be seen as normal and acceptable practice.
- Training and increasing awareness of good care practices is essential.
- Managers should lead by example.
- All members of a caring team should be able to seek help, including management. To seek help is strength not a weakness.

Case history three: Psychological abuse

Mr K went to live with his son and daughter-in-law in 1992. He had lived on his own in Devon for ten years and due to his increasing frailty the decision to move father in with them was taken. There were three children, all in their teens, who had supported the move. He was clearly a much loved member of the family and for a period of time all went smoothly. In May 1994 it became evident that all was not well. He appeared to have fluctuating cognitive ability and had a number of falls. A diagnosis of Lewy Body dementia was made. As both his son and daughter-in-law had full-time jobs and the children were in the process of taking exams, the decision to place Mr K into residential care was made.

Mr and Mrs K were delighted with 'The Nursing Home' and the care given to their father. He had settled more quickly than they could ever have hoped for. In September 1994, Mr K became aware that his father was unsettled. He appeared fearful and was constantly on the move, which in turn had increased his number of falls. When he visited his father, he would repeat the same words: 'The devil comes at night.' This went on and on and, in spite of reassurances that this was possibly a recurring visual hallucination, Mr K continued to worry. One day his father was so disturbed that he decided to revisit in the evening. The night nurse was sympathetic and endeavoured to reassure Mr K. She advised him that at the time of the visit Mr K was asleep, but promised she would keep a close eye on him throughout the night.

At 11.30 pm the nurse in charge told the care assistant that she was taking her break. She had settled down when she realized she had not seen Mr K. It would have been impossible for her to relax knowing she had promised his son she would monitor Mr K. On entering Mr K's room she found the care assistant bending over the bed. When the care assistant heard the nurse enter the room, she turned round. It was clear to see the reason for Mr K's agitation. The care assistant was wearing a devil's mask. When challenged the care assistant stated that it was one way to keep him quiet. (See Box 16.5.)

Case history four: Financial abuse

Mrs Y lived in a bungalow in Buckinghamshire. She had one married son who lived 30 miles away. Mrs Y was a chronic arthritic with poor mobility and a marked short-term memory loss. The district nurse, doctor and social worker were getting increasingly concerned at Mrs Y's ability to remain in her own home, in spite of the package of care in place. As a result, a case conference was arranged. The son attended it and was unhappy when it was suggested that maybe the bungalow could be sold to pay towards residential care. He asked for time to consider alternatives.

Box 16.5   Psychological abuse

- The first step must be the safety and welfare of the victim.
- Unqualified staff cannot be reported to a professional body.
- To refuse to give a reference may speak volumes.
- The unexpected can so often happen.
- Contact with an abuser can leave a care team feeling vulnerable and exposed.
- Counselling may be required.
- Training on all aspects of abuse and the need for sound core values is essential.
- It is important on finding abuse to take responsible action.
- The law offers limited help in psychological abuse, even when the abuse seems significant.

Mr Y contacted the social worker the following week to say that he and his wife would be moving in with his mother and would be there to support her. They sold their own property and used the proceeds to open a new business on a nearby industrial estate. Although there continued to be a very gradual deterioration in Mrs Y's condition, six months passed with minimal occurrences. Shortly after the six-month period, the district nurse sensed that all was not well with Mrs Y. By this time she was completely immobile, doubly incontinent and aphasic.

On a Tuesday morning the district nurse visited Mrs Y. The electric fire in the bedroom was on, but the room felt chilly. On taking Mrs Y's temperature, the nurse found it to be 34 degrees centigrade. As the weather was cold (mid-February), the nurse explained to the son the dangers of hypothermia and the need to keep Mrs Y's room at a constant temperature. The next visit was planned for later in the afternoon, some five to six hours away. Due to her concerns the district nurse decided to call back after two hours to check Mrs Y. On entering the house via the back door (an arrangement previously agreed) and going immediately to see Mrs Y, she found the room cold with no heating on. Her temperature had dropped to 33 degrees centigrade. Following consultation with the doctor, Mrs Y was considered unsafe and was admitted to hospital. She died in hospital two weeks later. (See Box 16.6.)

Case history five: Institutional abuse

By statute, all nursing and residential homes must be inspected at least twice yearly by the health and social services inspectorate. Many additional out-of-hours visits are also made. It was on one of these visits that the following cases of abuse were discovered.

> **Box 16.6   Financial abuse**
>
> - All persons have the right to have their finances safeguarded so that they are used for their benefit.
> - Financial abuse often leads to or links in with other types of abuse.
> - The other types of abuse included neglect, physical abuse and psychological abuse.
> - Recognizing abuse can leave a care team at risk, especially when one person is visiting alone in the victim's home. Where suspicions arise, visiting in pairs is advisable.
> - The importance of multidisciplinary working is paramount. It is also essential that common agreed policies and procedures are in place.
> - Good support, documentation and communication within the team are essential.
> - Financial abuse is very often difficult to prove and can often be indirect.

'The Nursing Home' was registered for 25 elderly mentally frail residents. The two inspectors arrived at 'The Nursing Home' at 11 pm. There was one registered nurse on duty and two care assistants. All was very quiet and everything appeared to be in order. All fire doors were closed and staffing was in accordance with the minimum levels laid down by the registering authority. Training was discussed with each member of staff and it was evident that training on fire safety, moving and handling was being strictly adhered to. Each member of staff stated that they had had an induction period on commencing work at the home and enjoyed working there. In fact all seemed correct.

One inspector asked the nurse to take them through a typical night and explain their work patterns. All appeared to be going smoothly until the nurse reached the early morning period. The statement went: 'At five thirty we put all the lights on.' When asked to clarify the statement as to which lights actually went on, she stated without any possible concern 'Why, all of them.' When asked why, the inspectors were informed that it was to allow the residents to wake up slowly and for them to check that no one had died during the night. The nurse was asked if it was acceptable to wake up the residents so early and would it not be more beneficial to let them sleep. The reply was simply that it did not matter; they all had dementia and did not know what day it was, let alone what time. It was simply the best routine for the home. The nurse was advised of her professional accountability and the inspectors made it abundantly clear that her actions amounted to professional misconduct.

A meeting with the proprietor and the matron of the home was held the following morning. Both stated that they were unaware of the early morning routine and would not have approved it. This claim to ignorance was not

---

Box 16.7   Institutional abuse

- The actions taken by 'The Nursing Home' staff were also discriminatory abuse and physical abuse.
- Persons with dementia have the same rights as any other person.
- Different forms of abuse often co-exist.
- Abuse can be indirect and unintentional.
- Leadership and supervision of all staff is essential. It is totally unacceptable for management and senior staff to be unaware of poor practice.
- Training is essential in all homes to ensure that staff are aware of the different types of abuse.
- Intervention and monitoring is often the better solution.
- Work undertaken within a home can become so routine that the persons undertaking the work no longer see the error of what they are doing.
- Setting routines that deal with work in a collective way is to totally ignore each resident as an individual.

---

accepted. They were the people in charge and it was their responsibility to know how work was managed. The need for training was discussed at length. (See Box 16.7.)

Case history six: Neglect and acts of omission

Mr M was admitted to 'The Nursing Home' on 21 May from the local general hospital. His admission to the hospital had been the result of a fractured femur that had required surgical intervention. Prior to his admission, Mr M had been living in sheltered housing and had been managing relatively well with the support of the community services. However, the period of time in hospital had been fraught with difficulties due to the fact that Mr M had Alzheimer's disease and the trauma had accentuated any difficulties that were beginning to emerge. On admission to the nursing home the initial records stated: 'Reluctant to stand and will require two nurses to transfer. Necrotic area on his left heel, small broken area on back of right calf, left heel has a blister which is broken.'

On 23 May the records stated: 'Ability to mobilise – no pressure sore risk assessment – very high risk. Patient incontinent of urine and faeces. Incipient sacral sore.'

On admission Mr M was placed on a duvet-style overlay, designed to improve patient comfort and reduce but not relieve pressure on relevant parts of the body. Records identify repeated requests for more effective pressure-relieving equipment due to 'skin breaking down in all areas'.

Ongoing reports identify Mr M as having constant diarrhoea, severe pain and unable to take adequate food and drink. There were no records of any turning regime to relieve pressure until 14 June. A pressure-relieving mattress was not provided until 1 July. There was minimum evidence of attention being paid to the severe pain, which was constantly recorded night after night. Statements were recorded such as 'cries out at the least touch' and 'appears to have considerable pain and discomfort, even when at rest'. There were constant references to diarrhoea, but little or no intervention noted. There was no nutritional assessment and no records of supplementary feeds. No referral was made to a continence advisor, dietician, tissue viability nurse or pain control specialist. There was no evidence of any sensory stimulation of any kind.

On 8 July a statement from the records read: 'ulcer to sacrum eight inches in length, open a further two and half inches of tissue ulceration, approximate depth of wound six inches tracking to the right under the skin for approximately a further two inches'. Mr M died on 16 July with a diagnosis of septicaemia. The care given was all to little and too late.

The above situation was identified when the son complained to the health authority about the lack of care given to his father whilst a resident at 'The Nursing Home'. The complaint was made following Mr M's death. During the process of investigation the above points, being just few of many, came to light. The senior nursing staff were adamant that Mr M had received good care. They advised the inspectors that they had endeavoured to contact the tissue viability nurse without success. They also stated that the doctor had visited frequently. Unfortunately, not all the doctor's visits were recorded and there was no evidence of any attempt to contact any specialist nurses or doctors. Pressure-relieving equipment was too little and too late. Only minimal assessments of individual needs had been made. No efforts were evident with regard to any sensory stimulation. (See Box 16.8.)

Box 16.8 Neglect and acts of omission

- Care can only be as good as the information on which it is based. A full assessment of all care needs, mental and physical is essential.
- Requests for visits, discussions with relatives and contacts with other professionals should be recorded. It is impossible to remember days, weeks, months or years later what happened and in what order.
- The suffering and anxiety felt by the relatives when reading their father's notes should not be underestimated.
- Ongoing training is essential.
- Withholding access to other professionals is a denial of rights and a form of physical abuse.
- Relatives should be encouraged to be partners in care. Their contribution can be invaluable.

Case history seven: Sexual abuse

It was in 1993 that Mr K noticed some marked changes in Mrs K. They had been married 47 years and had reportedly been a happy couple. His initial concerns were her forgetfulness and the fact that she had become quite distant, especially when discussing important family issues. When challenged she would become quite angry and Mr K found it easier to back down and take the line of least resistance. He confided in his son, but Mrs K seemed adept at putting on a good social facade when other people were present, which hid the forgetfulness and her fluctuating changes in behaviour.

In 1994 Mr K finally consulted his doctor, who in turn referred Mrs K to the consultant in old age psychiatry. A diagnosis of Alzheimer's disease was made. By this time Mrs K had deteriorated considerably and was visibly disorientated in both time and place. The total responsibilities of running the home were left to Mr K.

Added to the above Mrs K developed marked mood swings and had a reluctance to be in the same room as her husband. Mrs K also wandered around the house during both the day and night, often making repetitive noises and motions. The family were concerned for their mother, but also for their father. It was agreed after a family conference that Mrs K should be placed in residential care. A residential home was chosen near the family home, making daily visiting possible. Mr K spent considerable time at the residential home and felt a weight had been lifted off his shoulders. He requested that he should have a key to his wife's room to allow them some privacy. The manager of the home willingly gave this. It soon became evident to the staff that the purpose of the key was to allow Mr and Mrs K to have an intimate period of time together. As husband and wife they had no concerns about this; Mr K seemed a most devoted husband.

Three months after admission to the home the care staff noted changes in Mrs K's behaviour following her husband's visits. She would become quite distraught, sometimes for hours, and say 'no, no, no, don't touch, bad, bad, bad' over and over again. She was also unable or unwilling to make eye contact and would cower in a chair and cry. Staff members were upset as they found it impossible to comfort Mrs K. Eventually the carers went as a group to management to seek advice on how best to proceed. At first management took no action, until a strong-minded carer advised them that if no action were taken she would take it upon herself to go to the police.

The management of the home requested a full reassessment and case review. In this instance the police were not involved. It was evident however that Mrs K no longer recognized or accepted Mr K as her husband and any attempt on his part to be sexually intimate would constitute, at the very least, indecent assault. Abuse can so often be indirect and unintentional. Mr K was indeed a caring husband and he was clinging on to what had been such a normal part of their married life. He had failed to understand that

---

Box 16.9   Sexual abuse

The indicators, which give warnings of abuse, need to be understood. Mrs K's change in behaviour and her attempts at trying to avoid being with her husband were clear messages to staff for help. Abuse procedures are essential and must be followed. They should include:

- Initial action required.
- Planning the investigation.
- Multidisciplinary involvement.
- Planning, discussing and deciding the most appropriate way forward.
- Discussing and deciding on the need for a medical examination (welfare needs and/or evidence gathering to be balanced).
- Ensuring accurate contemporaneous records are in place from the first indication of abuse. They must all be signed and dated.
- Ongoing support for staff should be in place for as long as required.
- All agencies must work together in partnership to ensure that every person in care is protected and has their rights upheld.
- The idea of an elderly person still being sexually active is a foreign one to many young people. This should not be the case. If both adults are able to consent and there is no unlawful reason to prevent them from forming a sexual relationship, this should be respected.
- Vulnerable adults may not be able to make an informed decision because of lack of capacity and/or reliance on other people who may not feel as aggrieved as they do. They simply may not be able to communicate and may not realize they have been abused. Despite these problems, every person has a right to justice and to have their rights both understood and upheld.

Mrs K no longer knew him as her husband and was unable to take part in sexual activities. (See Box 16.9.)

Case history eight: Discriminatory abuse

A popular residential home was set in six acres of landscaped gardens. There were numerous quiet areas to sit in. A large conservatory adjoined one side of the residential home and was specially designed for all-year use. There were three other lounges in the home; two had views of the garden but one was part of the original building and had large leaded windows, which let in minimum natural light. The walls were dark wood and although they had a degree of elegance they were rather dull. This room was specifically used for the residents with dementia. It was out of the way and, according to the director of the home, 'restful for this type of resident'. The residents were seated in chairs placed against the walls. Not surprisingly, there appeared to be no interaction between residents.

Box 16.10   Discriminatory abuse

- Persons with dementia have a right to:
  - privacy but not isolation, carers should facilitate social inclusion
  - respect as an individual
  - be assisted at all times with a high standard of personal presentation
  - be given as much sensory stimulation as possible
  - be understood as an individual.
- Persons with dementia have a right to be cared for by knowledgeable, competent and suitably qualified staff. Training and understanding of the needs of persons with dementia is paramount.
- Working patterns within a home can become common practice/routine.
- Those in charge are too close at times to see more appropriate ways of caring or making changes.
- It is easy to make assumptions and stereotype people.
- Isolation is a form of psychological abuse.

The proprietor was advised to send staff on a care-giving in dementia course, 'A Positive Vision'. Many changes were made as a result. A section of the conservatory was set aside for the residents with dementia and the seating arrangements enabled better eye and body contact. The subsequent change in many of the residents was remarkable. (See Box 16.10.)

The way ahead

The 1990s have witnessed a significant growth of interest in adult abuse. Many documents giving advice, new books, support groups, joint disciplinary policies and procedures are emerging at a rapid rate. All lead to the same conclusion that vulnerable adults should be enabled to live and receive services in an environment which is free from prejudice and safe from abuse. Where there is any suspicion of abuse the agencies involved should aim to provide a responsive service, which is prompt, sensitive, effective, balanced and aware. Persons with dementia are among the most vulnerable people in society. The Department of Health document (Wright 2001) states:

> Point 11. No one can give consent on behalf on an incompetent adult. However, you may still treat such a patient if the treatment would be in their best interests. 'Best interests' go wider than best medical interests, to include factors such as the wishes and beliefs of the patient when competent, their current wishes, their general well-being and their spiritual and religious welfare. People close to the patient may be able to help to give you information on some of these factors. Where the patient has never been competent, relatives, carers and friends may be best placed to advise on the patient's needs and preferences.

There should be documentation of a patient's life history, and important preferences, collected from the person themselves, their family and important others. However, where this is not so, carers must be detectives in uncovering what the choices, desires and beliefs are, for the person no longer able to let their wishes be known.

Persons with dementia have the right to be free from abuse in all its forms and remain a respected and valued individual in a civilized society. It requires willingness, honesty and some degree of risk (courage), on the part of all caregivers to acknowledge that adult abuse exists. The case studies illustrate some of the complex and harrowing situations with which professional workers are faced when working with vulnerable persons. Adult abuse has equal status with other forms of violence such as child abuse. To be aware and to take no action is to condone and be 'guilty by association' as a consequence. There is a duty to care.

References

Bennett, G. and Ogg, J. (1992) *Elder Abuse in Britain*, London: Department of Health, Care of the Elderly.

Biggs, S., Phillipson, C. and Kingston, P. (2000) *Elder Abuse in Perspective*, Buckingham: Open University Press.

Dunn, P. (2000) *No Secrets*, London: Dept of Health.

Johnson, T. (1986) 'Critical issues in the definition of Elder Abuse', in K. Pillemer and R. Wolf (eds) *Elder Abuse*, Dover, MA: Auburn House.

Law Commission No 231 (1995) 'Mental Incapacity'.

Nursing and Midwifery Council (2002) *Practitioner–Client Relationships and the Prevention of Abuse*, London: Nursing and Midwifery Council.

Professional Conduct Committee UKCC (2001) 'More nurses are being struck off', *Nursing Times* 97, 11: 7.

Stevenson, M.L. (1999) *Elder Abuse Alert – Considerations about a Hidden Problem*. Virginia State University and Virginia Polytechnic Institute and State University, Virginia Cooperative Extension. Publication No: 350–251, July 1999.

Wright, C. (2001) *Twelve Key Points on Consent. The Law in England.* London: Dept of Health.

Additional reading

Alzheimer's Society (1998) *Mistreatment of People with Dementia and Their Carers: What to Do if You Suspect Mistreatment*, 2nd Edn, London: Action on Elder Abuse.

Anderson, P. (1999) 'Enough is enough', *Nursing Times* 1: 4.

Briggs, K. and Askham, J. (1999) *The Needs of People with Dementia and Those Who Care for Them*, London: Action on Elder Abuse.

Bright, L. (1994) *Harm's Way*, London: Counsel and Care.

Bunce, C. (2001) 'Adding insult to injury: Residents with dementia are being hit the hardest', *Nursing Times* 97, 36: 22–3.

Jenkins, G. (1995) *Taking Action on Elder Abuse – Everybody's Business*, London: Action on Elder Abuse.

Jenkins, G., Asif, A. and Bennett, G. (2000) *Listening is not Enough: An Analysis of Response of Calls to Elder Abuse Response, Action on Elder Abuse's National Helpline*, London: Action on Elder Abuse.

Macdonald, A. (2000) 'The vicious circle of the system: Who is responsible for abuse of people with dementia?', *Dementia Care Journal* 8: 5.

Manthorpe, J. (1999) 'The great taboo', Conference papers on sexual abuse of older people, London: Action on Elder Abuse.

McCreadie, C. (2001) *Making Connections: Good Practice in the Prevention and Management of Elder Abuse*, London: Kings College Age Concern.

Papadopoulos, A. and Fontaine, J.L. (2000) *Elder Abuse: Therapeutic Perspectives in Practice*, Oxford: Winslow Press.

Pritchard, J. (1999) *Elder Abuse Work, Best Practice in Britain and Canada*, London: Jessica Kingsley 585–8.

Register UKCC (2002) 'Verbal abuse and inappropriate restraint of patients'. UKCC Winter, 38.

Slater, P. and Eastman, M. (1999) *Elder Abuse: 'Critical Issues in Policy and Practice'*, London: Age Concern.

Stratham, D. (1992) *What if They Hurt Themselves?* London: Counsel and Care.

Wagner, G. (1991) *Not Such Private Places*, London: Counsel and Care.

Wolf, R. and McMurray Anderson, S. (eds) (1996) *Journal of Elder Abuse and Neglect*, Howarth Maltreatment and Trauma Press 8: 3.

Useful addresses

Action on Elder Abuse, Astral House, 1268 London Road, London SW16 4ER. Registered Charity no. 1048397.

Alzheimer's Society, Gordon House, 10 Greencoat Place, London SW1P 1PH. Registered Charity no. 2115499.

Counsel and Care, Twyman House, 16 Bonny Street, London NW1 9PG. Registered Charity no. 203429.

Relatives and Residents Association, 5 Tavistock Place, London WC1H 9SN. Registered Charity no. 10201194.

Part V

Ethical issues

Chapter 17

Between autonomy and security

Ethical questions in the care of elderly persons with dementia in nursing homes

Cees Hertogh

Every day Mrs Johnson asks to go home: she has to collect the children from school. Why is she locked up here? Around five o'clock she is always at the big glass doors of the ward entrance, asking people to let her out and constantly rattling the door handle.

Mr Billings roams about the nursing home all day, proud and upright. What wretches all these other residents here are! Luckily he can help them a bit now and then. He refuses all help himself when the care staff want to help him wash and dress in the morning: he's an adult and can do it himself.

Introduction

Ethical questions do not only arise in psychogeriatrics when difficult decisions have to be made about medical treatment, when it is a question of whether or not to comply with a euthanasia request or a compulsory admission. A lot has been said and written about these subjects already. The more mundane problems like those of Mrs Johnson and Mr Billings are also examples of care situations, in which ethical questions arise. The way in which caregivers deal with these situations and respond to the behaviour outlined above always begs the question of whether they are doing the right thing. These examples are just two of many in which the question of doing the right thing plays an important part – either in the foreground or the background. The management of persons with dementia therefore has an undeniably ethical dimension. But which maxims and values should we apply? Why do caregivers regularly feel that they are not doing the right thing, even when they are doing their best?

These questions are central to this discussion of ethical problems in the care of persons with dementia. A number of them, and definitely those outlined above, in one way or another relate to the principle of respect for autonomy, the central principle of current ethics. Many nursing homes have specified in their mission statement that respect for autonomy must be the basis of care: 'It means that patients can lead their own lives and make their own choices where possible and despite a dependency on care' (NVVz, 1993).

Naturally no one would deny or negate the importance of such an endeavour and of course care staff make every effort to make this possible for their patients. But persons with dementia are usually admitted into nursing homes because they have largely lost the ability to make their own choices and live their own lives. They often already need assistance with the most simple action or choice. Simply respecting the freedom of choice of Mrs Johnson and Mr Billings would place them in a situation of inadequate care. By reasoning here, as the current ethic proposes, on the basis of the incompetence argument, care staff are given a legitimate reason for not respecting the person's choice, but they are not given any guidance to help them respond to the questions and wishes these now 'legally incompetent' persons still express. This leads us to consider whether the ethical framework defined by respect for autonomy and competence is really suitable for the life situation and care requirements of persons with dementia.

In this discussion we will demonstrate that respect for autonomy definitely has a place in the care of elderly persons with dementia, but not as the sole or dominant maxim. This does not do justice to persons with dementia, and even less so to their caregivers, and results in a situation in which practical dilemmas can only be managed inadequately, as the unilateral emphasis on autonomy gives this principle an importance over and above that of more or less all other moral considerations. In Callahan's words (1985) 'autonomy thus becomes more an obsession than a moral principle'. This bias has meant that in recent decades prevailing biomedical ethics have increasingly come under fire, not just from the practical point of view but also from the point of view of ethical theory. Alternative ethical approaches have been sought from various perspectives in order to do better justice to the moral intuitions and experience of care staff and to the specific nature of care-giving and caring relationships. One of these is what is referred to as the 'the ethic of care', which draws attention to other dimensions of human existence, such as relationality, interdependence and mutual involvement, as a response to the current dominance of values such as independence and autonomy. Various ideas and views have also grown out of pychogeriatric practice in relation to 'proper care' for persons with dementia, which share a common feature in that they try to connect with the subjective experience of the person with dementia. In the Netherlands this is known as the 'perception-based approach'. For many this primarily calls to mind psychosocial therapies (validation, reminiscence, snoezelen sensory therapy) and environment-related measures, and not immediately ethics. Such a view incorrectly misses how such methods are linked to ethics. The following section shows how such 'perception-based care' methods respect and disseminate ethical values. These are closely related to the above-mentioned perspective of the 'care ethic' and are relevant to the creation of an ethical framework that better supports psychogeriatric care practice than a (unilateral) ethic based on 'autonomy and self-determination'. First of all however, we must look at the meaning and background of 'respect for autonomy'.

Respect for autonomy as a guiding moral principle

The emergence of the principle of respect for autonomy within health care and its ethics dates back to the 1970s and is primarily the result of patient emancipation. Democratization, which had already taken place in many areas of society, was also extended in the 1970s and 1980s to the field of health care. In this process the authority to make decisions relating to care and treatment was moved from the physician to the patient. Medical treatment is not permitted without free and uncoerced consent from the patient, and patients cannot actually exercise their (decisional) autonomy without accurate and full information.

In itself this is a positive development which we all wanted: everyone at first sight wants to be in control over what happens to them in matters relating to their health and welfare and we prefer others not to make decisions for and about us. In the meantime legislation passed in the 1980s and 1990s formalized the demand for self-determination in the Medical Contract Act (WGBO), a statutory provision which in the view of many can be seen as completing and affirming patient emancipation. In both this law and in modern ethics respect for autonomy is embodied in: (a) the doctrine of informed consent; (b) the reassessment of the doctor–patient relationship in terms of a contractual agreement with mutual (enforceable) rights and obligations.

Philosophical background

The principle of 'respect for autonomy' however has elderly philosophical roots, which we need to look at here in order to be able to assess its implications and meaning, because it also specifically expresses a well-defined anthropology and a vision of human relationships. The term 'autonomy' is made up of the Greek words *autos* (self) and *nomos* (law) and literally means: 'making one's own laws'. The term originated from political theory and until the sixteenth century it was only used to indicate the administrative independence of cities and states, which was expressed in their power to make their own laws. The extent to which individual lives were independent within the political community is a different question, which only becomes significant in terms of political theory in the seventeenth century, when philosophers started to consider society in terms of a social contract: an agreement between independent individuals with the aim of ensuring peaceful coexistence, whilst recognizing mutual rights and obligations. 'Respect for' autonomy in this context means guaranteeing the freedom of action of the individual within society. In principle this is a *negative* freedom: I am free to the extent that no person or authority interferes with my actions. According to John Stuart Mill, it is 'the only freedom which deserves the name'. Only if I damage the interests of others in the pursuit of my own interests is there reason to restrict my freedom. However, Mill clearly understood that the freedom he prized so highly had to be subject to certain conditions for people to be able to live with it. In his view, negative freedom is only given to people 'in the maturity of their faculties', in other words not to children or the mentally ill, because they do not have the necessary and required capacity for freedom of action.

This indicates a second aspect of the principle of respect for autonomy, an aspect which has its roots in the ideas of the Enlightenment. The essence of the emancipatory thinking of the Enlightenment philosophers focuses specifically on the view that people can control their own destiny by making use of their intellect.

Immanuel Kant refers in this respect not to autonomy but to 'Mündigkeit' and Enlightenment, which he – in terms, which sound quite contemporary – describes as 'the withdrawal of people from the "Unmündigkeit" [tutelage], for which they only have themselves to blame'. People are incapable of 'Mündigkeit' as long as they allow themselves to be led and controlled by others and do not have the courage to think for themselves. Their tutelage does not result from a lack of intellect but a lack of determination to rely on their own thinking and power of judgement. Power of judgement, rationality and intellectual appraisal are therefore important conditions for negative freedom and respect for autonomy therefore refers to autonomy as a faculty or capacity and assumes its existence.

On the basis of this brief summary, the principle of respect for autonomy can now be described as follows. Respect for autonomy means: offering people a negative freedom (Mill) on the basis of the assumption, which is also a condition, that – because of their rationality and power of judgement – they are individuals who make decisions for and about themselves and are self-determining (Kant) (Komrad 1983). In other words, it means offering the space to act and make decisions to – literally – self-sufficient individuals.

Further characteristics of this concept, which are clear from its background in political philosophy and thinking about the organization of society, are that the normative significance of this principle primarily relates to the public realm of interactions between equal citizens with rights and obligations in respect of each other and the government. The question which then arises is whether or not such a 'respect' for autonomy can also be considered to apply to other sorts of human relationships, such as those between caregiver and care receiver, carer and the person being cared for. Caregivers are not primarily motivated by a desire to implement respect for autonomy, even though they do attach a high level of importance to respectful treatment and freedom of choice. In health care, morally speaking, the primary focus is on a concerned response to human vulnerability, as demonstrated in illness and dependence (on care). How can these diverging moral perspectives be reconciled?

Criticism of the dominant position of (respect for) autonomy

This search for the link between respect for autonomy as an external maxim and the internal morality of health care practice has been high on the medical ethics agenda in recent decades. In their influential and frequently reprinted *Principles of Biomedical Ethics*, Beauchamps and Childress (1994) tried to establish this link by stating that medical treatment is governed by four equivalent moral principles: (respect for) autonomy, beneficence, non-malificence and justice. In the words of Childress (1990): 'Respect for autonomy does not exhaust moral life. Other principles are important, not only where autonomy reaches its limits. For example, focusing narrowly on the principle of respect for autonomy can foster indifference; thus the principles of care and beneficence are necessary. But without the limits set by the principle of respect for autonomy, these other principles may support arrogant enforcement of "the good" for others.' In this view respect for autonomy is a restricting but also a restricted moral principle. It is restricting in that it prevents or should prevent third parties (here read physicians and other caregivers) interfering illegitimately with the freedom of choice of the patient, but it is also of restricted application in that it must be balanced against other moral principles.

This may be the case, but in the meantime enforceable rights have been associated with respect for autonomy, enshrined in the legislation and regulations, which have given this principle relatively greater validity than the others, specifically the practical internal maxims of medical practice. This greater validity also comes to the forefront in what is referred to as the autonomy–paternalism debate, to which medical ethics have been confined since then. As proposed by Dworkin (1971), paternalism was described as a form of coercion exercised on patients, justified by motives such as beneficence, the promotion of welfare, good fortune, etc. This discussion has not been very fruitful. In it the relation between helping professionals and patients was considered unilaterally from a sort of conflict model and the main focus was on the conflicting interests of professionals and patients. As a result, 'paternalism' became a sort of modern term of abuse, used for anyone who questions autonomy as a value. Essentially however, the concepts autonomy and paternalism are no more than two sides of the same coin: both relate to the contours of the portrait of mankind outlined above, in which humanity is automatically identified with being autonomous and independent. This portrait of mankind is a long way from the experiences of disease and illness. In fact its abstract and unilateral nature is clearly demonstrated by the very existence of such things as care-giving and caring practices.

The focus of ethics on values like autonomy and self-determination is understandable against the background of the autocratic medical culture of the 1950s and 1960s and the prevailing social relationships at the time, in which the physician's authority dominated the patient's view to too great an extent. But the reaction to this resulted in such compartmentalization of ethical thinking that the vision of the moral specificity of caring and health care practice was lost. In recent years criticism of this unilateral autonomy-based ethic has become increasingly strong. Attention has been drawn, for example, to the excesses to which it has led in some areas of health care, such as in psychiatry, where the right to self-determination has, according to Applebaum and Gutheil (1979), become 'a right to rot'. Reference is also made to the need for ethical theory to be more closely linked to care practice, in order to see the practical context not just as an area of application for moral concepts but also as a source of moral knowledge. This is why we are going to look now at the 'practice of care for persons with dementia' and the ideas that prevail there about 'good care' for persons with dementia.

Perception-based care

Ilse Warners (1998) makes a strong plea for an approach to persons with dementia, which subsequently became known as 'perception-based' care in elderly care. She criticizes the preconception that persons with dementia are not fully aware of their situation: 'The assumption that persons with dementia do not perceive their situation or environment results in an attitude on the part of other people, which encourages dementia, both at microlevel, in personal contact and on a larger scale in care-giving policy.'

This criticism and the related plea to caregivers and care staff to seek contact with the subjective world of persons with dementia retrospectively marks a change in thinking on the subject of elderly care: a move from care based mainly on activities of daily living (ADL) deficiencies to an approach which no longer sees the language of persons with dementia as gibberish and which no longer confronts their behaviour as problem behaviour. Thus, the perception-based approach advocates emancipation of the person with dementia, but this emancipation follows a different pattern from that of the emancipation of competent patients. Based on a psychodynamic perspective of dementia, perception-based care focuses on the 'otherness' of persons with dementia and demands recognition of their specific care needs and the necessary expertise of care staff.

The fact that persons with dementia experience their situation and can suffer as a result is the essence of perception-based care. Persons with dementia can therefore rightly be called 'patients', without implying selection of the medical model. On this basis perception-based care does not just oppose the restricted and restricting view of a simply custodial approach, it also opposes what is referred to as the 'strategy of normalization' in elderly care; in other words the tendency to present life in a nursing home and that of its residents as being as normal as possible. As a result persons with dementia are possibly confronted to a lesser degree with their disabilities, but there is also the risk that their problems become less visible. Third and finally, the perception-based approach is a response to the disappointing results of the reality orientation therapy (ROT) of the 1970s. 'Good care', from a perception-based perspective, is care which tries to use the subjective experience of patients as guidance for treatment and communication. 'Keeping time' with persons with dementia is more important than 'keeping up to date' at all costs for those who find it hard to keep up with the times. This 'keeping time' does not mean indiscriminate confirmation of feelings and perceptions, but pursuit of contact with the aim of bringing order and cohesion to the way in which persons with dementia experience themselves and their reality. It is a matter of seeing persons with dementia as 'people who are open to influences from their environment but who can no longer fit all the information into a meaningful structure' (Warners 1998). This also assigns to perception-based care a certain therapeutic nature, where the care objectives are formulated not in terms of cure but in terms of well-being and in terms of restoration of the relationship with the environment.

Theoretical models

Despite a certain correspondence in respect of (moral) principles and practical starting points, there is (as yet) no complete theory as a basis for perception-based care. Research in this field is methodologically complex, as persons with dementia – as the disease progresses – are increasingly less able to share their experience with others. 'Delirium patients' are sometimes able to recount some detail of how they felt in this confused state after their delirium has passed, but persons with dementia do not have this option. Perception-based theories are often based on more or less characteristic behaviour of persons with dementia.

Miesen bases his theory of attachment and parent fixation on the typical way in which persons with dementia ask for their father and mother. He explains this behaviour on the basis of Bowlby's views of the role of attachment and attachment behaviour in developmental psychology. From this perspective the fact that persons with dementia ask for their parents is not so much indicative of memory problems but of feelings of fear, which are aroused by dementia. Parent fixation and attachment behaviour (seeking attachment figures) according to Miesen primarily represent the need of persons with dementia for safety and security. Such behaviour illustrates that persons with dementia experience their cognitive decline as an alienating and stressful situation (Miesen 1993).

Verdult (1993) draws on the work of Piaget and humanist psychology and takes the phenomenon of persons with dementia living increasingly in the past as a basis for his hypothesis that dementia is a reversal of the life course. The memories of persons with dementia roll up, as it were, and patients increasingly return to their childhood, relive experiences from their past and increasingly revert to early childhood experiences.

Dröes (1997) starts from the hypotheses that problem behaviour in persons with dementia (for example, suspicion and agitation) can be interpreted as an attempt to cope with and adapt to the disease. In this respect she assigns a central significance to both Lazarus and Folkmann's adaptation-coping theory and what is referred to as Moos and Tsu's 'crisis model', based on studies of seriously somatically ill patients (Dröes 1997).

All these theories, and I have limited myself here to a few examples from Dutch-speaking regions, offer meaningful starting points for care practice, but they cannot be generalized to all phases of dementia. There is also the question of how these different psychological approaches to dementia relate to the biomedical perspective and the neuropathological changes the disease brings at substrate level, as it were in the 'hardware' of the cerebrum. A lot of research still needs to be carried out and intensive cooperation is required between researchers working in the field of psychogeriatrics from different disciplines, including medicine, psychology and neuropsychology.

The moral challenge of dementia care: 'mending a fractured world'

Saying that persons with dementia perceive their situation – the basis of perception-based care – does not mean that they are aware of their dementia or that they have insight into the developing problems; on the contrary, illness insight disappears in many patients during the course of their disease, not infrequently at a relatively early stage. There are various explanations for this, both psychogenic (denial) and neurogenic (frontal damage) (see also chapters 1, 3 and 12), but the effect is the same: caregivers and the people they care for no longer share the same reality with regard to the trauma of dementia and its consequences (Bahro 1995; Zanetti 1999). Loss of insight (or anosognosia) marks the first stage in the gradual loss of a commonly shared world of experience, which in a relational sense is so characteristic of dementia. This is one of the most important causes of stress and overload for informal carers and a frequent reason why partners and family have to transfer care to the nursing home. Also, this lack of insight demonstrates a crucial difference between palliative care for people with somatic disorders and (palliative) care for persons with dementia. Denial is also a known phenomenon in palliative oncological care, where it impedes contact between patients and care staff. But if their mental faculties remain intact, many oncology patients develop a definite understanding of the fate their disease has in store for them; a process in which patients and their partners can support each other on the basis of a shared reality. This perspective of commonality is absent with dementia and this absence causes confusion for both informal and formal caregivers. The absence of illness insight in persons with dementia can fill them with feelings of impotence and inability when it comes to justifying and legitimizing their actions in respect of patients. How can they deal with feelings of suspicion and incomprehension in patients in respect of their admission to a nursing home, when the actual reason for this – their cognitive decline – is itself 'absent' from the subjective world of persons with dementia? How can they comply with the right to (objective) information based on respect for autonomy, when such information only meets with disagreement and denial?

Perception-based care tries, as it were, to build a bridge between the two worlds – that of the caring environment and the world of perception of the person with dementia. It emphasizes that persons with dementia – despite any appearance to the contrary – are actually actively occupied with keeping their identity and world intact, however strange the means they use to do so may appear in the first instance. So perception-based care tries to compensate as it were for the person with dementia's loss of insight and competence by improving the caregivers' expertise and understanding in order to maintain contact and communication between both parties. However, the tragedy of dementia is that this contact is ultimately doomed to decrease and ultimately to be lost. This unavoidable pattern characterizes the moral responsibility care staff have to face again and again. They must enter into a relationship that can only be developed to a limited degree because the progress of dementia means that there can be no permanent basis of trust from which contact between care receiver and caregiver can grow. Any contact that might be established seems unavoidably to disappear again during the course of the disease process, which is why Martin and Post (1992) refer to caring for persons with advanced dementia as a 'labour of Sisyphus'.

Nevertheless some perception-based authors suggest that persons with dementia have a need and are able to maintain contact with their environment at all stages of their dementia. Verdult (1997), for example, asserts that persons with dementia remain 'intentional' until the last phase of their illness. As the ability to communicate via language diminishes, the use of sensory stimuli and physical contact replace it as means of achieving proximity, in which persons with dementia can experience themselves and their environment. This idea legitimizes the role of techniques like snoezelen sensory therapy or sensory activation in care for persons with severe dementia. Care staff often set great store by this. On the one hand these techniques give them the opportunity to do 'more' for the persons in advanced stages of dementia than just washing them, changing their clothes and giving them food. On the other hand they often experience a form of contact and reciprocity in the reactions of patients to snoezelen activities, even if only transitory, in the form of a glance or smile. Given what has just been said above about the progress of dementia, the question is whether such physical signs can be assumed to indicate a world of internal perception. Neuropathological and neuropsychological research in any case tends to indicate a negative response to this question. As the disease progresses, the ability of patients to experience feelings and emotions and to experience themselves as distinct from their environment progressively decreases. An important psychological point in this process is the loss of recognition of the patient's own reflection, a stage towards the disappearance of self-consciousness. In the final stage of dementia, according to Antonio Damasio (1999), patients in fact remain awake and respond in simple ways to people and objects, but no longer have normal consciousness or sense of self and other. Where this sense of self is absent, so too are emotions, according to Damasio (1999).

Many caregivers are however unwilling to agree with such a conclusion. It does not correspond to their experience and even seems to be denied by their experience. But the one does not exclude the other. That care staff assign significance to facial expressions and physical language perceived in persons with dementia indicates an essential characteristic of care as a relational process. In the literature this phenomenon is reflected in the relationship between mother and newborn. There are processes of assigning significance to physical language here too, the 'crying' and 'laughing', which by no means correspond to conscious experiences on the part of the newborn, as the newborn is simply not capable of such, due to the immaturity of its central nervous system. The mother interprets a behaviour, still predominantly governed by reflexes, within a world of meaning to which the newborn does not yet have access. But such interpretations are necessary in order to establish a relationship in which care can be given. This applies both to the mother–child relationship and equally to the relationship between care staff and patients with severe dementia. Something which appears not to be possible (any longer) from a neurological perspective – the existence of emotions and mutual contact – is 'added' by care staff themselves to their management of patients as a necessary condition for care and carefulness. For without human relatedness, without any form of reciprocity – even if it is just the illusion of this – care not only loses its value and meaning, it also becomes almost impossible to give.

A perception-based ethic?

The limitations of the concept of autonomy in relation to care for persons with dementia have of course not escaped the attention of ethicists. None-theless the focus on autonomy as independence and respect for autonomy as a negative freedom for many ethicists remains at the forefront of their attempts to explain the moral questions which arise due to the acquired dependence of persons with dementia. An illustration of this is Oppenheimer's (1991) proposal that persons with dementia should be given a 'protected milieu of autonomy'. The dementia process means that whenever choices or decisions have to be made, the question may be asked whether persons with dementia can assess their situation and are able to make a decision. According to Oppenheimer, this is an undesirable and unnecessarily restrictive approach. He therefore proposes starting from a protected milieu of autonomy: a 'space' in which persons with dementia have freedom of choice and behaviour, until it becomes clear that this freedom results in danger to life and welfare. Only then is there reason to assess the decision-making capacity of the person and possibly take over responsibility for choices and decisions.

The advantage of this approach is that it offers persons with dementia freedom of action, even if they act unwisely. People without dementia have that right, so why not people with dementia? Within this approach they do not have to earn their freedom from choice to choice and their behaviour is respected, even if there may be reason for doubting their decision-making capacity. The concept of a 'protected autonomy' therefore offers a guarantee against excessive protection while at the same time endorsing the need for a protection system in the background. However, it is a very formal concept, which still has a strong focus on respect for autonomy as a negative freedom and the associated dichotomies of autonomy versus paternalism, (negative) freedom and coercion.

Safety and autonomy

In perception-based care, persons with dementia are not given negative freedom to the point of danger. Morally speaking this care gives priority to 'care for the threat of abandonment' over 'the threat of interference by others' (Hertogh and Verkerk 2002). The ethical values at the centre of this are expressed in the objectives of such care: offering safety and security, in order to make the suffering of persons with dementia (more) tolerable. As already stated, this suffering does not involve being weighed down by dementia as such. It is better described in terms of the negative feelings that can be aroused in patients by the loss of control of their functions, their identity and their environment. 'Good care' for persons with dementia requires that care staff not only look out for these feelings, but also know which situations and events may foster such feelings, so that they can then – as it were preventively – take them into account in care, treatment and communication. This does not just require competence and expertise, it also requires a readiness to become engaged in affective interaction. Perception-based care cannot therefore simply have a functional focus. Caregivers themselves very much play a central role here. In this context, Miesen (1993) asserts that care staff will function as 'attachment figures' for persons with dementia sooner or later during the disease process, and Verdult (1993) typifies the care relationship with a term borrowed from Winnicott as 'good enough mothering'. Care staff here act as mother figures, who do not have to be perfect but must be in harmony with and respond to what is happening in the world of perception of the person with dementia.

This emphasis on safety and security does not however mean that respect for autonomy should only be of peripheral or secondary significance in the context of perception-based care, but such respect has a different, more relational significance. We should look again in this context at the case of Mr Billings, one of the two cases at the beginning of this chapter.

Mr Billings is a retired captain. He was at sea until his retirement. His job meant he was in charge of the crew. He walks that way too – upright and proud. You cannot really help him wash and get dressed or show him the way. His response is to the effect that I can do it myself; I'm in my right mind; I don't need any help. He walks about the corridors and occasionally a member of staff's pager goes off. He looks up, surprised. The member of staff tries to explain to him what a pager is. He says, 'You don't have to explain to me. I know what it is. I can beep as well.' He sees his fellow residents as 'poor wretches', whom he regularly takes by the arm, as they wander around, aimlessly searching.

This example is a striking illustration of the efforts made by persons with dementia to 'stay on their feet'. It is also literally expressed in Mr Billings's behaviour, in his proud and upright posture; the posture of a captain who has control but now also a sign of his need to keep control of his innermost self and to maintain a feeling of competence. His fellow residents are 'wretches' whom he has to help. They are different from him; he is in his right mind. By saying that he 'can beep as well', he is clearly telling the member of staff that he does not need an explanation. Needing or accepting an explanation would mean that he does not understand. He does not accept care because he would then be one of the wretches or he would have to accept that something is happening to him, but he cannot do things himself (Hoveling 1995). Acceptance of his refusal of care not only means that his personal hygiene deteriorates, but also that he gets into a panic because he does not know the order in which he should put on his clothes, but he is aware that what he is doing is not right. If the care staff allow him space to make his own choices (what clothes he will choose, when he will get up) and employ a task segmentation strategy (putting various items of clothing out ready in order and giving verbal support), they can help him maintain a positive self-image and Captain Billings feels that his autonomy is recognized and respected. Respect for autonomy here is not a goal in itself, not simply a negative freedom. For the captain, the feeling of being able to control himself, of autonomy or self-determination in the original sense of the word, is of primary importance because he derives something from it: self-respect and self-esteem, the feeling that he is being respected and recognized by others as a competent player, the doer of his deeds.

However, this need is not exclusive to persons with dementia. It characterizes the existence of all people: autonomy is not possible without recognition from others. In the last section of this chapter we will look at this again.

An ethic of space

Perception-based care and the values it stands for not only impose requirements on the (quality of) interaction between persons with dementia and their caregivers but also on the physical environment. They amount in a certain sense to an ethic of space. It is also useful here to make a distinction between perception and reality, between the perceived and the objective space. A room or preferably an apartment of the patient's own with contemporary décor is a priority for family members in particular when choosing a nursing home. That is understandable because they make their selection and choice primarily on the basis of their own perception of life in a nursing home. The quality and aesthetic assessment of the material environment, together with the importance mentally healthy people attach to privacy and what this involves, regularly play a more important role in such a choice than the quality of the care offered. But does a luxurious nursing home with a high level of privacy always offer a safe haven for persons with dementia? Privacy and an own apartment can also mean deprivation and social isolation.

From a perception-based perspective, organization of the physical environment first and foremost involves looking for the psychological significance of concepts like 'living', 'at home' and 'domesticity'. The philosopher Gaston Bachelard referred to the importance of these in the 1950s when – in response to the existential mode of the time – he pointed out: 'They (the existentialists) talk about the "en soi" and the "pour soi", but they forget the "chez soi".' Before people experience the threat of the world, they inhabit it and nothing is as important to their feeling of control and familiarity as the safety of the space they live in and the experience of intimacy they can experience there (Bachelard 1969). It is security, not privacy, that is the most important aspect of 'living'. In this context privacy has a derived meaning: it is important but as a function of security and not in itself. The feeling and experience of 'feeling at home with yourself' is therefore more fundamental from a perception-based perspective than the objective space of your own room or apartment. In care practice persons with dementia generally make little use of their 'own' space. A specific place in the sitting room, their own chair, a painting or a chest which awaken memories of an earlier intimate space, for them often have more value and meaning than a single room, especially when spatial agnosia or topographical disorientation change and distort their experience of three-dimensional space.

This approach to perceived space also has consequences for the organization of the objective space. It must not only be safe in the ergonomic sense, so that persons with dementia can move about easily and without danger, but also in a psychological sense: persons with dementia must not get lost there and the space must not confront them with 'clues' which may arouse feelings of fear and insecurity. One example of this is the design and location of doors, specifically outside doors. Mrs Johnson, from the beginning of the chapter, wants to go home to her children. She feels confined and therefore insecure. The locked glass door reinforces her negative feelings and significantly increases her agitation. The world passing her by beyond that glass is a world she cannot reach because the lock on the door will not yield, but it is the world where her children go to school and where they come back home and their mother is not there to meet them. The result of her banging and knocking on the door is that other residents become agitated so by the end of the day there is quite a crowd at the locked door. If the door is hidden from them behind a curtain, such agitation diminishes considerably. Mrs Johnson still asks for her children, but now she asks the care staff. There is no longer an agitated crowd at the 'outside door'.

Ethic of care

The values expressed in perception-based care and the care-giving they inspire do not fit in well with the model of (negative) autonomy and the associated vision of human relationships, in which individual independence is primary and the social dimension of human existence appears to restrict rather than to promote autonomy. Moral questions in caring are primarily formulated in such a model in terms of rights and obligations. But ethics is not just a matter of what people owe to others. Put more forcefully, people who simply fulfil their obligations and respect other people's rights are not necessarily good caregivers.

The 'ethic of care' offers a perspective of ethics that fits in better with perception-based care and its moral values. It demands attention to dimensions of human existence, which remain in the background in autonomy-based ethics. They relate to a layer of human existence which is there all the time, but in an area neglected by modern ethics. Thinkers who focus on care ethics therefore criticize the portrayal of mankind on which modern ethics are based. People are not only independently occupied with giving shape and meaning to their own lives, they are not only free and equal, they are also vulnerable and dependent on others. These last characteristics do not just apply to a specific group of people: to a certain degree they typify the situation of all people. The extent and nature of dependence and vulnerability and the associated care of course vary depending on life situation, but people are involved in care in all phases of their lives, whether as care recipients or caregivers (Tronto 1993).

By emphasizing that care relationships are essential to human existence – how 'autonomous' would we be if others did not concern themselves with us? – the ethic of care not only allows criticism of life structures, which are based too unilaterally on the maxim of autonomy and independence, it also makes the case for changes, in which the provision of care is recognized as a vital activity that is an essential part of living. Although it is not a professional set of ethics for care staff and caregivers, important insights can be derived from the ethic of care for the professional care relationship.

First, care from this perspective means a marriage of functional caring and interpersonal communication. This requires a professionalism which goes beyond instrumental and technical nursing skills. Treatment is not an external value added to care, which can be omitted if time and means do not suffice. The 'attachment figure presence' and 'good enough mothering' of perception-based care are fundamental forms of involvement in the care demands of persons with dementia, which should not be sacrificed to task-based treatment in times of shortage. Second, the ethic of care attaches great importance not only to values like attentiveness and responsivity, but also to competence: care can only be good care if it is provided competently. It is not just the policy makers and managers who are responsible for this but also the caregivers themselves (Tronto 1993). It is paradoxical that within health care stringent requirements are imposed on the expertise of intensive care nurses while many feel that a bit of affectionate concern should be adequate for the intensive care of vulnerable elderly persons with dementia. Such concern is indeed an important and necessary condition, but it is not enough to turn care into good care. Lack of competence is a frequent cause of abuse in care, which causes suffering to both the people being cared for and their carers. For care receivers it gives rise to a feeling of not being understood or respected. For caregivers it causes frustration and demotivation. Good care for elderly persons with dementia therefore does not just require a focus on the people being cared for, it also requires a focus on the experience and skill of their professional caregivers. Training and promotion of skills alone are not enough in this context. Given the moral responsibility of caregivers, as outlined above, to seek contact time and again without any guarantee (and sometimes only the illusion) of reciprocity, supportive 'care for carers' is also urgently required. This is an important task for nursing home physicians and psychologists.

References

Applebaum, P.S. and Gutheil, T.G. (1979) 'Rotting their rights on: constitution theory and reality in drug refusal in psychiatric patients', *Bulletin of the American Journal of Psychiatry in the Law* 7: 308–17.

Bachelard, G. (1969) *The Poetics of Space*, Boston: Beacon Press.

Bahro, M., Silber, E. and Sunderland, T. (1995) 'How do patients with Alzheimer's disease cope with their illness? A clinical report', *Journal of the American Geriatric Society* 43: 41–6.

Beauchamps, T.L. and Childress, J.F. (1994) *Principles of Biomedical Ethics*, 4th edn, New York: Oxford University Press.

Callahan, D. (1985) 'Autonomy: a moral good not a moral obsession', *Hastings Center Report* 14, 5: 40–2.

Childress, J.F. (1990) 'The place of autonomy in bioethics', *Hastings Center Report* 20, 1: 12–17.

Damasio, A.R. (1999) *The feeling of what happens: Body and emotion in the making of consciousness*, New York: Harcourt Brace and Co.

Dröes, R.M. (1997) 'Psychosocial treatment for demented patients; methods and effects', in B. Miesen and G. Jones (eds) *Care-giving in Dementia: Research and Applications*, 2, London: Routledge.

Dworkin, G. (1971) 'Paternalism', in R. Wasserstrom (ed.) *Morality and the Law*, Belmont, CA: Wadsworth, p. 108.

Hertogh, C.M.P.M. and Verkerk, M. (2002) 'Wilsbekwaamheid en verpleeghuiszorg, een ongemakkelijke verhouding' [Competence and long-term care: an uncomfortable relationship], *Gerontologie en Geriatrie* 33: 212–18.

Hoveling, P. (1995) *The perception oriented approach of elderly persons with dementia*, Houten/Diegem: Bohn Stafleu Van Loghum.

Komrad, M.S. (1983) 'A defence of medical paternalism: maximising patients' autonomy', *Journal of Medical Ethics* 9: 38–44.

Martin, R.J. and Post, S.G. (1992) 'Human dignity, dementia and the moral basis of caregiving', in R.H. Binstock, S.G. Post and P.J. Whitehouse (eds) *Dementia and Aging. Ethics, Values, and Policy Choices*, Baltimore/London: Johns Hopkins University Press, pp. 55–70.

Miesen, B. (1993) 'Alzheimer's disease, the phenomenon of parent fixation and Bowlby's attachment theory', *International Journal of Geriatric Psychiatry* 8: 147–53.

NVVz [Dutch Federation for Nursinghome Care] (1993) *Eerste Aanzet tot basiskwaliteitscriteria voor verpleeghuizen* [First draft for basic quality criteria for nursing homes], Utrecht: NVVz.

Oppenheimer, C. (1991) 'Ethics and psychogeriatrics', in S. Bloch and P. Chodoff (eds) *Psychiatric Ethics*, Oxford: Oxford University Press, pp. 365–89.

Tronto, J.C. (1993) *Moral Boundaries. A Political Argument for an Ethic of Care*, London: Routledge.

Verdult, R. (1993) *Dement worden: een kindertijd in beeld* [The process of dementia: pictures of a childhood], Baarn: Intro.

Verdult, R. (ed.) (1997) *Contact in nabijheid. Snoezelen met ernstig demente mensen* [Close contact. Snoezelen with severely demented people], Leuven: Acco.

Warners, I. (1998) *Terug naar de oorsprong* [Back to the beginning], Houten/Diegem: Bohn Stafleu Van Loghum.

Zanetti, O., Valloti, B., Ecismi, G.B. *et al.* (1999) 'Insight in dementia: when does it occur? Evidence for a nonlinear relationship between insight and cognitive status', *Journal of Gerontology, Psychological Sciences* 54B: 100–6.

Chapter 18

Autonomy, competence and advance directives

The physician proposes, the patient with dementia disposes?

Cees Hertogh

Introduction

At the beginning of the twenty-first century, dementia has become a widely feared and common disease. It is a disease that primarily affects older people. While around 6.3 per cent of people aged 55-plus suffer from dementia, this percentage rises to 43.2 per cent for people aged 95-plus and it is easy to understand why older people fear this. This fear is heightened by the fact that the disease process is often insidious, gradually sneaking up and taking over the people in question. Some persons with dementia, in the early stages of their disease, feel that they start to lose a grip on their inner self and that feeling can sometimes be associated with a dreadful fear. But in many cases they are not fully aware of their decline and do not even deny it, gradually slipping into the changed mental state that is called dementia. At present there is no way of curing, preventing or predicting dementia, so older people have no option other than to learn to live with the fear of dementia, because if dementia is your lot in life you cannot escape it, or can you?

In this chapter we look at some ethical and practical aspects of respect for autonomy and self-determination in relation to caring for persons with dementia and the significance of 'advance directives' in this context in the Netherlands. We cannot cover all the ethical questions facing psychogeriatric care-giving staff but we will look at the most topical, which are the subject of intense discussion even outside the psychogeriatric care sector. In this chapter we cover:

- seriously damaged mental faculties
- self-determination and respect for autonomy
- competence
- living wills (written declarations of intention): when should they be used?
- the euthanasia declaration in dementia cases.

Seriously damaged mental faculties

The Watsons made a living will five years ago. They did this because they were deeply saddened by what happened to a mutual friend. This friend suffered from Parkinson's disease. In the end he had to be admitted to a nursing home. They not only abhorred the environment in this institution, where all the residents had serious handicaps, but the end of their friend's life was also darkened by confusion and dementia. After his death, Mr and Mrs Watson spent a long time discussing the possibility that they themselves might end up in the same situation. Their GP referred them to the Dutch Voluntary Euthanasia Association (NVVE). They applied to this association for an advance directive, which they both signed. In this document they named each other as having enduring power of attorney in case of decisional incapacity and they both signed the 'refusal of treatment' and 'euthanasia declaration'. They gave a copy of their living will to their GP. Their minds were at rest.

A few weeks later they were sitting together on the sofa watching TV when Mr Watson suddenly collapsed. In a panic, his wife grabbed the telephone and dialled 999. The ambulance arrived quickly. Mr Watson was taken straight to the A&E department at the hospital and from there he was admitted to a nursing home. He appeared to have had a stroke. After a few days of drowsiness and confusion he recovered consciousness. His left side was paralysed and he had significant cognitive failure. He had little awareness of his illness and could often not remember what had happened the previous day. Proper conversation was almost impossible but he was always pleased to see his wife: tears trickled down his cheeks and he immediately took her hand as if he would never let go. But what Mrs Watson found saddest of all was that her husband embraced his handicapped existence with a will to live that bore absolutely no resemblance to his earlier views. He eagerly consented to all the treatment offered and when he suffered serious breathing problems as a result of pneumonia, he actually asked for the physician himself. In fact she no longer recognized him as her earlier life partner, with whom she had reached the long considered decision that the precise situation he was now in was not what they considered to be a dignified state. Out of desperation she gave the nursing home physician their living will. It set out what her husband had 'actually' wanted and requested, but at the same time it upset her greatly that she could no longer communicate with him about this 'actual' wish. And she also felt guilty. It was she who, despite her earlier promise, had dialled 999 and was therefore responsible for his fractured but continued existence.

Self-determination and respect for autonomy

Western society today sets great store by the right to self-determination. It may not be an enforceable right but it inspires our legislation and our ethics.

In health care ethics this is evident from the central focus on the principle of respect for autonomy. Physicians, nurses and other health care professionals are bound by this principle to the wishes and views of their patients. If they do not agree to treatment, it is not permitted. Many older people fearing dementia see this as a way of influencing their future fate. 'If I start to suffer from dementia, I no longer want to be treated,' they claim. But it is a fact that for various reasons people with dementia often see their situation quite differently from the way they saw it before their dementia – and for example still want to be treated or endorse the prospect of a life which previously would have horrified them. With this in mind, an increasing number of people draw up what is an advance directive or living will: a document in which they set out their wishes with regard to care and treatment in the event of, for instance, dementia. Many of these written instructions also contain a request for euthanasia in case of dementia. But it is far less simple than it may seem. A living will is not automatically implemented when someone starts to suffer from dementia. The document only becomes significant when someone with dementia is also found to be incompetent and it is then up to the family and care-givers to decide jointly how the living will should be effectuated.

As outlined above, the principle of respect for autonomy has become a central maxim in health care ethics. But what does it actually mean and where did the maxim originate? We should try to find an answer to this first, before we look more closely at changes in ethics and legislation in relation to the role of advance directives in the care of people with dementia.

Respecting autonomy essentially means not interfering with the freedom (of choice) of the other person. The idea is that everyone has the right to shape their own lives according to their own standards. This means that people have the right to pursue their own interests without being obstructed by others, provided that they do not damage the interests of these others (Childress 1990; Agich 1993). In health care the maxim of respect for autonomy is particularly significant, on the one hand because people are in a vulnerable position due to the nature of their health problems, and on the other because medical treatment is often very invasive, both physically and psychologically. Treatment must therefore come with specific safeguards. This is why the prior consent of the patient is always required, and this consent can only be valid if appropriate information has been provided beforehand about the nature, object and risks of the proposed medical treatment. We refer to this as *informed consent*, in other words consent based on adequate information.

This probably sounds pretty obvious but it has not always been so. It was not so long ago that physicians were particularly non-communicative about their findings and treatment plans. 'But few people would reproach a physician for not telling an elderly man, without any clear symptoms or complaints, that a routine x-ray had shown up an incurable lung cancer,' wrote Lindeboom (a Dutch physician and historian of medicine) around 50 years ago. White lies like this have no place in the teaching of medical ethics today and the modern physician would only have recourse to them in very exceptional circumstances.

The doctrine of *informed consent*, the most significant manifestation of the autonomy principle, originated in the context of scientific research. Influenced by the wave of democratization in the 1970s and the growing rebellion of increasingly articulate patients against the authoritarian nature of medical culture, the rules of informed consent were extended from experimental treatments to all decisions relating to medical care and treatment. What had already happened in various areas of society now also happened in medicine: public morals were applied to the core of the care and treatment relationship. Medical ethics, until then primarily a matter for physicians, became an applied general ethic. Professional medical ethicists made their appearance and looked over the shoulders of physicians and other care staff to see whether the interests of patients, interpreted as 'respect for autonomy', were being adequately served.

Current health care ethics are therefore to a significant extent the product of patient emancipation. This in itself is a positive development, which we all support. We hold our freedom of choice dear and prefer others not to make decisions for and about us. This wish and that desire are active in all people, at least while they 'have control' of their lives and bodies. But in care and treatment relationships, different aspects of human existence become evident: not proud independence, but vulnerable dependence; not only the wish to make autonomous decisions, but also the desire to be helped and supported; not only the claim to 'have control' of their lives and bodies, but also the hope and need to rely on someone else. It is precisely these aspects which address the moral sources from which care staff such as physicians and nurses draw their motivation. After all they do not choose their careers to give expression to respect for autonomy but to implement ideals such as beneficence, concern and involvement. While the principle of 'respect for autonomy' is imposed, as it were, from the outside on (health) care practice, these ideals interpret something of the internal morality of this practice: the values and virtues care staff try to implement in their actions. This internal morality shows us – as if through a magnifying glass – something which is essentially an intrinsic feature of human existence. After all people are not just self-determining and autonomous beings. They are also vulnerable and reliant on others at all times of their lives. It is not just professional care relationships which testify to this, but in their personal lives too people constantly occupy themselves in different ways with caring for each other: for partners, friends, children. So our independence is only relative and when it comes to the crunch it is not the most important aspect of human existence (Tronto 1993; Van Delden, *et al.* 1999).

Competence

'Respect for autonomy' is thus closely linked to freedom, to negative freedom that is. Negative freedom means being free from, released from. It is the freedom to be left in peace by others (Berlin 1958): again a notion which is actually at odds with what is involved in human relationships and in particular in care relationships (Agich 1993). But the philosophical advocates of the autonomy principle, such as Immanuel Kant and specifically John Stuart Mill, were not such impassive thinkers that they claimed negative freedom for everyone. This concept of freedom, according to Mill, 'is meant only to apply to human beings in the maturity of their faculties'. It therefore assumes the capacity of people to shape their own lives independently and since the Enlightenment this assumption has been closely linked to the belief in human rationality. Being autonomous literally means making your own laws and, according to Kant, people do this by 'living in the light of reason', by which he meant in contemporary terms that people should live their lives according to the principles of reason and allow their minds to rule their feelings. Respect for autonomy as a negative freedom thus relates to autonomy as an (intellectual) faculty or capacity. In modern ethics we refer in this context to competence. Being competent means possessing the ability and capability to perform a certain task, such as to make an informed decision. In some countries the term competence technically refers to a formal judicial determination of an individual's legal authority to make his or her own decisions, while the related term capacity refers to the more implicit practical evaluation made by helping professionals of the (decisional) abilities of the patient. In others as in the Netherlands, the terms competence, decision-making ability and decisional capacity are used interchangeably. In the Dutch Medical Contract Act (WGBO), competence (although the term itself is not actually used there) is described as being able to make 'a reasonable assessment of one's relevant interests'. This is a broad and open formulation and one which raises a lot of questions. What do we understand by 'a reasonable assessment'? What does 'reason' mean in this context and what are 'relevant interests'?

These are important questions because the central focus of the principle of respect for autonomy (or self-determination, according to the legal formulation) implies that the wishes and views of the patient should not simply be ignored. Being too quick to doubt a patient's competence may result in an unjustified restriction of his (negative) freedom. On the other hand, too rigorous an assertion of competence may result in the patient ending up in a position where he is inadequately protected.

Clarity concerning competence is also of great importance with regard to the implementation of living wills, because such a will takes effect when the author has become incompetent. Before looking more closely at the concept of competence, we must first examine the significance and legal status of advance directives.

Advance directives under Dutch law

In situations where people can no longer be involved themselves in decisions about care and treatment, according to the prevailing ethics and the laws governing health care, physicians and other care staff cannot simply fall back on their own assessments of such people's interests but must discuss them with someone who can make decisions on behalf of them. These representatives are then required to adhere as far as possible to such people's earlier views. A living will can offer guidance here. Morally such a document can be typified as an expression of precedent autonomy. Through the living will the maker or principal exerts his rights prior to the moment that specific decisions need to be made. If someone who has become incompetent has produced such a document at an earlier stage of their life, the views in this document prevail over any wish reconstructed or assumed by third parties. In situations where partners or families want something different from the living will, the physician is legally bound by the written instructions of the principal. Since the WGBO came into force, living wills have been enshrined in the law; at least negative declarations of intention have been. These are documents in which people refuse consent to specific, explicitly defined medical treatments. Examples include the NVVE non-resuscitation declaration and the refusal of treatment declaration. Positive advance directives, in which physicians are specifically asked for certain actions or treatments, have not had as clear a legal status until recently, but change now seems to be imminent for one specific form, as a result of the recently adopted legislation concerning euthanasia and assisted suicide (referred to in short as the euthanasia law). This law allows physicians to act in accordance with a previously drafted euthanasia declaration in circumstances where someone is no longer able 'to express their will'. There is however a significant difference in the way in which physicians are bound by the two types of living wills: more strongly in the case of negative instructions than for positive written euthanasia requests. The WGBO states that in cases of incompetence physicians are required to act in accordance with a negative advance directive, 'unless there is good reason' not to do so. The new euthanasia law imposes no obligation on physicians but simply offers them the option of acting in accordance with the euthanasia declaration. This type of living will therefore only has the status of a non-binding request.

A closer look at competence

The closer look below at the concept of (in)competence is based on the Ministry of Justice guidelines for the assessment of competence (1994), the policy documents of the KNMG (Royal Dutch Medical Association 1997) and the NVVA (Dutch Association of Nursing Home Physicians 1997) on this subject. An important common basis is what is referred to as the 'presupposition of competence'. In other words people are deemed to be competent until the contrary is proven and the burden of proof in this instance lies with the care staff. Given the moral basis of respect for autonomy outlined above, it should be expected that care staff assume competence in principle and where possible. An explicit judgement concerning the patient's decisional capacity is only indicated when 'there is clear reason for this'. This is a fine and noble aspiration, but what does it mean in practice? In the case of persons with dementia, their competence may be questioned every day. Lay persons often assume, wrongly, that people with dementia are de facto also incompetent. Because the gradual progression of the dementia process also means that their decisional capacity changes by degrees. Persons with dementia do have competent wishes and ideas which should be discussed with them, although this does require care-givers to take into account their limitations in communication and not to 'over-question' them. Competence should therefore not be considered to be a characteristic of a person (with a specific diagnosis) but is linked to a certain task or skill in a specific context. A person with dementia can be incompetent to make certain decisions, but this does not imply incompetence for every decision. The more complex the situation about which a decision has to be taken and the more far-reaching the consequences, the more stringent are the requirements to be applied to the competence of the person in question. This means that a high level of competence is required in relation to consent to a very burdensome intervention or vice versa to refusal of not very burdensome but vital treatment. Conversely a relatively low level of competence is required if the consequences of refusal or consent would be neutral or would not harm them much. Some examples of the type of decision referred to here include the following:

1   The decision whether to analyse an unexplained anaemia is a complex decision. There are a number of causes, varying from innocent blood loss from the gastro-intestinal tract (for example, due to the use of certain drugs), to various forms of cancer. The diagnostic procedures can be burdensome and very taxing for the patient and the therapeutic consequences are sometimes invasive. In such a situation therefore stringent requirements are applied to decision-making ability and it is not enough to consider consent to such procedures alone as a sign of competence.

2   The decision whether to relieve urine retention by bladder catheterization and the decision whether to treat high blood glucose levels with an insulin injection are examples of – in the medical sense – less burdensome interventions. Less stringent (competence) requirements are applied to consent here but more stringent requirements are applied to the refusal of treatment.

3   An example of a relatively neutral decision – with regard to the benefits and disadvantages – is the choice of whether or not to have a senile wart removed. Consent and refusal should be given equal weighting here with regard to competence.

An important consequence of this task-related approach of competence is its asymmetrical character. This means that consent to medically indicated treatment is weighted differently from refusal of such treatment. Just because a person is competent to consent to a proposed therapy, it does not follow that he is also competent to refuse the same proposal (Wilks 1999). A person with dementia who suffers pain due to bladder inflammation should be more likely to be judged competent if they consent to antibiotic treatment than if they refuse such treatment. The asymmetry is clearest in decisions where life is at stake. After all a very high competence threshold should be applied in the event of a request for termination of life, but the threshold is low for requesting or consenting to a potentially life-saving treatment which is expedient according to prevailing medical understanding. Of course this does not mean that everyone who wants to live must always be judged competent, but that physicians are expected – as their profession requires – to be more willing to comply with the moral appeal of a wish to live than a wish to die. In other words a positive wish, a choice of life, is therefore assessed differently with regard to competence than a negative wish, the choice of death.

Advance directives: when do they take effect?

So how should physicians deal with the living wills of persons with dementia? It is clear from the above that this is not as simple as many people think. A living will is never automatically implemented when a person starts to suffer from dementia. Persons with dementia are also entitled to respect for their autonomy and their present wishes, whether or not they have a living will focusing on the dementia situation.

However, such living wills place professional staff and the person with dementia in a strange, if not alienating position; in the literal sense too as the author and potential executor to whom such a document is addressed do not know each other. They have never actually met face to face. The physician to whom such a document is addressed is an abstract other person to the future person with dementia at the time of signing, just as the earlier pre-dementia person is to their subsequent (nursing home) physician. The case of a patient with dementia with a living will is an example of a situation in which it is frequently necessary to assess competence specifically, because the practice of nursing home medicine teaches that there are often discrepancies between the former values and wishes in writing and the current desires of the person who now has dementia. This often results in tensions in relationships between physicians and patients' representatives, usually their partners or children, who at the time when the living will was made, undertook to ensure that it was complied with, without at that time fully realizing the moral responsibility they assumed with this promise.

In the foregoing we pointed to the mutual link between respect for autonomy, competence and living wills. Respect for autonomy is the moral basis of the living will but that principle is also the root of the 'presupposition of competence', which requires that care staff focus primarily on the current wishes and views of the person with dementia. The moral problems of dementia show how this dominant principle as it were cuts off its nose to spite its face. Respecting autonomy and the resulting presupposition of competence in practice often mean crossing the boundary, which was drawn as the absolute limit, in a living will considered as an expression of precedent autonomy. The example of the Watsons earlier in this chapter can help clarify the resulting moral dilemma.

The condition previously feared

Mr Watson did not suffer from Alzheimer's disease; his dementia was due to a CVA (vascular dementia). The more or less abrupt change to his life situation due to the stroke usually occurs much more gradually, more sneakily even, in people with Alzheimer's. The same applies to their changed view of life, which was expressed in Mr Watson's case in the positive embrace of a once reviled prospect of existence. It is true that such a change in attitude is not a systematic consequence of the dementia process, but it is such a frequently occurring phenomenon that it is important to look at it here, as it complicates the management of advance directives.

Scientific research strongly indicates that even in its early stages dementia is associated with a diminishing of illness insight. Illness insight means that people know what is happening to them and are able to understand the consequences of this. Clinicians and researchers have differing views about the reasons for this: some think that this loss of insight into a person's own mental decline is linked to cerebral damage to the frontal lobe; others argue that this is a form of gradual adjustment to the restrictions and changed circumstances. Denial, as a defence mechanism, may also be part of it. Persons with dementia unconsciously protect themselves, as it were, from an awareness of the failure of their mental faculties. A number of mechanisms are probably involved, but that is not so relevant here. Whatever the reason, the effect is the same, namely that dementia patients often experience their situation differently and no longer have access to their earlier views about their current condition. This does not mean that they are not aware of their situation; on the contrary. But the awareness that something is escaping and eluding them is different from the insight which leads them to conclude that this is the condition they feared beforehand and the reason why they made a living will. The continuity between present and past is broken by dementia and the awareness of loss results in a search for something to hold on to, such as affirmation and security from partners and care staff. Many of the fears and feelings of unease experienced by persons with dementia in the early stages of the disease are associated with reactions from their environment. A sympathetic attitude can remove or prevent many feelings of insecurity. If persons with dementia are addressed about their options rather than their limitations, there is a good chance that they – like Mr Watson – will 'consent' to a life which they once judged impossible. However, for partners and family members this is an important reason why they no longer recognize the actual demented person as the person they once were, and plead incompetence, whilst at the same time finding it difficult to ignore the wishes and desires of their family member now suffering from dementia, as Mrs Watson's situation illustrates. 'This is no longer my husband,' she might say, because his current consent to the care and treatment offered to him in her view no longer fits in with his previous set of values: his behaviour is 'out of character'. But does this mean that he should be judged incompetent and should the living will therefore prevail over Mr Watson's current wishes and desires? Our moral intuition suggests a negative response to this question and the task-dependent, asymmetric model of competence indicates the same. This does little to ease Mrs Watson's pain. She remains torn between the earlier promise to her partner and his current wishes, but that's another story.

Interpretation of the living will

So does this mean that an advance directive is a worthless document in practice? Definitely not, but it does mean that such a document offers no protection against dementia. Unlike the case of someone in a vegetative state, whose incompetence is evident, in the case of dementia, whenever a decision has to be made, care staff must ask themselves whether they must fulfil their obligations in respect of the present person with dementia or whether they should act in accordance with the living will. This means that they constantly have to ascertain the competence of this person with regard to the decision in question. This is the first rule when dealing with living wills. Because, as we have said, competence or incompetence is not a characteristic of a person or a direct implication of a diagnosis but a judgement concerning a specific choice or decision, where the threshold for competence varies depending on the nature and gravity of the decision.

The next important rule is that advance directives always require interpretation. Sometimes the literal text is sufficiently clear, but in many cases the formulations are relatively general and impersonal and offer the reader little information about the lives behind them, about the personal considerations of the authors and about what moved them to make such documents. Time and again the question is about what the author intended with this document; what were his considerations in making an advance directive? The replies to these questions to a large extent determine how the advance directive should be managed. In this respect consulting with the patient (if possible) and/or with their representative at as early a stage as possible is indicated.

Very often the intention of the directive appears to be much more important than the literal text, because following the 'letter' of the declaration can often result in conflict with its 'spirit'. To illustrate this, we will look here at what is referred to as the 'refusal of treatment' produced by the NVVE. In the event of a disorder in which 'I for example no longer recognize my loved ones', or 'if I have to be confined to stop me wandering', the author 'refuses and prohibits any further medical treatment, apart from the relief of pain, breathing problems and other ailments'. If physicians were to keep to the letter of this text, it would follow that dementia patients in locked wards with such a 'refusal of treatment' would have to be denied any medical treatment, even if this was solely intended to maintain or improve the quality of life. It would mean that antibiotics could not be used to treat erysipelas or a urinary tract infection and prostheses could not be used to replace fractured hips, with all the negative consequences this would have on the patient's quality of life. Such documents clearly manoeuvre future persons with dementia into situations of inadequate care and deprive their future physicians of almost all the means and options available to alleviate their situations. But that was of course not the intention at the time when the person, before having a dementing illness, made his living will. At that time such people wanted to spare themselves medical treatment solely aimed at extending their lives and to give their physicians an opportunity not to reject death as an unwelcome option when it beckoned round the corner. At least this is how nursing home medicine understands the 'refusal of treatment' directive, so that people who have made such a directive can nonetheless count on good palliative care if they start to suffer from dementia (NVVA 1997).

The euthanasia declaration in dementia cases

Finally, some comments on the most problematic type of living will – at least morally – the written euthanasia request. The criteria for justified administration of euthanasia until now emphasized intense discussion between physician and patient, because without dialogue with the patient how can a physician satisfy the conditions for justified euthanasia? How else can he ascertain that the request is voluntary, sustained and well considered on the one hand and that the patient perceives his/her situation as unbearable and hopeless on the other? The new euthanasia law states that an adequate living will can replace an oral request from the patient, if he/she 'is no longer able to express his/her will'. Some people, usually advocates of euthanasia for persons with dementia, feel that this is an important step towards legalization of life-terminating interventions applied to dementia patients with a euthanasia declaration. But it is not as simple as that. The criterion of incompetence used in this law differs from the one in the WGBO, where it is stated that a patient is incompetent when he is unable to evaluate his own interests to a reasonable degree. The euthanasia law states that a patient is incompetent when he can no longer 'express his will'. This difference actually means that the option of terminating life in the case of dementia on the authority of a living will actually only arises in the final stage of the disease when patients no longer have a 'will' to express. In this respect the new law, instead of clarifying difficulties, simply creates new problems. For if a living will, holding a request for euthanasia in case of dementia, can only replace a well-considered verbally expressed request – the first criterion for justified euthanasia – when current (expression of) intention is no longer possible, this is in a phase of the disease where the second criterion – that of unbearable suffering – can no longer be satisfied. In the last phase of their disease, demented patients are barely receptive to the experience of suffering and thus they can no longer suffer intolerably due to an awareness of their dementia. If it is so, that such suffering does not exist, there is no place for life-terminating treatment by a physician. Also, the authors of such living wills do not want to have their lives terminated only in the last phase of their dementia: the time for that was much earlier, in the phase when 'they play with dolls and no longer recognize their children', as Els Borst, Minister of Public Health, Welfare and Sports in the second Kok cabinet (1998–2002) tersely expressed it.

The big dilemma, which is glossed over in most discussions and was totally ignored in the debate on the euthanasia law, is that probably even the Minister and her supporters would no longer be able, in this feared state of humiliation, to evaluate their interests to a reasonable degree in respect of an entire range of tasks and decisions, but also would not want to die. On the contrary, it is astonishing how strong the will to live of persons with dementia often is and how valuable a perception-based approach and treatment, which includes offering cuddly toys and dolls, can be for their welfare and well-being. As in the situation of Mr Watson, with the loss of the continuity between present and past, dementia has more or less deprived them of their more abstract values relating to life in dependency, but this does not mean that the ability to express values and wishes has been lost entirely. Some values and recognitions become even more prominent in the behaviour of persons with dementia than in people without cognitive limitations: for example, values such as safety and feeling secure with attachment figures. These are general human values, which threaten to become less important in a culture based on independence and autonomy. In this sense, people with dementia hold up a mirror to us, because how autonomous would we be if others did not care about us? Autonomy is not a natural phenomenon. It is a vulnerable achievement, which would be inconceivable, even intolerable, as a form of existence without the care and presence of other people. The care and presence that people with dementia need from us are indicative of a more radical need which seems in principle to stand in the way of earlier written euthanasia requests, so that implementation of this type of living will morally becomes almost an impossible task (Hertogh 1999).

Conclusion

Respect for autonomy has become an important ethical maxim in present-day health care. Advance directives are a typical phenomenon of modern culture and an ethic with a strong focus on autonomy and self-determination. They come in all shapes and sizes, but the refusal of treatment directives and euthanasia declarations outnumber all other types. Although they can offer valuable support when making medical decisions, there are also situations where the presence of such a document causes at least as many problems as it solves. This is certainly true in dementia cases. The core of the moral dilemmas generated by the types of living wills discussed above is based on the fact that dementia does not immediately result in total incompetence, but is characterized by a gradual change in perception, cognition and competence, as a result of which a discrepancy can arise between current wishes and ideas from a forgotten past.

Given the already serious burden a disease like dementia brings for all those involved, it is therefore recommended that GPs and geriatricians together consider the question of how they can help people with the formulation of realistic living wills.

References

Agich, G.J. (1993) *Autonomy and Long-term Care*, Oxford: Oxford University Press.

Berlin, I. (1958) *Four Essays on Liberty*, Oxford: Oxford University Press.

Childress, J.F. (1990) 'The place of autonomy in bioethics', *Hastings Center Report* 20, 1: 12–17.

Delden, J.J.M. van, Hertogh, C.M.P.M. and Manschot, H.A.M. (1999) *Morele problemen in de ouderenzorg* [Moral problems in the care for the elderly], Assen: Van Gorcum.

Hertogh, C.M.P.M. (1999) 'Oud en der dagen zat' [Old and full of days] in J.J.M. van Delden, C.M.P.M. Hertogh and H.A.M. Manschot, *Morele problemen in de ouderenzorg* [Moral problems in the care for the elderly], Assen: Van Gorcum, pp. 203–26.

KNMG (1997) *Medisch handelen rond het levenseinde bij wilsonbekwame patiënten*, Utrecht: KNMG. [Royal Dutch Medical Association, end of life interventions in incompetent patients.]

Ministerie van Justitie (1994) *Handreiking voor de beoordeling van wilsbekwaamheid*, The Hague: Ministerie van Justitie . [Ministry of Justice, Guidelines for the evaluation of competence.]

NVVA (1997) *Medische zorg met beleid. Handreiking voor de besluitvorming over verpleeghuisgeneeskundig handelen bij dementerende patiënten*, Utrecht: NVVA. [Dutch Association of Nursing Home Physicians, Medical decision-making concerning demented patients. Directive of the Dutch Association of Nursing Home Physicians.]

Tronto, J.C. (1993) *Moral Boundaries: A Political Argument for an Ethic of Care*, London: Routledge.

Wilks, I. (1999) 'Asymmetrical competence', *Bioethics* 13: 154–9.

Chapter 19

Care-giving in dementia

An emancipatory challenge

Bère Miesen

Introduction

The term dementia has never been a uniform concept pointing to a well-established entity of human behaviour; that has to do with, among other things, how human behaviour in general is valued, and the process of valuing changes over time. In this way also the valuing of deviant or abnormal human behaviour changes, together with the 'right' or 'good' way of coping with it. From a certain perspective, at a certain period in time, the only, or right, way of coping with deviant human behaviour was not to cope with it; to isolate people as soon as possible; to get them out of (our) sight, so that we did not have to see them. So the valuing was not relational.

In the meantime it has been obvious that a lot of the behaviour of people with dementia, as an example of deviant behaviour, has been valued from a relational perspective. This immediately happens at the moment when there is real contact with persons with dementia, and especially if there is a continous relationship or contact. Then deviant behaviour is no longer viewed as deviant or is viewed as less deviant than before.

The discovery that behavioural changes in dementia have specific organic correlates in the brain increased the understanding of people with dementia, but the person as a whole remained out of sight and lacking consideration. The person with dementia was fully identified with his disease. He remained the patient.

Today the (deviant) behaviour of a person with dementia has slowly been valued, understood and coped with within the wholeness of the person. That was surely the case from the moment that it became obvious that his behaviour must be seen in the light of (normal) coping with (the disease of) dementia. The individual perception (and thus coping) with dementia is now always connected with the stage of the dementia process, the individual life history, personality and the way a person with dementia is dealt with.

Sooner or later everybody has to deal with major or minor catastrophes in life. From these human experiences we are able to imagine the specific nature of dementia as a catastrophe for the patient and as a catastrophe for the family, which follows its course from a general to an individual disaster scenario. Both types of catastrophe require a specific care-giving approach and therefore have a special impact on professional caregivers and care staff. Some can deal with it better than others. From this perspective a psychology of dementia can be developed which should always form the basis of a culture of care-giving in dementia and/or agreements about how (professional) caregivers themselves should deal with each other. This vision has to describe the consequences of this psychology; not just for the person with dementia, his family and professional caregivers, but also with respect to the ways in which all three 'parties' cope with it. The following practical sketch is intended to provide an initial outline of the development of such a psychology.

A brief psychology of care-giving in dementia

The term 'dementia' is used when there are specific permanent (tissue) changes in the brain. It is only possible to determine whether phenomena such as forgetfulness, restlessness, mistrust and confusion are due to dementia by extensively screening the person in question. If dementia is diagnosed, this means that an irreversible process has been triggered in the brain, for which there is currently no medical cure. This has far-reaching consequences for the person who has been diagnosed, as well as for his or her family. Care for dementia sufferers should mainly be aimed at making sure they are dealt with and managed as pleasantly and satisfactorily as possible. Insight and understanding are necessary, so that care can be given that is satisfactory for the patient as well as for his or her family.

Memory impairment forces people with dementia to seek structures to hold on to in their actual lives or in their memories. They hold on to what they perceive for as long as they are able. Staying in contact with dementia sufferers means quite literally staying close to them. If you want to comprehend and understand them as an outsider, you must always make sure that you are in contact via the various senses. They must be able to perceive – to touch, smell, feel, see and hear, as it were – what you want to say.

People with dementia remain attached to what is actually happening to them for longer than has so far been assumed. We refer to this as their awareness, or 'awareness context'. Denial and avoidance do not mean there is no awareness. Because their memory is beginning to desert them, they often have feelings of upheaval and not belonging. This makes them look for security, which can be expressed, for instance, through attachment and proximity-seeking behaviour. Parent fixation and parent orientation are examples of this. In cases where these phenomena are apparent, it is important to comfort the dementia sufferer and offer him or her security, helping to overcome the parent fixation and restlessness.

It is not just dementia sufferers who find it difficult – their families and in particular partners have a very difficult time. They have to tackle a whole host of practical as well as emotional problems. They have to slowly say goodbye to their nearest and dearest, whether they want to or not. It involves a process of dealing with their loss, a grieving process, with all the inherent behaviours and feelings. The thing that makes the dementia process all the more difficult for the family to bear is the lack of clarity. This situation is similar to what is felt if a loved one goes missing indefinitely. The person with dementia may well still be alive, but all emotional contact has now disappeared. It is only possible to say goodbye properly when the dementia sufferer has actually 'gone', in other words, when he or she has died.

Giving care to a person with dementia involves more than just offering help. Over the course of time, a closer and deeper relationship builds up between most caregivers – whether professional and volunteer carers or members of the family – and their patients. This bond can sometimes become so strong that it leads to a kind of adoption. In other words, the caregiver feels that he or she has become a member of the patient's family as it were. It is only possible to look after another person effectively if you look after yourself effectively. So it is important that caregivers accept their own skills and limitations. They should therefore, whether in conjunction with each other or not, keep an eye on their own behaviour, be aware of their own motives for giving care, and look into ways to put their skills into practice and develop them.

To ensure effective care-giving, in other words to give care that meets the needs of dementia sufferers, it is important that caregivers (professional and volunteer carers and members of the family) impartially take on board the various experiences of patients, as well as their feelings and needs. In practice, professional and volunteer carers and members of the family usually all manage in their own ways to take this on board without partiality. Both caregivers and dementia sufferers tend to project emotions and experiences from the past onto the present. This greatly affects the relationship between caregiver and dementia sufferer. We refer to this situation using terms such as transference and countertransference. It is important that caregivers are aware of possible transference or countertransference situations in which they may find themselves, and that they have insight into the effects of these projections. In other words, they must be aware of how experiences and unresolved losses may affect their own behaviour and that of dementia sufferers.

When dealing with dementia sufferers on a daily basis, there are frequently occasions when certain forms of power (may) become apparent; for instance, when family or professional staff have to take decisions on behalf of the dementia sufferer. They are forced to because of the dependence of the person with dementia. But power also resides in concern and a paternalistic attitude. Whatever decisions the family or staff have to take, they have to be taken to the best of their belief. All is well if decisions are made in an atmosphere of understanding, respect and acceptance of the limitations of the patient, as well as those of the family or member of staff. If decisions are not taken in this atmosphere, the patient will be excluded.

As their cognitive skills are declining, people with dementia increasingly use non-verbal means of communication to express what they are thinking, wanting or feeling. Touch then becomes the most important way of communicating, because dementia sufferers are starting to show more proximity-seeking behaviour. The relationship between caregiver and patient increases in intimacy as the dependence grows. In such a situation, it is easy to misinterpret expressions of intimacy and sexuality as 'undesired intimacies'. It is important for caregivers to realize that these sorts of expression are not usually meant in that way, but more as a desire for warmth and tenderness on the part of the dementia sufferer. The extent to which caregivers accept 'awkward' situations like these depends on their own limitations, values and norms.

People with dementia may display aggressive behaviour. This causes difficulties in their dealings with family members and caregivers. If the family and caregivers are able to understand and identify the possible causes, they will be able to have a better idea of the patient's own perception of the world. This gives them a means of preventing aggression. The dementia sufferer does not degenerate into an unknown stranger. A natural progression of this is that the aggressive behaviour is not felt to be directed at oneself. What is more, feelings of insecurity or one's own guilt tend to decrease and it is still possible to see the dementia sufferer as a nice, friendly, likeable or endearing person.

Dealing with people with dementia cannot be separated from dealing with the next of kin. It is important to note that the perspective from which the family experiences and perceives the situation is different to that of the caregiver. The main reason for this is that caregivers are busy dealing with the care aspects and do not have to free themselves from the emotional bond built up by the shared life history, whatever this may be. The family looking after a dementia sufferer has to do that out of necessity. In my opinion, this affects their behaviour, both as regards the person with dementia and as regards the professional caregiver. It is therefore important that care staff take into account the process of dealing with loss on the part of the family when they decide what to do and what not to do, as well as what to say and what not to say.

Review

Part I: Models and theories

The chapter by **Thomas Arendt** contains a realistic overview of the neurobiological correlates of functional impairment in Alzheimer's disease. The cause of it and the mechanism whereby a neuron dies are still not understood. At short notice the benefits for the person with dementia will not come from this basic research. Nevertheless, it guides caregivers to anticipate the (forth)coming functional impairments of the person with dementia, and it challenges to deepen the compassion and mercifulness in care-giving in dementia even more.

Hilda Flint's chapter contributes to a question which, against all present idolization of the autonomy of the individual (the individual who wants to stand on his one feet), society is asking more and more: what is the meaning of a life in dementia? Her voyage along several modern models of God points to an answer which is given by many caregivers today: it is the caregiver himself who gives a person with dementia meaning by never abandoning him.

In a didactically thought out chapter, **Gemma Jones** links recent neuro-pathological knowledge with memory, cognitive and behavioural staging in dementia. Using a practical model it offers both insight and understanding of the process which immediately improves the communication with demented persons and their families. The model is transferable in a way that caregivers themselves can educate the latter. It is well known that psycho-education leads to (a feeling of) control, which in turn raises well-being.

The last chapter of Part I is written by **Clare Morris**. Her chapter makes an example of theorizing person-centred care. She suggests Kelly's personal construct psychology as a framework to conceive the individual experience of both the person with dementia and the (professional) caregiver. In this way the 'personhood' of both 'parties' is validated. If caregivers are constantly supported both personally and professionally, two different worlds will belong together without denying the changing perspectives of perceiving.

Part II: Interventions in care facilities

There is substantial empirical evidence that direct relating to the persons themselves increases their quality of life. The chapters in Part II give various approaches of how this can be done. **Anne-Marth Hogewoning-van der Vossen** describes a process of changing the focus in care-giving in dementia from a traditional medical to a psychosocial one in a Dutch nursing home. By introducing the 'lifestyle' approach – after admission the person with dementia chooses a ward (out of six) in which his previous way of living is continued – the attitude of the professional caregivers themselves also changed. However, this cannot happen without totally restructuring the organizational model of the nursing home.

Another approach, treated by **Rosemary Hamill** and **Terry Connors**, comes partly as a reaction to the well-known negative effects of (total) institution-alization. Sonas aPc is a multisensory intervention which aims at activating the potential for communication. It represents a holistic traject of training which brings about positive changes both in caregivers and in cognition, mood, self-maintenance and communicative capacity of people with dementia. Sonas aPc is relevant both in residential and community care.

Neil **Mapes**'s chapter deals with various practical issues in running memory groups. Today memory groups are used more to support persons in coping with dementia than to train their memory functioning. The group he studied in a day-care setting is more focused on experience than on memory, and focuses upon psycho-education and sharing feelings and individual coping strategies. In this way the group aims to encourage persons with dementia to talk openly about living with dementia and invites caregivers to do the same.

The last chapter of Part II, about music therapy and dementia, is written by **Mariëtte Broersen** and **Niek van Nieuwenhuijzen**. Music is already without doubt an established and widely recognized intervention both for persons with dementia and their families. Describing theories and research results, the authors succeed in giving a varicoloured impression of how the many characteristics of music and the music therapist can be used in treatment and care-giving.

Part III: Topics related to care-giving issues

These days, clinicians, therapists and researchers accept that persons with dementia are more or less aware of the process of dementia, and that their families wrestle with intangible loss. From there, **Bère Miesen** starts a psychology of dementia (care) on the grounds that both 'parties' always try to live a normal life for as long as possible. From a 'coping' perspective he outlines the implications for psychosocial interventions such as psychotherapy and psycho-education. He places special stress on the meaning of denial and avoidance as being crucial to explore.

The psychological and physical vulnerability of family caregivers in dementia is meanwhile well documented. **Rose-Marie Dröes** and her colleagues review the results of more than 40 studies of various types of interventions for caregivers over the last 20 years, such as the already classic support groups, respite care, individual tailored interventions, and comprehensive integrated support programmes. They conclude that the main question both for practice and research is which intervention is effective for what kind of caregiver and person with dementia.

Ann Marshall's chapter continues the psychology of dementia by studying groups for persons with early dementia which generally offer both psycho-education and emotional support. She examines a few psychological models and their implications (process and content) for running these kinds of support groups. Despite methodological scepticism, she dares to conclude that there is evidence that these groups are useful notably because of the mutual support persons with dementia share with each other.

In the last chapter of Part III, **Gemma Jones** relies on Bowlby's attachment theory to understand behavioural changes in the process of dementia based on the attachment history of the person. She suggests that 'attachment objects' are extensions of 'attachment figures' to which persons with dementia meaningfully, be it often symbolically, relate. She offers the implications of this for both residential and home care-giving. The core of this is that caregivers must be aware of the symbolic role that they and many objects play in the lives of persons with dementia.

Part IV: Family and professional caregivers

The burden of the caregiver generally brings with it a number of emotional and physical health problems. In **Anne Margriet Pot**'s chapter her starting point is the tremendous amount of recent research in which she explores in detail the care-giving stress process. From there she develops a theoretical model that aims to understand, predict and intervene in the individual process by analysing the various factors involved. Special attention is given to what causes a caregiver's violent behaviour against the person with dementia and the decision about admission.

People with dementia are the focus of the Alzheimer Café concept which intends to break through the pain of denial. In the first part of their chapter **Bère Miesen** and **Gemma Jones** explain the theory that underlies the development of this new type of support. As opposed to superficial impressions, the Alzheimer Café stands for a careful combination of education and counselling. The second part of this chapter offers a detailed manual to help properly to set up this new type of support.

Effective care-giving requires insight into the interaction between subjective and objective burdens. **Mia Duijnstee** and **Wynand Ros** concentrate especially on care-giving at home where the family and the professional caregiver must become a team that works at the cutting edge of normal daily life and the dementia process. To grow from 'cooperation' to 'care-giving together' requires a professional caregiver to be aware of the relational, functional and organizational aspects of the situation. This is not self-evident but necessary indeed.

Abuse of people with dementia may take place in any setting, even in places that may be thought to be exceptionally safe. The last chapter of Part IV is a moving argument concerning adult abuse by **Gilda Newsham**. Drawing on 40 years of professional experience and observations, she deals with eight types of abuse and illustrates each with case history material: physical abuse, verbal abuse, psychological abuse, financial abuse, institutional abuse, abuse by neglect and acts of omission, sexual abuse and discriminatory abuse.

Part V: Ethical issues

No wonder that recent knowledge contradicts old societal assumptions about (care-giving in) dementia. **Cees Hertogh** asks the intriguing and challenging question as to whether respect for autonomy, a leading principle in general health care, is maintained in care-giving in dementia. He discusses respect for autonomy by holding it up to the light in the practice of care-giving. He calls attention to the fact that it clashes with a new culture of care-giving inspired by other principles such as mutual involvement and interdependency. He points to the necessity to support the caregivers in this daily surfacing of ethical dilemmas.

Western society today sets great store by the right of self-determination. In the last chapter of Part V **Cees Hertogh** again confronts some ethical and practical aspects of this principle with practical care-giving in dementia in The Netherlands. He considers, for example, the doctrine of informed consent, written declarations of intention, and euthanasia declarations in the case of dementia. He concludes that the mistaken assumption of total incompetence (instead of a gradual changing one) in dementia causes a huge amount of misunderstanding.

Care-giving in dementia: a developing specialty

Many experts working in the field of care-giving in dementia will undoubtedly be able to tell their own stories about the negative image that outsiders have of their field. The same applies to me. In 1970, when I was 23 years old, I started my career as a psycho(geronto)logist working at what was then called a 'nursing home for elderly people with dementia'. For years I had to put up with people saying it was a mortal sin to waste my expertise – even my life – in this field of work. I am sure these criticisms sometimes made me doubt my chosen course. On the other hand, they didn't at all. Somehow or other I stuck at it – and I believe so did many of my colleagues alongside me. In retrospect, I would like to have told all these critics 'we realize that working with vulnerable older people, especially the elderly with dementia, is a very unique and special field'. This emancipation means that all disciplines in the field of care-giving in dementia have (necessarily) acquired a positive image. This positive image is excellent to build on, as the field of work itself has developed its own theories and models. Treating, supporting and caring for people with dementia, their families and their professional carers is quite rightly 'a field of its own'. Having said this, I would like to outline a few developments, without mentioning them all, that give me cause for concern as well as joy.

Expertise and responsibility

Working in multidisciplinary teams is (becoming) quite prevalent to care-giving in dementia; certainly as far as analysing problems/problem areas is concerned. But this multidisciplinary aspect is not reflected or translated back into the organization of concrete responsibilities and tasks, for instance, with respect to the multidisciplinary treatment plan. This is too ridiculous for words. The quality of the products – for example, in terms of good treatment, support and care for people with dementia and the system involved – depends too much on the people involved or on how well they interact (it either works or it doesn't) instead of (priorities in) the expertise required at a certain point in time in the process of the disease. Generally speaking, (far) less medical care is needed in daily treatment than in the terminal phase of the dementia process. In daily treatment, the treatment plan is usually more focused on psychosocial or paramedical work than on somatic interventions.

Expertise and power

Over the last few years, nursing home doctors, especially in The Netherlands, have become so 'broadly' trained – for instance, they are now aware of or realize the psychosocial dimensions of the (somatic) problems – that they are tending to assume they also have expertise in the very fields or disciplines which broadened their basic training. In other words, psychologists are teaching nursing home doctors how to understand or behave in a multidisciplinary environment, but not so that they can then be priced out of the market in their actual workplace. The danger is that nursing home doctors (believe they have to) get involved in aspects that fall within the specific expertise of other disciplines. I believe the best solution is to understand each other in a multidisciplinary environment, analyse problems in a multidisciplinary team, but continue to adopt a monodisciplinary approach to the work itself. So we have a powerful medical expert and a powerful psychologist who get along well together. The problem is that the power does not always reside with the person with the (most) expertise.

Transfer of psychosocial 'expertise'

The same development can also be seen in non-medical disciplines, without any (explicit) processes of power playing a role. By working in a multidisciplinary environment, activity assistants, physiotherapists, occupational therapists and social workers, not to mention caregivers, have come to 'learn' (glean) so much psychosocial knowledge – reflected, for example, in the terms in which they couch their observation reports – that either unintentionally or with the best of intentions, they assume they have psychological expertise in areas in which they actually have insufficient or no competence/authority. The (dangerous) consequence of this is that, in particular if psychologists are short of time (this is usually a matter of staff shortages), essential treatment, support and care will be available admittedly more cheaply but with an ever-decreasing amount of expertise.

Individual disaster plan

Focusing on dementia, if we assume that the disease dementia is the same as a 'Type III (psycho)trauma' for people with dementia and their families – in other words, a *constant* battle against powerlessness, disruption and upheaval that only ends once the person with dementia is dead – then it is clear that an individual disaster plan has to be drawn up for every person with dementia as well as for his or her family. It goes without saying that (para)medical treatment, support and care play an essential role in this, but the way in which this individual disaster scenario is handled (tailored care!) requires expertise in the psychosocial field without any question. This view has still not become an automatic guiding principle in the provision and especially the organization of the necessary treatment, support and care.

Continuity in treatment, support and care in dementia

From the above – assuming the disease dementia is a 'Type III (psycho)trauma' – it can be said that continuity in treatment, support and care is a prerequisite. From the beginning, if possible, the same multidisciplinary (treatment) team should stand by the family going through the dementia, regardless of (changes in) living situation, although continuity in the care team is not feasible for the entire course of the dementia. Why do we need the same treatment team from the beginning to end? Because the whole thing is about always giving treatment in the short term but from a long-term point of view. In the beginning, knowledge/expertise is needed about everything that is going to happen; at the end, knowledge/expertise is needed about everything that has happened. It is only with this support that people with dementia and their families can find the security and control they need to continue living their lives as normally as possible for as long as possible, despite the disease dementia.

Emancipation of people with dementia and their families

Despite progress in the disease, it is not easy to maintain control over your life and therefore maintain a feeling of security. It is therefore important first of all to get a rapid and reliable diagnosis, so that you know what you are up against. The second thing to do is to waste as little time as possible denying and avoiding what you are up against. It is here in particular that caregivers must focus. Because if denial persists – and there may be all kinds of reasons for this – many different forms of treatment, support and care (by third parties) will either be impossible or barely possible or simply too late. It is therefore a matter of caregivers helping people with dementia and their families (both are victims of an ongoing catastrophe) take control of their fate (again), often with the help of others.

Emancipation of caregivers

Giving care to victims of a catastrophe – we are talking here about a 'Type III (psycho)trauma' – will sooner or later always have an (emotional) impact on the caregivers. They will have to constantly be aware of this impact and the way in which they deal with it, to ensure they prevent countertransference (projections) which may end in burn-out. To help them in this, they need supervision, an encouragement of expertise, and above all an open approach about the specific and complex (difficult and fascinating) aspects of this field of work – which in turn will promote a positive image.

Conclusion

Care-giving in dementia is a special field of its own that requires multi-disciplinary cooperation as a basic criterion. But this cooperation, especially given the expertise and commitment of psychosocial specialists, can easily lead to an erosion or degradation in their actual expertise and to them being undervalued in favour of cheaper 'experts' from other disciplines. This may be why some psychosocial experts are moving (willingly) towards management positions. In this respect, nursing home doctors in The Netherlands have organized themselves more astutely over the last few years and – if you look at the firm rooting of subject areas in academic faculties – they have safeguarded and strengthened their positions more effectively than the older psychologists. Perhaps it is a question of missed opportunities. Care-giving in dementia clearly shows that far more is involved in this field of work than purely medical input. Care-giving in dementia demedicalizes by definition and at the same time promotes the multidisciplinary nature of this area of work. In fact the immense complexity of this fascinating field automatically promotes its positive image – and in turn its emancipation.

Index

Index compiled by Frank Pert